How Strange the Change

STANFORD STUDIES IN JEWISH HISTORY AND CULTURE

EDITED BY *Aron Rodrigue and Steven J. Zipperstein*

How Strange the Change

Language, Temporality, and
Narrative Form in
Peripheral Modernisms

Marc Caplan

STANFORD UNIVERSITY PRESS

STANFORD, CALIFORNIA

Stanford University Press
Stanford, California

This book has been published with the assistance of the Department of German and Romance Languages, the Leonard and Helen R. Stulman Program in Jewish Studies, and the Office of the Dean of Arts and Sciences at the Johns Hopkins University.

"Ev'ry Time We Say Goodbye" (from *Seven Lively Arts*). Words and Music by Cole Porter. © 1944 Chappell & Co., Inc. Copyright Renewed and Assigned to John F. Wharton, Trustee of the Cole Porter Musical and Literary Property Trusts / Publication and Allied Rights Assigned to Chappell & Co., Inc. All Rights Reserved. Used by Permission of Alfred Music Publishing Co., Inc.

Cover image: *Aqua Allure*, 2005, by Sonya Clark. Combs, Thread, and Holographic paper. Photo credit: Tom McInvaille. This piece evokes one of the central figures of this study, the modern pan-African spirit Mami Wata (the "Mother of Water"), through an alternation of colors and shapes that suggests the inverted letters "M" and "W." Its commitment to abstraction, its innovative use of materials, and its creation of a peripheral aesthetic between image and text offers a model for everything to which this comparison aspires.

Printed in the United States of America on acid-free, archival-quality paper

Library of Congress Cataloging-in-Publication Data

Caplan, Marc (Andrew Marc) author.
   How strange the change : language, temporality, and narrative form in peripheral modernisms / Marc Caplan.
      p. cm. — (Stanford studies in Jewish history and culture)
   Includes bibliographical references and index.
   ISBN 978-0-8047-7476-5 (cloth : alk. paper)
   1. Yiddish literature — 19th century — History and criticism. 2. African literature — 20th century — History and criticism. 3. Comparative literature — Yiddish and African. 4. Comparative literature — African and Yiddish. 5. Literature — Minority authors — History and criticism. I. Title. II. Series: Stanford studies in Jewish history and culture.
PJ5120.C37 2011
 839'.109002 — dc22

                                                    2010050574

*To my grandmothers, Jeannice Caplan, o"h,
and Lilian Bloomenstiel, zol lebn;
to my children, Zipporah Glikl and Asher Rafael, biz 120;
and to the golden chain of memory and storytelling linking them all.*

There's no love song finer
But how strange the change
From major to minor
Ev'ry time we say goodbye

—Cole Porter
"Ev'ry Time We Say Goodbye"

Contents

Acknowledgments

There's an episode of *The Simpsons* memorably titled "E-I-E-I-(Annoyed Grunt)" in which Homer seeks refuge from a threat on his life in Springfield by moving his family to the farm where he grew up. Bemoaning the barrenness of the soil to Marge, she suggests to him, "Maybe it needs more fertilizer?" Indignantly, he replies, "I'm only one man, Marge." Much like Homer Simpson, I am grateful to report here that the labor, material, and support for this project have been much more than the work of one person.

First and foremost, I wish to thank Norris Pope, Sarah Crane Newman, and Tim Roberts at Stanford University Press for their interest, help, and esteemed editorial advice in turning this work from a manuscript into a book. Professor Steven Zipperstein at Stanford University has been an ideal interlocutor since I first approached him about publishing this project; his belief in the value of my research is what has made the appearance of this book possible. Professor Mikhail Krutikov at the University of Michigan and Professor Ato Quayson at the University of Toronto provided superlatively constructive criticism for the entirety of this manuscript. From the time I first began writing this comparison these two scholars were the readers I was addressing in my mind, and I am grateful for their comments as well as their generosity in revealing their identity as external readers to me. Professor Henry J. Drewal and Sonya Clark have both been encouraging and kind with their help and permission in securing the cover image that magnificently amplifies and visualizes the aspirations of this book's contents.

When this project began as a vague idea of comparing Yiddish and African literatures, my thoughts and my writing were refined considerably by the advice, instruction, and support of Professors Manthia Diawara and Kristin Ross at New York University (NYU) and Professor David Roskies at the Jewish Theological Seminary. In addition to their essential guidance, I received marvelous insight into the study of literature and the responsibilities of a scholar from Professor Dan Miron at Columbia University and Professor Ngugi wa Thiong'o at NYU and previously at Yale University; both of them continue to be my role models for everything that a writer and a critic should be. Professor Benjamin Harshav, Professor Avraham Novershtern, and the late Dr. Mordkhe Schaechter have my eternal gratitude for animating my love and knowledge of the Yiddish language and modern Yiddish culture. Throughout the writing process I have also benefited from the solicitous and supportive correspondence of Emeritus Professor Timothy Reiss at NYU and Dr. Alan Rosen, both of whom have my sincere thanks. A Vivian Lefsky Hort Fellowship in Jewish Studies from the YIVO Institute for Jewish Research, as well as a Penfield Fellowship from the Department of Comparative Literature at NYU and a Maurice and Marilyn Cohen Fellowship from the National Foundation for Jewish Culture (now the Foundation for Jewish Culture), made my writing and life itself possible in the early days of this work.

Thereafter I had the good luck to be employed in the Department of Comparative Literature at Indiana University; as a Betty and Morris Shuch Term Fellow at the Center for Advanced Judaic Studies (now the Herbert D. Katz Center) of the University of Pennsylvania; and as a Harry Starr Fellow at the Center for Jewish Studies of Harvard University. These institutions, my colleagues there, and their staff have my gratitude for their generous financial and intellectual investment in my work. In this context I would like to thank in particular Professor David B. Ruderman at the University of Pennsylvania for his ongoing engagement in and mentorship of my scholarship. My affiliations now with the Department of German and Romance Languages and the Leonard and Helen R. Stulman Program in Jewish Studies at the Johns Hopkins University have provided me with two equally welcome academic homes. Of my uniformly stellar colleagues there, I wish to thank in particular Bill Egginton and Steven David for their support and mentorship; Rochelle Tobias, Elisabeth Strowick, Katrin Pahl, Andrea Krauss,

Deborah McGee Mifflin, and the irreplaceable Rüdiger Campe for their collegiality in the German program; and Rebecca Swisdak, Sherron Bullock, and Mary Otterbein for making the complex machinery of our scholarly and pedagogical life run efficiently, promptly, and smoothly. Thanks as well to the scholars and staff of the *Kulturwissenschaftliches Kolleg* at the University of Konstanz, and especially to Professor Uwe Hebekus, for the productive and stimulating sabbatical semester I spent there in 2009 — the first of many visits, I can only hope!

Beyond my many professional debts (to say nothing of my gambling debts), I can only begin to express my gratitude and love to my family for their assistance and sustenance before, during, and after the long journey this manuscript has undertaken. My wife Brukhe has provided me with compassion, kindness, and patience from the day I first met her. My parents, David and Norrine Caplan, not only made this book possible at the outset, but also provided me with an invaluable anecdote for its conclusion. My brothers and their respective families have been the source of much good humor and welcome distraction: Sonny, Mr. Jeeves, I'm sorry about the incident in Havana, but I promise I'll make it up to you when we get together again in Tahoe — Fredo. And to my growing menagerie of in-laws across the pond — Mr. Charles, Miss Brendel, Hannah, Peter, Deborah, Nick, the kids, and the chickens — thank you for your love, your support, and your interest in my work; see you all soon, I hope.

Thanks additionally and especially to Benyomin, Khane, Itsik-Leyb, and Aron-Volf Moss, along with Sholem, Celeste, Beylke, and Mikhl Berger-Sollod for making downtown Baltimore an unlikely but thriving center of modern Yiddish language and culture. A few blocks away, Rabbi Zev and Rebbetsin Chana Gopin have provided me with wisdom, understanding, and knowledge since my arrival at Hopkins; every visit with them provides a model of kindness, welcome, and joy for which I am truly grateful. Across the tracks in Pikesville I wish to thank Joel and Jen Bader as well as Ken and Barbara Lasson for opening their homes to me and my family with unfailing graciousness on holidays of all description. Thanks also to Zelig Zumhagen and Afrodesia McCannon, as well as Liz Rosenkrantz and Steve Lancman, for their friendship before, during, and after this project. To Beth Lemoine and Susan Jenkins—it's wonderful being in touch again, after so long an absence. With enduring appreciation for three friends taken too early: Naomi Kadar, Isaac Meyers, and Ray Westbrook, may their memory be a blessing. To my three "wonder students," Kathryn Coers Rossman, Eleanor Vanden Heuvel, and Eléonore Veillet; as Van Morrison once put it, "You've made a happy man very old." *Akhren Akhren hoviv*, Dr. Sara Nadal-Melsió has given her encouragement, insight, and grace to this project from beginning to end, and beyond; I might have been able to write this book without her engagement, but it wouldn't be as good, and it wouldn't have been as much fun.

If as the preceding indicates this book is truly the work of more than one person, I can only hope that its entirety is greater than the sum of its many parts. Of what follows, everything that is meritorious is due to the generosity and wisdom of my family, friends, and teachers—those whom I've thanked by name, and those whom I am only able to honor in spirit. Any shortcomings, all of which will become apparent soon enough, are my own. In a just world, their merits will outweigh my shortcomings.

Portions of Part 2 first appeared as "*Nos Ancetres, les Diallobes*: Cheikh Hamidou Kane's *Ambiguous Adventure* and the Existential Roots of African Negritude," *Modern Fiction Studies* 51, no. 4 (Winter 2005): 936–957. © 2005 Purdue Research Foundation. Reprinted with permission by The Johns Hopkins University Press. Portions of Part 3 were previously published as "The Smoke of Civilization: The Dialectic of Enlightenment in Mendele Moykher-Sforim's *Di Klyatshe*," in *Beyond the Modern Jewish Canon: Arguing Jewish Literature and Culture, A Festschrift in Honor of Ruth R. Wisse* (Center for Jewish Studies at Harvard, Harvard University Press, 2008), 445–466.

How Strange the Change

Introduction   Apples and Oranges
On Comparing Yiddish and African Literatures

> " . . . [A]s a Jew, I was acquainted, as perhaps a Negro might be,
> with the alien and the divided aspect of life that passed from sight
> at the open approach, but lingered, available to thought, ready to
> reveal itself to anyone who would inquire softly. I had come to
> know a certain homelessness in the world. . . . The world is not
> entirely yours; and our reply is: very well then, not entirely. There
> were moments, however, when this minor world was more than
> universe enough."
>
> —Isaac Rosenfeld, *Passage from Home* (1946)

Just as Eleazar ben Azaryah declares in the Passover Haggadah that
"I am likened to a man of seventy years but lacked the merit to claim
that one recalls the exodus at night until I heard the explanation of Ben
Zoma," so too had I been at work on a comparison of Yiddish literature
with Anglophone and Francophone African literature for what felt like
seventy years without being able to articulate my motivations, until I
attended my teacher Ngugi wa Thiong'o's lecture at the 2001 Modern
Language Association (MLA) convention in New Orleans, Louisiana,
entitled "Out of Africa: Language, Knowledge, and Empowerment."
As always, Ngugi gave an inspiring presentation, defending the right
and necessity of Africans to preserve their native languages against the
hegemony of globalization, American popular culture, and the English
language. These comments offered a rejoinder to the often-implicit assumptions that intellectual work in Africa necessitates writing in a colonial language; that an African culture ceases to exist when it is not
perceived by the colonizer; and that the processes of globalization are
inevitable, irresistible, and irreversible. Yet the highlight of Ngugi's address occurred at the end of his remarks, when the Native American
poet Simon Ortiz[1] addressed Ngugi in his native Acoma Pueblo language. The audience reacted ecstatically, and more so when Ngugi re-

I

sponded to Ortiz in *his* native language, Gikuyu. Here two languages provided a paradoxical community, founded on the pleasure of mutual incomprehensibility. For the moment of their exchange, English, *the* global language, became a dispossessed language, spoken by everyone, belonging to no one.

Dispossession, the means by which peripheral cultures are confronted with their own marginality, is what originally brought Ngugi and Ortiz together. If this phenomenon is the consequence of commercial and political empires, then perhaps utopian moments such as the one that transpired between these two champions of peripheral languages, moments that in fact *constitute* globalization as much as they resist it, offer an antidote to the homogeneity of both global and national cultures that insist on speaking in a single voice. Although the embrace of unintelligibility can only take place with the safety net of a common language when communication becomes necessary, the commitment to a peripheral language or culture, the insistence on its centrality in a personal space within a public one, can be an expression of dissent not only in the context of political or commercial institutions but even in the supposedly liberal and inclusive enclave of academic institutions such as the MLA. Indeed, one feature of academic life that impresses the student of peripheral literatures is how consistently most academic culture mirrors the larger forces of the social order. Just as the nation-state is the means by which global capitalism is regulated, the study of national literatures regulates the concept of world literature. By contrast, peripheral cultures—cultures neither defined nor limited by national boundaries—experience difficulty in gaining access to resources or even obtaining recognition of their legitimacy as modes of being and fields of study.

This book thus proposes to affirm the paradoxical *centrality* of peripheral literatures to a theory of global modernism. As such it offers strategies whereby these literatures can be studied comparatively—where authors such as Ngugi and Ortiz can be rendered intelligible to one another without the difference of their respective languages being translated away. The specific literatures under consideration in this study are narratives written in Yiddish during the nineteenth century and those written in English and French in mid-twentieth-century Africa. The first part of the book considers two pioneering figures in these respective cultures, Reb Nakhman of Breslov and Amos Tutuola. This discussion culminates with a comparison of Reb Nakhman's first story, "The Story of a Lost Princess," and the "Complete Gentleman" episode from Tutuola's first novel *The Palm-Wine Drinkard*. Part 2 considers the first consciously modern ideologies in Jewish Eastern Europe and Francophone Africa, *haskole* (the "Jewish Enlightenment") and negritude. This comparison will focus primarily on the first edition of the didactic tale *Dos Vintshfingerl* ("The Magic Ring") by Sholem Yankev Abramovitsh (Mendele Moykher-Sforim) and the novel *L'aventure ambiguë* ("Ambiguous Adventure") by Cheikh Hamidou Kane. Part 3 discusses the breakdown of *haskole* and nation-state nationalism by analyzing two later Abramovitsh novels, *Di Klyatshe* ("The Mare") and *Masoes Benyomin hashlishi* ("The Travels of Benjamin the Third"), in comparison with the novels *The Interpreters* by Wole Soyinka and *Les Soleils des indépendances* ("The Suns of Independence") by Ahmadou Kourouma. The book as a whole concludes with a consideration of Jewish literature after the Holocaust, when Yiddish no longer serves as an intrinsically Jewish, international, peripheral language, and a discussion of the linguistic options available to African writers at the beginning of the twenty-first century.

The theoretical point of departure for this comparison is the "minor" literary theory of Gilles Deleuze and Félix Guattari.[2] In addition to incorporating the main principles of this theory, the discussion that follows will also propose a reexamination of the historical prerequisites for the creation of a "minor" or peripheral literature. To the three essential characteristics with which Deleuze and Guattari define "minor" literature—deterritorialization of language, political immediacy, and the assemblage structure—the comparison of Yiddish with African literature compels a focus on orality and its relationship with literacy, as well as a more complete understanding of the linguistic tensions that "minor," peripheral authors exploit. These emendations to Deleuze and Guattari's concept of "minor" literature require a greatly expanded theoretical field that encompasses an understanding of modernization and nationalism, the development of novelistic prose, and the linguistics of languages in contact and conflict—as well as a focused contemplation of the historical, ideological, and aesthetic development of Yiddish and African literature, respectively.

Through a consideration of these concerns, this book poses a question, prompted by Ngugi's encounter with Ortiz: What do two cultures have to teach one another, even when speaking in different languages? I would contend that they teach each other how to communicate in the *absence* of a common language. The significance of this question is all the more acute when considering the current generation of Yiddish scholarship, typically undertaken by students first acquiring knowledge of Yiddish as adults. To the question of what Yiddish can teach other cultures comes an additional set of problems at once philosophical and psychological—how, and why, does one choose a *mame-loshn* ("mother-tongue") not one's own?

I come to these questions by a perhaps representatively circuitous route. As an ill-fed and poorly socialized high-school student from rural Louisiana, I arrived at Yale with the solitary ambition to understand literary modernism—a task I continue to set myself today. In my first two years as an English major, I took every seminar in modernism my department offered, however improvident the course of study I set for myself may have been; is a nineteen-year-old really prepared to make sense, for example, of W. B. Yeats or Wallace Stevens? (I wasn't.) Nonetheless, by my junior year, I was in need of additional courses in order to complete my major, when I stumbled—I was expecting a seminar on Algernon Swinburne, but had misread the room assignment—into a class offered by the late Michael Cooke on the African novel in English.

The African novel of the 1950s and 60s, I discovered, narrated the same problems of modernity and modernism I had come to college to study in the first place. The defining characteristic of this literature is its temporal *belatedness* in assimilating the techniques of modernist narrative, while at the same time struggling against the social and epistemological demands, as well as the typically frustrated political promises, of modernity that had been assimilated in the colonial nations of Great Britain and France over the course of centuries. This belatedness, paradoxically enough, empowered the African novel to speak with greater urgency about the grand themes of modern literature—the relationship of the individual to society, the conflict between generations in demonstrating the transition from traditional culture to modernity, the limiting power and limitations of the nation-state as a mode of social organization, the recognition of philosophical subjectivity as a mode of historical agency (formulations that are in fact synonyms for one another)—than much of the contemporaneous fiction of the United States and Europe, for which these questions had already been too long embedded in everyday life to allow the dramatization of recognition.

Given the historical burden that these novels assume for themselves, it is perhaps not surprising that the literary genres they often inhabit tend to be associated with the early history of the novel—the satiric parody, the picaresque, the pseudo-autobiography, the *Bildungsroman*—though while enacting these genres, African novelists typically demonstrate corresponding familiarity with the technological and aesthetic characteristics of contemporary twentieth-century culture.[3] When at the end of my senior year I found myself in need of an additional course in order to graduate, I settled on Benjamin Harshav's "Transformation of Jewish Literature in the Modern Era." There I discovered, perhaps unsurprisingly, that Yiddish writers such as Mendele Moykher-Sforim and Sholem Aleichem, whom I was reading in translation for the first time, were in an attenuated sense also "postcolonial" writers, coming of age in the Czarist Pale of Settlement during the last half-century of the Russian Empire's existence, and often used similar genres, rhetorical gestures, and thematic dilemmas as the African writers I had been studying over the previous two years. This picaresque itinerary through world literature is how I discovered my subsequent course of study; at the same time, it was only through such an itinerary that I could come to focus on Yiddish, and thereby use the choice of Yiddish to understand my own picaresque path from the rural South to the metropolis of academia.

My comparative scholarship on Yiddish literature can thus be considered a continual process of translation: from the American South, by way of New Haven, then vicariously through literature to Africa and Eastern Europe; from English (and French) to Yiddish and back again; from the "minor" perspective of underexamined literatures to the "major" perspective of overdetermined literary theory; and from the periphery to the center (and back again). I come to Yiddish via this textual itinerary as much of an outsider as when I came previously to African literature—though with the added difficulty that by virtue of my status as an Ashkenazic Jew, there is an expectation that I am not an outsider, but a native informant. I am frequently asked as a student of Yiddish literature if my parents speak Yiddish (they do not), whereas I have never been asked if my parents are Nigerian (they are not). My use of Yiddish as a vehicle for scholarly self-expression is thus predicated on the fact that as much as I am a Johnny-come-lately or outsider to Yiddish culture, I am equally belated and dislocated from the world of academia, much like Yiddish, or African, literature itself.

The exchange between location and dislocation, of identifying with a mother-tongue not spoken by my mother (or either of my grand-mothers, or even two of my great-grandmothers), is the character-istic position of Yiddish scholars in my generation. The challenge of working with and in Yiddish today is the problem of locating oneself between languages, affiliating oneself with Yiddish while function-ing, professionally, in another language. This may be a problem every scholar working in a "foreign" language experiences when employed in the United States, but with Yiddish the dilemma is compounded by the fact that unlike *national* languages—Portuguese, Spanish, Jap-anese, and so forth—Yiddish does not dwell somewhere else. There is no Budapest, Bucharest, or even Bamako to which Yiddish schol-ars can travel to connect with "their" language and culture; at best there is a Boro Park or Bnei Brak, where the Yiddish scholar's status as *scholar* (modern, typically secular—a secularity perhaps felt most deeply when the scholar is to whatever degree religious) further re-moves him or her as observer rather than participant. Unlike ancient ("dead") languages, such as Latin or Sumerian, Yiddish not only re-tains an animated, oral character, but in spite of its written legacy re-mains, *except* for the precincts of contemporary scholarship, primarily a spoken language, even if it is a language increasingly misheard, mis-used, or misunderstood. This fact also connects Yiddish with other postcolonial vernaculars, as well as the peculiar phenomenon of im-perial languages filtered through postcolonial consciousness: English in Nigeria, India, or Trinidad is as resourcefully, mutably positioned between standard English and oral vernacularity as Yiddish is among [*hmm...*] the linguistic components from which it derives.

By contrast, I would argue, these questions seldom arise in the study of, for example, German, Italian, or Russian because the language already possesses a specifically national and territorial identity, even as this identity can also be deterritorialized via diaspora, colonization, tourism, and similar means of distension. Yiddish by contrast implicates its scholars and speakers in larger problems of identity and identification precisely because of its historical deterritorialization and its contemporary invisibility or inaudibility. In the negative space of contemporary Yiddish silence, modern Yiddish scholarship inherits a series of unstated negations: not-Hebrew, not-Hasidic, no longer the language immigrants use to keep secrets from children, no longer the language of the Jewish-socialist Bund or the *beys-medresh*,[4] but instead the language of the dead, the spectral, the thwarted possibility.

The spectrality of Yiddish resonates for students of postcolonial African literature insofar as this writing is typically conducted in a language distinct from what its subjects speak—a condition bemoaned by Ngugi and the few writers who have followed his lead back to their mother language.[5] For scholars of both literatures there is a fundamental disconnection between spoken language and written language, between the language of experience and the language of analysis. Indeed, Jacques Derrida articulates an analogous dilemma that, although not considering Yiddish directly, nonetheless engages the historical and philosophical questions that Yiddish and African literatures respectively confront. In his essay *Monolingualism of the Other*, Derrida, writing explicitly as a North African Jew, declares, "I only have one language, yet it is not mine."[6] For the contemporary Yiddish scholar, in ways similar to what Derrida refers to as his own "Franco-Maghrebian passion" (19), the study of Yiddish becomes a means of claiming—inhabiting—an identity signified by absence, dislocation, and loss. In contrast to Derrida's assertion of Algerian Jews in his generation, "as for language in the strict sense, we could not even resort to some familiar substitute, to some idiom internal to the Jewish community, to any sort of language of refuge that, *like Yiddish*, would have ensured an element of intimacy, the protection of a 'home-of-one's-own' against the language of official culture" (54, emphasis added), Yiddish for contemporary scholars typically functions less as a *chez-soi* than a borrowed address, halfway between a guest house and a ghost house.

If, as Derrida writes, "language is for the other, coming from the other, *the* coming of the other" (*Monolingualism of the Other*, 68), then for whom does the contemporary Yiddishist speak? Who is this other with whom he or she can speak, and in what language? These dilemmas center equally on the status of Yiddish in contemporary Jewish culture and the anxiety of the scholar confronting them; as Derrida writes, "in a grievance like this, one takes on lastingly a mourning for what one never had" (33). In committing to Yiddish, how do contemporary scholars represent themselves, and how does this representation at the same time figure as a displacement of self? These are questions that contemporary postcolonial theory has already begun to address, for encoded in both the term "postcolonial" and the field of study the concept signifies is a relationship at once psychological and political between the self and the other. The field of postcolonial studies offers a politicized consideration of the ways in which one establishes subjectivity both in relation to, and at the expense of, the object-position of other subjects. Postcolonial theory, and more fundamentally the literature that this theory *belatedly* and almost inevitably from the perspective of the metropolis tries to explicate[7]—theory, using the discourse of rationalist analysis, is always several steps behind literature, using the more compressed and propulsive discourse of metaphor—demonstrates that for both colonizers and the colonized, the moment of self-recognition confronts the subject with his or her essential *doubleness*, particularly with respect to language.

Thus, despite Derrida's consciously ironic assertion that the Other possesses no language, bilingualism or multilingualism is ultimately a precondition for all peripheral writing. Reacting against the limits of more than one language simultaneously signifies the dislocation of language commensurate with the necessary *defamiliarization* of ordinary life that calls writing into being. To find a literary voice, the peripheral writer must first lose his or her (native) language—even in the case of Ngugi, where creating a literary voice is a process of *return* to Gikuyu, via English.

This process, so painstakingly traced in various articulations of post-colonial theory, is inherent to Yiddish as both a language and a culture—so that the study of Yiddish in tandem with postcolonial theory reformulates this theory as much as it reconceptualizes Yiddish—and therefore the study of Yiddish is a crucial means of making apparent the doubleness of Jewish identity otherwise effaced in contemporary, monolingual Jewish cultures conducted in English or Hebrew.[8] In linguistic terms every student of Yiddish knows that it is a fusion language, in which the components that constitute it (Middle High German, Hebrew-Aramaic, and Slavic, to list only its most recognizable elements) remain discernable and for the most part unhomogenized. As Benjamin Harshav writes of modernist Yiddish poetry, contrasting it with High Modernism in national literatures: "Like the ideal of 'pure poetry,' pure art to the avant-garde meant the acceptance of one language that dominated each work. . . . For them, at any given moment, the poetics of their art was like a spoken language: one speaks either French or English or Russian, but not all in the same sentence. In Yiddish, however, one *can* speak several languages in the same sentence."[9] The cultural, rhetorical, and even linguistic multiplicity of Yiddish derives from its social origins as a language of translation and mediation, simultaneously, between the sanctified rabbinic tradition and everyday life, as well as between the coterritorial, non-Jewish world and the porous domain of Jewish values and tradition.

Premodern Yiddish literature functioned exclusively in these mediating and translating capacities—there are essentially no fictional Yiddish narratives published before 1815 that cannot be traced either to a Hebrew/Aramaic source or an adaptation from a contemporaneous, often contiguous language—and until the end of the nineteenth century the primary motivation for writing in Yiddish was to neutralize the danger of foreign ideas by clothing them in traditional Jewish rhetoric, so that modernity was translated into the discourse of tradition, while the tradition was reconfigured for a readership that was increasingly urban, secular, and politicized.[10] The doubleness of Yiddish therefore is at once linguistic and cultural, but also spatial and temporal; Yiddish idiom evokes the frame of reference, the sensibility, the memory of the shtetl marketplace and *beys-medresh*, even when it was spoken or written in Shanghai, Buenos Aires, or Melbourne.[11] But with the profound disruptions occurring over the course of the twentieth century, Yiddish became transformed from the language of tradition, even when used unconventionally, to its current status as a language subsumed by scholarship except in the ultra-orthodox world, where it is employed as a means of insulation against modernity, changing from a language of translation into a language that must be translated.

In social as well as cognitive terms, this transformation is most profound in the reversal of Yiddish from a spoken to a written language. This reversal therefore upset the balance of Jewish discourse between a largely written *Loshn-koydesh* (the "language of holiness," a fusion of Hebrew and Aramaic in which all sanctified literature, including rabbinical correspondence, traditionally was written) and a primarily, though of course never exclusively, spoken Yiddish. Out of this upheaval came not only the respective impulses for modern Yiddish literature and a modern, spoken Hebrew but also the competition between these languages that in part—together with the Holocaust, the Stalinist repression of Yiddish culture, and the monolingual demands of American civic culture—accounts for the eclipse of Yiddish as a modern vernacular today.

Where for modern scholars Yiddish is typically a language read, therefore written but not spoken, in the nineteenth century, this incomplete relationship was inverted—as language also was for African writers similarly negotiating between native vernaculars and colonial written languages. Whereas Jewish intellectuals turned Yiddish, often with great reluctance, from a vernacular language into a literary one, for nearly all African writers working with colonial languages, the task was to make a literary and administrative language into a vernacular, even if a vernacular typically used only by an educated elite. Linguistically, the aim of African writers to create a vernacular out of the colonial language is analogous to efforts of the maskilim (proponents of *haskole*) and their successors to create a modern Hebrew vernacular; the juxtaposition of Yiddish and African literatures thus allows the reader to see them not as repetitions but inversions of one another. This in turn empowers the recognition of a historical commonality between these cultures and among peripheral modernities (and modernisms) in general. Indeed, for both of these emerging literary cultures, writing as such was an act of resistance against the hegemony of colonial culture and the hierarchies of traditional culture simultaneously: a means of speaking out of turn and trespassing borders, but also of effacing oral traditions. The transformation of language in these two cultures therefore serves an explicitly political purpose, at least for those few intellectuals using language in the self-conscious way of creating belletristic literature. Although this politicization of language reflects a broader phenomenon in the development of a peripheral modernity, the specific condition of literary language in African and Yiddish cultures serves to connect these two deterritorialized literatures as well as to distinguish them from the literatures created in tandem with a territorial nationalism.

For example, the best-known theorist of territorial nationalism, Benedict Anderson, offers an analysis of the first Latin American novel, José Joaquín Fernandez de Lizardi's *El Periquillo Sarniento* ("The Itching Parrot," 1816):[12] "Here . . . we see the 'national imagination' at work in the movement of a solitary hero through a sociological landscape of a fixity that fuses the world inside the novel with the world outside. This picaresque *tour d'horison* . . . is nonetheless not a *tour du monde*. The horizon is clearly bounded: it is that of colonial Mexico."[13] By contrast, what distinguishes early modern Yiddish literature, as well as the first works of postcolonial African literature about a century later, is the typicality of their use of purely imaginary spaces: Reb Nakhman's wilderness, Tutuola's Bush of Ghosts, Yisroel Aksenfeld's Lohoyopoli ("a city that never was"), and the development by Mendele and Sholem Aleichem of prototypical *shtetlekh* (Glupsk, Kabtsansk, Kasrilevke, etc.). By design, the landscapes that dominate the early development of African and Yiddish fiction, respectively, could be anywhere, everywhere, or nowhere, at the same time. Their spectral character—most vividly invoked in Y. L. Peretz's 1895 short story *Di Toyte shtot* ("The Dead Town")—alerts the reader to their fundamentally conflicted temporality, perched uneasily between tradition and modernity, invoking both simultaneously, while inhabiting or affiliating themselves with neither fully.

There is of course a parallel tradition of explicit territoriality in both Yiddish and African fiction, exemplified first and foremost by Peretz's *Folkshtimlekhe geshikhtn* ("stories in the manner of folklore") and *Khsi-*

dish ("Hasidic-styled stories") genres, which create a symbolic geography for Yiddish literature by frequently invoking specific place names in Czarist-controlled Poland. Similarly, the Lagos of Nigerian novelists such as Chinua Achebe, the late Cyprian Ekwensi, and Wole Soyinka is as historically specific and dramatically vivid as Charles Dickens' London or Marcel Proust's Paris. In all these counterexamples, territoriality signifies a later phase of modernization in the respective history of these literatures that nonetheless competes with radically deterritorialized writers who preceded them yet continue to write in a deterritorial mode. The coexistence of territorial and deterritorialized landscapes in these literatures—and in the instance of writers such as Peretz and Soyinka, among genres or phases of development within the work of a single author—signifies a choice between two modes of modernist critique, and develops for both African and Yiddish literature in historically parallel ways, despite the geographical and cultural boundaries that otherwise separate them, and despite the chronological affinities that might connect these two literatures with contemporaneous, fundamentally territorial nationalist literatures. As might be anticipated, the deterritorialized model for African and Yiddish fiction dominates my comparative research, and through it I am attempting to define a historically and formally grounded theory of peripheral literature as an integral component in global modernism. Indeed, the defining focus of Yiddish in this theory is the anticipatory role played by a *belated* modernity in creating an *anticipatory* modernism.

In purely chronological terms, this identification of the origins of Yiddish modernism might seem counterintuitive, since the first Yiddish writer this study considers, Reb Nakhman, died in 1810—at least three-quarters of a century before the commencement of any standard dating of the Modernist revolution in literature.[14] Reb Nakhman's stories for the purposes of this discussion are modernist even though he precedes the canon of metropolitan Modernism; to make this semantic distinction more precise, these narratives can be considered modernist, even if Reb Nakhman cannot be considered a Modernist. Modernism in this reformulation thus functions coincidentally with modernization. It is modernity becoming self-conscious of itself, which occurs in peripheral cultures through the remainder, the persistence and resistance, of a traditional discourse in an era of crisis. Where a canonical literary Modernism develops in metropolitan culture at a moment of anxiety over a dying or lost tradition, in peripheral cultures this phenomenon anticipates the metropolitan canon because the tradition refuses to submit to a regime of forgetting necessary for the "business" of modernization to proceed.

Indeed, in the example of Reb Nakhman writing in Yiddish and Hebrew, and Tutuola in English, the modernist critique precedes the belletristic exposition of modernization, by the maskilim in Eastern European Jewish culture or among the first Anglophone realists in Nigeria such as Chinua Achebe or Cyprian Ekwensi. The anticipatory character of peripheral modernism responds with the production of narrative—stories—to historical developments such as the emergence of new political structures, urban industrialization, and the disruption of local traditions through linguistic, technological, territorial, and social dislocations and innovations. This anticipatory character, itself a consequence of modernity's belatedness in the peripheral context, demonstrates the significance of the periphery to the center: one can never identify a center without recognizing how it differs from and relates to the margins. Because modernity must emanate from the center out, modernism must correspondingly migrate from the periphery in.

One might fairly ask in response to this description of an anticipatory, peripheral, or "minor" modernism, "If Reb Nakhman of Breslov is a modernist, who, then, is not?" This question can be answered decisively: modernism develops on the periphery in advance of the metropolis because modernism itself occupies a position of peripherality, a "grievance" that Derrida defines in the dual sense of mourning and protest. Reb Nakhman, Tutuola, and the other writers in this analysis are modernists because their work incorporates peripherality on a formal and structural level. Their many contemporaries who disguise or dismiss this peripherality either by writing in Russian or in a "Germanized" Yiddish (in Eastern Europe), or else by imitating the dominant modern aesthetic of literary realism (whether in Europe or Africa), signify less, except when their narrative structure betrays similar anxiety over language, form, and cultural capital; hence my discussion in the second part of this comparison of an unfinished manuscript by Isaac

Meyer Dik, perhaps the most popular representative of a "decorous" Yiddish literature during the nineteenth century, rather than his more polished, ultimately ephemeral, published works.

One essential yet complicating concept in the formation of Yiddish literature's anticipatory modernism, a concept that distinguishes classic Yiddish fiction from contemporary (Hasidic) Yiddish culture, is that of secularization—as distinct from secularity. Though modern Yiddish literature is not secular insofar as it never loses contact with the rhetoric, symbol system, and cosmology of traditional Judaism, it plays an integral role in the social and intellectual modernization program of nearly every ideological movement available to Eastern European Jewry.[15] Yiddish literature reconciles the paradox of a literary discourse communicating its secularizing intentions through the rhetoric of religious tradition by employing myth and satire, two premodern narrative discourses capable of reconciling logical contradictions beyond the limits of rationalism. As Max Horkheimer and Theodor Adorno's discussion of Homer's *Odyssey* in *Dialektik der Aufklärung* illustrates,[16] the epic as a mode of enlightenment subordinates and domesticates myth to the same extent that "enlightened" civilization dominates and marginalizes the cultures it subordinates. Implicit in the epic struggle of man against nature, though explicit in later tragedies such as Euripides' *Medea*, is the conflict between Greek and Barbarian; from a "mastery" of nature, Greek civilization moves inevitably to the domination of other groups of people, a process duplicated in every other imperial culture. As Horkheimer and Adorno suggest, enlightenment's repression of myth creates a psychic wound, what Adorno refers to as "a damaged life," that modernity inflicts on others as well as the self.

The resistance to this act of aggression, as well as to the expectation that enlightenment's violence always be internalized, constitutes itself in Yiddish and African fiction as the return of the repressed mythical culture via satire and fantasy. Both fantasy and satire liberate myth from the straightjacket of purely rational thought, but they do so by rendering myth demotic; Yiddish literature, as well as most of the African examples chosen for this comparison, responds to the epic demands of rational subjectivity with a mock-epic sensibility. The creation of an autonomous Yiddish literature over the course of the nineteenth century thus not only removes the language from its subordinate status to *Loshn-koydesh*, but also determines the focus of this literature away from the realm of sanctification, into the everyday. This strategy can be effectively contrasted with the other great deterritorialized literature of the nineteenth century, the writing of the African Diaspora, particularly African American narrative. The foundational trope for Black authors in the nineteenth century is predicated not on the bathetic contrast between the cosmic origins of a collective identity and the tragicomic fate of the individual confronting a modern society unwilling to acknowledge his or her subjectivity but, instead, on the elevation of an individual to the political, social, and metaphysical level of subjectivity through the divine agency of a literary device that Henry Louis Gates Jr. describes as the "Talking Book."[17] As this trope appears in several slave narratives of the late eighteenth and early nineteenth centuries, the enslaved African acquires insight into his or her political condition, as well as mastery of the culture of the slave owners, by understanding and participating in the linguistic transaction whereby words on a printed page become human speech. The book that almost always empowers this process is the Bible—precisely because at stake in the slave's elevation into literacy is his or her moral and spiritual status as a child of God, and thus he or she is the metaphysical equal of the slave owner.

The slave narrative as a foundational genre of African Diaspora literature therefore does not domesticate myth as part of a secularizing project; it creates new myths to fill and dramatize the void created by the unique trauma of slavery. Distinctive in the production of these new myths are the roles played by the book as a technology of modernization and English as a language of global modernity. It is therefore not coincidental that the Bible by which the slave-narrator establishes his or her humanity, a narrative act that only gains in moral and dramatic force with its reiteration in successive formulations, is the King James Version, the translation used at the time throughout the Anglophone world. Subjectivity is not only constructed in this context through reading a sacred text, it is explicitly revealed to the narrator by a sacred text *in English*. The trope of a Talking Book could not exist in either Yiddish or postcolonial African literature. In traditional Ashkenazic culture, not only does the Bible speak *constantly*—via the public reading of the

Torah—but at all levels of religious instruction, it speaks through oral translation and commentary in Yiddish. Indeed, the origins of bathetic comedy in modern Yiddish fiction derive from the disconnection between the Torah as the sacred Truth and the mundane, inadequate uses to which its rhetoric is put in the fallen world of the everyday.

In the multiplicity of contexts out of which postcolonial African literature emerged, missionary Christianity through which colonial languages were taught is only one textual and spiritual system in which the writer's consciousness develops. In Francophone Africa, for example, which in the colonial era lacked a vernacular tradition of biblical translation and where missionary activity alternately competed and collaborated with an ostensibly secular administrative authority, the primary sacred book for most people was the Koran, which for most Francophone writers was read and recited, but *not* translated or understood;[18] Islam in this context counts as much as Christianity for an earlier imperial presence and modernizing strategy. In Anglophone Africa, as well, the Bible and missionary Protestantism[19] compete both with Islam, particularly in northern Nigeria, and with native religious traditions that, although not transcribed alphabetically, nonetheless constitute themselves textually.[20] Thus Michael Thelwell writes in his introduction to Tutuola's *The Palm-Wine Drinkard*, the first internationally recognized Anglophone novel in Africa, "[Tutuola] was born into a powerfully traditional household—to Christian parents. . . . Though nearly all of his children adopted the new faith, the *Odafin* [Tutuola's grandfather] never did. While he lived, he was master of a traditional household in which all the *Orishas'* festivals were celebrated. . . . Every Thursday the household awakened to the sound of ritual drumming. . . . On Sundays the Christians went to church" (182). Where the early African American trope of the Talking Book emphasizes the singularity not only of the reading subject but also of the language of literacy, in both the Yiddish and perhaps more crucially the African context, subjectivity is paradoxically predicated on multiplicity and proliferation—of languages, temporalities, and modes of identification.

The two literatures out of which I attempt to construct a theory of peripheral writing therefore affirm not only Derrida's paradoxical formulation "We only ever speak one language," but also his corollary, "We never speak only one language" (*Monolingualism of the Other*, 7). The linguistic precondition for understanding these two literatures in turn suggests both a metaphor and a methodology for comparative literature in general. I would propose as well that it offers a mode of expression for life lived on the margins, a location possibly most comfortable for anyone attempting to engage in critical thinking. This mode of expression presents its own paradoxes, particularly with respect to temporality; how, for example, can life even on the margins be articulated in a spectral language? This question refers back to the status of Yiddish literature as a secularizing phenomenon, never a secular one: it is a literature of becoming modern. Once the modernization process has concluded, almost inevitably with the assimilation of a national language (English, Russian, Hebrew, etc.), it becomes defunct or, in linguistic terms, obsolescent.[21] By studying, and in turn speaking, an obsolescent language, the speaking student enters into a critical relationship with his or her own modernity. This, then, is the perspective I had sought to acquire for my own precarious modernity, traveling from Louisiana to college in order to understand the aesthetic and political potential of modernist literature. It is also the reason that I have chosen Yiddish not only as a scholarly affiliation but also as the language I now speak to my four-year-old daughter and eight-month-old son (who nevertheless speaks Yiddish at a nine-month-old level!). For them, Yiddish is not a language of use-value—to speak with an extended family, to foster identification with a homeland, or to use in order to make a way in the world—in any sense other than the abstract affirmation that all knowledge is useful. Ultimately for them Yiddish will someday soon be a choice and a challenge, but one that I present to them with the hope that they will choose the possibilities created beyond the boundaries of identity that are constructed when one is confined to speaking, thinking, and dreaming in only one language.

Part One *The Origin of Stories*
A Story of Origins

The comparison that animates this book, between modern Yiddish and postcolonial African literature, mimics the controlled conditions of a scientific laboratory in order to test a difficult and far-fetched hypothesis: Can two literary cultures using different languages, in different centuries, on different continents—in the absence of contact or even, for the most part, awareness of one another—nonetheless, when taken in comparison, illuminate the interdependence of literary form and social history in a way that makes both of these cultures more comprehensible? Can this comparison serve as a model to explain more general phenomena in the development of minority literature, or, indeed, the proper relationship between peripheral and metropolitan cultures in the development of literary modernism? Or will this discussion retreat, in the face of its own relativism, to the assertion, merely, that various people, in various places, at various points in history, have written books?

Before succumbing to the nihilism of this final rhetorical question, one should consider the critical theory that has developed in the last two decades around questions of "minor" literature, minority cultures, and postcolonialism.[1] Abdul JanMohamed and David Lloyd, for example, describe in characteristically polemical terms the academic context and critical objectives that the present comparison seeks to address:

> In the past two decades, intellectuals . . . have enabled fresh examinations of a variety of minority voices . . . repressed or marginalized by a society that espouses universalistic, univocal, and monologic humanism. Although this archival work has generated provocative theoretical analysis . . . the dispersal of the intellectuals in underfunded "special

programs" has . . . reinforced the . . . marginalization of nonhege-
monic cultures . . . in academic as well as other spheres. . . . [M]inority
discourses and their theoretical exegesis continue to flourish, but the
relations between them remain to be articulated. Such articulation is
precisely the task of minority discourse, in the singular.[2]

Like JanMohamed and Lloyd, this discussion will take as one of its
starting points the concept of "minor literature" as proposed by Gilles
Deleuze and Félix Guattari.[3] Deleuze and Guattari are helpful not only
for the particular model they provide for reading "minor" literature but
also because they chart useful exegetical ground by resisting the tendency to submit to reductive, allegorical, or symbolic interpretations
that deny the force and significance of a narrative *as it is written* (or, in
the case of oral narratives, enunciated). Thus in theoretical terms, the
opening premise of this comparison is the definition of "minor" literature formulated by Deleuze and Guattari: "The three characteristics of
minor literature are the deterritorialization of language, the connection
of the individual to a political immediacy, and the collective assemblage
of enunciation" (*Toward a Minor Literature*, 18).

Despite the usefulness of these thinkers' terminology, as well as their
sympathy for the literature they seek to theorize, Deleuze and Guattari
themselves *do* acquiesce to the biases of a "monologic humanism"; witness, for example, the assertion that "talent isn't abundant in a minor
literature" (*Toward a Minor Literature*, 17).[4] The callousness manifest
in this statement serves to warn that no literary theory can long endure
without reference to specific writers and their work. This discussion
will commence, therefore, at the beginning of the respective histories
of Yiddish and African writing in modern forms. In this section, the
primary authors under consideration will be the Hasidic leader Reb
Nakhman of Breslov[5] (1772–1810)—whose posthumous collection of
stories, *Seyfer sipurey mayses*[6] (1815; roughly, "The Holy Book of Stories"), can be considered the first volume of original, autonomously
conceived stories in modern Yiddish—and the Nigerian writer Amos
Tutuola (1920–1997), whose 1952 book *The Palm-Wine Drinkard*[7] is the
first novel written in English by a Nigerian writer, and the first by a
West African to receive international distribution and recognition. At
the same time, this comparison seeks to evaluate the respective claims

of postcolonial and poststructural theory, among other methodologies. Such a comparison, and perhaps all comparisons across cultural and linguistic lines, risks a certain arbitrariness. The intention of this study is not to make categorical statements about these literatures in their entirety, but rather to construct a series of analogies between modern Yiddish and postcolonial African literature that will throw the development of both into relief.

As to the status of Reb Nakhman and Tutuola as instigators of a modern revolution in the literary history of their respective cultures, such an assertion can be affirmed by default with respect to the relative paucity of belletristic writing that precedes them. In the case of Anglophone African literature, in contradistinction to traditional oral forms of creativity in native African languages, the precedents to Tutuola can be summarized in a half dozen examples. As Charles Larson writes, "In 1906, the South African, Thomas Mofolo, had written a novel in his native language, *Sesuto*, which was later translated into English under the title *The Traveler of the East* and published in London by the Society for Promoting Christian Knowledge (1934). . . . Two later writers of historical interest were both from Ghana. In 1911, E. Casely-Hayford published a novel which (in a later English translation) was called *Ethiopia Unbound*. Much later, in 1943, R. E. Obeng's *Eighteenpence* (written in English) was published by Arthur H. Stockwell, Ltd. (London)."[8] More significant than the works that Larson cites is the writing of Chief Daniel Olorunfemi Fagunwa (1903–1963), a serious and respected novelist writing in Yoruba, whose books were widely studied in the colonial school system of Yorubaland, and who undoubtedly exerted an influence on Tutuola. Despite Fagunwa's importance as a literary figure in his own right, the significant differences between his writing and Tutuola's—a subject unfortunately beyond the scope of this discussion[9]— underscore Tutuola's greater stylistic and philosophical affinities with "minor" literature, and therefore with literary modernism.

Although writing in Yiddish has been traced as far back as 1272[10]— with most linguists extrapolating the presence of the language at least two hundred to three hundred years prior to that[11]—serious belletristic writing in Yiddish remained in a state of arrested development throughout the premodern era, at least when compared with other European vernacular literatures or the parallel growth of poetic, rabbinical, and mystical writing in *Loshn-koydesh* within Jewish culture. "Literary" books in Yiddish, some of remarkable quality, were published from the fourteenth to the seventeenth centuries in Germany, Switzerland, Bohemia, Italy, and the Netherlands. This literature was inevitably adapted, however, with varying degrees of interpolation, from the Hebrew Bible (e.g., *Dos Shmuel-bukh*, 1544); the Talmud and Midrash (e.g., *Tsene-rene*, 1622); oral or stylized legends of Jewish sages (e.g., parts of *Dos Mayse bukh*, 1602); Aesopian folktale collections (e.g., *Dos Ku-bukh*, 1595); or, perhaps most remarkably, medieval Christian romances (e.g., *Dos Bove-bukh*, 1541).[12] None of this literature, however, was produced in Eastern Europe, where Yiddish culture was concentrated from the beginning of the eighteenth century until the era of mass emigration (1881–1939), and none of it was created, though much of it was frequently repackaged, in the hundred years prior to the publication of Reb Nakhman's collected stories.

Moreover, in formal terms, Jewish writing lacked autonomous narrative traditions before the modern era.[13] The character and function of premodern Yiddish literature is therefore ultimately more significant than the premodern circumstances, form, or language in which it was produced. In this respect, one must acquiesce to the assessment of Max Erik (1898–1937) of premodern Yiddish literature fundamentally as a "mediation," either between the common reader and the elite *Loshn-koydesh* textual tradition, or between the Jewish people and contemporaneous, coterritorial cultures.[14] To return, however, to the comparison of Reb Nakhman with Tutuola: although both Reb Nakhman and Tutuola use their creativity "modernistically," to redefine the function and significance of the traditional cultures that shaped them, the relative stature of these authors in their respective cultures is nonetheless a further study in contrasts. Reb Nakhman was a controversial leader of a dissident sect within the early Hasidic movement, but also an unassailable scholar and master of the religious tradition; Tutuola, though well-exposed to both Yoruba and Christian traditions, received only the equivalent of a sixth-grade education in English. Unlike Reb Nakhman, who attracted a small group of followers within the Hasidic movement that holds his teachings sacred to this day, and who has been a romantic hero in secular Jewish culture for the past century,[15] Tutuola has, at least until the occasion of his death, occupied an uncertain position in the history of African literature, and has attracted the suspicion and at times hostility of better-educated African intellectuals.

Moreover, one crucial difference between these writers emerges from the outset: Tutuola, unlike Reb Nakhman, never publicly envisioned his writing as part of a messianic or cosmological project; he never claimed that his writings could, for example, "lead lost souls to repentance . . . make barren women fertile . . . heal blind eyes [or] restore, somehow, the unity of a shattered world."[16] In fact, relatively little is recorded as to how Tutuola regarded his writing or its significance. One can nonetheless deduce part of his aim by examining the rhetorical strategy that he employs. Tutuola, like Reb Nakhman, seeks to "redeem" these traditional stories, to "liberate" them, if not for a messianic project, then at least to transfer their relevance to the modern world of literate, Anglophone Nigeria.

Tutuola's artistic project can best be described as "recuperative" rather than "restorative"; rather than seeking to exert an influence on the external world through his stories, he seeks to preserve a folk tradition as a "thing-in-itself" in great danger of disappearing because of modernization and the gradual shift in the public sphere from Yoruba to English. As Michael Thelwell quotes him in the introduction to *The Palm-Wine Drinkard*: "[T]he time I wrote it, what was in my mind was that I noticed that our young men, our young sons and daughters did not pay much attention to our traditional things or culture or customs. They adopted, they concentrated their minds only on European things. . . . [S]o if I do this they may change their mind . . . to remember our custom, not to leave it to die" (*PWD*, 186–187). Indeed, one can interpret the overriding motif of the novel, the quest for a *dead* palm-wine tapster, as a search for a mythic past already cut off from contemporary Nigeria. This anxiety over the viability of the folkloric past, furthermore, had already been observed at least two generations earlier, as Ato Quayson notes: "Newspapers of the period give evidence of the concern of the people that 'our Folklore, Legends, Histories, Parables, Aphorisms, Allegories & Co., are within the ready grasp of Oblivion.'"[17]

Part of the anxiety surrounding the survival of these folk narratives, and therefore the motivation for Tutuola's novel, derives from the conflict between oral and written culture in colonial Nigeria. Unlike traditional Eastern European Jewish culture, in which a largely oral Yiddish and written *Loshn-koydesh* interacted, by design, through complementary social functions, the conflict between orality and literacy in colonial Nigeria was one in which a written English literally threatened to erase the oral memory of traditional Yoruba culture. In this instance, therefore, it is particularly significant that Tutuola harnesses the technology of modernization, namely, the production and distribution of books—as well as English, the language of modernization—to his radical recontextualization of tradition. These two writers share one function in relationship to their respective cultures, however, that validates a comparison on personal, artistic terms as well as a social, historical level. Each writer possesses an exceptional command of the preoccupations and rhetoric of very complex belief systems, and they each channel this knowledge into a new form of writing that enables them to recast their traditions along personal, idiosyncratic lines. As such, they each represent for their respective cultures, on both personal and historical levels, the transition between tradition and modernity.

One   Defining Peripheral Modernism

The terms "tradition" and "modernity," to say nothing of "transition," are complicated and procrustean enough to elude succinct definition. One can nonetheless summarize the aspects of life transformed through modernization in terms identified by Michel de Certeau: "The generalization of writing has in fact brought about the replacement of custom by abstract law, the substitution of the State for traditional authorities, and the disintegration of the group to the advantage of the individual."[1] Certeau's synecdochal model for modernity as the transition from orality to literacy can be characterized as "supersessionist." Where previously a culture functioned exclusively through the oral transmission of information, values, and collective narratives, the introduction of writing, whether gradually through technological development or suddenly through the imposition of a new social order, fundamentally transforms the formerly traditional culture. This model seems to be apt for understanding the dramatic transition that took place in the purely oral Yoruba culture when it was subjugated in the nineteenth century by the modern, literate British Empire.

With respect to Eastern European Jewish culture, however, writing was always a factor in cultural life, though Yiddish was primarily reserved for oral purposes (with *Loshn-koydesh* being used primarily in written contexts). In the context of Eastern Europe, it is helpful to modify an apparently rigid dialectic between the oral and the written with reference to an observation by the medievalist Brian Stock: "Understanding how a textually oriented society came into being presupposes a basic chronology of medieval literacy. If we take as our point of departure the admittedly arbitrary date of A.D. 1000, we see both oral and written traditions operating simultaneously in European culture, sometimes working together, but more often in separate zones, such as oral custom and written law."[2] Stock's starting point coincides with Max Weinreich's ultimately no less arbitrary date of 1000 C.E. for the birth of Yiddish, and underscores therefore both the mediating function of Yiddish *between* "oral custom and written law," as well as the essential proximity of Reb Nakhman's writing, eight hundred years later, to medieval cultural norms.[3]

In terms of the transition from tradition to modernity, however, it is important to stress that for *both* Eastern European Jews and Independence-era Africans—in contrast with, for example, Western Europe during the Industrial Era, or China in the postimperial era[4]—tradition and modernity do not separate into discrete, generational demarcations, but rather continue to coexist, interact, and compete with one another for several generations.[5] In fact, in imperial contexts such as colonial Africa and nineteenth-century Eastern Europe, tradition is often a site of political contestation, and is itself a means of resistance against a modernity imposed *from above*. The reconfiguration of "tradition" from a position of authority within a culture to an oppositional force in the face of an imperial hegemony will be a recurring concern of this comparison.

The use of tradition as an oppositional force takes on added significance when one considers that ethnic-Yoruba writers such as Tutuola are preeminent among Africans in using folk traditions to illustrate the transition from tradition to modernity. In a characteristic strategy for peripheral literature, the Anglophone writing of Yoruba authors has typically used the motifs of folklore to apprehend modernity, rather than using the language of modernity—as in the case of, for example, Chinua Achebe's use of narrative realism in *Things Fall Apart*, or Camara Laye's use of quasi-anthropological discourse in *L'enfant noir*—to interpret an ostensibly closed-off past.[6] The decision, therefore, to begin this examination of postcolonial African literature with Tutuola not only accords the author appropriate historical status as a pioneer, but also identifies him as a representative of the enduring and adaptive folk tradition itself. The Anglophone literary tradition that he calls into being derives from oral narrative not only themes or examples of "local color," but a formal model for the evolving relationship between tradition and modernity, orality and literacy.

For both Yiddish and African literature, one of the ways that oral, folkloric culture exerts a structural and thematic influence on written narrative is through the pronounced *fantastic, supernatural* character of the first books in these respective traditions. It thus comes as no surprise that both the Hasidic worldview from which Reb Nakhman emerged and the traditional Yoruba culture of Tutuola's youth are distinguished by the prominent role each accords to modes of esoteric knowledge that combine features of oral transmission with written semiotics: *kabala* (in general, the mystical "branch" of the tree of Jewish knowledge) for the Hasidim; divination and transformation rituals among the Yoruba. In Tutuola's example, particularly, despite the power disparity between native and imperial belief systems inherent in the colonial situation, a synthesis between the Yoruba and Christian religious traditions in which he was raised was possible because of the syncretism of Yoruba culture as well as the heterogeneous pluralism of modern life. Both Reb Nakhman and Amos Tutuola, with apparently quite different aims, have therefore fashioned literature out of the folkloric traditions of their cultures. In each instance the narratives that these writers create highlight fantastic situations and spontaneous, supernatural transformation. In the narrative world of both Tutuola and Reb Nakhman, *anything can happen*, and therefore the formal contours of their writing are distinguished by open-ended, rhapsodical structures and development that is analogical, rather than logical.

That Tutuola and Reb Nakhman should fashion their narratives as associative juxtapositions of sacred and profane sources within their traditions, incorporating both autochthonous and coterritorial folkloric motifs, comes as no surprise, given the relative absence of autonomously literary models in either colonial Africa or Jewish Eastern Europe. Belletristic literature both in Africa and among Jews in Eastern Europe was, after all, a new concept when Tutuola and Reb Nakhman, respectively, began writing. This points to two trends simultaneously within "minor" literatures: their dependence on oral sources for much of their subject matter, particularly at their inception, and their social function as an agent of collective consciousness—though often in pa-

rodic, anti-authoritarian terms—in the breakdown of traditional hierarchies at the onset of modernization. As Deleuze and Guattari write:
"[B]ecause collective or national consciousness is 'often inactive in external life and always in the process of breaking down,' literature finds
itself positively charged with the role and function of collective, and
even revolutionary, enunciation. It is literature that produces an active
solidarity in spite of skepticism, and if the writer is in the margins or
completely outside his or her fragile community, this situation allows
the writer all the more the possibility . . . to forge the means for another
consciousness and another sensibility" (*Toward a Minor Literature*, 17).
In Tutuola's Nigeria and Reb Nakhman's Eastern Europe, the "collective consciousness," when conceived along religious or ethnic lines
rather than national ones, was in fact neither inactive nor in the process
of breaking down, but was being repoliticized through conflicts within
the writers' respective communities and between these "minor" cultures
and the dominant hegemony. The writing of Reb Nakhman and Tutuola serves as an artistic correlative to these political struggles.

    The political motivations of modern Yiddish literature were not lost
on the first critics of Yiddish literature—although the political implications of Reb Nakhman's stories often were. Soviet critics during the
1920s and 30s, the only period in which an objective study of Yiddish
literature was permitted there, were particularly acute in articulating
the sense that Yiddish literature, with its strong emphasis on parody
and satire, was the product of what could be termed a "minor" sensibility. Thus Meir Wiener (1893–1941), the most talented of the Soviet
Yiddishists, writing about the emergence of Yiddish satire during the
haskole, the so-called Jewish Enlightenment, concludes: "These maskilic
[proponents of *haskole*] writers . . . used 'humoristic irony,' each in his
fashion and each according to his circumstances, so that in the Jewish setting they could overcome the backwardness of [traditional] life."[7]
Wiener recognized the political significance of maskilic satire, though
not of Reb Nakhman's stories.[8] The modern reader, however, can understand the "revolutionary" character of Reb Nakhman's stories. One
reason for adapting Deleuze and Guattari's model to interpret Reb Nakhman, therefore, is the need to liberate him from the conventions of
a religious "orthodoxy"—to invoke an anachronism—that he neither

identified with nor was accepted into and, at the same time, to resist the agonistic psychoanalytical readings of twentieth-century scholars such as Joseph Weiss or Arthur Green (however impeccable their research), in order to recognize Reb Nakhman, like Kafka, as "an author who laughs with a profound joy"[9] (*Toward a Minor Literature*, 41). In so doing, Reb Nakhman emerges, like Tutuola, as a new paradigm for "minor" literature. In order to demonstrate the relevance of this paradigm, it is necessary to consider the three essential characteristics of "minor" literature, as Deleuze and Guattari define it: the "deterritorialization" of language, the connection to a political "immediacy," and the "collective assemblage of enunciation" (18).

Considering the first of these characteristics: Tutuola represents more conventionally the type of deterritorialization that Deleuze and Guattari have in mind, that of a colonized writer "forced" to use the imperial language and thus displaced from his native means of expression. For want of more precise terminology, one might refer to this type as "extrinsic deterritorialization." Reb Nakhman's language, whether Yiddish or *Loshn-koydesh*, represents, by contrast, a kind of "intrinsic deterritorialization" in the sense that both languages are identifiably and deliberately *Jewish*, yet both are unbound by national borders or political authorities.[10] Reb Nakhman further deterritorializes both languages, and in so doing modernizes Jewish writing, by eroding the traditional division of labor that had instituted a hierarchy of dominant *Loshn-koydesh* and subordinate Yiddish. Both Tutuola's English and Reb Nakhman's bilingualism represent, to use another Deleuzian term, "paths of escape," and it is clear that each writer plays his linguistic status against the stylistic norms of either language that he draws from. Thus Tutuola consciously bends English to the rules of Yoruba syntax and grammar, reterritorializing the colonial language under the auspices of the colonized. Reb Nakhman, analogously, lets Yiddish determine the *Loshn-koydesh* versions of his stories, literally and figuratively, from below.[11]

In general terms, such deterritorialization serves four functions, all of them relevant in varying degrees to understanding the peculiar linguistic character of both Tutuola's and Reb Nakhman's respective work: "vernacular, maternal, or territorial language, used in rural communities or rural in its origins; a vehicular, urban, governmental, even worldwide language, a language of businesses, commercial exchange, bureaucratic transmission . . . ; referential language, language of sense and of culture . . . ; [and] mythic language. . . . [V]ernacular language is *here*; vehicular language is *everywhere*; referential language is *over there*; mythic language is *beyond*" (*Toward a Minor Literature*, 23).[12] Thus, the fusion of native Yoruba grammar and imperial English vocabulary ensures for Tutuola an underlying *vernacular* to an otherwise foreign, *vehicular* language, while his free and fantastic mix of modern technology and traditional cosmology provides simultaneous *referential* and *mythical* layers to his discourse. For Reb Nakhman, similarly, Yiddish is both a *maternal vernacular* and a *vehicular* language of commerce linking Jews, at least throughout the Eastern Europe of Reb Nakhman's day, otherwise separated by governmental boundaries and local customs. Like Tutuola, Reb Nakhman's Yiddish moreover is often *referential* in its frequent mention of non-Jewish customs, political institutions, and instruments of warfare and *mythical* in its extravagant dependence on the *Loshn-koydesh* component of its fusion vocabulary.

Furthermore, between the two versions of his stories, there is a continuous linguistic porousness: thus, Yiddish words and even whole phrases appear throughout the *Loshn-koydesh* versions, while unusual and occasionally even unique verbal coinages from *Loshn-koydesh* are one of the stylistic markers for Reb Nakhman's Yiddish.[13] Both the interrelationship of the *Loshn-koydesh* and Yiddish versions of these stories, and their subversive potential as deterritorialized discourses, have been overlooked by all but two recent commentators—the major exceptions are David Roskies and Chone Shmeruk[14]—who have usually focused on the *Loshn-koydesh* versions, to the exclusion of the Yiddish.[15] According to the "conventional wisdom" of these commentators, the Yiddish versions of these stories were published merely to make them accessible to an audience unable to read *Loshn-koydesh*.

In this manner, Arnold Band writes, "The Hebrew text [of Reb Nakhman's stories] . . . conveys a dimension of connotations lost in the Yiddish. . . . 'Ilan' in Hebrew means a tree and is translated or appears as 'boim' in the Yiddish, but the Hebrew 'ilan' evokes associations with the Kabbalistic 'tree of the spheres' (the world-tree in folklore and anthropology) while 'boim' remains nothing but a tree. In this sense, the Hebrew text must be treated as the primary text first consulted by the translator. . . . " [16] By way of response, just as one can ask of Freud, "when is a cigar just a cigar," so too must one wonder when a tree is merely a tree! The exegetical method that Band's comments exemplify—in which virtually every word of *sipurey mayses* derives from a previous mystical source—denies, unwittingly, the creative force and bewildering originality of Reb Nakhman's narration, and often distorts a basic comprehension of the stories themselves. Considering the Yiddish version of these stories, analytical deadwood for too many commentators, offers a solution to the dilemma of the Jewish tradition and Reb Nakhman's individual talent. Thus, the Yiddish version of these stories possesses an independent *status*, though not an autonomous *function*, from the *Loshn-koydesh*. If the *Loshn-koydesh* version of these stories more fully conveys the "multiple levels of Scripture, Talmud, and Zohar operating beneath the narrative surface" (*A Bridge of Longing*, 30), then the Yiddish version more fully articulates equally important aspects of social satire, creative improvisation, and moral challenge. In such terms, Reb Nakhman's imagery should not be understood as allusions *to* the tradition so much as metaphors derived *from* the tradition that reflect the crisis of values confronting Jews at the onset of modernity in Eastern Europe. By focusing exclusively on the *Loshn-koydesh* and its points of correspondence to the Jewish tradition, contemporary commentators ignore the significance of oral discourse to the structure of the tales and their commentary on the social landscape opening up around Reb Nakhman. To overlook either of these versions is to misapprehend the full range of implications of these stories and their centrality to the development of modern Jewish literature. [17]

The relationship between Yoruba and English in Tutuola's ostensibly monolingual novels has, fortunately, received more thorough scholarly attention, from both linguists and literary critics. Adebisi Afolayan, for example, has offered a formal linguistic analysis of *The Palm-Wine Drinkard*, and has thereby demonstrated that "Tutuola's English is 'Yoruba English' in the sense that it represents the expression of either Yoruba deep grammar with English surface grammar or Yoruba systems and/or structures in English words. . . . " [18] Afolayan further quotes from Tutuola's characteristically aggregative sentence structures to demonstrate that his style "results from the conventional orthography in Yoruba which allows the stringing together of several sentences as a single orthographic sentence" (*Critical Perspectives*, 196). Tutuola's English therefore is a by-product not only of the Yoruba oral tradition but of its *written* conventions, as well. His writing, far from either a "simple" reduction of oral narrative to writing or a "simple" adaptation of Fagunwa into English, is indicative of a fundamentally literate consciousness that adapts oral tradition to self-consciously literary forms—even if both the narrative and stylistic models for these forms are bilingual to an unusual degree.

In stylistic terms, Tutuola's language has given him an advantage over other, typically better educated or more fluent African writers in English. As Omolara Ogundipe-Leslie wrote in 1970, "Tutuola could never have been articulate in the Queen's English, but he becomes fluent, even eloquent, in a language of his own making" (*Critical Perspectives*, 153). But the political significance of his language—his "revolutionary" status as a "minor" writer ("There is nothing that is major or revolutionary except the minor," *Toward a Minor Literature*, 26)—has never been fully schematized. One can begin to understand the subversive potential of his language, and therefore the significance of his aesthetic choices, through reference to Reb Nakhman's bilingual strategies.

Reb Nakhman's precedent, for example, offers a vehicle for fruitful speculation into a mystery of Tutuola's career: the absence of a published Yoruba translation of *The Palm-Wine Drinkard*.[19] What would such a translation have been like? A "straight" translation of *The Palm-Wine Drinkard* "back" into the elevated, heroic stylistic norms of Yoruba narrative would not accurately recreate Tutuola's English style; more likely, such an effort would count as an attempt at rationalization that both linguistically and thematically would efface the narrative's strangeness, its existential location between languages, temporalities, and metaphysical worlds.[20] Part of the joy in reading Tutuola's work, after all, lies in the very political thrill the reader receives from seeing the author's native, "minor" language subvert—not unlike Mark Twain's linguistic subversions in *Huckleberry Finn*—the stylistic and even grammatical norms of the dominant language of his colonizers. What effect would the author have created if he had tried to reverse this power relationship, this revenge fantasy? It would seem, indeed, that the status of Yoruba folktales, as the author would later acknowledge to Michael Thelwell, was already too imperiled to permit further "corruption" by parodying the language in which they were originally conceived. The imbalance of power between English and Yoruba ultimately is pitched too profoundly against Yoruba to allow for a further deterritorialization, a further diminishment of the language's signifying authority and autonomy from what it already had lost under colonialism.[21]

This, in fact, relates to a fundamental distinction between Reb Nakhman and Tutuola: the difference between an intrinsically bilingual culture and an extrinsically bilingual one. But if Tutuola's linguistic strategy is intended to realign the cultural politics of Yoruba and English at the moment of nationalistic awakening in colonial Nigeria, what, then, is the object of Reb Nakhman's linguistic rebellion? The revolution that Reb Nakhman's writing achieves, the only successful one of his career, derives primarily from its *emancipation* of Yiddish; he paradoxically modernizes Jewish literature by granting Yiddish, if only in his tales, an equal or ultimately superior status to *Loshn-koydesh* — thus reinstituting the oral foundation of Jewish learning and devotion. This "return of the repressed" language, given the centrality of *Loshn-koydesh* writing to the rabbinic tradition that Reb Nakhman would be expected, because of his status and birth, to command, and also given the anxiety that early Hasidic leaders faced in establishing the intellectual "bona fides" for their movement (an anxiety that to a lesser extent persists today), can only be interpreted as an act of willful rebellion. Indeed, for Reb Nakhman, the subversion of the roles that Yiddish and *Loshn-koydesh* had played for centuries gives voice to his desire, essentially, for a revolution in Jewish culture *from within*, a reinvigoration of Jewish faith to withstand both the economic and political transformations affecting Eastern Europe as well as the perceived abandonment of Jewish observance encouraged by the inception of *haskole*.

For both of these writers, therefore, the problem of language comes to represent an *existential* moment in the creation of a new subject: the linguistic representation of modernity itself.[22] For Tutuola — and this is ultimately the crucial distinction between him and Fagunwa — the crises of the modern world cannot be articulated in Yoruba, and even the relevance of the Yoruba tradition as an antidote to modernity's rootlessness and atomizing values cannot be communicated to an urban, modern readership in the language of tradition. Nor can Tutuola discuss these problems in the standard English of the colonial power structure. If the streets of Lagos are as fantastic and dangerous as the endless forests of Yoruba folklore, then Tutuola's novels offer a metaphor for the wildness of the modern city through reference to the folkloric tradition; the point of interaction, of metempsychosis, between these worlds is the densely polyphonic language that Tutuola employs.

Similarly, for Reb Nakhman, the crisis that occurs in the first decade of the nineteenth century, whether understood primarily as theological or social, a personal catastrophe in his own messianic expectations or a public collapse in Jewish life brought on by the corruption of Hasidism's original vision and the fledgling emergence of *haskole*, can no longer be addressed in either the traditional forms or even the sanctified language of preexisting Jewish writing.[23] Historically speaking, Hasidism is a complicated, diffuse, and contested phenomenon in the development of Ashkenazic Judaism. Nonetheless, one can summarize its early history, beginning about 1772, as the coalescence of a charismatic movement around the popularization of previously esoteric concepts and literature, which was devoted to a newly influential class of mystic preachers, faith-healers, and kabalists: the Hasidic rebbe or *tsadik*. By the time of Reb Nakhman's ascendancy in the first decade of the nineteenth century, Hasidism was no longer a new "revivalist" movement; it was increasingly the hegemonical force within Jewish religious life, and Reb Nakhman objected to the ostensible complacency of other rebbes as well as to the competition they posed to his own authority.[24] Storytelling, for Reb Nakhman as for Tutuola, offers a series of metaphors through which to represent these public and private conflicts simultaneously. The language of these stories therefore had to convey the immediacy and urgency of personal speech, as well as the sanctity and profundity of holy writing—hence the bilingual strategy that he adopts.

Having addressed the "deterritorialized languages" of Reb Nakhman and Tutuola, it is necessary to consider some of the ways in which these two writers are connected to the "political immediacy" of modernity.

For Reb Nakhman, the conditions of modernization included the 1772 and 1795 partitions of Poland that brought the Ukrainian provinces in which he lived under Russian domination for the first time;[25] the Napoleonic wars and their itinerant discourse of *liberté, égalité, et fraternité*; the tentative beginnings of industrialization[26] and the emergence of a mobile, quasi-urban Jewish mercantile class;[27] and the consolidation of the Hasidic movement. This final point is itself the subject of controversy among Jewish historians. Although it is beyond the intentions of this discussion to adjudicate among the competing theories as to why Hasidism emerged in the second half of the eighteenth century,[28] a sense of the contrast in Eastern European Jewish culture before and after the advent of Hasidism can suggest the political influences on Reb Nakhman's storytelling, specifically, and his radical version of Hasidism in general.

With these questions in mind, Moshe J. Rosman describes the background of social divisiveness out of which the Hasidic movement emerged: "[I]n Miedzybóz[29] there were several vectors in the vortex of social confrontation. In addition to élite versus plebians, there were also different versions of the élite versus élite as well as artisan versus artisan and poor versus poorer. The array of power relationships was not rigid; alignments could shift."[30] Rosman's research suggests two possibilities for a sociopolitical understanding of Hasidism. First, the fact that rich and poor equally participated in the rise of a new, revivalist religious movement suggests that Jews in Eastern Europe, regardless of their economic status, were essentially a *subaltern* group, and therefore they channeled the frustration over the loss of their communal autonomy, which occurred with the partition of Poland, into a spiritual reorganization of communal life.[31] Second, the fact that Hasidism experienced its most significant "growing spurt" in the last third of the eighteenth century suggests that the dissolution of the Polish kingdom by the superior Prussian, Austrian, and Russian empires was a catalyst for the realignment of Jewish life in the era. This would imply that the growth of Hasidism is in part a reaction to the newly "colonized" status of the Jews, primarily in the outer reaches of the Russian and Austrian empires.[32]

The use of the term "colonized" is relatively unusual in the context of Yiddish culture and contemporary Yiddish studies. Nonetheless, the dismemberment of Poland over the years 1772 to 1795 by the empires surrounding it counts as colonization in the most literal sense. In certain respects, especially in contrast with the decentralization of Polish rule, the early years of imperial domination—particularly in Austrian-controlled regions—brought about an expansion of guaranteed rights and economic mobility for Jews. Similarly, imperial policies toward Jews changed over time in relation to other dominated ethnic groups, particularly the Poles, the one group under imperial control that had a recent history of political self-determination. This inconsistency of imperial power is typical of colonialism. In the Russian context, for example, where Yiddish literature experienced its most intense development over the nineteenth century, the colonial atmosphere derived from the fundamental *capriciousness* of autocratic power. John Klier thus explains:

> As [Polish] Commonwealth territories were gradually Russified through the erosion of rights and the removal of pre-partition institutions, special representative bodies for Jews were also eliminated; the deputies of the Jewish people were dispensed with after 1825. The Russian state certainly did not consult the Jewish communities about the introduction of military service. . . . [I]n the reign of Nicholas I [1825–1855], when the government began to pursue a policy of state-sponsored Haskalah, the so-called rabbinical commissions were created to advise the government on matters of Jewish religious practice. These bodies were completely undemocratic, however; their members were appointed by the government and they operated on an ad hoc basis.[33]

As in most colonial situations, the dominant powers in Eastern Europe turned to the elites in the Jewish community to administer policies, enforce communal obligations—such as military service—and collect taxes. Although Hasidism did not arise merely to meet these imperial needs, it did establish a new elite among Eastern European Jews. Part of the early success of Hasidism, coincident to the conquest of Poland, can be attributed to its ability to adapt, evade, and transcend, via the extraterritorial nature of this new elite, the hegemony of imperial power.

Moreover, it is important to stress the immense social change in Eastern European Jewry that Hasidism created because of the internal revitalization of Jewish intellectual life—including, of course, the learned polemics against Hasidism from both proponents of *haskole* (maskilim) and traditionalist rabbis (*misnagdim*)—that Hasidism stimulated. Indeed, in contrast to the social instability that influenced, or appears to have influenced, the formation of the early Hasidic movement, the intellectual climate of Eastern European Jewry immediately before the appearance of Hasidism was essentially stagnant. As Max Weinreich writes, "Ashkenazic Jewry [in the eighteenth century] experienced a period of decline that must have had an impact on its literature. The light reading of this era was for the most part reprints: *Bove-bukh*, *Zigmunt un Magdalene*, etc. Glikl Haml's memoirs are fresh and lively . . . but this hardly counts since they were written only for her family, without a thought for publicity or a broader audience. The historical chronicle *Sheyris yisroel* (Amsterdam, 1743) makes an altogether respectable impression . . . but this can scarcely be considered belletristic. . . . " [34] Although recent historians of Hasidism's origins—Rosman, Gershon Hundert, the late Shmuel Ettinger[35]—are doubtless correct in examining with skepticism the claims of earlier scholars that Hasidism originated essentially as a social, crypto-political movement of discontent against the status quo, these more recent scholars veer to the opposite extreme in dismissing nearly all evidence of social and intellectual unrest, and all populist sentiment, at the root of the early Hasidic movement.

A consideration of Hasidic literature can begin to modify this imbalance. Weinreich's remarks regarding the austerity of European Jewish literature in the seventeenth and eighteenth centuries, for example, underscore the departure of Hasidism from the norms of Jewish self-expression that preceded it. The astringency of eighteenth-century public writing in Yiddish, which consists primarily of lachrymose ethical tracts such as *Lev Toyv*, and often more lugubrious "women's prayers" or *tekhines*, conforms to a broader tendency against "frivolity" or socially disruptive entertainment.[36] One departure of early Hasidic storytelling from the forms of writing that held sway in the generations preceding its advent is the extraordinary prominence this genre accords to the fantastic. The stories of *Shivkhey haBeSh"T* ["The Praises of the Baal Shem Tov," 1815][37] and Reb Nakhman's *sipurey mayses* are the first volumes after a gap of more than 150 years to compete with the great works of medieval Yiddish narrative in captivating and stimulating the creativity of the traditional Jewish audience. The opportunity to participate, however vicariously, in the life and deeds of the Hasidic rebbe—a figure simultaneously holy and charismatic, religious and social—both epitomizes the social aspirations of the new movement and transcends them at the same time. In this sense the figure of the rebbe signifies a new mode of leadership and social organization among Ashkenazic Jews. His rise to prominence over the latter half of the eighteenth century initiates a revolution, expressed in mystical and religious terms rather than political ones, that cuts across formerly rigid lines of class, education, region, and local custom.[38]

Furthermore, as hagiographical testimonials of the Baal Shem Tov's character, the stories in *Shivkhey HaBeSh"T* establish the model for subsequent Hasidic tales. They also depart from earlier Yiddish genres in that they are not, at least explicitly, reworkings of previous narratives from either coterritorial or venerable Jewish sources but are dynamic, heroic descriptions of real individuals who had lived in nearly the same time and place as their audience. In this regard, Simon Dubnow offers a sense of the creative novelty of Hasidic storytelling that helps explain both psychologically and socially the environment out of which Reb Nakhman's own storytelling developed: "In these generations, the spirit of which has yet to depart even from our own surroundings, a mystical cult, a new type of miracle tale, was created in the 'broad daylight' of our history . . . the heroes of which did not emerge from primordial legend, but were human beings who lived in the most recent past."[39] With little exaggeration, Dubnow identifies precisely the thrilling mix of historical verisimilitude and wondrous mythology—the notion that miraculous events occurred not only in the legends of the medieval German rabbis, or in biblical times, but also in the lifetime of the Hasidic audience of the early nineteenth century—that characterizes Hasidic storytelling. Nothing in Reb Nakhman's stories is more fantastic than the legends told about the Baal Shem Tov, and therefore the precedent of these hagiographies, particularly in their precanonical, oral form, provides Reb Nakhman with the stimulus and legitimacy to tell his own stories.

For Tutuola, the analogous factors that would connect him to a "political immediacy"—a presumably simple enough task, given the extensive theoretical and historical research that has developed around postcolonialism in Africa—include the urbanization of Yorubaland (which he experienced), World War II (of which he was a veteran), the creation of a civil service class in Lagos (of which he was a member), and the rapid growth of nationalism throughout Western Africa. Each of these developments occurred within the first thirty years of Tutuola's life; the conclusion of World War II brought the advent of the independence movement in Africa that developed rapidly in the seven years separating Tutuola's military discharge from his publication of *The Palm-Wine Drinkard*. In purely literary terms, moreover, the appearance of a new form of popular literature, in English and Igbo, occurred in the markets of the southeastern Nigerian city of Onitsha at the same time that Tutuola began writing in the 1940s.

Much of the scholarly interest in this literature derives from its demonstrable connection with the modernization and development of national consciousness in the postwar era. This locally produced market literature, which as a variety of "organic," popular narrative occupies an analogously parallel position in relation to Tutuola as the "standard" Hasidic hagiographies do to Reb Nakhman's idiosyncratic storytelling, is in fact seldom invoked in discussions of Tutuola. As Charles Larson states, "Amos Tutuola's universe is almost totally different from that of the Onitsha pamphleteers. While theirs is a world of urbanization and neorealism, Tutuola's is one of jungle and bush—fantasy, supernaturalism, and surrealism" (*The Emergence of African Fiction*, 93). Moreover, as a phenomenon concentrated in Nigeria's southeast among the Igbo ethnic group, market literature would presumably fall outside the parameters of Tutuola's southwestern Yoruba culture. And yet, without arguing for a direct interaction or influence between these distinct literary phenomena, it is worth considering that this popular literature is linguistically hybrid in almost exactly the same way, and for the same reasons, as Tutuola's fantastic novels; both coincide with the formulation of a new idea of the Nigerian "nation" that occurs with the adoption of the 1947 constitution and the convening, for the first time, of a regionally elected legislature encompassing the whole of the British colony.[40] They are therefore among the first productions of what can be referred to as a Nigerian national culture.

Because market literature engages directly with social and political themes that Tutuola addresses only obliquely,[41] considering the way that political factors shaped these homegrown, populist pamphlets offers a means of understanding the political factors in Tutuola's writing. Thus Emmanuel Obiechina writes: "[The] period from the late 1930s onward was marked by intense political activity. It was the era of the soap-box political rhetoricians and spell-binders. . . . The tendency towards thinking and reacting in clichés and slogans further developed during this intensely political age and has persisted ever since. The pages of the pamphlet literature bear eloquent testimony to it. They are sprayed with stock expressions from newspapers, the cinema, romantic magazines, the Bible and other religious works, literature books and so on" (*An African Popular Literature*, 79–80). The language of Tutuola's writing derives from a comparable variety of sources, among them religious sermons, technical terms, and Yoruba idiom. But the effect of Tutuola's writing, unlike that of the market pamphlets, is never clichéd or jingoistic. Tutuola's writing, though persistently calling attention to the diversity of its inspirations, is at the same time always greater than the sum of its parts. One can, however, understand the motivation for Tutuola's heteroglossia by considering the rudimentary attempts of his contemporaries to create a literary language from the various jargons around them.

By way of analogy, one can compare Onitsha market literature with what the musicologist Mark Slobin has written about the "vulgarity" of Jewish American popular music at the beginning of the twentieth century: "[A] complexity of motivation reflects the cultural confusion of the situation being described [in these songs]. . . . Linguistic variety and hyperbole, along with cultural excess, reflect the disarray of immigrant life."[42] Just as Slobin argues that the aesthetic character of supposedly vulgar entertainment—linguistic variety and hyperbole, cultural excess—reflects the confusion of immigrant life, so can one understand that the lack of control that the Onitsha authors maintain over their language expresses a similar confusion of values. The lack of a discourse to articulate the situations these writers seek to describe signifies deeper psychological and moral ruptures among the writers personally and their audience generally.

By contrast, there can be little question that Tutuola is in control of his literary materials. It is remarkable, moreover, that Tutuola, particularly in the West, has been accepted in the ranks of serious literature without his ever attempting to mimic the values or aesthetics associated with contemporary Western literary genres. It is even more remarkable that his relative canonization has occurred at the expense of precious little energy to understand the structural and aesthetic features that he offers in place of, for example, Chinua Achebe's neorealism or Wole Soyinka's neomodernism. In lieu of a critical terminology with which to characterize his writing, one can point with ease to the theme of disorder—chaos—that resonates everywhere in his work. The very obscurity of the symbolic language that he employs, the compulsion he feels to create a private literary language, therefore offers proof that he seeks to reflect, *on the level of literary language itself*, the rupture in values portrayed less self-consciously by the "popular" writers of his day. Because Tutuola's aesthetic choices, unlike those of his contemporaries, are so self-conscious, they are an ideal focus for a literary interpretation of modernity in the new Nigerian culture.

It is now possible to consider the third characteristic that Deleuze and Guattari assign to "minor" literature, the "collective assemblage of enunciation." The theorists define the "assemblage," their central concept for describing Kafka's writing and its significance, simultaneously in formal and psychic terms:

> [I]t is segmental, extending itself over several contiguous segments or dividing into segments that become assemblages in turn. . . . The segments are simultaneously powers and territories—they capture desire by territorializing it, fixing it in place. . . . But we must declare as well that an assemblage has points of deterritorialization; or that it always has a line of escape by which it escapes itself and makes its enunciations or its expressions take flight and disarticulate . . . or that the assemblage extends over or penetrates an unlimited field of immanence that makes the segments melt and that liberates desire from all its concretizations and abstractions or . . . fights actively against them in order to dissolve them. (*Toward a Minor Literature*, 85–86)[43]

Stated more directly, an assemblage is a structure that never concludes or resolves itself into stable hierarchies. It is a neurotic structure, forever vacillating between the imperatives of desire and power—and thus forever generating new compartments within its "field of immanence." With respect to the unresolved nature of the assemblage, it is noteworthy that both *The Palm-Wine Drinkard* and *Seyfer sipurey mayses* conclude on a note of radical "incompleteness": Reb Nakhman's tale of the Seventh Beggar will remain untold until the final redemption; the problem riddles that the Palm-Wine Drinkard must solve defy resolution, though not interpretation, in the realm of logic and remain unanswered at the book's end. This resistance to literary closure is characteristic of both the evolution of literary structures—in which evolution itself serves a narrative and structural function—and the historical situation into which these two writers enter.

In terms of literary form, *The Palm-Wine Drinkard* is an assemblage in that Tutuola constructs a single narrative out of a proliferation of adapted and reworked folk tales, each of which by itself contains more than one narrative "segment," and hence can be considered an "assemblage" in turn. Leslie Ogundipe-Leslie remarks in this capacity, somewhat clinically, that "[Tutuola] has given . . . *The Palm-Wine Drinkard* an asymmetric form. . . . Roughly twenty-one episodes made up the Departure, that is, the journey to Deads' Town; five bring him back to the river which all too frequently in folk imagination demarcates the land of the dead from the land of the living; and about four episodes comprise the events taking place after his return from his Quest. . . . Of the twenty-nine episodes in the book, sixteen are unoriginal, taken from folklore, or from Fagunwa, or from popular wit . . . " (*Critical Perspectives*, 147–148). As an autonomous narrative, *The Palm-Wine Drinkard* incorporates an additional "point of deterritorialization" by making reference to the "two-headed creature" from *The Wild Hunter in the Bush of Ghosts* (*PWD*, 235)—even though the latter narrative did not appear in book form until nearly thirty years after the former[44]—as if each book were a segment within a larger assemblage.[45]

Internally, the proliferating series of monsters in the endless forest also forms an assemblage that represents, in various guises, "a concretization of power, of desire, of territoriality," and so forth, each of which the protagonist must overcome, only to encounter new concretizations in the guise of a new monster that further proliferates the assemblage as a whole. The more general thematic preoccupations of the novel, as well, create assemblages: the porousness between languages (a feature Tutuola shares with Reb Nakhman) and the porousness between belief systems (a tendency that Reb Nakhman rejects!) resist the concretization of power, of "transcendental law," so that generic, linguistic, biological, and cosmological classifications are *never* fixed but always in a state of "becoming," of merging and recombining. These assemblages are therefore reflective of the *unfixed* character of Nigerian life in the era *between* colonialism and independence, power and desire—for a generation *between* tradition and modernity. Indeed, Tutuola's response to the dislocations of his time is more radical than that of any of his contemporaries writing either in realist English (Achebe) or fabulist Yoruba (Fagunwa). Tutuola responds to the unsettled character of his time by creating structures that mirror the transformational nature of Nigerian society in their refusal to be tied to a stable social or aesthetic formation. That these structures are the only ones he was capable of creating, due to his education and experience, is testimony not to the weakness of his aesthetic but to its inevitability.

Deleuze and Guattari's vocabulary acquires further relevance in this context when one considers the ultimate affinity of the structures they describe to oral narrative forms and consciousness. For example, Walter Ong recalls among many proofs of the oral origins of Homeric poetry the observation that "the organization of the *Iliad* suggests boxes within boxes created by thematic recurrences. . . . " [46] This model, in Deleuzian terms, is an assemblage, and this coincidence points to the ultimate compatibility of an "oral/written discourse" analysis with Deleuze and Guattari's poststructuralism: the assemblage itself, whether employed by Kafka[47] or Reb Nakhman and Tutuola, represents a return to oral narrative habits. More specifically, Tutuola and Reb Nakhman—neither of whom demonstrates a particular consciousness of postmodern theory—are attuned to the structures that Deleuze and Guattari have designated as "minor" by virtue of their proximity to oral structures.

The concept of the assemblage further resolves questions of exegetical and narrative unity in Reb Nakhman's collected stories. In this regard, both the assemblage as an expanding structure and the fundamentally oral character of Reb Nakhman's *toyre* (Hasidic teaching) are recognizable in the uncollected, uncollectable state of his writings. His various unpublished, suppressed, and burned manuscripts[48] form missing cogs in the assemblage of Reb Nakhman's praxis of Hasidism and, thus, eternal paths of escape from a finite or fixed meaning that Reb Nakhman so heroically resists. In philosophical terms, moreover, Reb Nakhman's teaching abjures the status of "transcendental law" because this stature can only be accorded to the Torah, itself given by a God whose transcendence signifies for Reb Nakhman an ineffable inscrutability.[49] The "immanence" of Reb Nakhman's own teaching, by contrast, is confirmed with respect to its incompleteness; most of Reb Nakhman's "missing" manuscripts continue to circulate surreptitiously, seeming to confirm for genuine Breslover Hasidim the idea—whether as belief or necessary fiction—that the Rebbe is not dead, even after two centuries. These "subterranean" manuscripts extend the assemblage of his teachings to offer new, previously "unrecorded" teachings. Indeed, the entire production of the Hasidic *seyfer*, from oral performance to memorization to transcription/translation to publication, is itself an assemblage, a bureaucracy, unparalleled by anything else in modern letters.

If the relationship between Reb Nakhman's stories and his other teachings does not justify referring to the *Seyfer sipurey mayses* as an integrated narrative—and there is no reason to suggest that it does—it is worthwhile to point out that despite the conscious organization of *The Palm-Wine Drinkard*, Tutuola nonetheless highlights, to a greater degree than his contemporaries, the rupture between individual episodes and the novelistic design as a whole. In this respect, it is worth recalling the episodic nature of vernacular narratives earlier in history—the discrete narratives of the *Decameron* in connection with the marvelous digressions of *La Vie de Gargantua et de Pantagruel*, for example. That such diffuseness is characteristic of emerging literature derives precisely from its connection with the folktale. The difference between Reb Nakhman's stories and Tutuola's novel is therefore one of degree, not kind.

If Reb Nakhman's *seyfer* (holy book) is thus not, like *The Palm-Wine Drinkard*, a novel, or even a unified narrative, it is nonetheless possible to discuss thematic and motivic patterns and recurrences that provide at least a loose structural unity: of the thirteen tales, eleven (1, 2, 4–7, 9–13) deal with a king and kingship (or empire); six deal with father-children relationships or intergenerational conflicts (1, 2, 5, 8, 10, 11); six deal with disguised, mistaken, or reversed identities (i.e., the great become lowly and vice versa: 2, 4, 7, 9–11); five or perhaps six deal with explicitly Jewish themes (4, 5, 8, 9, 12 [also 13? Is the wedding in the "Tale of The Seven Beggars" a Jewish wedding?]); and four focus exclusively on non-Jewish characters (1, 2, 7, 11). Moreover, even though the collection as a whole does not create a unified narrative, specific sequences within the *seyfer* suggest thematic, if not narrative, development. Hence the ninth tale, *A mayse mit a hokhem un a tam* ("A Story of a Sophisticate and a Simpleton"), a parody of the maskilim, the leading opponents to Hasidism in the nineteenth century, directly follows *Meyrav uveyn yokhid* ("A Rabbi and His Only Son"), a Menippean satire directed at the *misnagdim*, the traditional, rabbinically oriented Jews who were Hasidism's principal opponents in the eighteenth century. In broadest terms, the simultaneous preoccupation with kingship and paternity consciously refers both to differing aspects of God's relationship to the world—God in Jewish liturgy is, famously, *avinu malkeynu*, "Our Father, Our King"—and to crises in the public and private authority of men in Reb Nakhman's day. Similarly, the alternating focus on Jewish and non-Jewish characters, as well as the sometimes surreal interaction between them, suggests that the political anxieties in these tales relate to both internal and external Jewish politics.

The assemblage structure also manifests itself in the relationship of these books to the writers' career as a whole through the ambiguous correspondence of these two "minor" figures to what Michel Foucault describes as the "author function."[50] In Reb Nakhman's case, any evaluation must reckon with the fact that Reb Nakhman is, literally, *not* the person responsible for committing the words of his stories, or any of his other public writings, to paper. He can thus be reckoned the *creator*, but technically speaking *not* the author, of his stories; Reb Noson (Nathan) of Nemirov (1780–1844), Reb Nakhman's devoted scribe, was the actual person who recorded the Rebbe's thoughts and edited them for publication, in most cases after the Rebbe's death. This fact makes interpretation of Reb Nakhman's work particularly difficult: Are the ruptures, digressions, and inconsistencies that dot the surface of the *sipurey mayses* attributable to poor narration, poor transcription, or a discrepancy between the two? Have Reb Noson's inevitable editorial decisions—and no one doubts his scrupulousness in this regard—improved or diminished the quality of these stories? The unanswerability of these questions, and the controversies they generate among scholars, attest to the problem of assigning conventional functions, such as "author," "plot," "closure," and so forth, to literatures that lack fixed conventions in these matters.

The same problems recur with respect to Tutuola. Even his authorship of *The Palm-Wine Drinkard* caused sufficient anxiety for his publishers that they made the unusual decision to print a page from his (rather elegantly handwritten) manuscript in the published edition of the book (*PWD*, 208). And although no doubt exists today that Tutuola in the physical sense committed the words of his novel to paper, controversy continues to rage around his "authorship" of the narrative—more acutely in Nigeria than in the West. According to his negative reviewers, the origin of *The Palm-Wine Drinkard* can variously be traced to the moralistic/allegorical tradition of such colonial-school staples as *Pilgrim's Progress*; to D. O. Fagunwa's Yoruba classics; to the oral folk traditions of western Nigeria; indeed, to anyone, it seems, but Tutuola himself. In both Reb Nakhman and Tutuola, furthermore, there remains the unresolved tension between linguistic traditions—*Loshn-koydesh* and Yiddish for Reb Nakhman, Yoruba and English for Tutuola—and, perhaps more fundamentally, an unresolved tension between collective, oral traditions and the demands of modern, autonomous writing.

One can therefore appropriate from Antonio Gramsci—as if he hadn't suffered enough already—yet another concept for schematizing the differences between the authors under consideration in this comparison and conventional literary figures in "major" traditions: that of the "organic intellectual."[51] Although in the narrowest sense, Gramsci means by this term the specialists within each profession by which capitalism implements its technical innovations, he evokes through the concept of the organic intellectual the intellectual activity that each individual engages in, regardless of whether or not he or she is engaged in a specifically scholastic or academically certified occupation. Gramsci writes, "There is no human activity from which every form of intellectual participation can be excluded: *homo faber* cannot be separated from *homo sapiens*. Each man . . . outside his professional activity carries on some form of intellectual activity . . . he participates in a particular conception of the world . . . and therefore contributes to sustain a conception of the world or to modify it, that is, to bring into being new modes of thought" (*Prison Notebooks,* 9). In Reb Nakhman's era, the eighteenth-century conflict between traditional rabbinical scholars (*misnagdim*) and the charismatic Hasidic movement can thus be understood in part as an instance of the dialectic between traditional, institutional intellectuals and organic ones.

Similarly, the nineteenth-century conflict between exponents of the Jewish enlightenment (maskilim) and Hasidim represents the equally relevant conflict between urban and rural intellectuals.[52] Even though the vast majority of Eastern European Jews in this era resided in towns (*shtetlekh*),[53] just as many Hasidic rebbes were as learned as their misnagdic enemies, Gramsci's terminology is useful insofar as it refers to the orientation and source of values for these respective intellectuals. Because the connection between intellectual authority and political or economic self-determination is quite attenuated, *misnagdim*, maskilim, and Hasidim are all in effect competing simultaneously for the allegiance of their folk and for economic privileges from the governing classes.

Tutuola, as well, reflects and refracts the Gramscian model in that he is economically and politically an urban intellectual. Nevertheless, he is *not* an elite (!) but rather part of an urban, Anglophone industrial class who exercises his intellectual authority, seemingly, in an entirely rural fashion (by manipulating the folk tradition). More paradoxically, he is an organic intellectual who could not function without a thoroughly modern economic industry of publishing and distribution—his original English publishers were Faber and Faber, then headed by none other than T. S. Eliot—and whose inspiration to write derives as much from the boredom of modern bureaucratic labor as from a desire to preserve rural folk traditions. A profile of Tutuola published in the May 1, 1954 issue of *West Africa* reports that the author began to consider writing "[t]o free his mind from the boredom of clock-watching" while working as a messenger with the Labour Department in Lagos. "Of his first written story, *The Wild Hunter in the Bush of Ghosts*, he says 'in a day I cannot sit down doing nothing. I was just playing at it. My intention was not to send it anywhere'" (*Critical Perspectives*, 36).

The intellectual problems that Gramsci and Foucault isolate converge on the peripheral writer to illuminate another aspect of the correspondence between Reb Nakhman and Tutuola: the similarity with which critical authorities in their respective cultures have willfully distorted their creative achievements. Thus, Simon Dubnow, for example, dismisses Reb Nakhman's literary activity by writing; "In all his . . . 'tales' the author [Reb Nakhman] follows the path of old-wives tales of the worst sort. The majority of them describe a king who wanders aimlessly over various lands; a prince and a princess who are lost and magically found; or bandits and pirates . . . such as are found in children's tales."[54] Dubnow, by contrast, devoted his entire career to the establishment of Judaism as a "major" culture within European civilization; he once articulated his own mission as a historian by writing, in Russian, "[l]et us demonstrate that as Russian Jews we constitute a branch of the 'most historical' nation, are in possession of a rich past, and know how to give it value."[55] For Dubnow, nothing calls more glaring attention to the persistent "minority" of Jewish culture than the origins of its modern literature in the intellectual *minority* of children's fantasies.

And yet, children's stories—fables, folktales, and fairy tales—are a natural source for literature in a peripheral culture, which lacks formal belletristic structures for an autonomous "adult" literature. Peripheral literature reworks the motifs of children's tales, releasing them from the obligation to impart specific moral lessons, and thus enabling them to become a vehicle for experiment and engagement with the modern world. As Quayson writes, in this connection, about Tutuola:

> The interesting thing about Tutuola's handling of these [folkloric] materials is that he brings together a whole range of oral genres such as riddles, proverbs and etymological tales so that his narratives become concatenations of several elements from Yoruba storytelling traditions and thus cannot be easily limited to one mode or genre. Furthermore, he interweaves the cautionary vein with humour, giving the cautionary mode an inflection that does not seem to be present in the oral

contexts in which cautionary tales are used to frighten and inform children about the spiritual world. (*Strategic Transformations*, 46)

In keeping with the traditional Jewish interpretative model of *Kal Va-Chomer*—inferring from an apparent case to a more obscure one—one can argue that if Tutuola has liberated Yoruba storytelling from its homiletic and therefore generic strictures, how much more radically has Reb Nakhman achieved such freedom for the Yiddish tale!

Tutuola has not escaped, however, either the obscurantism of many academic researchers or the hostility of his native audience. Of the former, one need only note the following citation from one Paul Neumarkt: "In a study of Amos Tutuola, there are certain psychiatric categories, such as the syndromes of paranoia and lycanthropy which will have to be taken into consideration" (*Critical Perspectives*, 183).[56] A more provocative complaint against Tutuola can be represented by an indignant letter to the editor by Babasola Johnson, published in the April 10, 1954 issue of *West Africa*: "*Palm-Wine Drinkard* should not have been published at all. The language in which it is written is foreign to West Africans and English people, or anybody for that matter. . . . The language is not West African Patois as some think. Patois is more orderly and intelligible than the language of *The Palm-Wine Drinkard*. . . . How many English readers know that 'Unreturnable Heaven's Land' [see *PWD*, 238] is Mr. Tutuola's version of 'The undiscovered country from whose bourne no traveler returns'?"[57] Although one is free to decide if Johnson's translation of "unreturnable heaven" is superior to Tutuola's, what is significant about this letter is the anxiety that Tutuola's English provokes among his own countrymen. Johnson presents three options for the postcolonial Yoruba novelist: directly translated Yoruba, very rhetorical standard English, and colloquial Nigerian "street" English. He or she could write in Yoruba—this letter mentions Fagunwa favorably—or in standard English, or in "patois." Each of these languages is ostensibly valid, provided that it remains "pristine." The one option that is unacceptable is Tutuola's strategy, to write in a mixture of the three.

The status of Tutuola's English in fact parallels, uncannily, the status of Yiddish both as a fusion language and as the haven of Jewish folklore for Jewish intellectuals in the nineteenth century. Indeed, one of the interesting insights that a consideration of Reb Nakhman in the context of "minor" literary theory reveals is the fact that Yiddish has already occupied a peripheral space within traditional Judaism before the advent of modernity—and that Reb Nakhman seizes on the revolutionary potential of Yiddish to articulate both the innovative political and theological presence of Hasidism within the tradition, and more particularly the revolutionary spiritual vision of his *toyre* within the Hasidic subculture of his day. His seemingly incomprehensible stories, the only work among his voluminous writings to have been published originally in both Yiddish and *Loshn-koydesh*, thus signify not only the exceptionality of his teachings within traditional Eastern European Judaism but also the more general status of Yiddish as a language in which the sanctity of *Loshn-koydesh* can be at least provisionally bypassed and the hegemonic seriousness of rabbinical Judaism, therefore, can be overcome.

More generally, the reader of "minor" literatures must confront the question of whether mixed languages in literary contexts are inevitably comic and subversive—that is, parodic. It seems that they are, as long as they are perceived as a fusion, a mismatch, a *mishmash*. Complaints about fusion languages, whether voiced by maskilim against Yiddish or by "Anglicized" Nigerians against Tutuola's English, are thus a consequence of peripherality itself, a response to the powerlessness of the marginal group forced to struggle with the mixed, "degraded" language. The responses of these intellectuals refer back to a dream of *re*territorialization, the dream that by means of linguistic *purity*, a marginalized folk can recenter itself, and thereby reposition its greatness, by fiat. Tutuola and Reb Nakhman attempt something more difficult: they poeticize the despised language as it exists. One can therefore learn much from Deleuze and Guattari's observation that the power of writers such as Kafka and Beckett—or Tutuola and Reb Nakhman—resides in their ability to capture the *intensity* of a deterritorialized language (*Toward a Minor Literature,* 19). In structural terms, as well, one can consider Gerald Moore's early comment, that "even those who have always been inclined to dismiss [Tutuola] as a 'freak' will at least admit that he is now too sizable a freak to be ignored" (*Critical Perspectives,* 49), as a complement to the linguistic anxiety that Tutuola and writers

like him provoke. The label "freak" is neither accidental nor imperti-
nent; one can better understand the term as a pejorative designation
for a writer who is, in fact, sui generis. In theoretical terms, Tutuola
represents the "minor" writer in a mixed-language culture. In artistic
terms, he is unique.

Two   One Tale, Two Tellers

Having proposed the theoretical foundations for this comparison, it is possible, at last, to engage directly with these two writers in detail. The most apt focus for this discussion is the structural and thematic similarity between Reb Nakhman's *mayse aleph* ("Tale the First"; Y 1–17, E 31–54) and the "Complete Gentleman" episode (*PWD*, 200–213) of *The Palm-Wine Drinkard*. By way of introduction, Reb Nakhman's *mayse aleph*, *Meyaveydas bas-meylekh* ("About the Loss of a King's Daughter") was first told on Saturday, July 25, 1806 (E 31). This story describes a king's daughter, his seventh child, who vanishes one night after her father "lets slip a word that the no-good should take you away."[1] The following day, a viceroy goes out in search of her, accompanied by a servant, a horse, and some money. Traveling over deserts, fields, and forests, he comes upon a beautiful castle. Abandoning his horse, he enters the castle unmolested by its many guards. In the main hall he encounters a vast and opulent court awaiting the arrival of the queen—the lost princess. Recognizing her, he asks how she arrived there. "It happened when my father said 'no-good' should take you away. This place is No-Good" (Y 4–5; E 39). In order to take the lost princess out of the castle, she commands him to seclude himself for an entire year, after which he must fast and remain awake for twenty-four hours. Heeding her order, he endures the test until the very end, when he eats an apple, which causes him to fall asleep for many years.

52   Upon awaking, he seeks the princess out again, who commands him to hide himself another year and on the last day abstain from wine in order to remain awake. But on the last day of the second test he finds a spring from which wine flows. Again he falls asleep for seventy

years. In that time, the princess leaves the castle and passing him in his slumber she leaves him a note written in tears on a kerchief, explaining that she would now be found in a pearl castle atop a golden mountain. When he awakens, the viceroy abandons his servant to search for the lost princess. Along the way in the wilderness he encounters three giants who together summon the animals, birds, and winds to assist him in his quest; only the last giant summons a final wind to carry him to the golden mountain, where he could only enter by bribing the soldiers standing guard at its entrance. Reb Nakhman does not tell how the viceroy freed the princess. But in the end he did free her.

The Palm-Wine Drinkard describes the quest of a rich man's son, who bears the auspicious name "Father of gods who could do anything in this world," to find his dead palm-wine tapster in the "Deads' Town"; along his journey he encounters and captures death, acquires a wife, fathers and then abandons a demon-child born from his wife's thumb, encounters numerous fearful ghosts, enjoys a respite from his travails in a casino found inside a white tree, evades a plot to scapegoat him for the murder of a king's son, then arrives at the Deads' Town only to find that he is unable to bring the tapster back with him "because a dead man could not live with alives and their characteristics would not be the same" (*PWD*, 279). When after further adventures the Palm-Wine Drinkard returns to his home he discovers that a great famine rages as a result of a dispute between heaven and earth. Armed with the gift of a providential egg from his dead tapster, the Drinkard ends the famine and feeds the whole world until the revelry accompanying the famine's end causes the egg to break. Only when a sacrifice is brought to heaven do rains fall again and the natural order, apparently, is restored.

Within this fantastic, picaresque narrative, "The Complete Gentleman" episode describes a daughter unwilling to accept any of the suitors with whom her wealthy father arranges her to marry. One day at the market, she is lured into the "Endless Forest" by a man far more beautiful than any she has ever seen before; Tutuola describes this figure by writing, "He was a beautiful 'Complete' gentleman, he dressed with the finest and most costly clothes, all the parts of his body were completed, he was a tall man but stout. As this gentleman came to the market on that day, if he had been an article or animal for sale, he would be sold at least for £ 2000" (*PWD*, 202). On finding herself lost in the forest, however, the girl discovers that his beauty is an assemblage constructed from various body parts that he has borrowed or rented from other creatures, and in reality he is a skull.[2] The girl's distraught father commissions the Palm-Wine Drinkard to rescue his daughter, who is now held captive somewhere in the endless forest, in the realm of the skulls. Disguised as a lizard, the Drinkard follows the "Complete Gentleman" back from the market to his lair, where the rich man's daughter is held captive on a large frog, with a cowrie shell tied to her neck to prevent her from speaking. When he attempts to rescue her, the cowrie sounds an alarm that could be heard four miles away (*PWD*, 210). To save himself, the Drinkard transforms into a sparrow. Transforming again into a lizard, he discovers the cure for the daughter's captivity: a leaf that the Complete Gentleman/Skull had ripped in two which must be pieced together again. When he cooks the leaf and feeds it to her, the cowrie disappears and they are able to escape. And this is how the Palm-Wine Drinkard acquires his wife.

Despite the superficial disparities of cultural reference between the two tales—there are no cowrie shells in eastern Europe, nor pearl castles in the symbol systems of western Nigeria—there are enough morphological similarities and direct correspondences to suggest a fundamental structural relationship between them. A comparison of these stories thus demonstrates that although they share a common theme and draw on similar folkloric devices, in both instances the authors have modified the "logic" of the folktale to convey the newly unfixed, unsettled quality of life in their respective cultures at the onset of modernization. In formal terms, a basic distinction must be drawn between these two episodes: for Reb Nakhman, *mayse aleph* is a tale unto itself, whereas for Tutuola, "The Complete Gentleman" is an incident on the Palm-Wine Drinkard's journey, both demarcated from and integrated into a larger narrative. One can nonetheless see that both Reb Nakhman and Tutuola violate the formal rules of the fairy tale, with which their tales share the essential plot structure of a hero's charge to rescue a maiden by magical means.[3] That they violate the conventional structure of the material they use is already evidence that in both cases the reader must deal with independent writers, in belletristic terms, rather than with mere transcriptions or reductions of oral narrative performance.[4] Nonetheless, it is illuminating to consider in what ways these two authors violate the generic conventions of the fairy tale. One can venture to say that Reb Nakhman achieves his transformation of archetypal folkloric structures into personal, "literary" expression through compression and ellipsis, whereas Tutuola achieves his "writerly" effects through elaboration and deferment.

In both narratives, the author begins with an initial situation that already calls attention to the porousness of literary demarcations. The "Complete Gentleman" episode is, as Sunday Anozie demonstrates, the third discrete incident in *The Palm-Wine Drinkard*.[5] Reb Nakhman is already "midway through life's journey" when he begins to tell his first story: "On the way I told a story, and whoever heard it was moved instantly to repentance. And this is the story" (Y 1; E 31). In fact, in each incident, the narrative is set into motion by introducing the various members of an incipient family drama. Only after these characters have been assembled—which in Tutuola's case requires a fundamental shift away from the protagonist of the novel—does the primary protagonist of the incident emerge to accept the charge of finding the missing daughter. In each version, the story develops when both the Lady and her ostensible Rescuer are in the domain of evil, though the external appearance of this domain varies considerably between the two narratives.

In the second half of the narratives, correspondences begin to intensify: Tutuola's Lady attempts to escape and Reb Nakhman's Viceroy attempts to rescue the King's Daughter from the lair of evil. At precisely this point, a curious inversion of great thematic significance occurs—the Palm-Wine Drinkard begins his quest with an otherwise "functionless" palm-wine *binge* (PWD, 206), whereas the Viceroy attempts to abstain from earthly comforts, culminating in the calamitous *fast* at the end of his yearlong trial. Thereafter both tales provide a recapitulation of sorts, with the Palm-Wine Drinkard retracing the Lady's steps, and the Viceroy returning to the King's Daughter for a second trial. When the Viceroy and the Drinkard next encounter the captive maidens, and both heroines are unable to communicate directly with the heroes, further trials await the male protagonists. For Tutuola, the Palm-Wine Drinkard is able to carry the Lady out of the Skulls' lair in a dramatically apt nick of time, just as Reb Nakhman provides the third and final wind to arrive in the instant when the Custodian of the Winds is about to send the Viceroy away. Both narratives then provide an analogous climax, with the Palm-Wine Drinkard returning a third and final time to the endless forest to discover the cure for the Lady's muteness, and the Viceroy bribing the guards to gain entry, at last, to the Pearl Castle on the Golden Mountain. Both narratives then conclude each incident without providing conventional closure; the Palm-Wine Drinkard marries the Lady, but new problems and adventures follow them immediately, whereas the Viceroy takes the King's Daughter out of the Pearl Castle, but how this takes place or what follows remain unnarrated.

Having suggested some of the parallels apparent in these two narratives, one can now consider the ways in which they draw upon and adapt traditional tale genres; as Propp states, "The hero of the tale may be one of two types: (1) if a young girl is kidnapped . . . and if Ivan goes off in search of her, then the hero of the tale is Ivan . . . (2) if a young girl or boy is seized or driven out . . . then the hero of the tale is the . . . banished boy or girl" (*Morphology of the Folktale*, 36).[6] In both narratives, elements of each type freely intermingle: Tutuola's Lady is both the errant girl who must be punished for disobeying her father *and* the captured maiden who must be rescued by a drunken Ivan, whereas the King's Daughter is simultaneously the kidnapped object *and* the self-valorizing instigator/antagonist of the Viceroy's quest. In both Tutuola and Reb Nakhman, the basic motif of a beautiful girl, a "princess," stolen away to the realm of evil is transformed from a story about the princess to a story about her rescuer—though with different narrative functions. For Tutuola, the transformation carries the folkloric motif over to the broader novelistic structure by linking the rich man's daughter to the Palm-Wine Drinkard, not only dramatically, but also thematically, in that they share analogous characteristics of self-centeredness, indifference to traditional norms of behavior, and impracticality or poor planning. For Reb Nakhman, an almost diametric narrative motion occurs, insofar as the narrative action of *mayse aleph* becomes reflexive and internalized, thus unintegrated into a larger narrative. It is unfinished and unfinishable (at least until the coming of the Messiah).

For both Tutuola and Reb Nakhman, the emphasis is not on the actual rescue of the maiden, but on the obligations of the hero; hence the shame that the Palm-Wine Drinkard feels when he recalls that his name is "Father of gods who could do anything in this world": "I was about to refuse to go and find out his daughter . . . but when I remembered my name I was ashamed to refuse. So I agreed to find out his daughter" (*PWD*, 201). In Reb Nakhman, the emphasis shifts onto the hero's personal trials, which appear to have little to do with the rescue of the King's Daughter as such. The "hero as rescuer" is what distinguishes a narrative as a *folktale* (i.e., in Propp's diagnosis, an attenuated species of myth [*Morphology of the Folktale*, 90]). The hero as *protagonist* in a multidimensional experience, of which external events form only part of the reader's (or listener's) understanding, is what distinguishes these narratives by contrast as dialogical works of *literature*, belonging to a different age and consciousness from collective oral narrative.

Though the feminine protagonists of both narratives are in part the hero, in part the victim, it is essential to note that Tutuola's Lady *must be rescued* from the lair of skulls, whereas the King's Daughter in Reb Nakhman *cannot escape* the Palace of the *nisht-guter*. The King's Daughter, like the Emperor's Daughter in *mayse beys* ("Tale the Second," Y 18–47; E 55–81), is a maiden seemingly in no need of rescue; she is both the "victimized hero" (*Morphology of the Folktale*, 30) and an imprisoned donor (40) assisting the Viceroy on his quest, assigning him tasks through which to prove himself and offering clues toward her own redemption, neither of which he accomplishes at the close of Reb Nakhman's telling. In this regard, it is significant that in their first encounter in the Palace of the *nisht-guter*, she seeks the Viceroy out, rather than, as is conventional, vice versa:

> Afterwards the queen [of the *nisht-guter*'s realm, i.e., the King's Daughter] looked around and saw someone lying in a corner whom she recognized. She stood up from her chair and went to him and touched him. When she asked, "do you know me?" he answered, "yes. I know you, you're the king's daughter that was lost." He asked her, "Why did you come here?" She answered, "Because my father let slip

from his mouth that word (namely, that the *nisht-guter* should take you) and this is the place that is *nisht gut*" (Y 4–5; E 39).

The *nisht-guter* in Reb Nakhman's story is, similarly, a seducer but not an adversarial villain—although there are guards surrounding his opulent palace, they make no effort to interfere with the Viceroy's mission, and there is no indication that the King's Daughter is held against her will. In theological, or psychological, terms this story's Satan is not the negative face of the Law, but the unseen hand of desire.

The basic situation of the protagonist in a foreign and menacing royal court recurs throughout the *sipurey mayses*, and it suggests on the most fundamental level of meaning that evil, the *nisht-guter*, can be found primarily in a place where material decadence and political power coincide; the similarity between the palace of evil and the Christian courts of Eastern European noblemen can hardly be accidental.[7] Similarly, *mayse khes* ("Tale the Eighth," Y 122–129; E 154–159), "The Rabbi and His Only Son," underscores the connection between evil and materialism by describing an encounter with the devil on the open road, disguised as a merchant. As such, this tale articulates anxieties toward the materialism, mobility, and treachery of the modern commercial order as much it satirizes the opposition of traditional rabbinic elites to Hasidism.

Reb Nakhman's equation of evil with materialism refers to the modern commercialization of Eastern European Jewish life, which was casually associated with the rise of *haskole*,[8] and therefore, from a Hasidic worldview, with the decline of religious observance, even though in point of fact there were most likely more successful businessmen associated with Hasidism in the nineteenth century than *haskole*. However contemporary Reb Nakhman's frame of reference is, though, in moral terms this critique differs little from traditional Jewish pieties—or, for that matter, the ascetic impulses of any religion. The beginnings of industrialization and modern capitalism in Eastern Europe provide the impetus for these preoccupations, but the substance of his critique derives straightforwardly from the traditional worldview.

His depiction in *mayse aleph* of the devil, however, as the passive agent of human desire psychologizes and relativizes the conflict between the spiritual and the material: instead of the victim of a power-ful cosmic malevolence, the characters in this story are victims of their own seemingly mundane choices. This is the central concern of the tale, and it too resonates throughout Reb Nakhman's collection. Indeed, it is to this idea that Reb Nakhman returns in his last story, *mayse yud-giml* ("Tale the Thirteenth," Y 405–489; E 354–437), *Meyhashivoh betlers*⁹ ("About the Seven Beggars"), told over six nights in the last months of Reb Nakhman's life (E 354), and left deliberately unfinished at its conclusion. This story describes the wedding of two orphaned beggars, followed, according to Jewish custom—virtually the only overt Jewish reference in the story—by seven nights of feasting at which the newly-weds are entertained by seven wondrous beggars; Reb Nakhman tells the tales of six of these beggars, but the world would not be ready for the tale of the seventh until the coming of the Messiah (Y 487; E 436).

On the third day of the story (Y 437–459; E 383–390), the third beggar, whom the married couple had known as a stutterer, explains to them, in a parable that is characteristic of this tale's structure, that far from speaking with a stammer, he was in fact the most eloquent speaker in the world, and that his speech contained all the wisdom in the world (Y 437–439; E 383–384). To demonstrate his wisdom, this beggar describes a mountain, a stone, and a spring (Y 442; E 385). "Everything has a heart," Reb Nakhman explains:

> And the world in its entirety also has a heart. . . . And the mountain with the spring stands at one end of the world. The heart of the world stands at the opposite end of the world. The heart of the world faces the spring and constantly longs and fervently yearns to come to the spring. . . . The spring longs for the heart as well. . . . And consider-ing that its longing is so great, why doesn't the heart go to the spring? But as soon as the heart decides to approach the mountain from which the spring flows, it would no longer see the peak. It then could not see the spring, and as soon as it stopped looking at the spring, it would die. . . . When it stands facing the mountain, it can see the peak from which the spring flows, but as soon as it comes close to the mountain, the peak is hidden from its eyes. . . . If it could not see the spring, then it would die. If the heart died, God forbid, then the entire world would cease to exist. . . . It is for this reason that it cannot go to the

spring. It only stands eternally facing it, yearning and crying out endlessly (Y 442–445; E 386–388).[10]

At the end of his life, Reb Nakhman thus conceives of existence itself balancing precariously on the pivot of a tortuous cosmic desire—a desire imperceptible in the course of ordinary reality—the consummation of which would bring the destruction of the universe. In this respect, the fragmented, inconclusive structure of both *mayse aleph* and *mayse yud-giml*, as well as many stories in between, reflects the harsh lesson taught by the parable of the heart and the spring; providing artistic closure to these passion-infused narratives, uniting these irrevocably estranged lovers, would mean acquiescing to a temptation that for Reb Nakhman threatens to undermine the foundation of the world. Reb Nakhman ultimately could not provide a resolution in the fictional world that he created when God had withheld such harmony from the real world,[11] and therefore, as his disciples state at the end of the last tale, these stories must remain incomplete until the final redemption.[12]

Returning to the morphology of *mayse aleph*, however: although the tale's structure is fragmentary, it is by no means inscrutable. Indeed, the story can be seen to fall into two symmetrical halves: the first half involves the disappearance of the King's Daughter and the Viceroy's putative rescue of her; the second, starting with the command that he choose a place and remain there for a year, fasting on the final day of his isolation, narrates the Viceroy's inner struggle, no longer to liberate the King's Daughter, but seemingly to liberate himself from earthly desires. The "action" in *mayse aleph* begins with an inverted interdiction—a curse, that the *nisht-guter* should take you away—followed by an *absentation* (*Morphology of the Folktale*, 26), in which the King's Daughter vanishes overnight, to reappear in the palace of the *nisht-guter*. This interdiction is not only inverted, but occurs passively, in that the King "lets slip from his mouth that the *nisht-guter* should take you away" (Y 1, E 34). In keeping with a tendency in this story and the *sipurey mayses* as a whole, the male character is passive, letting words slip from his mouth, whereas the female character is active, taking the initiative from her father and falling, perhaps willfully, into the clutches of the *nisht-guter*. The dynamism of Reb Nakhman's heroines might well be on one level representative, as has been suggested,[13] of the *shekhinah*'s—the Divine Immanence in creation, traditionally figured as female—interaction with the physical world (why not?), but what is singular about this feature of the tale is not the symbolism, but the means of representation.

In this respect, the crucial moment in the story occurs when the Viceroy approaches the castle of the *nisht-guter*. At first fearing the soldiers standing guard around the palace, he quickly changes his mind and decides to go forward on his quest: "He considered, I will try myself" (Y 3; E 37–38). This elliptical sentence provides the central textual clue as to how this story can be interpreted. The central component of the narrative is not the Viceroy's rescue of the princess, and certainly not how this rescue comes about. Instead, the central drama of this story is the Viceroy's test of himself—*ikh vel mikh pruvn*.[14] The unresolved tension between a test of the self and the rescue of another that animates this tale can perhaps be understood with respect to the unstable, triangular relationship that Hasidic rebbes such as Reb Nakhman engaged in with their Hasidim and, ultimately, God. In such an interpretation, both the King's Daughter and the Viceroy need one another to achieve liberation *and* reunification with the Father, the King, and thus to reconcile the fundamental existential tension between free will and obedience to divine law at the heart of monotheistic religion, particularly Judaism. That Reb Nakhman is unable to narrate this reconciliation between freedom and obedience offers evidence of the experimental nature of storytelling as an aspect of his theology, as well as the aptness of the assemblage as a structural principle for his narratives.

By way of elaboration, it is useful to consider a passage from one of the first and most important Hasidic texts, *Toldes yankev-yoysef* (roughly, the "chronicles of Rabbi Jacob Joseph," 1780; Ya'akov-Yosef of Polnoye, d. 1783, was one of the original disciples of the BeSh"T): "The common people (likened to a beautiful woman who is imprisoned and whom you desire), and whom you draw closer to God's service, you would not call on them to take on the burdens of Hasidism [and change their nature] from one extreme to the other."[15] From this earlier source, which Reb Nakhman and his disciples were quite familiar with,[16] one can contend that the analogy of "the common people" to an imprisoned, desirable woman like the King's Daughter—a woman both captive and captivating—provides a metaphorical basis for the interpretation of *mayse aleph* along both personal, psychological lines and social, historical ones. It is striking therefore, that Reb Nakhman's portrayal of the common people in these terms is far more radical than Reb Yankev-Yoysef's. Although the rebbe must liberate the captive woman, the woman (the people) must also liberate the rebbe from his own desires.

But if the source of Reb Nakhman's imagery in fact is Reb Ya'akov-Yosef's admonition to potential Hasidic rebbes not to impose the same burdens on ordinary Jews that they would on their devoted followers, then the triangular relationship between the King, the Viceroy, and the King's Daughter no longer plays out along symmetrical allegorical lines; if in Reb Ya'akov-Yosef's scheme, the common people are the beautiful woman, then the king they are estranged from is not God, but His ostensible representative on earth, or at least His primary intermediary, the Hasidic rebbe. Is the King in *mayse aleph* in fact God, or Reb Nakhman? Is the King's Daughter the captive Jewish people, or the feminine immanence of God, the *shekhinah*? Who, among these allegorical alternatives, is the Viceroy: Reb Nakhman, or his Hasidim? (And will the real *nisht-guter* please stand up?)

In fact, the overlapping allegorical possibilities for this story can be unraveled—and therefore in effect dismissed—with reference to the mystical thinking that inspired both Reb Ya'akov-Yosef and Reb Nakhman. In the kabalistic doctrine of Reb Isaac Luria (1534–1572), the concept of *tikkun olam* (repairing the world) constitutes the process by which Creation is completed through the performance of the ritual commandments of the Torah; the fulfillment of each act of observance, when accompanied with prayer and mystical understanding, redeems and unifies the shards of divinity scattered throughout the universe at the traumatic moment of creation. In existential terms, these religious observances bring the individual closer to God. In cosmological terms, these acts bring humanity closer to the ultimate experience of redemption, the coming of the Messiah.[17] From this perspective, the actions, and interactions, of the individual Jew *in this world* have consequences for the universe as a whole. Understood through this concept of *tikkun*, the Viceroy can represent, *simultaneously*, the Hasidim in their efforts to bring the common folk closer to the rebbe *and* Reb Nakhman in his efforts to bring his followers closer to God, because either the downward momentum of the Hasidim reaching out to other Jews or the upward movement of the rebbe toward God constitute the *same movement*. Seen within the framework of *tikkun*, the social orientation of the Rebbe's relationship with his Hasidim, and the cosmic orientation of the believer's relationship with God, are part of an all-subsuming mystical process.

Though the concept of *tikkun* can, arguably, reconcile the social and cosmological implications of the story, it cannot provide an ending to the story itself. Introducing this concept therefore invokes an irony at the reader's expense: a story that illustrates the process by which a rebbe establishes intimacy with the "common people" *in order* thereby to experience a more intimate relationship with God in fact draws attention to the *inability* to achieve *tikkun* in the world by underscoring its own fragmentary narrative structure. If this is a story that promises on an allegorical level the reconciliation of ordinary Jews, Hasidim, the rebbe, and God, such unification is left unachieved at the story's end.

In this respect, one should recall that the primary effect of this story, according to Reb Nakhman, is to provoke *instantaneous thoughts of repentance*.[18] Whoever heard this story immediately repented, yet the ending of the story remains unnarrated: "And he [the Viceroy] went to a rich man and hired himself out to him, because one had to stay there [in the realm of the Pearl Castle] for a long time. Because one must see with wisdom and good sense in order to bring the King's Daughter out. (And how he brought her out, he didn't say.) But in the end he brought her out. Amen selah" (Y 17; E 54). Thus *only* Reb Nakhman, presumably, has "heard" this story in all its details; he is both the narrator and the audience, just as in the tale itself the Viceroy is simultaneously the hero and the victim. Reversing the relationship of cause-and-effect, one can infer that the Rebbe himself is in greatest need of repentance, and this he can achieve only with the help of the captive King's Daughter, already identified by Reb Ya'akov-Yosef with a rebbe's Hasidim. And yet, paradoxically, one of the desires that imprisons the Rebbe, and for which he must repent, undoubtedly, is the woman herself—whether understood as a literal object of desire (woman as woman), or a symbolic object of power (woman as the people over whom a rebbe exercises authority). Instead of narrating a messianic vision of the redemption of the Jewish people, the rescue of the King's Daughter, *mayse aleph*, as evidenced by its narrative dissipation, becomes a private apocalypse induced by the temptation to believe in a redemption unattainable in the world as Reb Nakhman experienced it. The temptation thus requires its own repentance—the deferral of a conclusion is in itself an act of penance.

In general terms, *mayse aleph* establishes a number of rhetorical and thematic patterns that recur and develop over the subsequent twelve stories in this collection. Rhetorically there is here, as elsewhere, an instability in narrative voice, as when this story concludes with Reb Noson, the transcriber, interjecting that Reb Nakhman failed to reveal how the King's Daughter was rescued, thus conflating the narrator with the protagonist. This story also introduces the motif of the desert, which remains throughout the collection "a place of both seduction and purification" and "the favored setting of radical self-confrontation" (*A Bridge of Longing*, 35). Significantly, both Tutuola and Reb Nakhman, in spite of the obvious cultural differences separating them, have both chosen, habitually, the wilderness as a setting in which to express the chaos of the world outside their tradition and their community. The wilderness as a physical description of the unknown and the threatening is for both writers a spatial analogy for the temporal, social dislocations that their societies undergo in the transition from an autonomous traditional culture to a colonized, belatedly modern one.

But in both thematic and rhetorical terms, the most significant concept introduced in *mayse aleph* is the verb describing the Viceroy's state of mind when he decides simultaneously to test himself and rescue the King's Daughter: *myashev zayn zikh*, "to deliberate, to contemplate, to change your mind." This quintessential term in Reb Nakhman's thought, the one verb that appears in virtually every story,[19] is, aptly, a verb of introspection. Such introspectivism is a crucial distinction of Reb Nakhman from both traditional fairy tales and the hagiographic legends of other Hasidic rebbes, which are typically tales of action, even when the action is the rebbe's clairvoyance regarding the soul of his interlocutor. As with the personal, individualistic consciousness of

Tutuola's narrative voice, this introspectivist turn is an essential index of Reb Nakhman's own modernity—one in keeping with the coincidental affinities that Roskies, Wiskind-Elper, and Green, among others, have noted between Reb Nakhman and the Romantic writers of his generation.[20]

Just as the introspection of *mayse aleph* distinguishes it from the premodern story genres that remained active in Reb Nakhman's generation, so too does the quest motif on which the story is built represent an innovation. As Arthur Green writes, "The motif of spiritual quest is not a common one in the literature of Judaism. The idea that human life is a constant search for a hidden God would have struck most premodern Jewish authors as a rather strange one. God had already spoken, already revealed Himself and issued His command. . . . If there is any single feature about Nakhman's tales . . . that makes them unique in the history of Judaism, it is just this: their essential motif is one of quest" (*Tormented Master*, 366). By contrast, the Yoruba cosmology that undergirds the plot of Tutuola's novel is everywhere portrayed as a journey. Efforts to locate Tutuola's narratives in an allegorical or archetypal scheme thus fall flat when one considers the centrality of the journey to the structure of traditional Yoruba divination.[21] In this light, one could consider the Palm-Wine Drinkard to be a type of diviner, though perhaps a diviner in reverse, transforming himself by traveling from the earth to heaven, and back again. The structural precedent of traditional Yoruba divination therefore places in relief the centrality of magic (juju) to the Drinkard's adventures; juju is, in the clearest sense imaginable, the objective correlative to the protagonist's moral and spiritual transformation. Paradoxically, Reb Nakhman, a spiritual leader in a relentlessly antisyncretic religion, adopts a less conventional literary structure for his purposes than does Tutuola, the unorthodox Yoruba Christian whose ultimately Christian morality expresses itself by means of traditional Yoruba religious motifs!

To turn, then, to a consideration of the "Complete Gentleman" episode, one can note that although both the Lady in *The Palm-Wine Drinkard* and the King's Daughter in *mayse aleph* are disobedient daughters, Tutuola—unlike Reb Nakhman—begins his narration not with a focus on the daughter, but with an exchange between the Palm-

Wine Drinkard and his future father-in-law.[22] The "Complete Gentle-man" episode lacks the centrality of introspective struggle essential to Reb Nakhman's story. *As a novel*, however, Tutuola's narrative provides opportunities for psychological and dramatic development that Reb Nakhman rejects in favor of the immediacy of the unintegrated spiritual conflicts depicted in each individual story, and in favor of the autonomy of the individual oral-narrative situation in which these stories were originally told. Tutuola consciously violates the autonomy of oral story forms by constructing a larger, written narrative out of oral narrative components. As Quayson writes, "[B]y stringing such stories as he does, he [Tutuola] prevents the affirmation of closure that these formulaic endings would signify in the context of oral storytelling. . . . Good examples are the interruptions in the tale of the 'complete gentleman' when, instead of going right ahead and telling us how he rescues the young lady, the hero digresses to tell us the circumstances of her kidnapping" (*Strategic Transformations*, 58). This digression, in fact, makes for a morphological irregularity when compared with actual folk narration: though the Palm-Wine Drinkard knows what has happened to the Lady, there is no narration of how he acquires this knowledge.

One can nonetheless resolve this difficulty by referring again to Propp: "One of the most important attributes of a helper is his prophetic wisdom: the prophetic horse, the prophetic wife [the function that the Lady will come to fulfill later in the novel], the wise lad, etc. When a helper is absent from a tale, this quality is transferred to the hero. The result is the appearance of the prophetic hero" (*Morphology of the Folktale*, 83). The Drinkard's own prophetic gifts, later displaced onto his wife, must be counted, at least for the duration of this episode, when such gifts serve an integral narrative function, among the protean traits that his magical abilities (juju) afford him. A similar morphological anomaly occurs when an interdiction is issued to the Lady; this interdiction comes from the Complete Gentleman himself, who warns her not to follow him into the forest: "But as she was following the complete gentleman along the road, he was telling her to go back or not to follow him, but the lady did not listen . . . and when the complete gentleman had tired of telling her not to follow him or to go back to her town he left her to follow him" (*PWD*, 202). He simultaneously warns the Lady and seduces her into following him, and this instability of function is represented graphically in his status simultaneously as a figure of beauty (a complete gentleman) and a figure of terror (a skull). Such instability, of course, is both functional in terms of his generic relationship to the narrative, and metaphysical in terms of his cosmic role in the Endless Forest. These idiosyncrasies, which cause most readers little difficulty, in fact violate crucial features of traditional folklore by which different occurrences within the tale are logically linked.

In Proppian terms, moreover, there can be no definitive "liquidation of lack" (*Morphology of the Folktale*, 53) at the close of the "Complete Gentleman" episode because the episode itself is a combination of two different tale types. Since only one of the two can be resolved at a time, it is the author's intention that the Lady's tale should be resolved first so that further adventures can develop the Drinkard's "tale" (the novel as a whole). In formal terms, therefore, the episode should end with "This was how the Lady got a husband" rather than with "This was how I got a wife" (*PWD*, 213). But with respect to this episode in particular, one should note that the protagonist's marriage to the Lady does not close the episode of the "Complete Gentleman"; the monster-baby born from his wife's thumb does (*PWD*, 214). This is not only important structurally, but also thematically, in that both the Complete Gentleman and the baby are reflections of the Palm-Wine Drinkard's monstrous and wonderful character because they both reflect his capacity for magical transformation and exploitation of others. These two characters thus frame the story of the protagonist's marriage to underscore the deficiencies in his personality that his subsequent experiences will correct.[23]

To consider further, however, the thematic and structural significance of the "Complete Gentleman," one should recall that the term "complete gentleman" originates in the discourse of English colonialism. It was the "complete gentleman" that the Victorian Englishman aspired to be, and it was the colonial, imperial project that enabled this class stereotype to emerge.[24] Although the motif of a figure (or evil spirit) renting body parts from other people (dwellers of the Endless Forest) stems from Nigerian folklore—Bernth Lindfors duly notes that this episode corresponds to Items G369* and F501* respectively in two indexes of folk-motifs[25]—Tutuola alone, writing in English, is responsible for connecting this folktale to the political context of colonial Nigeria. What emerges from Tutuola's literary adaptation of this folktale, in fact, is a durable metaphor of colonial acquisition and its psychological effects on the *colonized*. Thus, the lady who follows the Complete Gentleman into the "Endless Forest" discovers that "every part of this complete gentleman in the market was spared or hired and he was returning them to the owners" (*PWD*, 204).

Colonialism has enabled the colonizer to construct his beauty from various "rented or borrowed" parts taken throughout the world. The resulting image is indeed alluring, as Tutuola states—"[I]f I were a lady, no doubt I would follow him to wherever he would go, and still as I was a man I would jealous him more than that, because if this gentleman went to the battle field, surely, enemy would not kill him or capture him and if bombers saw him in a town which was to be bombed, they would not throw bombs on his presence, and if they did throw it, the bomb itself would not explode until this gentleman would leave that town, because of his beauty" (*PWD*, 207)—but it is ultimately an illusion that conceals terror, entrapment, imprisonment, and death. In more explicitly psychological terms, Tutuola depicts the negative, punitive consequences of the Lady's relationship with the Complete Gentleman as the repression of silence, enforced by a cowrie shell, a unit of currency in precolonial days thus associated with the humiliating rate of exchange during the time when England first conquered Nigeria. It should be noted as well that the colonial associations with the Complete Gentleman are reinforced by Tutuola's use of the British currency system to appraise his value (£ 2000: *PWD*, 202); by his appearance in the marketplace,[26] with its inevitable connection to the slave trade; and by the imagery of modern warfare, occurring in a novel completed by a World War II veteran less than seven years after his tour of duty. Indeed, references to currency appear throughout the novel, signifying, or mocking, the bourgeois system of reference—in which everything has its price—that critics such as Georg Lukács have identified as the epistemological origin of the novel.

In formal terms, Tutuola has hinged this episode on the status of the "Endless Forest," a narrative space where *anything* can happen; in this practice, he does not deviate from Yoruba writers such as Fagunwa, or from traditional oral narrative. It is moreover significant that this episode occurs immediately after the protagonist's first "test," the "binding and bringing of death" (*PWD*, 195–199), which introduces a simultaneously supernatural and parodic dimension into the narrative, in which the fantastic and the absurd reinforce one another to create a comic harmony that affirms, cosmically, the renewal and circularity of life over the finality of death. Indeed, one might compare Tutuola's strategy in these episodes to the logic of a dream, in which contradictions coexist unresolved, and in which, crucially, metaphors are rendered *literally*. In this sense, death can function both as a character and a metaphysical condition—but even as a metaphysical state, it is neither absolute nor omnipotent.

Thus, the Endless Forest in which the next episode occurs is not, unlike the use of space in contemporaneous African narratives written with a Western audience in mind—for example, the bombax tree of Camara Laye's *L'enfant noir*, or the "Evil Forest" in Chinua Achebe's *Things Fall Apart*—an anthropologically or sociologically constructed space against which the protagonist or his community define themselves. Nor is it an allegorical landscape in which a place or a figure encountered represents a counterpart in the actual environment, in Nigeria or elsewhere. Rather, the Endless Forest is a *psychological* space constructed for the dual narrative aims of reflecting the narrator's emotional, ethical development and furthering his quest.

In this sense, the forest setting has become analogous to the "road of life" so crucial to Mikhail Bakhtin's description of the Menippean satire. That this road is both endless and cluttered with the chaotic activities of fantastic creatures makes this setting a modern narrative space for the unfolding of the protagonist's experience, and the construction of his narrative voice. The Palm-Wine Drinkard himself stands at a crossroads among metaphysical, linguistic, and social phenomena, and his narrative mediates these tumultuous manifestations of existential and rhetorical polyphony. More significantly, the language in which Tutuola renders his protagonist's experiences—a stylized discourse in which juju, evil spirits, petrol barrels, and telephones form a coherent, heteroglossic reality—crafts a perfect metaphorical critique of his society on the hopeful eve of independence and modernity.

In this respect, Anozie is correct to identify the dialectic between traditional magic and modern science, or modern science fiction, as one of
the central tensions on which Tutuola's novel pivots:

> Whether or not there is in this [the scenario of *The Palm-Wine
> Drinkard*] an unconscious allusion to the European experience in pre-
> colonial Africa (the appearance of the Drinkard in that strange world
> of the dead presents a kind of analogy with Achebe's vision of the ap-
> pearance of the first white man in precolonial Ibo society), Tutuola . . .
> poses the scientific imagination against the imagination fastened upon
> traditional folklore, and opposite the time machine or the interplan-
> etary spaceship, he places traditional magic, the external means by
> which the hero undergoes the desired metamorphoses. (*Critical Per-
> spectives*, 241)

Instead of imagining the Palm-Wine Drinkard as an unwitting representative of the European in Africa, however, it is more constructive to
assume that his story is, in fact, a *conscious* representation of the consequences of colonialism on the African tradition itself. The Drinkard is
therefore not the figure for colonialism in this episode; the Complete
Gentleman is. It is the Complete Gentleman who has bewitched and
seduced the traditional African maiden, only to reveal that the charms
he advertised externally are, as he made clear from the outset, only a
trap leading her to confinement, captivity, and potential or metaphorical death. The Palm-Wine Drinkard can use the full battery of traditional magic to struggle against the supernatural agents of this new,
unheard-of world, but he cannot finally restore the life he knew before
he confronted them. The utopia Tutuola offers at the end of his narrative—remarkable as much for its dystopian aspects as its idyllic ones—
signifies a return to the harmony and bliss that had characterized the
Drinkard's life before his quest, but it no longer resembles that world
in any of its particulars: too much has occurred to both the Drinkard
himself, and to his world, to allow for a "seamless" reassertion of the
past.

Conclusion

If this comparison has stressed the "radical inconclusiveness" of both Reb Nakhman's and Tutuola's respective narratives, it is only appropriate that the discussion itself should also end on an inconclusive note. Admittedly, a comparison between one of Reb Nakhman's stories with one episode in *The Palm-Wine Drinkard*, however intensive, cannot begin to account for the full richness and complexity of these works in their entirety. And yet, the problems introduced in this discussion will remain relevant throughout this book, which will continue to trace the parallel development of Yiddish and African literature through subsequent generations and social contexts. Although the dilemmas posed by orality and literacy, tradition and modernity, native cultures and the metropolis, periphery and center will remain essentially constant—as will the importance of literary form to understanding how these conflicts are mediated by particular authors—the serendipitous affinities between Reb Nakhman's *mayse aleph* and Tutuola's "Complete Gentleman" episode will remain unique. Never again in this comparison will two narratives share a common structure to the extent that these two do; never again will subsequent African or Yiddish writers maintain the intimacy with oral narrative that will allow for the analysis suggested by Propp's formal model.

Indeed, never again in the subsequent history of African and Yiddish writing will two writers single-handedly represent so fully the challenges facing the creation of modern literature from these cultures, nor will the response to these problems ever again be so idiosyncratic as the narratives of these two figures. After Reb Nakhman and Tutuola, there are talented writers and less talented ones, original writers and conventional ones—but never again are there sui generis writers to the extent of these two. Unlike conventional conceptions of literary development that trace cultural progress from primitiveness to sophistication, Yiddish and African literatures emerge in a condition of bewildering complexity and only gradually converge with the conventions of mainstream, "major" literature. Not only do subsequent generations fail to supersede the achievements of Tutuola or Reb Nakhman, but the structural solutions they devise for the "problems" posed by these pioneering figures are inevitably simpler—more transparent and less challenging—than these authors' work.

The subsequent parts of this book therefore not only will compare more than one writer from each culture—thus obligating comparisons within the two cultures as well as across them—but also will discuss to a much greater extent than this chapter the development and influence of *ideology*, both aesthetic and political, in the narratives of African and Yiddish authors. With the development and adaptation of *national* ideologies within these two cultures comes, perhaps inevitably, an analogous adoption of common strategies among writers with respect to literary form, genre, and language. For example, in subsequent generations of Jewish intellectuals, the dialectical relationship between *Loshn-koydesh* and Yiddish so central to Reb Nakhman's purposes is bridged by a change in attitude toward Yiddish and the Jewish masses that speak it, as well as by subsequent developments in both spoken and written modern Hebrew. To a great extent, as will be discussed in the next chapter, the evolving attitude to these Jewish languages is directly related to the secularizing objectives of these intellectuals; this is certainly the most fundamental distinction between these writers and Reb Nakhman. As general attitudes toward the Yiddish and Hebrew vernaculars modernize (and later concretize into competition and polemic), and the literatures developed in these languages acquire greater fluency and directness in discussing contemporary social issues, the spiritual and cosmological dimensions that Reb Nakhman encodes as an integral part of his creative vision and storytelling technique recede ever further in the background as allusion, symbol, and allegory—generally as expressions of the mythological Jewish past rather than as clues toward the redemption of the Jewish future.

Similarly, as formally educated intellectuals come to dominate African literature in the postindependence era, folklore as such becomes increasingly isolated from the structural character of African literature. Folkoric motifs shift from an objective correlative to the situation of the contemporary African to become in the work of these later writers a symbol of the archaic past—proverbs, in Wole Soyinka's memorable phrase, "to bones and silence."[1] It would take more than a generation before this attitude toward folklore and its underpinning in traditional cosmology would be reappraised, along with the particular, generally dystopian, aspects of modernity introduced during the era of independence; it is hardly incidental that Soyinka is among the authors most responsible for this reevaluation. Language, as well, plays a role in this reassessment, and from the stylized "pidgins" of Ahmadou Kourouma in French and Ken Saro-Wiwa in English to the adoption of native African languages by Ngugi wa Thiong'o and his followers, Tutuola's groundbreaking mediation of imperial English form and native Yoruba expression, whether acknowledged or not, has borne much fruit.

The significance of these developments will be discussed in the subsequent chapters of this comparison. For now, however, the essential objective of this study between Reb Nakhman and Tutuola has been to show that these particular representatives of tradition, as *representers* of tradition, cannot be understood as opponents of modernity, but as part of the process of modernization itself. This returns the reader to the insights of Margaret Drewal: When ritual and the traditions that ritual encodes and enacts are no longer seen as unchanging or static hegemonies against which modernity and change must be mobilized, then the narratives of Tutuola and Reb Nakhman, and the oral traditions they utilize, can be understood as self-conscious, dynamic responses to modernity itself. Far from the immovable force that modernity must subvert, tradition in the work of Reb Nakhman and Tutuola is the most significant and elastic resource in the struggle for autonomy from the new, imperial hegemony of the modern world. Seen from this "minor" perspective, these works provide for their readers an alternative—particular, multivocal, dialogical—to the "universalistic, univocal, and monologic humanism" critiqued by Lloyd and JanMohamed. The articulation of such a humanism, at once individual and rooted in a community of tradition and belief, is surely an achievement of enduring and universal value.

Part Two Eyn Kemakh, Eyn Toyre; Eyn Toyre, Eyn Kemakh

The first self-consciously modern protagonist to appear in the Yiddish narratives of the nineteenth century is paradoxically not a product of the *haskole*, the "Jewish enlightenment," but the *hokhem* (alternately "wise man" or "wise guy" in Yiddish) of Reb Nakhman's *mayse tes, mehokhem vetam* ("Tale the Ninth, of a Sophisticate and a Simpleton" [1809]). Reb Nakhman's tale opens, as traditional tales often do, just outside the gates of Eden: the fathers of the two main characters have lost their wealth, and are left with only their houses. By means of this setting, Reb Nakhman confronts the contemporary Eastern European Jewish crisis, in which the society at large, and possibly even the Jewish tradition itself, stands bankrupt and dormant, with the only apparent options open to its members either a passive adherence to tradition and custom—the decision of the *tam* (alternately a "simpleton" or a "person of perfect faith") to remain in his father's house and work as a shoe-maker—or travel, as the *hokhem* does, in search of the fortunes offered in the world.

Like many maskilic heroes, Reb Nakhman's *hokhem* begins his progression through the world by apprenticing himself as a servant to a group of merchants en route to the metropolis, Warsaw. In fact, the *hokhem* receives his education through a series of jobs, venturing out of the Pale of Settlement, the western corridor of the Russian Empire where nearly all Jews of the realm were confined by law during the nineteenth century, as far afield as Italy and Spain, on the path, supposedly, to self-sufficiency. The *hokhem*'s travels and his pursuit of various professions and areas of knowledge bring him no peace of mind, however; he is truly modern in this respect. "I should learn such a trade that will always be important,"[1] the *hokhem* tells himself before embarking on a program of study that includes goldsmithing, gem cutting, natural science, Latin, medicine, and philosophy. For Reb Nakhman, however, only knowledge of the Torah can provide the certainty he seeks. When the *hokhem* returns to his hometown, he fashions a ring that could have brought him glory in Spain but that pleases no one among his own compatriots. Like many of the "enlightened" protagonists who will follow him, the *hokhem* learns that one consequence of modernity is estrangement from his original community.

A significant stylistic marker for the *hokhem*'s dissatisfaction, and therefore his spiritual error, is the recurrence of the verb *myashev zayn zikh*, "to deliberate." Reb Nakhman uses the term almost exclusively with respect to the *hokhem* alone; the only instance in which the verb is used with respect to the *tam* occurs after he has become governor of his province, and is given a chance to learn languages and wisdom (*hokhmes*).[2] He deliberates (*hot er zikh myashev geven*) and at last decides to study, but nonetheless he uses only his simplicity to govern (Y 156–158; E 180–183). The verb therefore—as in *mayse aleph*, discussed in the previous section of this comparison—signifies a type of contemplation mandated by existential choice. The frequency with which the term recurs with respect to the *hokhem* underscores both his spiritual crisis, and the repeated instances in which he makes poor decisions. For him, unlike either his counterpart the *tam*, or the Viceroy in *mayse aleph*, such contemplation invokes a despiritualizing, relativizing self-consciousness that has followed from the foundational credo of modern ontology: I think, therefore I am.

As the product of a Hasidic imagination, the ideological antithesis of *haskole*, the *hokhem* is hardly a valorization of the maskilic ideal. Indeed, this tale is arguably the most overtly satiric in Reb Nakhman's collection; notwithstanding its fire-and-brimstone conclusion—in which the *hokhem* on account of his blasphemy is cast to the fires of hell and saved only thanks to the *tam*'s intervention with a *baal-shem*, a Jewish wonder-worker, on his behalf—the humor he derives, toward the end of his narration, from reducing the *hokhem* and a newfound companion on his journey to Beckettian vagabonds as they deny the reality around them is apparent even in the most cursory reading. Nonetheless, the *hokhem*'s fate, in the first narrative to confront the burgeoning cultural war over the soul of the Jewish people, offers an instructive parable for tracing the consequences of the Jewish intelligentsia's embrace of European modernity as it was constituted at the beginning of the nineteenth century.

The first part of this study examined the transformation of folkloric motifs in the writings of Reb Nakhman and Amos Tutuola, writers who create modern narratives by reconstituting and recontextualizing oral traditions, in order to argue that this writing is by virtue of the historical circumstances that motivate it, as much as by its specific ideological implications, revolutionary. This section, by contrast, will focus on an alternate tradition within African and Yiddish writing that creates an autonomous, literary *voice*: not a deceptively oral voice for the reconstituted community, but the written voice of the modern individual. The comparison in this section examines the most intensive moment in the early history of these literatures during which the experiences of intellectuals, in the "institutional" sense of the word, take center stage; at this moment, the internal struggles of the neophyte intellectual serve to represent an incipient modernity for the culture as a whole. Connected to the construction of voice and ideology is the question of *audience*, and in this respect these literatures offer a useful study in contrast. Where the African literature in this section is inevitably addressed to metropolitan readers, the Yiddish literature with which it is contrasted explicitly addresses a local readership. With their focus on the intellectual, these literatures become preoccupied with the definition and critique of modernizing ideologies—*haskole* among Yiddish writers, negritude among Francophone African ones—not only to justify the existence of narrative but also to explain the appearance of new modes of thought, new departures from tradition, and new lifestyles.

To understand the development of *haskole* and negritude as a parallel to the writings of Reb Nakhman and Tutuola, rather than a superseding of them, requires a reconfiguration both of literary history and of the dynamics of cultural development. With respect to the development of

African literature, for example, Christopher Miller summarizes the dialectical thinking of Frantz Fanon by writing:

> There are three phases in the cultural development of colonized peoples: 1) assimilation, in which the artist proves that he/she has mastered the language and culture of the colonizer and can imitate received forms perfectly, but without originality . . . ; 2) recollection, in which the artist "becomes unsettled and decides to remember," but is not involved with his/her people; this sounds like the Mandarin side of negritude: elite and removed from the masses; and 3) combat, revolution, national culture, in which the artist awakens the people from their lethargy.[3]

This comparison, however, humbly submits a revision of Fanon's model. Even bracketing the Anglophone African tradition, with its very different relationship to English culture (in what sense does Tutuola "imitate received forms"?), one is hard-pressed to find in Francophone writing imitation or repetition without difference. Moreover, the struggle with form betrays the problem, at once aesthetic and social, of applying foreign modes of expression to native experience. Therefore the comparison between negritude and *haskole*, two ideologies animated by this struggle, helps illuminate this problem. Finally, Fanon's neat schema, obviously influenced by classical Marxism, suggests an ultimately chronological hierarchy in which previous stages of national culture are rendered obsolete.

In fact, recalling Margaret Drewal's observations on the persistent interplay between tradition and modernity in Yoruba ritual, one can see a competition between various political orientations and aesthetic approaches in these literatures, just as, at the same time, tradition and modernity as value systems and modes of cultural production continue to compete, conflict, and influence one another in the articulation of a "minor" culture. Most significantly, a careful consideration of the ideological literature of modernization indicates a thoroughgoing ambivalence toward the ideology invoked to define and justify modernity. The "past" of the premodern culture never disappears from the peripheral landscape—its persistence, in fact, contributes to the definition and location of the peripheral—while at the same time the modernizing ideology never succeeds in establishing a stable hegemony within either the consciousness of the ideologue or the culture as a whole.

The narratives discussed in this section therefore constitute not so much a second period in the linear development of either African or Yiddish literature as an alternate beginning. In the case of African literature, this alternative is formed along explicit linguistic and generational lines: the novels of Cheikh Hamidou Kane (b. 1928), Camara Laye (1928–1980), and Ferdinand Oyono (b. 1929) represent collectively an analogous force for Francophone literature that Tutuola represents for Anglophone literature; they signify the origins of a narrative tradition that coincides with the beginning of the postcolonial nation-state. The ideological dimensions of the linguistic divide in West African literature, already apparent in the polemics among and between Anglophone and Francophone writers that precede the era of the nation-state, can be further understood through a comparison with the ideological and, in a different sense, linguistic conflicts in Eastern European Jewish literature of the mid-nineteenth century, as reflected in the Yiddish fiction of Yisroel Aksenfeld (1787–1866) and Isaac Meyer Dik (1814–1893), as well as the early, pseudo-autobiographical narratives of Mendele Moykher-Sforim (Sh. Y. Abramovitsh, c. 1835–1917) and Y. Y. Linetski (1839–1915). Such a comparison will demonstrate the complex interrelationship between language and literary form in the formation (and deformation) of didactic narratives, and of ideology itself.

The essential difference between the polemical writers of this part of the comparison and the fantastic ones of the previous part can be summarized with respect to their attitude toward metaphor: fantastic writers render metaphors oblique by depicting them *literally*. The monster in Tutuola's Endless Forest cannot merely symbolize something else as long as it remains, for the other characters surely, but also for Tutuola's readers, *literally* a monster. References external to the narrative can therefore only be provisional, conjectural—metaphor in fantastic literature functions as an expanding series of analogies, a new assemblage of associations. The polemical writer, by contrast, depends on the transparency of his or her metaphors, the symmetry of allegory. For the ideological writer, images *have to* represent something more abstract, or the narrative fails as ideology. Because the literature discussed in this chapter concerns intellectuals writing about intellectuals, autobiographical and pseudo-autobiographical narratives understandably play an essential formal and thematic role in the development of African and Yiddish literature of this sort. The life stories of these authors' protagonists therefore become representative of the conflict, never fully resolved as transition, between the traditional and the modern.

Nonetheless, the distinctions between the modern era and what had preceded it were quite evident to the creators, ambivalent adherents, and sympathetic critics of the new ideologies. For example, the Soviet-Yiddish literary historian Nokhem Oyslender quotes from the serial column *Yidishe lebns-fragn* ("Jewish Crises") in the first Eastern European Yiddish newspaper *Kol mevaser* ("The Voice of the Messenger," 1862–1871), a leading (late-) maskilic organ for Russian Jews, to characterize the transformation of Jewish life in the Pale of Settlement:

> A hundred years ago the Jew lived in another world, under a Polish nobleman . . . from whom he received his livelihood. . . . Today [the mid-nineteenth century], everything has changed: the idle nobility doling out limitless funds no longer exists. The unification brought about by the railways between various lands has caused a revolution in commerce. New styles and machines have given a new face to most trades. Old-fashioned professions from old-fashioned crafts have been rendered worthless today. What can be earned from such sources of income today isn't even enough to buy water.[4]

That this disparity between tradition and modernity—understood in the above-cited passage as economic and technological disruptions of an outmoded way of life—recapitulates itself in the African context of negritude is acknowledged in cultural and philosophical terms by Cheikh Hamidou Kane in his novel *L'aventure ambiguë* ("Ambiguous Adventure"), a central work in an emergent critique of negritude, the dominant formulation of Francophone cultural nationalism in the era of decolonization and therefore a focus of the ensuing discussion.

In a conversation, or perhaps more properly an ideological catechism on behalf of secular modernity, between a French communist and the novel's protagonist, the communist, Lucienne, states:

> You have delved deeply into the Russian mind of the nineteenth cen-

tury . . . the Russian writers, poets, artists. I know that you love that century. It was filled with the same disquiet, the same impassioned and ambiguous torment. To be the extreme eastern end of Europe? Not to be the western bridgehead of Asia? The intellectuals could neither answer these questions nor avoid them. . . . [T]he milk that has nourished you, from the breast of the country of the Diallobé, is very sweet and very noble. . . . But know also that the more tender the mother is, the sooner comes the moment for thrusting her aside.[5]

With a little stretch, these remarks about Russia in the nineteenth century can be applied equally to the "Jewish question" of the same era, both in terms of the disquiet and torment that characterize it as well as the ambiguous position between Europe and Asia of which these intellectuals were so self-conscious. As the Hebrew poet Yehuda Leyb Gordon (1830–1892) wrote of his own transformation from a traditional Jewish youth to a young maskil in the late 1840s, "[T]he mask that veiled my eyes fell off, and I turned around to behold myself . . . and saw that I was a wild Asiatic in the midst of enlightened Europe. . . . I therefore resolved to correct what had been distorted by others, to repair the damage they had done, and I set myself to learning Hebrew grammar properly, as well as the Russian, Polish, German, and French languages and all the knowledge required of man."[6] And just as the voice of modernity in Kane's novel advises the traditional African to abandon his *maternal* culture, so did maskilim such as Gordon often see, and portray, themselves as orphans.

Literature in this context therefore seeks to justify not only its own existence but also the life of its creator and his dissent from convention in general. The creation of an autobiographical narrative for these writers signifies not so much the recontextualization of tradition as the explicit, often painful departure from it. The autobiographical voice therefore serves as a correlative to the conflict between tradition and modernity already observable in economic, political, and psychological terms. There is in these narratives a crucial introduction of foregrounded internalized consciousness, in contrast to the representation of an internal consciousness metaphorically, and obliquely, in Reb Nakhman's and Tutuola's work. Because of the centrality of autobiographical narratives in this period, childhood, *Bildung*, as a theme becomes the point of intersection that makes the comparison between negritude and *haskole* possible. Through the autobiographical narrative, the ambivalence of the author situated between tradition and modernity—the community inside and the society outside, the mythical and the referential, the oral and the written—comes into psychological and dramatic focus.

Three *Haskole* and Negritude Compared

In order to understand better the metamorphosis of individuals as both creators and protagonists in these narratives, it is necessary first to define and contextualize the ideologies that will provide the focus for this comparison, particularly since even within their own disciplinary fields these definitions are contested. Thus *haskole* begins in the Berlin salons of the philosopher Moses Mendelssohn (1729–1786) and his circle in the latter half of the eighteenth century, and it spreads gradually eastward — first migrating to the southeastern outposts of the Austrian empire, and then slowly northward toward Lithuania — into the Pale of Settlement.[1] *Haskole* in Eastern Europe reached its culmination in the 1860s, when the limited political and social reforms of Czar Alexander II briefly ignited and quickly extinguished the expectations of civil equality for Russian Jewry's small, westernized intellectual elite.

Modernization as a social development must be distinguished from modernity as a social condition; as with the Hasidim, modernity is not a construct that the maskilim created or chose for themselves; it was an obligation that was thrust upon them.[2] As was asserted in part 1 of this study, it is the pervasively coercive character of modernization in Eastern Europe, as it was instituted in the Austrian and Russian empires, that most intimately connects Eastern European Jewish culture to modern African culture specifically, and to the phenomena of colonialism and postcolonialism generally.[3] The maskilic response to this enforced enlightenment shares more with Hasidism and other neotraditional movements than meets the eye. In fact, both ideologies signify newly modern cultures *emerging from* the traditional world.[4] The modernity that the maskilim embraced was characteristically tentative and understood from the perspective of the tradition, just as the tradition that the Hasidim embrace—one that maskilim spared no expense in decrying as an outlandish degeneration of "authentic" Judaism[5]—must inevitably be reconfigured in terms of the modern reality. Moreover, at least in Eastern Europe, *haskole* should not be confused with religious reform.[6] Indeed, the paradoxical goals of most maskilim can be summarized as an effort to assimilate modern values of rationalism, secular education, industriousness, individualism, and capitalism into Jewish society without obligating Jews, for the most part, to abandon either observance of ritual law or most of the community structures through which Jewish life had constituted itself traditionally.

In the Czarist Pale of Settlement, just over the border from Austrian Galicia, the efforts of the maskilim to remain both autonomously Jewish and tentatively modern were easier to sustain, if for no other reason than the absence of a comparably modern non-Jewish social movement.[7] Because Eastern European Jews—and only a small minority among them, at that—embraced modernization in such isolated circumstances, it should come as little surprise that the Enlightenment, the version of modernity they accepted as their ideal, was already an anachronism when they begin to assimilate it. Jewish intellectuals therefore work their way up to the vanguard of eighteenth-century philosophy only at the moment when much of the rest of Europe was awakening to the "blood and soil" nationalism of the nineteenth—in reaction against both the Enlightenment's "universalist" ideal and the hegemony of supranational empires.[8]

Similarly, G. Wesley Johnson Jr. writes of his research on the Senegalese residents of Dakar, Saint Louis, Rufisque, and Gorée—Africans granted the status, unique on their continent, of French citizens[9]—who formed the core of *évolué* society during the colonial era: "This study has attempted to explain why an elite, famous in France and generally well known in the literature as the epitome of assimilated Africans, was not in fact totally assimilated and did not desire to be" (*Africa & the West*, 184). The comparison of *haskole* with negritude thus illuminates the relationship between two ideologies that seek modernization without assimilation to the modern hegemony: this strategy, indeed, is characteristic of "minor" cultures generally. *Haskole* as a philosophical movement attempts to Judaize a "universal" movement, the Enlightenment, by recasting ideas originating primarily in Great Britain, France, Germany, and Italy in the discourse, and usually the language, of the Jewish tradition; negritude as a philosophical movement attempts to universalize the Black experience, to represent Black people in a schematic relationship with other cultures, especially the French colonial culture, and to valorize social, cultural, and metaphysical principles ostensibly inherent in Black culture as an alternative to the materialism and nihilism of Western modernity.[10]

However much *haskole* resisted the erasure of difference between Jews and non-Jews that the coercive measures of both the Austrian and Russian empires seemed intended to ensure, the adherents of this ideology were nonetheless opposed to what they considered the stagnation and superstition of traditional Jewish life, and they did not shrink from a polemical campaign that characterized the majority of Jews in their day as irrational, immoral, and contemptible. *Haskole* is a specifically Jewish ideology, the first such philosophical movement that attempts to define Jewishness in modern, "cultural" terms rather than traditional, exclusively religious ones. Nonetheless, unlike later manifestations of Jewish nationalism, including Zionism, for which it serves both as a prototype and a point of departure, *haskole* premises its modernity on a rejection of the Jewish "folk"[11] and its quasi-mythical aspirations for a return to self-determination—the messianic "redemption of Zion"—in favor of an ultimately more utopian quest for equality within the imperial regime, achieved by appeal to universal values of reason, truth, and justice. The German-born maskilic rabbi Max Lilienthal (1815–1882) therefore wrote to an adviser of Czar Nicolas, "Once they [the Jews] have attained culture, they are offered emancipation; in the wake of knowledge—the rights of man" (quoted in *Tsar Nicolas*, 71).

In their rejection of "the folk," one of the most intensive and sustained maskilic campaigns focused on the folk language, Yiddish. Although Yiddish was of course the spoken language of the overwhelming majority of Eastern European Jews in the nineteenth century, and although a rich Yiddish literature of truly universal value would develop in the second half of this century, commencing with the time period under discussion in this chapter, the *haskole* movement at its inception approached Yiddish with relentless hostility, distaste, and extraordinary anger. Yiddish as a language was for the proponents of *haskole* the linguistic expression of the disorder and decay of traditional Jewish life. As Dan Miron explains in *A Traveler Disguised*, Yiddish violated the aesthetics of the *haskole* and its expectations for the rehabilitation of the Jewish people in at least three respects: (1) Yiddish was, and is, a specifically Jewish language that separated Jews from non-Jews without elevating them in the manner of biblical Hebrew; (2) Yiddish as a language that developed in the European Diaspora was an emblem of national impotence and degradation; (3) Yiddish as a fusion language that developed from Middle High German, the scriptural languages of premodern Hebrew and Aramaic, and the small but crucial contribution of coterritorial Slavic words and grammatical forms represented the hybrid, parasitic, and chaotic character of Jewish life.[12] Thus, when compared to German, which most early-nineteenth-century maskilim valorized, Yiddish was seen to possess not a different grammar but, rather, no grammar at all.[13]

In this regard, it is revealing to consider an incident in the career of Yosef Perl (1773–1839), one of the most radical first-generation maskilim—and paradoxically, the most talented of its Yiddish writers. Among many literary, propagandistic, and communal activities on behalf of *haskole*, Perl established a "modern" synagogue in which the homiletic language, though certainly *not* the liturgical language, was German. On one occasion, however, Perl addressed his congregation in Yiddish (though for the sake of correctness, he wrote out his sermon in Hebrew, as well). As Shmuel Werses writes, "Until then, he [Perl] had preached in German in his synagogue. He used the excuse that when speaking of more neutral, general subjects he could allow himself the luxury of speaking in a refined language—that is, German; 'but being forced to address a difficult controversy . . . was a different matter: and therefore I must speak with the parties to the dispute. With these I must speak their language, crudely: they won't feel a more refined one. And therefore I will preach today in Yiddish.'"[14] Yiddish for Perl is not merely a practical language for communicating with his fellow Jews, but also a psychologically necessary one. Maskilim were unable to sustain a polemic in a foreign language, especially not one that they associated with a forbidding sense of refinement. Yiddish for these writers therefore signifies not only a return to familiarity and intimacy but also a descent into transgressively indecorous, raw emotions. In Freudian terms, the balance between "major" and "minor" languages could not be more apparent: German was the superego, Yiddish, the id.[15]

The source of this antipathy toward Yiddish, like the motivation to modernize generally, derives from the encroachment of modernity and the suspicion that Jewish "particularism," in dress, social customs, and language, prevented Jews from participating in the modern, for them German, culture to the West. This harks back to the Enlightenment, and indeed pre-Enlightenment, complaint that Jews were categorically inassimilable to the general society because such external differences signified an inherent foreignness and danger.[16] Thus maskilic attacks against Yiddish can be seen to derive from a larger critique of Jewish exceptionalism, figured as cultural pathology, emerging from the German Enlightenment. The modernity of the Enlightenment therefore requires not only the assimilation of a new set of cultural values but also the rejection and suppression of the previous ones; there is no room for simultaneity in this dispensation, though in fact it is precisely the coexistence of traditional and modern temporalities that defines and determines the peripheral condition. As Sander Gilman argues, the maskilic antipathy toward Yiddish internalizes—and ultimately projects onto other, less modern Jews—the antisemitic discourse of the Enlightenment itself.

From the vantage point of the present day, of course, *haskole*'s antipathy toward Yiddish can be seen as a symptom of irrationality—none of the maskilim's objections against Yiddish pass critical muster, and one should not be surprised that these arguments in and of themselves exerted relatively little influence on most Jews during the nineteenth century, particularly when such arguments were typically formulated in manifestos written in German, Hebrew, or Russian. The credibility of these complaints notwithstanding, they do account in part for the almost complete absence of published Yiddish-language belles-lettres in Eastern Europe before the 1860s.[17] As Chone Shmeruk demonstrates, although maskilim produced dozens of Yiddish narratives and dramas in the first half of the nineteenth century, the fate of nearly all of them was to wait decades, and sometimes more than a century, for publication; or to be lost to history entirely.[18]

In this regard, the sad case of Yisroel Aksenfeld (1787–1866) is particularly instructive. A writer whose enthusiasm appears to border on graphomania, Aksenfeld wrote exclusively in Yiddish from at least the 1820s until his death; by his own estimate, he completed about thirty novels and plays,[19] including one novel, "A Jewish *Gil Blas*," that ran to nearly two thousand pages in manuscript.[20] To his misfortune, however, the two official Jewish publishing houses operating in Czarist Russia from 1837 to 1862, in Vilna and Zhitomir,[21] were unwilling to publish Aksenfeld's maskilic satires of Hasidic life for fear of offending their Hasidic customers—although the non-Hasidic Vilna publishing house did briefly consider publishing Aksenfeld's *Seyfer Hasidim*, which the author himself characterized as a "sort of [Jewish] *Don Quixote*," in 1840 (*Prokim fun der yidisher literatur-geshikhte*, 273).

His subsequent effort to open a maskilic publishing house in his own city, Odessa, in 1860–1861—the chronological high-point of maskilic expectation toward the Czarist regime—similarly failed to gain government support. In 1864, Aksenfeld and his supporters approached the newly formed St. Petersburg *Khevres marbey haskole b'yisroel* ("Society for the Promotion of Enlightenment among the People Israel")[22] to request that this organization of elite Jews, actually headquartered in Russia proper, consider publishing his works. The society's response is typical of "orthodox" *haskole* ideology: they rejected the petition "because according to its first principle, the society has authority to print books only in Hebrew and in Russian, and not in the spoken language (jargon)" (*Prokim*, 275). Only two of Aksenfeld's works, the novel *Dos Shterntikhl* ("The Headband") and the dramatic comedy *Der Ershter yidisher rekrut in rusland* ("The First Jewish Recruit in Russia"), appeared in his lifetime, in self-published editions dated 1861 and 1862, respectively, in Leipzig, over the border and potentially out of reach of his Eastern European audience. An additional three comedies were published after Aksenfeld's death, between 1867 and 1870; the rest of his work, which lay in manuscript, was most likely destroyed in a fire during the Odessa pogroms of 1871.[23]

Most poignant among the stations of Aksenfeld's itinerary—a narrative more profound and edifying than any of his surviving writ-ings—is the rejection of his work, *on linguistic grounds*, by a society of like-minded Jews dedicated explicitly to the same ideology as Aksen-feld. Though sharing Aksenfeld's objectives, these maskilim resisted his practical efforts to communicate Enlightenment philosophy in the one language actually comprehensible to the entirety of Eastern European Jewry. In this respect, it is important to consider Robert Alter's observa-tion that "[t]he pioneer [*haskole*] publication, *HaMe'asef*, probably had no more than 1000 subscribers at the outset; by the time it was falter-ing, in 1797, it had only 120 subscribers, and yet it managed to limp on, appearing sporadically, for another twenty-two years, still thought of in Haskalah circles to the east as an important source of ideas and literary models" (*The Invention of Hebrew Prose*, 11). As much as these statistics speak to the limited impact writing in Hebrew—and therefore *haskole* in general—had during the eighteenth and nineteenth centuries, they also serve to demonstrate how committed the maskilim were to expressing themselves in Hebrew, and to developing Hebrew as a mod-ern language. Nonetheless, because Yiddish was the only language in which the majority of Eastern European Jewry were fully literate, it was only a matter of time, though the advent of this era proved too late for Aksenfeld, before maskilim would of necessity turn to Yiddish.

In order to justify this turn to Yiddish, which amounted to a be-trayal, however necessary, of the commitment to "pure" languages such as German or Hebrew, the Yiddish writers of the *haskole* devised a lin-guistic and literary strategy that Miron describes as "a language as Cali-ban": to promote the ideology of *haskole*, these writers devoted works of satirical parody to the task of holding a mirror up to their culture in order to exhibit or uncover its distorted, grotesque, and excessive traits—starting with the language itself. If, like Caliban, the demotic language of the Jews is fit only for curses,[24] then the maskilic authors would use Yiddish not to praise the light of reason but to curse the benighted superstition, folly, and venality of provincial Jewish society. Miron's aesthetic description of maskilic narrative as essentially satirical and parodic should therefore draw the reader's attention to the function of this literature, primarily, as social critique. Because, moreover, the exposition of *haskole* in Yiddish can only proceed in negative terms, the

prominence of satire and parody to Yiddish literature lays the ground-
work for a subsequent critique and rejection of *haskole* in the final
decades of the nineteenth century; this ambivalence toward the modernizing ideology, as much as any other historical similarity, provides
the essential parallel between maskilic writings in Yiddish and the late
or postnegritude writings of the 1950s and 60s.

To better understand what kind of society maskilim envisioned for a
modern Jewish culture, and how it differed from the shtetl reality of
Eastern Europe, it is worthwhile to make the first of several digressions
in this chapter to consider a programmatic manuscript by the "moderate" maskil Isaac Meyer Dik. This uncompleted narrative, really a manifesto in tale form, was first published under the title *A Maskils utopye* ("A
Maskil's Utopia") in 1952.[25] Dik's version of *haskole*, as indicated previously, is less confrontational than that of his comrades to the south, and
yet many of the main themes of *haskole*—the role of Jews vis-à-vis non-
Jews, the need to reform social customs and education, the valorization
of "productive" labor over traditional Jewish occupations, the attitude
toward imperial rulers, and the status of Yiddish—are given an unusually comprehensive, if quite schematic, exposition in this fragment. The
story describes the author's visit to an imaginary town, Katloyke, and
his meetings with the local rabbi. Much of the long narrative is taken
up with descriptions of the ideal town, or polemical dialogues on the
state of Jewish life in Eastern Europe. Describing Katloyke, Dik writes:

> . . . The entire Jewish community there from small to large, men,
> women, and children . . . wore Christian clothing, and it was difficult
> to distinguish between the Jews and the non-Jews, especially regard-
> ing the youths, who went about unshaven (without beards). Second,
> everyone I encountered could speak and write Russian, and between
> themselves spoke a most refined Yiddish, really almost German.
> Thirdly, in the entire duration of my being there I did not see a single
> Jewish pauper or beggar. . . . Thirdly [*sic*], I never encountered in any
> of the shops or taverns there a single woman of quality (that is, of the
> well-to-do folk), and simply no young girls whatsoever, excepting
> women in the market. . . . Fourthly, the Jewish neighborhoods there
> were clean and tranquil, just like the Christian ones. . . . Fifthly, there

they know nothing of Jewish thieves, or pickpockets . . . or Jewish
tax-collectors or back-alley shysters. . . . Sixthly, I never encountered
there a single Hasidic synagogue, nor a reformed synagogue,[26] to say
nothing of a butcher's synagogue, a tailor's synagogue, and so forth,
as it is among us—no, there were only ten or eleven synagogues there,
or large houses of worship, and all of them only communal, and they
all were known only by the streets on which they were located. . . .
Sixthly [*sic*], I was greatly impressed by the cemetery there, which
was established fifty years previously. . . . The gravestones there were
simply arrayed, without large inscriptions, only with the name and
the date of death, and the name of the person who dedicated it. . . .
Seventh, I was pleased to see in Katloyke a Jewish public library, which
contained a club, a study-room, and this building consisted of two
large halls with various side-rooms, and it contained virtually every
Jewish holy book of worth, from the greatest to the smallest, all bound
identically, and all well sorted, so that it was very easy to find the book
you were looking for, and besides that they had entire runs of all the
Jewish newspapers, and the same with Russian and foreign papers, and
also several Russian and German works from their classic authors . . .
as well as many precious manuscripts. (*A Maskils utopye*, 157–161)

Two features distinguish themselves in this long passage: the inverse
invocation of contemporary realities, and the passion for conformity
that defines Dik's vision of an ideal society. The emphasis on order
and uniformity as a thematic feature of Dik's utopia is a reversal of the
"language as Caliban" strategy otherwise typical of maskilic satire in
Yiddish. Indeed, rather than using a "grotesque" Yiddish to reflect grotesque social conditions, Dik deliberately employs what he describes
as a "refined" Yiddish to reflect a modernized and "improved" vision
of Jewish life. Nonetheless, Dik's prose style undermines his ideological emphasis on order, harmony, and decorum; his long invento-
ries and run-on, indeed runaway, sentences more closely resemble the
ramshackle cemeteries and chaotic streets of a parodic shtetl than the
modern boulevards and industrious organization of his idealized "Katloyke." The "overgrown" state of his writing in this manuscript in fact
betrays his anxiety toward the reality that his utopia is meant to as-
suage, and this disparity between rhetoric and discourse is the only
sense that Dik's writing can, like Reb Nakhman's stories, be read as

"modernist." Where Reb Nakhman engages in storytelling in order to critique modernity, consciously, for Dik the critique betrays itself, unwittingly, through his use of language, even in a manuscript intended to sing modernity's praises.

Indeed, although Dik is a lively and resourceful storyteller[27]—less so than usual in this narrative, which is perhaps why he never finished it—as a literary stylist, he is typically quite awkward. For example, his character descriptions read like nothing so much as the descriptions found in lists of dramatis personae in printed editions of plays;[28] hence he describes the Katloyke rabbi, the hero of his utopia, by writing, "I encountered in him a person of highest masculine perfection (completion), of medium weight, healthy, equipped with a longish-round face which was surrounded (fixed as with a small frame) with a long, parted beard that was sprinkled with gray hair, indicating him to be in his 50s" (*A Maskils utopye*, 166). This weakness in Dik's style reflects the more general problem affecting the new Yiddish literature of imagining situations, or characters, divorced from immediate experience. Dik cannot write effectively about his utopia because he lacks the language, whether in terms of rhetoric or narrative, to create an alternate reality.[29]

Dik's prose style may lack novelistic fluency, but it possesses the polemical virtue of deliberateness, and in nine points the author outlines his vision for an entire society, encompassing individual dress,[30] language, economic life, religious life, the role of women, education (the library), and death (the cemetery). Each point mirrors the others through the repetition of identical sequences; the tombstones, like the library books, like the synagogues, are an interchangeable and proliferating assemblage, set out in the description of Katloyke clothing, "like the Christians," but somehow, at the same time, distinctly Jewish. Perhaps the greatest preoccupation of the excerpt quoted above is the concern that Jews in no aspect of their public life call attention to themselves as Jews, hence the stillness of the streets, the abandonment of traditional dress, and the repeated insistence on uniformity and anonymity, even in the grave. It is nonetheless important to note that—his frequent, incredible expressions of gratitude and loyalty to the Russian government notwithstanding[31]—when Dik uses words like "patriotism" and "nation," he clearly means the Jewish people, despite the absence of any feature defining the Jews of the Russian Empire as a nation in the modern sense (e.g., political institutions, ownership of land, economic autonomy, regional separatism from other ethnic groups, etc.). Dik therefore writes about assimilating Christian values, but not integrating with Christian people: the one place where Jews and non-Jews meet is the public library (see *A Maskils utopye*, 161), suggesting intellectual integration, but social contact of only the most superficial sort.

Indeed, Dik's simultaneous belief in modernization and autonomy betrays an incipient nationalism—at odds with the Enlightenment's ostensible emphasis on universality, yet equally distanced from the revolutionary nationalism otherwise proliferating in Central and Eastern Europe after 1848—and he accordingly defends his decision to write in Yiddish with an appeal to Jewish solidarity: "I must make known the quite noble foundation and principle that leads me on . . . to write in *zhargon* . . . and that is solely a pure and impassioned feeling of patriotism. . . . And what's more, only a critical spirit that has inspired me from earliest childhood, to remark upon her (the nation's) host of errors (deficiencies) and to correct them" (*A Maskils utopye*, 176). In schematic terms, one could say that the virtue of patriotism, loyalty to the "nation," trumps the prohibition against using Yiddish; nonetheless, both the positive attitude toward ethnic solidarity and the negative qualities associated with Yiddish are essential, if self-canceling, features of *haskole*, and where individual maskilim came down on this divide often went a long way toward distinguishing between "radical" maskilic anti-Yiddishism and "moderate" maskilic populism. That Dik believes the Yiddish language can be successfully reformed through "rapprochement" with German is the clearest evidence that his maskilic agenda is more conservative than his predecessors to the south, such as Aksenfeld or Perl.

The question of whether, and how, Yiddish can be modernized—an impossible task for radical maskilim, who reveled in Yiddish's "primitiveness"—leads this consideration of Dik to the linguistic question of *daytshmerism*. *Daytshmerism*, the conscious importation of modern German into Yiddish, is ultimately a verbal correlative to the larger maskilic project of assimilation without integration.[32] *Daytshmerism* is not an abandonment of Yiddish: it is, to take a concept of Houston Baker's, a *marronage*, in which "the discourse of lordship and bondage, controlled by the master, will be taken up and transmuted—deformed as it were—by the maroon [the fugitive slave turned guerilla warrior against the slave system itself]."[33] *Daytshmerism* is an attempt, however clumsy, to appropriate the prestige and modernity of German for a language and a people seen, by themselves as well as their antagonists, as lacking both prestige and modernity. As much as *daytshmerism* is an effort to remake Yiddish in the image of its antithesis, German, it is also an effort to remake, *deform*, German in the image of Yiddish. Seen from this perspective, *daytshmerism* is a masquerade in which Yiddish mimics German, to at times absurd extremes, while retaining its separateness, its *foreignness*, as a language.[34] Indeed, it is a paradox of *daytshmerism* that however much closer Yiddish approaches German, the intrusion of other linguistic components—Slavic, *Loshn-koydesh*—intensifies its sense of difference from German; linguistically speaking, it thus enunciates not only two languages or rhetorical conventions in contact with one another, but also two temporalities colliding into one another.

Daytshmerism therefore bespeaks a significant reconfiguration of the politics of deterritorialized languages and as such is a significant—if arcane—issue in nineteenth-century Yiddish. *Daytshmerism* illustrates how a "minor" culture creates a literary language by mimicking, however superficially, the appearance of a "major" language and culture. *Daytshmerism* is more common during the nineteenth century in Russian-controlled Lithuania[35] than in the Yiddish literature produced in the Austrian Empire.[36] At least during the nineteenth century, there is no Russian equivalent of *daytshmerism*, and in fact most Slavic words in Yiddish typically derive from Czech, Polish, or Ukrainian rather than Russian, and they usually signify primitivism, earthiness, not sophistication. *Daytshmerism* thus participates in a broader linguistic phenomenon of the early modern era that distinguishes culture-languages from ethnic "national" ones. As Benedict Anderson explains:

> [T]he major states of 19th-century Europe were vast polyglot polities, of which the boundaries almost never coincided with language-communities. . . . Rich eighteenth-century Dutch burghers were proud to

speak only French at home; German was the language of cultivation in much of the western Czarist empire, no less than in "Czech" Bohemia. Until late in the 18th-century no one thought of these languages as belonging to any territorially defined group.[37]

By approaching German to make Yiddish a culture-language, *daytsh-merism* exposes the deterritorialized status of both the imperial language and the vernacular one by unmasking the linguistic similarities they share. More significantly, it reveals that the real colonizing presence in the minds of Yiddish-speaking Jewish intellectuals was not the Russian Empire, per se, but a more abstract and insidious empire of Western modernity, for which the Yiddish word *daytsh* (German) could stand not just for a linguistic affiliation but also for a style of dress, a new attitude of worship, and a new habit of being.

Moreover, *daytshmerism* in nineteenth-century Jewish culture recapitulates the efforts of German reformers in the eighteenth century to refine German according to Romance-language models. As Pascale Casanova writes of Frederick II's attitude toward the cultural status of German:

> Frederick II, king of Prussia, published in Berlin in 1780 a brief essay in French . . . titled *De la littérature allemande, des défauts qu'on peut lui reprocher, quelles en sont les causes, et par quels moyens on peut les corriger* (On German Literature, the Defects for Which It May Be Reproached, the Causes of These, and by What Means They May Be Corrected). Through an extraordinary accord of language and argument, the German monarch called attention to the specifically literary domination exercised by French over German letters at the end of the 18th century. . . . To carry out his program for "perfecting" the German language, a "half-barbarous" and "unrefined" tongue . . . Frederick II proposed to Italianize (or Latinize) it.[38]

Frederick the Great's proposal—connected subcutaneously to a broader ambition of making Prussia into an empire and with it to establish the German language, by simultaneously disciplining and deterritorializing it through the importation of cosmopolitan elements, as a "European" language like French or Italian—demonstrates that German culture in the eighteenth century, like Yiddish in the nineteenth, had its own "inferiority complex" to overcome; it also suggests that language reform as such is a central factor in the modernization process. It furthermore offers proof that the model for modernization that the maskilim chose belonged, ultimately, more to the eighteenth century than to the nineteenth.

Returning to Fanon's "dialectic of national culture" with which the comparison in this section began, one can contend that *daytshmerism* does not represent a stage in the development of Yiddish literature, so much as an ongoing strategy based on the purposeful mimicry—fundamentally distinct from Fanon's concept of "imitation"—of a dominant culture. At the opposite end of the maskilic spectrum, the linguistic strategies of the southern radicals, foremost among them Yisroel Aksenfeld, also derive from an aesthetic of mimicry, and serve to locate these writers in the context of their anxious, unstable relationship with tradition and modernity. Aksenfeld's sole surviving full-length narrative, *Dos Shterntikhl*,[39] the first published Yiddish novel, follows the generic rules of domestic farce, which in all likelihood was the dominant theatrical genre that Aksenfeld, like the Yiddish dramatists preceding him, wrote.[40] The book opens on the eve of the Napoleonic invasion of 1812, when Mikhl, the protagonist, a young and enterprising scholar in the Russian shtetl Lohoyopoli ("the town that never was," felicitously translated as "Nosuchville" in Neugroschel's version), is engaged to the beautiful but immature Sheyntse, daughter of the poor synagogue custodian (*shames*). Sheyntse's fondest wish is to receive with her dowry a bejeweled headband, a *shterntikhl*, to wear on festive occasions, the height of fashion for women in the premodern shtetl (and not unknown among Hasidic women today).

When Mikhl is caught absentmindedly eating on a minor fast day, he's brought before a Hasidic rebbe—modeled according to Meir Wiener after Reb Borukh of Miedzybóz (1753–1811), a grandson of the Baal Shem Tov—who bankrupts him by imposing a fine, which leads to his engagement with Sheyntse being broken off. Mikhl leaves town and Sheyntse is engaged to Naftolke, the idiot son of a wealthy family in the next town over, but before they are married Naftolke converts to Christianity and joins the army to serve as a drummer boy (in an era before

Jews were conscripted). Sheyntse then disappears and the story shifts back to Mikhl, who has apprenticed himself to the maskil Oksman and earns a new fortune providing goods and services to the Russian army while learning about enlightenment in the German city Breslau. Arriving in disguise at Miedzybóz, Mikhl reunites Sheyntse with her parents, who, it turns out, had only adopted her at birth; her birth mother and father are also identified at the revelation. He also exposes a series of charlatans posing as pious Jews in the court of the rebbe, persuades the rebbe to marry him and Sheyntse, and presents her with a *shterntikhl* bedecked with fake jewels, reasoning: "When it comes to worldly things, when people are only after money or silly ornaments or other wasteful things, then they deserve to be punished, we ought to fool them" (Y 175; E 168).

To be blunt, Aksenfeld's narrative is a chore to read. As Dan Miron puts it, "the novel as a whole, although not very long, seems at times almost insufferable. We are saturated with the effect of the parodic dialogues before we have read a third of it, and we all but welcome the dull sections in which Oksman expatiates on the nature of the educational theater and on the tactics of the *Haskala* in general" (*A Traveler Disguised*, 260–261). Nonetheless, it is precisely the overdependence on this parodic dialogue that exposes Aksenfeld's paradoxical attitude toward language and, with it, his idiosyncratic approach to tradition and modernity. Nearly all of the traditional characters in *Dos Shterntikhl* are identified through a string of obsessively repeated words, often from *Loshn-koydesh* and always bearing no communicative function. Wiener describes this technique, which is characteristic of early-maskilic writing in Yiddish, as *shprakhfolklor*: "such figures, with which the author maintains a negative relationship . . . make use in their dialogue of unusually plentiful stereotypical, fixed phrases . . . clichéd figures of speech, idioms, *bon mots*, comparisons, etc." (*Di Yidishe literatur in nayntsntn yorhundert*, 71). Although Wiener argues that *shprakhfolklor* provides an early model for the hyper-idiomatic discourse of the "classic" Yiddish writers active later in the nineteenth century (Mendele, Sholem Aleichem, and Y. L. Peretz), it seems less like folklore than a caricature of Yiddish speech, akin to minstrel performance in the same era of American literature and popular theater.[41]

Indeed, minstrelsy insists in rhetorical terms on the absolute, immutable otherness of the object *impersonated*, while it always betrays in the performance of difference the ultimate closeness, familiarity, and similarity of that object to the creator-performer of the impersonation. Like minstrelsy, Aksenfeld's use of Yiddish is provoked by an ambivalent mix of fascination, affection, and revulsion toward the Hasidic culture that forms the object of representation; that Aksenfeld in this instance burlesques other Jews is hardly surprising given that American minstrelsy also constantly indulged in such "self-ridicule."[42] Moreover, as in American minstrelsy, the psychological use of this burlesque, like Perl's use of Yiddish in his sermons, is simultaneously to castigate, indulge, and project the unseemliness of the author's id onto the body, language, and identity of the other. Yiddish for Aksenfeld, a maskil based in cosmopolitan, modern Odessa, is a projection of provincial backwardness and primitiveness as much as it is a vehicle for depiction of actual traditional Jewish life in a self-consciously earlier, "historical" era at least a generation before the time when Aksenfeld actually wrote the novel.

Wiener elaborates on his discussion of *shprakhfolklor* by identifying it as a symptom of an older order's decline into cliché, repetitiousness, and stereotype: the fixity of language betrays the immobility of thought for a culture incapable of adapting to new intellectual and social circumstances (*Di Yidishe literatur in nayntsntn yorhundert*, 72). For Wiener, the use of *shprakhfolklor* is an effort toward realism in a culture not yet capable of integrating its factions within a unified historical temporality. But for Aksenfeld, *shprakhfolklor* does not illustrate the dependence of the older culture on stereotype; it stereotypes that culture itself, not for purposes of mimetic verisimilitude but for ideological contrast. What emerges from his depiction is not the decline and limitation of an older order, but the nervous energy of his own mimicry in projecting an ideological and cultural distance between himself and the characters he has created. In a sense, this "internal minstrelsy" underscores Sander Gilman's notion of linguistic difference lying at the heart of modern antisemitism.

The fact that Aksenfeld takes his narrative cues from comic drama points to the porous proximity between written and spoken conventions, for a literature that at the time lacked both a modern theater and a distribution system for popular fiction. Describing a tavern keeper, Reb Markl, Aksenfeld even writes, "Moreover Reb Markl, the once-mighty rationalist, became a Hasid and made Hasidic grimaces and with glassy eyes carried on worse than a born Hasid" (Y 92; E 90); the burlesque aspect of this description extends beyond speech to gesture. Aksenfeld thus "novelizes" the conventions of farce, primitively, not only because he lacks a tradition of narrative convention to draw from but also because as in dramatic farce his characters possess only surface mannerisms, not internal motivation. By contrast, although it could be argued that Reb Nakhman's characters, as creations of a much more fundamentally oral sensibility, similarly lack the representation of psychological depth already available in 1815 to the beginnings of a Realist tradition elsewhere in Europe—Jane Austen's *Pride and Prejudice*, for example, had appeared in 1813—the atmosphere of doubt, hesitancy, and silence that pervades these stories points to the psychological complexity of their origin and their significance.

Indeed, Aksenfeld's *shprakhfolklor* can be contrasted with Reb Nakhman's language in the *sipurey mayses*, which derives its force and rhythm through the repetition of periphrastic verbs such as *myashev zayn zikh* (to deliberate) that serve for him as shorthand for the fault line between spoken Yiddish and written *Loshn-koydesh*.[43] This compact, allusive complexity is reduced in Aksenfeld's parody, which depends on the repetition of extragrammatical interjections from *Loshn-koydesh*, to neurotic, foolish chatter. The rhetorical contrast between the two authors—in Reb Nakhman's case, perhaps more properly *auteur*—suggests in turn a fundamental temporal distinction in their respective grasp of politics and history. Specifically, the Napoleonic wars, which are central to the poetics of Reb Nakhman's later stories, all of which were narrated years before Napoleon's invasion of Russia, register in *Dos Shterntikhl* only as an economic opportunity for Mikhl, unironically, to profit off of business with the army: "The time in which Mikhl became a broker was a period of war, when the great Napoleon with the French army had invaded Russia. Russian officers were traveling back and forth through Lohoyopoli. An active youth, a young youth [*sic*!], a handsome youth, a clever youth, Mikhl gave first-class service to all the officers and everyday he earned good money from them" (Y 86; E 84).[44]

The ostensible recognition that the Napoleonic Wars are good for business exposes not only the economic underpinnings of *haskole*— as a mode of capitalism closely derived from an earlier Jewish role as mediator between economic elites—but also its inexhaustibly odd relationship to nationalism ideologically and the Russian Empire politically. For Aksenfeld, unlike Reb Nakhman's ambivalent combination of contempt and curiosity toward a generic non-Jewish aristocracy, the Russian incorporation of Poland offered an unmistakably progressive advance in the capacity of Eastern European Jews to modernize. Regarding the difference between Poles and Russians, he writes, "The Pole's overweening pride, the Pole's arrogance is never found in a Russian. When a Russian gets to know a Jew and deals with him a couple of times, he calls him 'brother' or 'little brother.' Even a broker. If he serves him loyally, the Russian gets to love him. Yes indeed, love him. Especially when he becomes acquainted with a Jewish merchant after doing business with him for a while: then even the greatest Russian becomes friends with the Jew. Yes indeed: friends" (Y 85; E 83). What distinguishes this passage is the tepidness of Aksenfeld's effusion toward Russian power, how low his expectations are; if one didn't know how fundamental the currying of favor with political authority was to the larger maskilic agenda, it might seem as though he was ironic in his response to subordination under both the Polish and Russian regimes.

More than an exercise in historical verisimilitude, however, the bizarre image of a friendly Czarist officer serves a structural function: to illustrate that the officer, like the maskil, is both an outsider and a redeemer of the corrupt and stagnant shtetl society. To underscore this contention, Aksenfeld in the next paragraph describes how Mikhl's older competitor Meshl remains obsequiously loyal to the old Polish aristocracy against the newer Russian hegemony. Once again the old, traditional Jew is explicitly associated with an outmoded and discredited political affiliation to promote an image of maskilic modernity as being seamlessly compatible with the new imperial order. The benign Russian occupies an analogously inverted relation to the malignant Polish aristocrat as the maskil does to the Hasidic rebbe; if Aksenfeld had been writing in Warsaw instead of Odessa, these non-Jewish stereotypes might well have been reversed. Just as Mikhl's maskilic mentor

Oksman, in a story he relates in the novel's fifteenth chapter, undermines Hasidic authority through mimicry and masquerade, betraying
the superimposition of one ideological affiliation onto the other, so too
can one recognize the opposing images of non-Jewish power as stock
characters with no inner reality and only a symbolic connection with
historical reality.[45]

There is a similarly deliberate contrast between Mikhl's "appropriate"
relations with the army as a businessman—by which one earns the respect of the officers—and Naftolke's inappropriate desire to convert in
order to serve as a soldier (but a childish, powerless imitation of a soldier, a drummer boy). Naftolke's presence in the narrative nonetheless
betrays more anxiety toward the outside world than Mikhl's decorous
service of the military elite; his "fraternization" with common soldiers
exposes the unvarnished stereotype of non-Jewish men that Aksenfeld's
praise of Mikhl's clients is intended to neutralize. When Naftolke makes
his first appearance in the novel, for example, he arrives in the company
of a soldier whom Aksenfeld describes by writing, "He [Naftolke] was
accompanied by a drunken soldier, who kept tugging and grabbing at
him. If the soldier hadn't been drinking, Naftolke wouldn't have been
able to escape, but since he was good and drunk, Naftolke had managed to drag him all the way home" (Y 73; E 71). Aksenfeld's faint praise
for Russian authority and his palpable uneasiness over physical contact
with actual Russians indicate how utopian Dik's (much later) vision of
Jews and non-Jews mingling in a Jewish library is. Aksenfeld reveals
how little the maskilim sought interaction with non-Jews. This attitude,
as will be seen, recapitulates in the attitude of the *évolué* toward colonial power in the French context, desiring a maximal knowledge of
French culture with a minimal contact with French people. This desire
ultimately proves to be illusory in the postcolonial moment of the first
Francophone African novels.

Just as *haskole* in Aksenfeld's presentation of it proves to be ambivalent and conflicted toward the non-Jewish world, it is of necessity equally fraught in its relationship with the tradition from which it
emerged. Arguably the exposition of *haskole* ideology in Yiddish fiction
exposes the circularity of maskilic reasoning more clearly than the more
purely polemical maskilic works in other languages. Aksenfeld's mouth-

piece Oksman, for example, cites the German maskil David Friedlän-der (1750–1834) to explain, "In Germany, there was no lack of scholarly Jews, but they had to be enlightened, they had to be shown that it's not enough to study the Talmud, you have to master other subjects and lan-guages as well, and this was demonstrated with the help of the Talmud" (Y 114; E 111). Though the tradition is ostensibly insufficient to sustain itself hermetically, the ability to rectify the tradition receives justifica-tion from within the tradition itself. The slippage among upholding, improving, and rejecting the tradition for modern, non-Jewish values betrays the uncertainty and instability of maskilic ideology: its frustra-tions with traditional Jewish life, its aspirations for approval from the very lines of internal authority against which it rebelled, and the ulti-mately conservative perspective from which it made uneasy efforts to incorporate the outside world.

Perhaps it is this instability that makes the prospect of masquerade offered by theater so attractive to Aksenfeld and other early maskilim. In this regard Oksman contends that the purpose of theater is to model good behavior and provide moral instruction, which it does more ef-fectively than a sermon in synagogue. This declaration precedes the tale of his crude burlesque of a Hasidic rebbe (Chapter 15) to demonstrate the foolish duplicity of Hasidism. The incident thereby demonstrates in concentrated form the methodology of the novel as a whole, which unfolds as a series of dramatized episodes in which ideological posi-tions are performed before the shtetl—a space lacking a private dimen-sion, which in its excessive intimacy obligates life to be displayed before others—and in which deception not only is justified in the service of ideological truth but also is the means by which objective truth and genuine values are established. Aksenfeld is the only maskil in the Rus-sian context to see performance and role-playing in these terms: for Linetski and Mendele, for example, role-playing is the means by which a picaresque character loses his identity and soul. Aksenfeld's embrace of role-playing underscores his creative and ideological debts to theater, where later writers represent, however tentatively, an approach via the picaresque toward the psychological and ethical complexity of novel-istic prose. The difference in this respect between Aksenfeld and later maskilic writers can perhaps be expressed as the narcissism of the small difference between farce and satire, but in this difference a temporal shift toward a later stage of modernization can be inferred.

Having therefore taken Dik's utopian manuscript and Aksenfeld's corrosive satire as representations of *haskole* ideology, one can at last summarize the paradoxical character of early Jewish modernization: an intellectual elite within Eastern European Jewry develops a national consciousness in apparent opposition to both the culture they would set about liberating and the modern hegemony that would provide the tools for liberation. As the literary critic Sh. Niger (1883–1955) character- izes this dilemma, "Dik suffered from the contradiction, from which several younger maskilim also suffered in the 'springtime,' as Mendele [Moykher-Sforim] called the period of the 1860s: on one hand he held that Jewish life could only be improved by internal means; on the other, he didn't believe in the internal strength of the Jewish people. . . . " (*A Maskils utopye*, 143). One can better understand these paradoxes by studying *haskole* comparatively in the context not of other forms of contemporaneous European nationalism—with which it shares nei- ther intimate contact nor a shared goal of establishing an independent nation-state[46]—but with other ideologies that redirect national aspira- tions into a "universalist" framework. It is for this reason that a com- parison between Eastern European *haskole* and West African negritude is so compelling.

By way of elaborating on these correspondences, one can define negri- tude as an aesthetic and cultural movement that developed in France during the 1930s among young Black intellectuals, *évolués*, from both the Caribbean and West Africa. Like *haskole*, negritude is essentially an urban, diaspora phenomenon. Indeed, it was the first effort by Black artists, primarily poets, to create an aesthetic that was both explicitly Black, pan-African and, at the same time, High Modernist—"a synthetic vision of universal black culture with its roots in Africa," as Bennetta Jules-Rosette has characterized it.[47] That is to say, negritude aspires to express a specifically Black sensibility in aesthetic terms that derive from cosmopolitan, ostensibly universal sources at the heart of Western culture. Negritude is preceded by Black nationalist and pan-Africanist theories dating to the same era as *haskole*.[48] Unlike these precursors, however, negritude is the first such ideology to create a native African belletristic literature.[49]

As a *synthesizing* position between traditional Africa and modern Europe, negritude articulates a situation that is analogous to the ambivalence toward assimilation and autonomy that characterizes *haskole*. Whereas maskilim often express this ambivalence through appeals to traditional authority—hence their valorization of biblical Hebrew and their commitment, generally, to the observance of ritual law—the ideologues of negritude, who unlike the maskilim shared no common language or culture *except* French, gravitated toward an ostensibly transcendental humanism. For example, Léopold Sédar Senghor (1906–2001), the leading African proponent of negritude, who became both the first president of Senegal and the first Black member of the *Académie française*, writes, "What all these [African] writers cry out for is . . . not to reject what the West brought them, not a return to the Africa of pre-colonial times, closed in upon itself; nor is it to be able to construct their own world totally separate from the white. What they want is . . . to contribute to the formation of a universal humanism, in collaboration with all races."[50] In more caustic terms, Alioune Diop (1910–1980), founder of the central negritude journal of the independence era, *Présence Africaine*, makes essentially the same claim: "As for Western civilization, it is definitely murderous—even towards itself. But it is the seat of the most powerful institutions to support democracy, justice, and love. . . . We all need the West. We also need it to master . . . an all too powerful appetite on its own part for domination—so that we may live harmoniously . . . with other human civilizations."[51]

In its African manifestations, negritude seeks to affirm a unifying African essence—a «*négritude*» to quote a phrase—and yet, this essence inherits the assumption of an immutable racial essence from the white supremacist doctrines propounded in Europe during the nineteenth century. V. Y. Mudimbe connects negritude's received racism not only to the fact of colonialism but also to the structure of colonialist ideology itself:

> The extreme violence of certain of these [African discourses] . . . is not in sum so different from certain "signs" that previously distinguished

the order and the manner of colonial thought. The principal difference that distinguishes them . . . lies in the fact that "African" discourse, as the articulation of a counter-ideology or of a cult of difference, in principle poses a challenge to the dominant ideology that, from the outset, regards itself as "scientifically" absolute. . . . [52]

One wonders if the structural parallels between negritude and colonial racism therefore speak to the "necessity," of an "anti-racist racism," as Sartre characterized negritude, or to the limitations of being the double of the West's science of the Other? In fact, negritude shares with previous pan-African ideologies the racialist double-bind: simultaneously accepting the belief in fixed, biologically determined racial identities, and rejecting the power imbalances that these racial categories were created to justify. But as Enda Duffy warns, "Racism . . . will always formulate discourses within discourses, reverse racism, to counter racism, which it is doomed never effectively to oppose because it merely imitates it."[53]

However problematic the intellectual premise for negritude is—and indeed its debts to nineteenth-century racial discourse are as extensive as the cues *haskole* took from Enlightenment-era antisemitism—one must note that the immediate political consequence of pan-African thought in general, and negritude in particular, is a rejection of the same type of nineteenth-century European nationalism that the *haskole* had rejected approximately a hundred years previously, in favor of a generalized Black consciousness, culture, and politics.[54] Though the founders of negritude intended their movement to be pan-African, uniting Black people from Africa and the New World in a new creative spirit, the ideology developed in parallel directions during the 1940s and 50s among Caribbean and African intellectuals. Among Caribbean thinkers, primarily from Martinique and Guadeloupe, negritude was associated with communism and surrealist aesthetics. In Africa, mostly Senegal and Mali, negritude, though somewhat nebulously committed to socialism, was far more interested in articulating a vision of the collective African *soul* and its symbiotic relationship with European and Arab cultures.[55] Where Caribbean negritude looked to André Breton for inspiration and ideological guidance, African negritude fell under the spell of the idiosyncratic German ethnographer Leo Frobenius (1873–

1938), a figure of great intellectual energy and enthusiasm but dubious scholarly rigor, who claimed in effect that every aspect of African culture was governed by aesthetics, and therefore every object created by African hands, regardless of its function, was a work of art.[56]

Like Dik's *daytshmerism* and Aksenfeld's "minstrelsy," the negritude of Senghor and his followers is characterized and compromised by its attitude toward language. Thus Senghor writes in his essay, *L'art négro-africaine*:

> The French always feel the need to comment and explain the meaning of images by abstract words. For the Negro poet this is rarely necessary. His public has this second sight spontaneously, because it is . . . gifted with inner eyes which see through walls. . . . There is no need to explain that the young girl who has just seen her fiancé triumph in athletic games is flooded with joy as she sings: I shall not sleep; I shall watch on the open square / The tom-tom of me is decked in a white necklace. (*Black Writers in French*, 88)

Senghor's idealization of the "spontaneous," unmediated rapport between the poet and his audience is undermined, however, by his decision to write exclusively in French. After all, how many of the Africans who could spontaneously comprehend his writing were actually capable of reading poetry in French?[57] Moreover, writing in French compels Senghor to adopt a cultural reference system quite removed from his ostensibly authentic African aesthetic; his appeals to literary authority in this essay, for example, aren't African griots, they are LaFontaine and Baudelaire.

None of which is intended to criticize his decision to write in French, per se;[58] it isn't merely lip service to say that Senghor is a gifted poet and an inspirational figure in the history of African thought.[59] Rather, the problem with Senghor's remarks is the gap between the imagined significance of this writing for an African audience and the political realities of writing in French. Senghor's presentation of an "organic" negritude is undermined by his choice of language, as much as it is by his location within the colonial system as an *évolué* living in France. Jean-Paul Sartre's living prototype of African authenticity, his Black Orpheus,[60] is in fact an example of Bad Faith. Comparing the rhetoric and ideology of negritude—particularly in its second-generation, novelistic treatments of the 1950s and 60s, when the limitations of the ideology had already become apparent to the intellectuals trained in its sensibility—to the often contrary sensibilities of *haskole* is therefore illuminating: though *haskole* expresses the desire to abandon the folk sensibility, with its corrupt values and degraded language (Yiddish), it inevitably returned to both in search of an audience. Negritude declares its identification with the folk, in a language only an estranged and self-conscious minority could understand.[61]

Both *haskole* in Yiddish and negritude in French thus meet one another coming and going between the universal and the particular; where *haskole* aspires to universal, enlightenment values, but must articulate these values in the language of the particular, therefore expressing them inversely, through parody and satire, negritude proclaims its particularity, its essentialism, but does so in a "universal," vehicular, imperial language. These values, in turn, are further attenuated in negritude's second phase, when novelists turn the self-scrutiny of autobiographical prose to an ideology originally formulated in the discourses of polemical essay and lyric poetry. The "negritude" novelist is thus as paradoxical in formal terms as a "Yiddishist" maskil is in linguistic ones.

The correspondence between *haskole* and negritude on the question of language leads the reader back to the question of universalism as it was understood during the eighteenth century, when the idea of a "world literature," analogous to the emerging global marketplace of mercantilism, first gained recognition. As Pascale Casanova has characterized Frederick the Great's conception of Germany's role in European culture, "Germany could not hope for a more brilliant destiny than to assume its place in a universal history of culture . . . in which each nation in its turn incarnated the classical ideal before stepping aside, overcome by decadence, as another slowly reached maturity" (*The World Republic of Letters*, 70). Frederick's "Vicoesque" assertion of the cyclical pattern of national domination notwithstanding, what is of interest in this context is the implication that, as considered previously, by mimicking the language and cultural practices of France or Italy, Germany could achieve France's hegemonic status. By analogy, it is worth considering whether this process of mimicking—*not* imitating—the "universal," dominant cultural language motivates the commitment to *francophonie* among negritude writers, particularly those partisans of negritude, like Senghor, who contributed to the establishment of independent nation-states in West Africa. This strategy thus speaks to the ambivalence of many negritude writers toward both the colonial culture that oppressed them and the conventional concept of the nation-state that ostensibly offered them the only viable means of achieving liberation.[62]

With negritude's focus on the universal, the decision to articulate African "authenticity" in the colonial language becomes indicative of the estrangement from the native culture affecting the ideology's formulators.[63] In practical terms, French is the *only* language for modern literary expression under the terms of negritude. Thus, Senghor writes, "We express our message in French since French has a universal vocation and since our message is also addressed to French people and others. In our languages the halo that surrounds the words is by nature merely that of sap and blood; French words send out thousands of rays like diamonds."[64] It may be noted that the opposition between the hardness, polish, and dazzle of French "diamonds" and the organic functionality of African "sap and blood" replicates an aesthetic and metaphysical dichotomy that recurs everywhere in the literature of negritude: Africans are closer to the earth, the spirit, and the life force of an authentic creativity—their humble culture is more natural and vibrant than the cold, technological symmetry of the West. But the French have the diamonds.

Given the decision to embrace the colonial language, the presence of the colonizer is much more palpable in, or just behind, negritude writing than Senghor's reveries would suggest. Thus Sartre writes in *Orphée noir*, "All those, colonist and accomplice, who open this book, will have the sensation of reading as though over another's shoulder, words that were not intended for them. It is to black men that these black poets address themselves; it is for them that they speak of black men."[65] Sartre's observation raises an important question: If it is to a Black audience that these poets speak, why has a white writer written a 35–page introduction to the anthology—an introduction itself addressed *exclusively* to a white readership? The decision to write in French, however necessary and inevitable, undermines the rhetoric of solidarity with Africa that everywhere characterizes negritude as an ideology. However "authentic" these authors imagine themselves,[66] they are everywhere implicated with the modern, metropolitan culture.[67] It is only in negritude's second generation that this ambivalence begins to be articulated and explored, as the novels under consideration in this part of the comparison will demonstrate.

One of the most explicit demonstrations of colonialism's "hidden hand" in the discourse of negritude occurs in Francophone Africa's first important narrative of the independence era, Camara Laye's *L'enfant noir*.[68] In the sixth chapter, the narrator describes his experience transferring from a Koranic school to a colonial one, a progression narrated again in Kane's *L'aventure ambiguë*. Critics of Camara's book who have bemoaned its ostensibly apolitical stance[69] have apparently overlooked this chapter; if this episode isn't political, nothing is. As Camara describes the arrival of the young children in the classroom, the same insistence on order and conformity that Isaac Meyer Dik had gleaned from the decorum of modernity becomes clear:

> Once at school, we went straight to our seats, boys and girls side by side, their quarrels over. So motionless and attentive did we sit, that it would have been wonderful to see what would have happened had we stirred. Our teacher moved like quicksilver, here, there, everywhere. His flow of talk would have bewildered less attentive pupils; but we were extraordinarily attentive. Young though we were, we regarded our schoolwork as a deadly serious matter. Nothing that we learned was old or expected; all came as though from another planet, and we never tired of listening. But even if we had wearied, this omnipresent teacher would never have given us an opportunity to interrupt. Interruption was out of the question; the idea did not even occur to us. We wanted to be noticed as little as possible, for we lived in continual dread of being sent to the blackboard.[70]

In a social system that stresses uniformity, nothing strikes fear so much as being distinguished from the crowd. Moreover, the chalkboard— and the color symbolism of its *blackness* is only slightly more explicit in translation than in the original—serves as a kind of mirror to the colonial students' intimidation in the face of a Western discourse that, as Mudimbe has stated, considers itself "scientifically absolute." Thus Camara writes, "This was our nightmare. The blackboard's blank surface was an exact replica of our minds" (F 84; E 80). This blankness reflects the narrative's voicelessness about the political situation, which itself is a voicelessness *because of* the political situation. Knowledge in the colonial school, like most pedagogical situations, flows only in one direction.

Nonetheless, in this context, the flow of knowledge becomes a pointed, if subtle, political synecdoche for the entire colonial enterprise. The teacher is an embodiment of Michel Foucault's concept of the "panopticon": "Hence the major effect of the Panopticon: to induce in the inmate [which for Foucault includes schoolchildren, as he states explicitly in the paragraph preceding this citation] a state of conscious and permanent visibility that assures the automatic functioning of power."[71] If understood as a "social mechanism," the teacher is an embodiment of the panopticon principle—everywhere at once, constantly monitoring his charges, his disciplinary functions indistinguishable from pedagogical ones, his dictatorial behavior inseparable from the flow of knowledge and information he imparts.

Camara makes explicit the connection between this colonial synecdoche and the epistemological problem of African orality vis-à-vis Francophone literacy when he describes the experience of the unlucky student—the exception, the inmate, the body under surveillance—called to the blackboard: "If we made one downward stroke not precisely of the same height as the others, we were required to do extra lessons on Sunday, or were sent during recess for a caning—a caning, I should add, one did not easily forget. Irregular downward strokes made our teacher furious. He examined our exercises under a magnifying glass, and dealt out his blows accordingly. He was indeed quicksilver, and he wielded his rod with joyous élan" (F 85; E 80). Unlike the Koranic teacher in *L'aventure ambiguë*, who similarly indulges in the sadistic pleasure of tormenting his errant pupils, the colonial schoolmaster here represents a new order imposing its power on the Africans, rather than the old order struggling to maintain its traditions in the face of a new hegemony. Aside from the railroad invoked in the first chapter, the schoolmaster is virtually the only explicit reference to the colonial world in Camara's narrative, at least until after the climactic series of initiations recorded in chapters 7 and 8. Moreover, as a Black teacher within the colonial system, this character is another mirror, a proleptic one, of the protagonist's eventual destiny as an *évolué*.

Significantly, the narrator doesn't even mention the subject he's studying when he receives, or at least witnesses, the teacher's blows: What subject requires absolute uniformity in downward strokes? Grammar? Arithmetic? Drawing? Spelling? The real subject of instruction, it seems, is conformity itself, the uniformity of submission to the colonial order and its self-justifying system of knowledge. An associative link can therefore be made between the downward strokes on the background and the downward motion of the cane. Both strokes are simultaneously forms of punishment and writing—like the tattoos in Kafka's "Penal Colony." They are each indelible acts of violence against the *enfant noir*.

Furthermore, these beatings are part of a more systemic violence in the colonial school. As Camara notes, "There were fewer beatings in the upper classes; other kinds of punishment, no more pleasant, took their place. I underwent a vast variety of punishments in that school, and only one thing did not vary—my anguish. One's love of knowledge had to be very strong to survive these ordeals" (F 85; E 80). Keeping in mind the teacher's role as part of the "panopticon," one might contend that Camara again anticipates Foucault's argument that the evolution of punishment in the modern era proceeds from public to private, external to internal, physical to psychological, torture to discipline. Camara's depiction of an almost identical development occurring in the evolution of his own education not only confirms Foucault's contention that education, like medicine, psychology, and labor, has been subsumed in a larger project of disciplining the individual but also makes explicit the connection of discipline, as both subjugation and punishment, to the colonial enterprise. What's more, the reader can at last understand that one of the crucial distinctions between the maskil's experience and the *évolué*'s—and therefore a fundamental difference in the literature these two ideologies produced—is the relative absence of contact between most shtetl Jews and the social disciplines of the modern regime; the very isolation from the social mechanics of modernity is what preserves the allure of modernity for the maskil.

Although Camara claims that the schoolmaster discontinues corporal punishment among the upperclassmen, these students have not only already assimilated his violent example but, in good neocolonial fashion, they become his surrogates—and it should be recalled in this context that the schoolmaster himself is merely an African surrogate for the French regime—distributing supplementary beatings on top of his lessons. As Camara writes, "That's how it was with our teachers. . . . And yet it seems that as yet I have scarcely said anything about the dark side of our school life, since the worst was what the older pupils made us younger ones suffer. These older students—I cannot call them 'comrades' since they were older and stronger than we, and less strictly supervised—persecuted us in every conceivable way. They were a haughty lot, and with reason, since no doubt they were repaying the treatment they had themselves received" (F 87–88; E 82). It may be noted that the presentation of strife and violence only within the confines of the colonial school system is itself a political gesture, perhaps an inverse one to Aksenfeld's strategy of presenting all Russian officers as benign and all Polish aristocrats as corrupt, that contrasts the idyllic traditional world with the modern one, which distinguishes itself through competition, domination, and exploitation.

Nonetheless, the purpose of this contrast is not merely to valorize the past, tradition, and Africa over modernity, colonialism, and the West. Rather, this contrast serves to underscore the weakness of the old order and the confusion that the conflict between modernity and tradition engenders among the colonial students. This in turn connects to a complicated relationship between fathers and sons that structures the narrative as a whole, and which becomes manifest when the narrator discusses the question of whether his parents should intervene on his behalf to protest his abuse at the school: "Possibly it would have been wiser to have informed our parents of what we were undergoing, but somehow or other this never occurred to us. Perhaps we remained silent because of pride, or because of loyalty to the school. I know now that whatever the reason, it was stupid of us to keep silent. Such beatings were utterly alien to my people's passion for independence and equality" (F 90; E 84). The last appeal to independence and equality makes more explicit the political subtext of this episode. And yet, at the same time, the equivocal tone of the passage as a whole is another instance of Camara's ambiguous rhetoric whenever he proposes to discuss the meaning of his experiences; virtually every explanation in this narrative is preceded, as in this example, by the word *"peut-être."*

In this instance, at least, the resistance to making definitive statements both about the experience in the colonial school and the way this experience changes the dynamic between Camara and his parents can be understood as a political statement in reverse, a political "aphasia." Camara and his friends fail to appeal to their parents, because the parents now represent a power system that no longer exerts authority in the new domain of the colonial school. Just as Camara here protects himself from the confirmation that the power of his parents has been rendered defunct, so too does he elsewhere protect other, secret manifestations of traditional power from too much scrutiny, to shield these vestiges of authority from the disempowering gaze of the Western reader.

Camara's father does, however, eventually intervene in the school and secures the protagonist's freedom from the bullies; the tradition does, in the end, exert parental, patriarchal power over the new order. In the metaphorical politics of this narrative, this assertion of authority seems to be part of the hope implicit in Camara's crypto-revolutionary affirmation of his people's "independence and equality." Moreover, it can hardly be accidental that the father's eventual intervention comes about because the narrator's best friend, the son of a griot (a traditional praise singer in Mande society), uses the griot's trademark of disingenuous flattery to trick one of the bullies into coming to the griot's house so that his father can beat him: "The next day, no sooner had Kouyaté arrived at the school yard than he went over to Himourana, the boy who had thrashed him so brutally the day before. 'My father is most anxious to meet the upper form boy who has been kindest to me. I thought of you at once. Can you come to dinner this evening?' 'I'll be happy to,' Himourana said. Himourana's brutality was only matched by his stupidity. He was probably a glutton as well" (F 92; E 85). The tradition thus reasserts its authority, if only in miniature, through the entirely traditional means of the griot's verbal art.

Moreover, the griot's authority is asserted through two power-systems working in tandem: when Kouyaté invites the bully to come to his house for dinner (and for just desserts, as well!), he tells his father that this boy was the one who had beaten him most viciously and had most frequently extorted his spending money. The griot cross-examines his son, asking, «C'est bien vrai au moins ce que tu me dis là»? Kouyaté replies, «Par Allah»! His father concludes, «C'est donc vrai» ("Is what you've said to me really true?" Kouyaté replies, "By God!" His father concludes, "Then it's really true") (F 93). With the bully standing in for the modern discontents to be found within the colonial school—and foreshadowing the brutality of the neocolonial power structure—Kouyaté analogously derives his authority from his status as a griot's son *and* a devout Muslim. Although in reality both the power of the griot and the authority of Islam would be co-opted into the neocolonial regime, at the moment of preindependence optimism to which *L'enfant noir* in general speaks, a faith emerges, as it does in Tutuola, that the tradition itself offers the best system of values with which to resist the depredations of the modern world.[72]

The power of the griot functions in an earlier, more celebrated moment in Camara's narrative, as well. In the second chapter, the narrator depicts his father's work as a goldsmith; describing the involvement of the griot in the ritual of smelting gold, Camara writes, "the praise-singer took a curious part . . . in the work. He was drunk with the joy of creating. He shouted aloud in joy. He plucked his *cora* like a man inspired. He sweated as if he were the trinket-maker, *as if he were my father*, as if the trinket were his creation" (F 34; E 38–39, emphasis added).[73] At the same time that Camara describes the griot's vicarious identification with his father, the goldsmith, he suggests, or rather inscribes, his own vicarious identification with the griot—"as if he were *my father*." If the griot is to be likened to the goldsmith in his creativity, then Camara is to be likened to the griot in his use of language. Indeed, Camara's own writing aspires to both the seductive fluency of the griot and the exalted permanence of gold jewelry. Yet it is, of course, neither; writing is different from both, conceived in another culture and temporality.

Thus here, as throughout the narrative, Camara announces his allegiance and identification with the culture of his father, even as he abandons it. The negritude he advertises is ultimately a masquerade; Camara hides his status as an *évolué* behind the drama of goldsmiths and griots.[74]

The crucial distinction between Camara and his "surrogate father," the griot, is the author's decision to tell *his own* story—unless the reader considers that the "I" in the narrative is "an other," itself a modernist, European formulation (yet one that informs any autobiographical narrative implicitly)—because a griot, by definition, is always speaking for someone else. The decision to invest significance in the awakening of a subjective consciousness is what distinguishes Camara's writing as different in kind, and not just in medium, from the oral, griotic narrative that precedes it and mediates the author's relationship to his own father, and his own past.

Negritude can therefore be seen as very much of a piece with the discussion of the assemblage in Tutuola's and Reb Nakhman's writing: negritude structures itself between polarities of desire, for an uncorrupted Africa, and of power, the French colonial regime. Yet in negritude literature, these two polarities blend and collapse into one another—the vision of an uncorrupted Africa can only be articulated through the language of the colonizer, while the need for mastery in the colonial system makes of French culture itself another object of desire. The diamonds of Senghor's poetry become a mirror reflecting back a desire for two power constructions, Africa and France, that on closer inspection prove to be equally unattainable.[75]

To interrupt the irresolvable contest between Africa and Europe that initiates negritude, it is useful to introduce a third term to the equation—already foreshadowed by Kouyaté's oath, «par Allah»—a cultural presence in Francophone Africa as significant as "Blackness" and "whiteness" but identifying with neither: Islam. Because negritude derives much of its intellectual dynamism from the dialectical opposition of Africa and Europe, as a formal ideology it has surprisingly little to say about Islam, a religion that arrived in Western Africa as part of a colonizing mission from the North that precedes European colonialism by several centuries, and yet which quickly became an integral and highly adaptive fixture of Western African life. Islam is, for example, the religion of over 90 percent of the nation of Senegal, but not the religion of its first president, Senghor (a Catholic), who belatedly formulated the concept *Arabité* as a complement to negritude not as an extension of his thinking about his native culture but apparently to cultivate a closer relationship with the Egyptian leader Nasser (!).[76] Nonetheless, the most pronounced and complex effects, or perhaps "aftershocks," of negritude on African literature, particularly African novels, can be found in the work of Muslim authors, for whom Islam in varying degrees of orthodoxy is an essential component in the understanding and interpretation of their work.

What can therefore be termed "Islamic negritude" provides a particularly apt point of comparison with *haskole* because in both movements one finds bilingual—in fact, multilingual—literate cultures caught in the struggle between tradition and modernity. In the analogous contexts of *haskole* and negritude, modernity signifies technology, secularism, the City, and the West (the "diamonds" of European civilization). Tradition, by contrast, not only refers to the culture and beliefs that precede, or at least appear to precede,[77] the imposition of modernity but also consists of the power formations that organize around these institutions of belief, education, and social organization. One of the essential contrasts, therefore, to be established between the writers under discussion in this chapter and Reb Nakhman and Tutuola in the preceding one is the depiction, through recognizably realist techniques, of tradition and modernity, not as polarities of order and chaos, home and wilderness, respectively, but as rival social and political *institutions*.

In these cultural conflicts, tradition and modernity are as likely to assert their respective authority through dissimulation, subterfuge, and negotiated interests as through open hostility or competition.[78] In Eastern Europe, for example, the Russian Empire proved much more willing to grant concessions and publishing rights to Jews who remained traditional in their religious and cultural orientation, and therefore politically acquiescent vis-à-vis the state, than to the maskilim with their agenda of social transformation; their Western, Enlightenment values of freedom and equality; and their noisy, extravagant declarations of loyalty to the Czar. In Africa, as well, colonial administrators typically made a separate peace with traditional authorities, and, indeed, when finding no authorities from within the tradition with which to deal, often set about creating them to fill the breach.[79] Thus the seeming inflexibility of African tradition can be understood as a consequence, at least in part, of a conservative imperial modernity's desire for fixity in the colonized administration in order to assure the passivity of the dominated population. In this respect, modernity *mandates* the immobility of tradition—traditional cultures are sometimes not only more dynamic than modernity understands them to be, but are also more elastic than the weighty apparatus of modernity itself.

In the context of French colonialism, specifically, modern education in French was available to a tiny elite of African students, for the purpose of training this cadre to administer the colonies, while the colonizers left the vast majority of the colonized Africans to traditional, premodern forms of education and initiation. Benedict Anderson connects this administrative policy both to the origins of negritude and the subsequent character of Francophone African nationalism:

> In its heyday, the École Normale William Ponty in Dakar [established in 1913], though only a secondary school, was still the apex of the colonial educational pyramid in French West Africa. To William Ponty came intelligent students from what we know today as Guinea, Mali, the Ivory Coast, Senegal, and so on. We should not be surprised therefore if the pilgrimages of these boys, terminating in Dakar, were initially in French (West) African terms, of which the paradoxical concept of negritude—essence of African-ness expressible only in French, language of the William Ponty classrooms—is an unforgettable symbol. . . . [T]he school's Old Boys went home to become, eventually, Guinean or Malian nationalist leaders, while retaining a "West African" camaraderie and . . . intimacy lost to succeeding generations. (*Imagined Communities*, 123–124)[80]

The absence of such a centralized bureaucracy in British colonial Africa helps to explain why there is no Anglophone equivalent of Francophone negritude.[81] At the same time, however, one should consider another historical cause of the cultural disparity between Anglophone and Francophone Africa: in Anglophone West Africa, the role of an indigenous elite had already been supplanted by Sierra Leone (and Liberia), which served to mediate between imperial and "native" cultures to a more complicated and—as events of the last two decades have made disastrously clear—agonistic extent than the Francophone alumni of William Ponty.

Nonetheless, like the pan-Africanism of nineteenth-century Creole intellectuals in Sierra Leone and Liberia, negritude creates a culture, though not a nation, in the *absence* of a community otherwise sustainable in traditional terms through religion, language, custom, or land. Moreover, Wole Soyinka comments on the political ambiguities that affect African Americans, Francophone Africans, and Anglophone Africans equally, while marking the last of these colonial subjects as estranged from the first two, but *not* from their native cultures:

> [A] sociological reality . . . accounts for the deep empathy . . . that existed between the Francophone emigrés and the American [writers of the Harlem Renaissance], one that left the British subjects as outsiders. Both, in contrast to the British-ruled colonials, were citizens, albeit alienated, second-class citizens—of European nations. True, in the case of the African continent, there was a further demarcation: the statutory French citizenry, usually those born in the colonies' capital cities and adjoining provinces and—the rest. . . . This was a totally different state of social identity from the colonial subjects of the British both in Africa and the West Indies. The former—whether American or Francophone—were trapped in their socio-political bind; the latter, though subjugated, had no crisis of alienated citizenship to contend with. . . .
> (*The Burden of Memory*, 127–128)

Soyinka's rueful comments, while accounting for the disparity in cultural reactions between Anglophone and Francophone Africans, bespeak an additional paradox. Because Anglophone Africans—with the troublesome exception of Sierra Leone and Liberian Creoles—have ostensibly escaped alienation from their native cultures, they are therefore estranged from the rest of the modern Black world.

This discussion of negritude can thus provisionally conclude with the observation that however dissimilar negritude and *haskole* may appear on the surface—given that the former lavishes extravagant praise seemingly on every aspect of African society, whereas the latter castigates traditional Jewish culture with equal immoderation—a focused comparison of these ideologies' cultural productions, particularly in the "second-generation" examples of maskilic Yiddish and "negritude" novels compared here, reveals that both arise from a common anxiety provoked by contact with Western, imperial modernity. As such, this comparison, while contributing to a developmental model of Yiddish and African literary history, suggests a more general conceptualization of the development, at once psychological, ideological, and aesthetic, of peripheral literature in its first intimate exposure with the metropolis. With these factors in mind, it becomes possible both to differentiate these literary histories from more conventional, hegemonic models of nationalism and to understand how African and Jewish writers, who are at one and the same time "early" and "late" moderns, *imagine*, in Anderson's now ubiquitous phrase, an alternative community to the nation-state.

Four Education and Initiation in the Narratives
of *Haskole* and Negritude

In the context of a modernizing ideology, literature in Western forms becomes for African and Jewish intellectuals—as well as for intellectuals in many other cultures, to be sure—a means to create a separate cultural space between systems of power organized around the polarities of tradition and modernity. Through the mediation of literary form, the peripheral intellectual creates an autonomous cultural space ideally independent from both the confines of the tradition and the coercive or repressive aspects of the imperial order. Nonetheless, Yisroel Aksenfeld's truncated career illustrates that the author's autonomy is ultimately dependent on social institutions, such as publishing houses, school systems, and political organizations, that are typically controlled by the power structures from which the writer seeks to liberate himself or herself. These institutional limitations notwithstanding, the mimetic quality of literary narrative, particularly when constructed either along satirical or realist lines, provides a means of understanding the complex interaction between tradition and modernity, and among these power formations and the individual. To demonstrate this process, the subsequent comparison will focus primarily on two narratives: *Dos Vintshfingerl* ("The Magic Ring," or "The Wishing Ring"),[1] the second Yiddish narrative by the classic Jewish author Sh. Y. Abramovitsh (Mendele Moykher-Sforim), and *L'aventure ambiguë*, the first novel by Cheikh Hamidou Kane.

By way of introduction, Sholem Yankev Abramovitsh created the alter ego Mendele Moykher-Sforim (Mendele the Book Peddler) as a pseudonymous publisher, editor, narrator, and often interacting character in Abramovitsh's Yiddish writings. In creating Mendele, Abramovitsh not only found a mask behind which to hide when violating the commitment to Hebrew promulgated by *haskole*, but also established an intermediary who could bridge the gap between modernity and tradition, between *haskole* and the folk, between the author and his material. Though Abramovitsh was only about thirty when he began writing in Yiddish, the Mendele figure, by contrast, is a traditional, Yiddish-speaking Jew of the Ukrainian shtetl in his late forties or early fifties. For the next fifty years of Abramovitsh's literary career, Mendele does not age or change—though the circumstances around him do, at least somewhat. Quickly the Mendele character came not only to occupy a constant presence in Abramovitsh's writing—commenting on nearly every event and perspective in these narratives with shrewd satire—but also to subsume the author's own identity, so that today it is the name "Mendele" that is synonymous with the foundation of classic Yiddish fiction, and not Abramovitsh.

Mendele as an alter ego for the maskil Abramovitsh becomes not only a bridge between the modern intellectual and his traditional "folk" but also, as a modern sensibility disguised in traditional trappings, a means for Abramovitsh to develop a voice in his native language.[2] Individuality as such is fundamentally a modern value, but it should be stressed that for Abramovitsh, Yiddish discourse, supposedly incompatible with the maskilic conception of modernity, provided a personal literary language by returning the author, in a critically ironic manner, to the tradition. One can therefore perceive a general rule in nineteenth-century Yiddish fiction: just as the radicalism of an author's agenda is usually complemented by the dependence on folk sayings and proverbs, what Wiener terms *shprakhfolklor*—only the more moderate maskilim attempt to "reform" Yiddish by mimicking German—so too is the author's persona most likely to become more seemingly traditional in direct proportion to the actual subversiveness of his agenda. "Moderate" maskilim such as Dik, the authors most associated with *daytshmerism*, advertise themselves as being far more modern than they actually are, whereas the more genuinely radical maskilim present themselves as deliberately rustic character types.

Dos Vintshfingerl is Abramovitsh's second Yiddish narrative; the first, *Dos Kleyne mentshele* ("The little man," or "The parasite")—where the Mendele figure made his debut—was serialized in 1864, in *Kol mevaser*, the first Yiddish-language weekly newspaper to appear in Eastern Europe. At the time these works appeared, Abramovitsh was known as a journalist and essayist in Hebrew primarily interested in literature and the natural sciences. Although maskilic narratives in Yiddish were written at least as early as 1819, it was only in the 1860s, thanks largely to the appearance of the newspaper *Kol mevaser*, that works in this form began to receive publication and wide circulation.[3] Despite the fact that Mendele belongs therefore to the second generation of maskilim in Eastern Europe, his works were among the first to receive wide circulation and to exert an impact on an audience.

Dos Vintshfingerl tells the story of a traditional Jewish boy, Hershele, who spends his time pining for a magical device that will grant all his wishes. The boy comes from Kabtsansk, literally "the pauper's town," and he achieves his wish when he arrives in the great city of Glupsk ("the fool's town," a large shtetl inspired by the Ukrainian economic center Berditchev, where Abramovitsh resided in the 1850s and 60s).[4] There he falls under the influence of a "Litvak," a Jewish rationalist from Lithuania. The Litvak teaches Hershele German, arithmetic, geography, and other subjects excluded from the yeshiva curriculum. Eventually, the Litvak takes Hershele with him on business to Leipzig, where—wonder of wonders!—Hershele enters the university, and discovers a genuine *vintshfingerl*, wisdom. "With wisdom," Hershele states, "a man can achieve everything that he desires. Wisdom is the natural magic ring, and through wisdom he can feel strong enough to satisfy all his needs through natural means" (*Dos Vintshfingerl*, 39). Hershele's journey to the home of a Litvak, an outsider in Ukrainian "Glupsk," parallels and inverts the biography of his creator: Abramovitsh himself was born in the Lithuanian sector of the Jewish Pale of Settlement, and after studying in characteristically antimodern, non-Hasidic (misnagdic) Lithuanian yeshivas, he discovered enlightenment by traveling south, abandoning the Lithuanian sphere of influence, and joining the bustle of what was for a time a major commercial hub in the Ukraine. If the mirror is the structuring metaphor of this comparison, one such mirror appears in the relationship between this author and his own protagonist.[5]

Dos Vintshfingerl in its first edition mixes a variety of genres—*Bildungsroman*, social satire, parodic fairy tale, moralistic sermon—in what is essentially a compressed pseudo-autobiographical narrative. As Marcus Mosley writes, the pseudo-autobiographical genre occupies a particularly significant role in the development of the eighteenth-century novel, one that predates, in fact, the development of autobiography as a modern genre: "Rousseau was the first to incorporate techniques of verisimilitude and psychological penetration deriving from the eighteenth-century novel within the non-fictional, extra-referential context of autobiography. In particular, he was indebted to . . . a 'new biographical model' of eighteenth-century providence—the novel that purports to be an authentic first-person account of the life of the protagonist."[6] By analogy, the "pseudo-auto" genre is all the more significant to the development of nineteenth-century Yiddish (and Hebrew) literature, in which almost no contemporary narrative conventions had existed, other than the Hasidic praise-story—itself a quasi-biographical genre. Just as maskilic philosophers had gravitated to eighteenth-century Enlightenment values to articulate their idiosyncratic modernity, Abramovitsh also chooses an essentially eighteenth-century genre to initiate a revolution in modern Yiddish prose.

Moreover, this pseudo-autobiography, of a maskil who achieves a utopian modernity in Leipzig, appears to owe its inspiration to the bona fide autobiography of a hero to Eastern European maskilim, the Polish-born Jewish philosopher Salomon Maimon (c. 1753–1800).[7] As Abramovitsh's contemporary Peretz Smolenskin (1842–1885) writes in the Hebrew "pseudo-auto" novel, *Hato'eh bedarkhey hakhayim* ("Mistakes on the Paths of Life," 1868–1870), "The thought just occurred to me several days ago upon reading the life-story of one of the renowned philosophers of that country [Solomon Maimon]. He also came from a poor background and suffered great privations. And, in his youth, he too suffered the persecution and disgrace of the *Yeshivah*. But after he left the Pale of Settlement and studied at a German university he became a great man and was widely acclaimed. I determined to follow his path, come what may" (quoted in *Being for Myself Alone*, 63). Though Abramovitsh, crucially, does not follow in Maimon's footsteps, which for Maimon in any event led to despair and dissoluteness, in *Dos Vintshfingerl* he creates a protagonist who does, thus allowing his readers to envision the modernity of the West without ever leaving the shtetl.

In structural terms, Hershele's narrative divides almost evenly in two: from page 12 until page 24 in the 1865 edition, Abramovitsh presents a typical shtetl satire, replete with fantastic parody, crowd scenes, and numerous asides, told from the point of view of a naive young child; from page 25 until page 40, the tone shifts abruptly to a polemic from the perspective of a maturing, "enlightened" skeptic.[8] Instead of crowd scenes, Abramovitsh focuses in the latter half of the narrative on the relationship of Hershele and the Litvak. Instead of parodic fantasy he restricts himself to philosophical speculation and sober polemic. Conceptually, the narrative shifts from the free associations of a comic monologue to the development of a rational argument. Thus, Abramovitsh's concern with the balance between two modes of thought that Hershele, as a personification of the *haskole*, is meant to engage reflects the divided character of the Jewish Enlightenment. Between the parodic comedy of shtetl life, and the valorization of the individual who resists the superstitions that the author so enjoys ridiculing, one observes Abramovitsh's dilemma in creating fiction that is both entertaining and meaningful. This dilemma involves not only the problem of modernity's relationship with tradition—a relationship schematized as the individual maskil's relationship with his community—but more specifically the uses of Yiddish as a literary language. The young Abramovitsh, like Aksenfeld and Dik, wants to use Yiddish, despite the negative qualities attributed to the language, to critique traditional society and suggest alternatives, but the result is a narrative that literally splits in half.

Cheikh Hamidou Kane, by analogy, was born in Senegal, and after receiving a rigorous Islamic education he studied philosophy and law (with equal rigor) at the University of Paris. He then returned to Senegal, where he made his career primarily in bureaucratic and diplomatic services. *L'aventure ambiguë* received the 1962 *Grand prix littéraire de l'afrique noir* after it was published in France. The novel relates the story of Samba Diallo, a child of the traditional African elite, and opens with an image of him nobly enduring the obligatory poverty and harsh—indeed, sadistic—instruction at the Koranic academy. As a young boy, Samba Diallo is required to learn the sacred text of the Koran by rote memorization: that is, as an *oral* narrative. Immediately preceding his initiation into manhood and more intellectually engaged study of the

Koran, the Islamic equivalent of the bar mitzvah referred to in the novel as the "Night of the Koran" (F 83; E 71), his aunt, *la Grande Royale*, withdraws him from the academy and places him in a colonial school. From there, he is launched on the ambiguous adventure of the book's title, traveling to France, where he falls in with the communist Lucienne and an old man from the Caribbean. Upon returning to Africa, he finds the master who taught him the Koran has died, and the only person who preserves his memory is "the fool" (*le fou*), a mentally disturbed man who, like Samba Diallo, has returned from Europe. When the fool takes Samba Diallo to the master's grave, the protagonist finds himself unable to pray. In reaction to his apparent apostasy, the fool murders him, and the novel concludes with Samba Diallo's dying thoughts.[9]

As Abiola Irele characterizes the novel, "[*L'aventure ambiguë*] is a work that summarizes and brings into brilliant focus the ideas, sentiments, and attitudes that lie at the center of inspiration of all French African writing. It can thus be considered to represent the most characteristic statement . . . of the French African intellectual in the colonial situation" (*The African Experience*, 152). Emmanuel Obiechina similarly refers to the novel as "a storehouse of negritude in prose."[10] Nonetheless, however vigorously these Anglophone critics have championed Kane's novel as an exposition of negritude values, one finds no similar description in the Francophone criticism of the novel, which typically treats it as a *repudiation* of negritude. Indeed, Kane himself foregrounds his ambivalence to the term, writing, "I confess that I do not like the word [*négritude*—translated in the English edition literally as "negroness"!], and I don't always understand what it would be meant to cover" (F 155; E 142). One can, however, split the difference between Anglophone and Francophone readings of the novel by recognizing in its ambivalence—arguably analogous to the ambivalence of maskilic satire in Yiddish—a distillation of negritude ideology and aesthetics *in negative form*. This negativity, in turn, signifies a void both in ideological as well as aesthetic terms for the peripheral intellectual to represent himself or herself; this negative space emerges, however, as a zone of autonomy and ultimate possibility.

Like Abramovitsh in the *haskole*, Kane was a young writer from the second generation of negritude, more properly the *post-negritude* generation, but among the first generation of Francophone African novelists.[11] With this historical parallel in mind, it is possible to see these two narratives as mirrors of one another, and to demonstrate how they represent a common historical and social crisis affecting each of these cultures. The generic conflicts in *L'aventure ambiguë*, like those in *Dos Vintshfingerl*, serve to represent psychological and ideological dilemmas. For example, when Samba Diallo first enters the colonial school, the perspective shifts from him to the children of the white colonial administrator: "The story of Samba Diallo is a serious story. If it had been a gay recital, we should have told you of the bewilderment of the two white children, on the first morning of their sojourn among little Negroes, in finding themselves in the presence of so many black faces. . . . But nothing more will be said of all that, because these memories . . . would bring gayety to this recital of which the profound truth is wholly sad" (F 62; E 50–51). In schematic terms, Kane suggests here that the difference between white and Black, between outside and inside, between modernity and tradition is the difference between comedy and tragedy; the triumph of modernity is a *commedia*, in Dante's sense of a tale with a happy ending, for those with access to power, a tragedy for its colonized victims. The shift in perspective between Black and white, tragedy and comedy, suggests that Kane is capable as an *évolué* of seeing both viewpoints,[12] but as a consequence he is suspended between these polarities.

The tendency to portray situations from alternating, self-canceling perspectives establishes a vacillating structure to the conflicting ideologies that inform this novel.[13] Indeed, Kane provides a metaphor for understanding this structure of ambiguity when he writes, "I walk. One foot before, one foot behind, one foot before, one foot behind: one-two, one-two. No! I must not think: one-two, one-two. I must think of something else. One-two, one-two" (F 140–141; E 128). Both the footsteps themselves and Samba Diallo's tortured self-consciousness in observing them bespeak an irresolvable tension between space and time, past and future, tradition and modernity. At the same time, Samba Diallo's resistance to the tyranny of binary thinking is illustrative of his efforts to break free not only of the various dialectics in which he is enmeshed but also of the lockstep conformity demanded both by colonial modernity of the *évolué* and by Islamic tradition of its adherents. That the novel as a whole incorporates this structural ambiguity can be seen in its formal designation as a *récit*, a term Kane took from André Malraux (*The African Experience*, 167), and which can suggest either a written, journalistic account or an oral narration, a "recitation."

The representation of the conflict between Black and white as an opposition between orality and literacy—therefore not only between tragedy and comedy, but between the epic and the novel—underscores an additional contest between two "logi": the Word of Western modernity against the Word of African Islam. In this regard, it is worth recalling that the Koranic study depicted in this novel is an almost completely oral undertaking. As Nouréini Tidjani-Serpos states, the rote memorization of the Koran "was perhaps adapted . . . to the oral character of African text production; however, this sort of memorization, without any accompanying explanation, corresponded perfectly with another trait of African culture: science is never more appreciated than when it is secret and when it demands years of wandering and suffering before it can be properly acquired" (*De l'école coranique à l'école étrangère*, 189). These observations therefore connect the conflict between Africa and the West not only to orality and literacy but also to further distinctions between secrecy and openness, the community and society, inside and outside, and, at its cosmic extreme, death (the ultimate closed community!) and life. As Tidjani-Serpos states explicitly, "The foreign school, as *life*, is, so to speak, the antithesis of the Koranic school, which is apprenticed to *death*" (*De l'école coranique à l'école étrangère*, 192, emphasis in original).

At the heart of these ambiguous structures, in both narratives, is an analogous crisis in religious faith and cultural identification. Before meeting the Litvak, Hershele, like Samba Diallo, tortures himself in pursuit of the magic ring and magical knowledge promised him by the mystical tradition: "We [Hershele and his friend Moyshe in the Glupsker yeshiva] secretly exhausted ourselves over the art of *roye v'eynoy nire* [seeing without being seen].[14] Moyshe even underwent this suffering without really wanting to. But I submitted myself fully to the regimen: we fasted voluntary fasts, recited psalms, immersed ourselves in cold *mikves* [ritual baths]—everything that might be required of us. But nothing helped" (*Dos Vintshfingerl*, 28). The difference between Kane's depiction of Samba Diallo's apparent apostasy and Abramovitsh's portrayal of Hershele's embrace of enlightenment is an outcome of the object of their respective religious quests; Samba Diallo seeks a spiritual enlightenment that becomes illusive after the encounter with colonialism and modernity, whereas Hershele seeks a providential form of magic to provide him with his intense physical needs through a violation of the laws of nature. But the real distinction between these two quests is more dependent on the generic conventions embraced by Kane and Abramovitsh, respectively, than on the inherent worthiness of the quests' objectives.

For Samba Diallo, too, is motivated by a fantastic goal, which he admits to himself at the grave of the old woman Rella: "For a long time, near his dead friend, the child reflected on the eternal mystery of death, and, on his own count, rebuilt Paradise in a thousand ways. When sleep came to him he had grown entirely serene again, for he had found the answer: Paradise was built with the Words that he used to recite, the same glowing light, the same deep and mysterious shadows, the same enchantment, the same power" (F 53; E 42–43). At the heart of his quest is Paradise, the transcendence of earthly strife and doubts, metonymically connected at the grave with death and a retreat to the past. As Kane describes Samba Diallo's quest, it is a means of escape from the difficulties and anxieties that both impending adulthood and the modernity of the colonial school have rendered inevitable. The quest itself is therefore doomed to failure by time, in both a chronological and historical sense. The Paradise that Samba Diallo pursues is the stasis, alternately, of childhood or of death; although adulthood demands the abandonment of this fantasy, the apostasy that adulthood, travel, and modernity engender in him creates the pretext for his premature death—at the hands of the fool, the only adult in the novel who refuses to abandon this dream of paradise.

Kane makes explicit that his novel elegizes the lost autonomy not just of childhood but of his native culture generally,[15] as Samba Diallo states, "I am not a distinct country of the Diallobé facing a distant Occident, and appreciating with a cool head what I must take from it and what I must leave with it by way of counterbalance. I have become the two. There is not a clear mind deciding between the two factors of a choice. There is a strange nature, in distress over not being two" (F 164; E 150–151). In this context, fusion becomes a source of anxiety over a death of sorts for the two cultures being fused. The ambiguity of being two means, of course, no longer being one—that is, identical with nature, God, and the other abstractions that negritude had valorized as essential to African culture. Samba Diallo, having become one with the West, is now, in Woody Allen's famous formulation, "two with nature," and as such he contrasts with his father, and more broadly with the first generation of *évolués* who had preceded Kane, who had approached the Occident from a distance and thus maintained their equilibrium in precisely the manner no longer available to Samba Diallo's or Kane's generation. By the standards of the previous generation, Samba Diallo has grown too close to the West and, like Icarus, is consumed, like a sacrifice to the sun, by the blinding rays of Enlightenment.[16]

Moreover, the fact that Samba Diallo has lost the ability to identify with his native culture is a consequence of the triangular competition of power structures—traditional African, Islamic, and Western—which define the protagonist's cultural predicament, and determine its characteristic ambiguity. Whereas in a typical negritude formulation, the West contrasts with animist Africa to the exclusion of Islam, in most respects *L'aventure ambiguë* depicts a conflict between Islam and the West, to the exclusion of the animist tradition long suppressed by Islam.[17] On an intertextual, or even metatextual, level, therefore, there is no African epic behind or beneath *L'aventure ambiguë* the way the *Sunjata* epic,[18] the most celebrated and widely influential traditional narrative in West Africa, informs and animates the symbolism of *L'enfant noir*. *L'aventure ambiguë* relegates the animist or syncretic tradition commemorated in epics such as *Sunjata* to the unspoken cartography of Samba Diallo's aunt *la Grande Royale*'s face: "[I]t was like a living page from the history of the Diallobé country. Everything that the country treasured of epic tradition could be read there. . . . Islam restrained the formidable turbulence of those features, in the same way that the little veil hemmed them in" (F 31; E 20–21).[19] For Kane, the Koran takes the place that *Sun-*

jata holds for *L'enfant noir*, the ancient and immutable mythic subtext for the ambiguous adventure of modern, written, colonized culture.

Nonetheless, the pre-Islamic African tradition does reassert itself, surreptitiously, in apparent alliance with the West, when *la Grande Royale* persuades the people to send their prize pupil Samba Diallo to the colonial school. Indeed, *la Grande Royale* acknowledges that her advocacy violates the public submissiveness demanded of women by traditional Islam, even as her arguments ultimately serve to subvert the power of Islam among the Diallobé: "I have done something which is not pleasing to us and which is not in accordance with our customs," she says (F 56; E 45). On the surface, *la Grande Royale*'s speech is an act of "defensive modernization"—to save the tradition, one has to destroy the tradition; to save the next generation, one must force them to forget their heritage. And yet, as a woman, *la Grande Royale* violates the tradition in a specifically gendered way. If her face, as Miller writes, is a "map" of the pre-Islamic Africa repressed by the Fundamentalist Diallobé, this speech is her revenge.

Indeed, given the subaltern status of the Diallobé as a whole, one can understand the struggle between *la Grande Royale* and the Islamic elites among the Diallobé as a competitive effort to reconfigure and preserve power in the face of colonialism's overwhelming force, perhaps akin to the competition among maskilim and Hasidim for influence with Russian authorities and hegemony over their people in the Pale of Settlement. For the Koranic Teacher and his allies, preserving power means resisting colonialism's efforts to remake the Diallobé in its image; for *la Grande Royale*, preserving power means making a strategic alliance with colonialism, subordinating the native aristocracy to the more powerful hegemony of the French. Seen from this perspective, *la Grande Royale*, like the maskilim who advocated the abandonment of certain Jewish customs in favor of an acculturation to modernity, represents political accommodation of imperialism. By contrast, the Koranic Teacher, like the Hasidim who accentuated their dissent from modernity, champions the minority culture, thus transforming the tradition from a hegemonic force to an implicitly anticolonial one.

Moreover, *la Grande Royale* is, symbolically, a reminder of a previous act of repression among the Diallobé, and it is significant that her campaign in favor of the colonial school sets her directly at odds with an Islamic tradition that had excluded her, as an animist and a woman, to begin with. In this context, what Philip Curtin describes as the difference between "neo-traditionalists" and "defensive modernizers"[20] is particularly useful; conversely, the conflict between these "neo-traditionalists" and "defensive modernizers"—the Koranic Teacher and *la Grande Royale*, respectively—serves to critique Curtin's terminology, and illustrates that these various ideological positions, each motivated by an overarching competition between tradition and modernity, can nonetheless be used to perpetuate conflicts from *within* the tradition. After all, *la Grande Royale* coordinates a "conspiracy" between herself and the colonial school against the Islamic tradition, a "conspiracy" that aligns these two forces against the Koranic school in a struggle, cosmologically, between life and death. As *la Grande Royale* tells Samba Diallo, "The teacher is trying to kill the life in you. But I am going to put an end to all that" (F 32; E 22). Seen from this cosmological perspective, only the Koranic school, as presented here, properly appreciates the inevitability, and therefore the significance, of death as the counterpart to a meaningful life, and perhaps this understanding is the only explanation for the attraction this austere regimen holds for Samba Diallo, and the only way to understand the novel's transfigured conclusion as a victory, both for the Koranic Teacher and Samba Diallo.

Whereas Kane offers an implicit, if sympathetic, critique of Samba Diallo's experiences by exposing and examining his internal anxieties about adulthood and the world at large, Abramovitsh uses the Mendele persona to deflate both the fantastic wishes of the child Hershele and the rationalistic triumphalism of the adult maskil. Thus, to Hershele's straightforward and rather heavy-handed didactic lesson, Mendele adds, if only in the 1865 version, a preface explaining how he ostensibly acquired the narrative: on a late-summer Monday morning after the fast of Tisha B'Av, Mendele the Book Peddler is on the road from Glupsk, drowsing in the middle of his morning prayers while riding in his book cart (so much for him as a figure of old-fashioned piety!), when suddenly he collides with another horse-drawn cart. At first fighting with the driver of the cart, he soon recognizes the other man as Reb Senderl, another book peddler who had collided with Mendele because he, too, had dozed off during his morning prayers.[21] Just as Hershele is a mirror image of Abramovitsh, Senderl is Mendele's double.

The two book peddlers quickly begin to discuss business, and Senderl gives Mendele the manuscript to *Dos Vintshfingerl*, supposedly written in German, in exchange for several of Mendele's maskilic chapbooks. Mendele is pleased with the bargain, because, as he makes clear, *haskole* publications don't sell [!]: "My heart began to dance with joy when I heard that word *vintshfingerl*. That's the genuine article. . . . Just like the *Bove mayse*, or *A Thousand and One Nights*" (*Dos Vintshfingerl*, 5). Mendele's delight at finding what he presumes will be a fairy tale in the tradition of *A Thousand and One Nights* foreshadows Hershele's own quest for a *vintshfingerl*; just as Hershele as an "unenlightened" young boy expects a magic ring to solve all his material worries, so Mendele expects a story about a magic ring to make up for the money lost on maskilic pamphlets. In differing respects, both Mendele and Hershele are conditioned by the fantastic literature they have read, and this folkloric tradition—which Abramovitsh clearly shares with his otherwise unacknowledged predecessor Reb Nakhman—is intended to shape the reader's expectations as well. Since everyone likes a good fairy tale, with a name like *Dos Vintshfingerl*, how can he miss? And so, Mendele arranges to have the story translated by the one maskil he knows, hence the reader's ability to appreciate Hershele's story in a native Yiddish.

The strategy of presenting *Dos Vintshfingerl* as a translation from German extends Abramovitsh's satire in a number of directions. It provides, in a manner typical of eighteenth-century satirical narratives, *accréditement* for the narrative as an "authentic" document, while enabling Mendele to exert his own stylistic presence to "improve" on the original; it gives cover for Mendele, a "traditional" Jew, in publishing a maskilic work that religious authorities would find impious; it betrays Mendele as a "naïve" figure insufficiently schooled in modern ways, and unlike his creator ignorant of German entirely, to distinguish between maskilic propaganda and the wonder stories which this propaganda campaigns against; it holds the *haskole* itself up for ridicule for its elitism in communicating its agenda in a language foreign to most Eastern European Jews. At the same time, it underscores an existential problem confronting both Jewish and African writers in this discussion: In what language can the "minor" writer communicate with, and through, modernity?

It is therefore worth considering momentarily the role of translation as a literary artifice, a strategy, in *haskole* and negritude narrative. In *L'aventure ambiguë*, for example, the name of Samba Diallo's native language is never mentioned, though it is clear that most conversations in the first part of the novel take place in this language, not in French.[22] Thus, in the first chapter, the (African) teacher of the colonial school tells Samba Diallo's Koran instructor that his school "only teaches men to join wood to wood—to make wooden buildings." Kane explains: "Pronounced in the language of the region, the word 'school' means 'wood.' The three men smiled with an air of understanding and slight disapproval of this classic play on words in connection with the foreign school" (F 19; E 9). Kane does not pretend that these characters would be speaking French, but he also does not go so far as to provide the actual wordplay from the unnamed African language. The best the reader can hope for is to have the colonial teacher's wordplay explained, *invoked*. This strategy prompts a question of how much access Kane grants the reader to the conversations and situations he describes, and therefore positions the reader as an interloper—possibly akin to the professional ethnographer who provided the bulk of France's knowledge about Africa prior to the advent of the postcolonial novel—in the world of the novel.

Kane's linguistic strategies as a Francophone, university-educated intellectual can be fairly contrasted with a small but significant class of Russian-trained Jewish intellectuals such as Osip Rabinovich (1817–1869) and Lev Levanda (1835–1888) emerging in the latter half of the nineteenth century.[23] The essential distinction between these Russian-language figures and Kane demonstrates the cultural capital of language: although the penetration of French into the everyday life of French colonial Africa was even more superficial than Russian among Jews in the Pale of Settlement, Francophone narratives such as *L'aventure ambiguë* constitute the canon of African writing in the region; there is no counterpart to this novel available in Fula, Wolof, or Bambara (to list just three of the many native languages active in French-colonized West Africa). The literature produced by Russian-language Jewish intellectuals in the Czarist era, paradoxically, is a far more ephemeral body of work, compared either with Russian-Jewish writing after World War I or contemporaneous writing in Yiddish or Hebrew; even Simon Dubnow's pioneering historical research sold incomparably better in Yiddish translation than in either the Russian or Hebrew originals. Although Yiddish maintained a largely oral function and subordinate status in the hierarchy of languages in nineteenth-century Ashkenazic culture, it was a language that essentially any literate Jew in the region could and did read.

By contrast, both the resources and the ability to read in native African languages during the colonial era, particularly in French colonies, were significantly smaller. Moreover, by the 1860s Yiddish publishing houses and distribution networks existed for intellectuals such as Abramovitsh to communicate with an audience in a way that never existed to the same degree either for Russian-Jewish or Hebrew-language publications at the same period or in the African context for native languages ever.[24] Moreover, at issue for this project as a whole is the identification of modernism not with a specific language, whether native or imperial, but with a tension *between* languages; the multilingual character of life on the periphery, typically confined in belletristic discourse to a monolingual mode of expression, is a fundamental characteristic of modernist literature, and in this tension a series of conflicts, between tradition and modernity, official discourse and subversive vernaculars, finds expression. The *disharmony* among languages connects postcolonial African literatures, in any language, to the analogously fractious contest among imperial, Rabbinic, and demotic discourses out of which modern Yiddish literature develops. The Russian-language literature of nineteenth-century Jews suggests that the Jewish experience with modernity can be fully articulated in the imperial language in a way that neither Jewish-language literatures nor postcolonial African literature in English or French could or would desire.

In this regard perhaps the most significant African use of translation as a literary strategy—certainly the one that most closely parallels Abramovitsh's strategy in *Dos Vintshfingerl*—occurs in Ferdinand Oyono's novel *Une Vie de boy*.[25] It is worth considering aspects of this novel in the context of Mendele's prologue to *Dos Vintshfingerl*, to understand both translation as a device and the positioning of the reader that this device entails. Oyono's novel, the fictional journals of an African servant to a colonial officer in Cameroon, begins in Spanish Guinea when the narrator of the prologue finds the protagonist, Toundi, dying of gunshot wounds after his escape from a Cameroon prison. Toundi's diary appears in a packet of his personal effects, along with a toothbrush, a stub of pencil, and "a large native comb made of ebony" (F 14; E 5)—a black object placed, strategically, among Western tools.[26] "That was how I came to read Toundi's diary. It was written in Ewondo. . . . In the translation which I have made . . . I have tried to keep the richness of the original language without letting it get in the way of the story itself" (F 14; E 5). The diary serves as a kind of written deathbed confession, a naturalistic "dialogue with the dead," and as such reinforces the ambiguous nature of Toundi's death, between public and private, murder and suicide.

Of equal significance are the narrator's somewhat cryptic remarks about his "translation" of Toundi's writing, a translation from inside to outside, from native to colonial language—exactly the opposite direction of Mendele's "translation" of *Dos Vintshfingerl*. For Abramovitsh, the prestige of modernity, unlike Oyono's Francophone modernity, cannot move beyond a symbolic, superficial association with German, because the audience he would enlighten through his writing is fully literate only in Yiddish whereas for Oyono the only available language is French. The study of "minor" literatures thus offers a particularly complex history of narrative development, and therefore an analogously complicated social history of modernity, precisely because of the inherently *evolving* nature of language in peripheral contexts, both with respect to the dominant language that surrounds the "minor" and with respect to the "minor" language's relationship to its own cultural past. For these reasons, the Francophone (or Anglophone) novel and the Yiddish narrative present themselves as mirror-images of the same heteroglossic *process*: every word of the postcolonial novel is double-voiced because of the tension—bemoaned by ideologists of linguistic purity[27]—inherent in a colonial language expressing the consciousness of African characters and situations that continue to develop *in the na-*

tive African language. By contrast, though the maskilic authors resort, reluctantly, to their authentically native language, they do so in service of an ideology derived explicitly from foreign (French, German, later Russian) sources, hence the *inverse* relationship of *Une Vie de boy* to *Dos Vintshfingerl.*[28]

Abramovitsh further ironizes *haskole*'s relationship with the language of modernity by having Mendele discuss *Dos Vintshfingerl*'s literary antecedents with Senderl—thus acknowledging these sources and parodying them at the same time. By way of Senderl's inquiry about his horse, Mendele states, "They say that there's a gentile writer, someone called Lessing or Essing—what difference does it make, let's call him Essing—who wrote some kind of ode to a donkey. A German[29] I picked up last year talked my ear off the entire way about some Sankho Pankho and his donkey, characters from a book named *Don S'kot . . . Kot . . . Kikhot. . . .* Whereas amongst us Jews there are even donkeys that can talk—Balaam's ass, for example. . . . Yes, amongst us Jews there are quite a few famous asses" (*Dos Vintshfingerl,* 4). The figure of the donkey both betrays Abramovitsh's shrewdness in placing his writing within the tradition of rationalist, Enlightenment satire and serves, again in time-honored satirical fashion, to equate Jews, even enlightened ones such as Hershele and the author himself, metonymically with donkeys.

The association of Jews with donkeys is in fact premised on another intertextual joke: Senderl's inquiry refers to a story about Mendele's horse that appears in Abramovitsh's first Yiddish narrative, *Dos Kleyne mentshele.* The connection between these two narratives, by means of Mendele's horse, thus creates an assemblage that in turn connects Abramovitsh to the Western literary tradition, not only through satire as a genre but also through free associations that link Mendele and Senderl with the Bible, Cervantes, and Lessing. This intertextual assemblage nonetheless differs from the assemblage of Reb Nakhman's *sipurey mayses* in that Abramovitsh, like so many maskilic authors, is preoccupied with the *textuality* of his narratives. Unlike Reb Nakhman, whose scribes extend such lavish efforts to preserve the oral character of his narration, particularly in the Yiddish versions of his stories, nearly all the maskilic authors choose narrative models rooted in the act of writing itself—that is, rooted in forms of communication that can only exist in written form. Abramovitsh's first narrative, *Dos Kleyne mentshele*, is a last will and testament (and as such is, like *Une Vie de boy* and the last chapter of *L'aventure ambiguë*, an attenuated "dialogue with the dead"); Yosef Perl's *Megale tmirin* ("The Revealer of Secrets," 1819) is an epistolary satire; *Dos Vintshfingerl* is ostensibly an autobiography translated from German.

This distinction applies to postnegritude novels as well; unlike Tutuola, the oral dimension in these narratives, though significant, is relatively inconspicuous. In Kane's novel, for example, the distinction between Africa and the West is represented in the conflict between the Koran and European philosophy—that is, between traditional and modern *texts*. And although the Koran is studied orally, it neither replicates nor compensates for the absence of a storytelling tradition. Similarly, Oyono's *Une Vie de boy* is the "confessions" of a dead African servant. *Mission terminée*, an antinegritude satire by Mongo Beti (*né* Alexandre Biyidi, 1932–2001), takes as its genesis the protagonist's failure of the French *bachot* and resembles both structurally and rhetorically the novels of Denis Diderot or Voltaire. In each of these narratives, the emphasis on literacy serves notice that these authors are consciously modern. Moreover, by mimicking "natural" written genres, these writers communicate to an audience no longer imagined as an intimate, traditional *Gemeinschaft* that can be reached through oral storytelling, but as an abstract, modern *Gesellschaft*. The difference between the two can be understood as the distinction between communion and communication, and it points to what Benedict Anderson has emphasized as the relationship between the "imagined community" of print capitalism—a relationship invoked and parodied by Mendele's occupation as an old-fashioned book peddler—and the imagined community of the nation.

Nonetheless, the community that these authors imagine is fundamentally different from the community imagined in the nationalist literature of, to cite Anderson's favored example, the revolutionary nation-states of nineteenth-century Latin America. The community in the "minor" literature of negritude and *haskole* is understood as an extension of the author himself, rather than configuring the author as an instrument of the nation; the maskilim and the authors of negritude imagine a readership, not a nation in the current sense of the term. Indeed, though much of the critical terminology that has developed around the concept of "narrating the nation"[30] is applicable to negritude and *haskole* fiction, the term "nation" as such is not. These ideologies respond to the impulses of modern nationalism in a decidedly non–nationalist manner—hence Kane's novel depicts the fate of the Diallobé "tribe," a community imagined along neo-traditionalist lines at once smaller than, but transcendent of, the boundaries of Senegal. Y. Y. Linetski's best-selling satire *Dos Poylishe yingl* ("The Polish Lad") similarly describes the life history of a Jew who did not live within the boundaries of modern Poland, at a time (the 1860s) when Poland did not exist as a nation-state.

The ironic connection of these narratives to literary antecedents—originating, for both *haskole* and negritude, in the Enlightenment—contrasts with a more fraught relationship that these writers maintain with the folklore of their respective traditions. Thus, despite the ostensible rationalism of Hershele's narrative, he indulges in one fantastic aside that the modernity of his personal history does not challenge,[31] the tale of Reb Shmelke, the grandfather of the town's one successful man, Reb Yudl. Reb Shmelke's story flows from Hershele's description of Kabtsansk's poverty: the town is so poor that every holiday the entire population travels to Glupsk to hire themselves out as functionaries in the synagogues of the larger city. One Purim, Reb Shmelke is left alone in Kabtsansk, and therefore is unable to fulfill the commandments for the holiday that require the presence, in traditional Judaism, of ten Jewish men. There soon appear, however, nine unexpected guests with whom he is able to celebrate Purim; only after these guests depart does Reb Shmelke learn the secret of their identity:

> The old rebbe, may he rest in peace, said that the group of guests was none other than the cream of the crop: the three old ones were the patriarchs [Abraham, Isaac, and Jacob], the one in the pointed fur hat was Mordecai [the hero of Purim], the one in the royal robes was Elijah the Prophet, the one with the red-currant nose was the notorious drunkard Lot, and the three wearing breastplates and aprons were Mattathias the High Priest [a hero of the Hanukah story] with two of his sons.[32] . . . The old rebbe said that before this group paid Reb Shmelke a visit, they came to him for permission, because Shmelke

was his Hasid, and Kabtsansk belonged to him. That is, the town actually belonged to a local nobleman, but the rebbe took in the kopeks; the nobleman had the cows by the horns, but the rebbe milked them. (*Dos vintshfingerl*, 16)

The legendary origins of Reb Yudl's wealth work their way down to Hershele's *kheyder*, where one of his classmates speculates that Reb Shmelke had received a *vintshfingerl* from Elijah after the Purim visitation. This remark sets Hershele on his quest for his own magic ring, and leads him eventually to the Litvak.

Just as Mendele's comic aside on literature culminates with an equation of Jews with donkeys, here Hershele compares Jews with cattle to critique exploitation in the traditional shtetl. The Hasidic rebbe works in tandem with the (Polish) gentry to keep the Jews pacified, exploited, and impoverished. Although Abramovitsh allows himself an ostensibly un-maskilic indulgence in fantasy, even intimating a kind of immaculate conception from this visitation—it is only after this Purim that Reb Shmelke's wife is able to conceive, and she delivers the child exactly nine months later[33]—he links this folkloric wonder-tale to an implicit critique of Hasidism and the mystifying irrationalism it inspires.[34]

It is worth considering in this regard the relationship, simultaneously parallel and contrary, between *Dos Vintshfingerl* and Abramovitsh's previous narrative, *Dos Kleyne mentshele*,[35] to understand how maskilic conventions shape the author's attitude toward both narrative form and traditional Jewish life. *Dos Kleyne mentshele* and *Dos Vintshfingerl* are conscious inversions of one another; each presents an "autobiography" of a young Jew from the shtetl as a representation of the backwardness and smallness of traditional life—the common use of diminutives in their titles itself suggests the "minor" function that Abramovitsh, like previous maskilim, envisioned for Yiddish—and as a suggestion of the alternatives to this society posed by a modern social, pedagogical, and moral order. Unlike Samba Diallo, neither protagonist is an exceptional individual. Indeed, Itsik-Avreyml, the protagonist of *Dos Kleyne mentshele*, states at the end of his narrative, "Thus I must now remark that by nature I was not a bad person or villain. I was simply misled" (Y 108; E 214). By following a typical, if picaresque, shtetl trajectory, Itsik-Avreyml demonstrates that traditional Jewish life itself corrupts young people. One can similarly deduce that chance alone brought Hershele in contact with the Litvak who takes him to Leipzig, and initiates his intellectual and spiritual migration from the shtetl when he lures him away from the yeshiva in Glupsk. In both narratives, the strategic use of chance is an indication of modernity, counteracting the analogous role of fate and the fixed social character of traditional life and the folktales that enact traditional values.

Itsik-Avreyml's lifelong quest for a *kleyn mentshele*, like Hershele's quest for a *vintshfingerl*, pivots on the ambiguities of language and on the confusion of spiritual values in traditional Jewish culture. Just as in the end Hershele discovers that "wisdom is the true magic ring," Itsik-Avreyml is unable to differentiate between the idyllic meaning of the "little man" that his widowed mother defines for him as the soul (Y 54; E 194), and the colloquial Yiddish sense of the term *kleyn mentshele*, a "parasite," that Itsik-Avreyml becomes over the course of his life. As the protagonist himself explains, "I assume that to be a *kleyn ment-shele* means to drain strange blood and to con money" (Y 90; E 207). Abramovitsh makes the metaphor of the *kleyne mentshele* literal not only in the colloquial sense of a man who lives off the labor of others, but also in a psychological sense: Itsik-Avreyml is a "little person" in that he lives in a state of arrested development, limited in his spiritual aspirations and his sense of self by the stifling atmosphere and corrupt values of the shtetl. This becomes explicit in a pivotal, "prophetic" dream—in structural terms not unlike the visitation of Reb Shmelke in *Dos Vintsh-fingerl* that gives birth not only to Kabtsansk's one self-sufficient citizen but also the "magic ring" legend that propels Hershele's narrative—in which Itsik-Avreyml encounters a "real" *kleyn mentshele*, a kind of homunculus or automaton. Upon waking, he realizes "that you can't become a *kleyn mentshele*, unless you first give up feeling and thinking" (Y 82; E 204–205). Thus, in each of Abramovitsh's first Yiddish narratives, psychology is externalized by rendering literal the rhetoric of folklore.

One should note, moreover, that the image of parasitism surfaces in the writing of contemporaneous pan-African activists. Thus Emmanuel Obiechina quotes the nineteenth-century pan-Africanist Edward Blyden (1832–1912) as characterizing the situation of colonized Africans in terms quite similar to Abramovitsh's depiction of Itsik-Avreyml: "From the lessons he every day receives the Negro unconsciously imbibes the conviction that to be a great man he must be like the white man. He is not brought up—however he may desire it—to be companion, the equal of the white man, but his imitator, his ape, his parasite. . . . The only virtues under such circumstances he develops are, of course, the parasitic ones" (*Language and Theme*, 72). The common denominator in both contexts is the sudden intrusion of a new standard of value. For both African and Eastern European intellectuals, therefore, the limits of the modern world encroaching on tradition create similar feelings of inadequacy—the former, because there is too much mimicry of Western customs; the latter, apparently, because there is not enough!

Although engaged in the same conflict between tradition and modernity, the periphery and the metropolis, as both Abramovitsh and his own pan-Africanist predecessors, Kane nonetheless bypasses the sociological impact of these tensions by typically portraying his characters in monologue or dialogue situations; even *la Grande Royale* addresses the Diallobé in a formal speech, not a palaver. Abramovitsh, by contrast, delights in describing collisions, crowd scenes, the tumult of a large group: on Hershele's first visit to Glupsk, he sits on a wagon with his parents, their possessions, and "various people, nearly a quarter of the shtetl. There sat together girls, women . . . and all types of men—beautiful Jews, kosher Jews, silken Jews, golden Jews with gold flowing in their veins, and just plain ole' Jewish Jews, and I sat among them all. And all that sat together sweat—even the silken Jews sweat like beavers" (*Dos Vintshfingerl*, 22). The various types of Jews in this inventory multiply in proportion to the number of people crowding onto the wagon, and their pretensions to elegance are undercut by the very intimacy both with their own bodies and the bodies crowding in on them.

Kane and Abramovitsh thus schematize the relationship between their protagonists and the community in contrary fashion: Samba Diallo is typically presented in isolation, either in dialogue with one person or communing with the dead in his memories. This tendency is inversely underscored by the autobiographical fact that Kane's own name in the Fula language is "Samba," a name traditionally given to second sons.[36] If Samba Diallo is, like the author, a second son, why is there no reference in the novel to his siblings? Indeed, perhaps the greatest distinction between *L'aventure ambiguë* and the great neorealist classics of African literature—*Things Fall Apart* and *L'enfant noir*—is the virtual absence of anthropological detail in its description of traditional (or at least "traditional") African life. In lieu of ritual ceremonies, family dynamics, culinary customs, or life cycle events, the study of the Koran, a tradition by no means associated exclusively with Africa, is the only representation of the tradition juxtaposed against the modern world. This is truly a curious synecdoche, one that reduces the difference between Africa and the West to exclusively ideological and religious terms.

One can better understand the differences between Abramovitsh and Kane with respect to the tradition by considering their contrary treatment of *sacred language*. In *Dos Kleyne mentshele*, for example, a decisive scene occurs in the *kheyder*, the traditional elementary school, when a visiting maskil asks Itsik-Avreyml to translate a verse from the Torah. This verse, "And Lamech spoke to his wives Adah and Zillah" (Genesis 4:23), refers, according to rabbinic interpretation, to the death of Cain at the hand of his great-great-great-grandson Lamech. As Itsik-Avreyml explains this passage, in accord with the traditional interpretation, "Lamech was blind and Tubal-Cain [his son] had to lead him; and as he [Tubal-Cain] suddenly saw from far-away his grandfather Cain, he thought he saw a wild animal (my teacher said a fox, so as to make the incident more understandable), and so he told the blind man, Lamech, that he should shoot at the fox. And so he actually killed him. And when Lamech realized that it was Cain, his grandfather, he clapped his hands together, and at that instant beat his son Tubal-Cain to death" (Y 56; E 195). Like Lamech, Itsik-Avreyml becomes *blinded* by his fear of the maskil, and so he is unable to translate or explicate the passage properly in the *kheyder*. The consequence of this blindness, over the course of the narrative as a whole, will be, as it was for Lamech, estrangement from his community, past, present, and future.

That the root of this estrangement is as much pedagogical as political or ethical can be understood with respect to Itsik-Avreyml's command performance before the maskil: "Having thoroughly confused myself, I began, *'vayoymer* [Thus spoke] a fox, *leymekh* [Lamech] a blind man, *l'noshev* [to his wives] Tubal-Cain led him thus, *ode v'tsilo* [Adah and Zillah] and he killed him'" (Y 58; E 195). Abramovitsh's parody at this moment does double-duty; this satire echoes the standard maskilic critique of traditional exegesis that, in the view of the *haskole*, needlessly interfered with the sublime poetry of the original verses.[37] At the same time, he exploits this rabbinic tradition, expecting it to be familiar to his readers, to provide a savvy foreshadowing and parallel to Itsik-Avreyml's own predicament. Indeed, as a result of the disgrace that Itsik-Avreyml's failure brings on the *kheyder*, he leaves the world of traditional education and begins the tragic-picaresque journey that culminates in his becoming a genuine *kleyn mentshele* in the pejorative meaning of the term.

It is worth noting in the context of this comparison, however, that the immediate object of Abramovitsh's ridicule, the fact that *kheyder* students acquire no rational understanding of the sacred texts they study, is the focus of nostalgic reverence in Kane's novel. In theoretical terms, the difference between these two narratives can be underscored with reference to Mikhail Bakhtin's remark on what he terms "authoritative discourse" in the novel: "It enters the artistic context [of the novel] as an alien body, there is no space around it to play in, no contradictory emotions—it is not surrounded by an agitated and cacophonous dialogic life, and the context around it dies, words dry up" (*The Dialogic Imagination*, 344).[38] Itsik-Avreyml's absurd commentary on the story of Lamech is nothing if not an instance of "play" in the space not only *around* the authoritative discourse but literally *between* its sacred words. This example is not only typical of Abramovitsh's parodic mimicry of Judaism's authoritative discourse—in its tone, phraseology, frame of reference, and worldview—but in fact becomes representative of the comic tradition within Yiddish literature and the relationship between modern Jewish belles-lettres and the sacred texts of Judaism. (Moreover, this relationship can be backdated, with considerable differences of intent and effect, to Reb Nakhman's stories.)

However much at odds Bakhtin's remarks about "play" and the sacred tradition are with Yiddish literature, though, they are quite to the point when considering the relationship of the sacred to the discourse of *L'aventure ambiguë*. It is significant, in this regard, that not only is the Koran never quoted, translated, or paraphrased in the novel but the study of this Holy Book is confined to the Koranic school, a narrative space that is not only separated emotionally from the modern world that engulfs the novel's protagonist but, indeed, becomes the victim of the "agitated and cacophonous dialogic life" that renders both the discourse of the Koran and the values that it represents "simply an object, a *relic*, a *thing*" (*The Dialogic Imagination*, 344, emphasis in original). In this respect, the juxtaposition of Itsik-Avreyml and Samba Diallo with their respective communities involves not only the generic differences between a satire and a philosophical novel but also the way in which the communities themselves are conceptualized. For Kane, the tradition must be elegized because, in 1961, he believes that it *is* a relic, one that is in ostensible danger of disappearing, along with the purity of the values that he associates with it. For Abramovitsh in 1865, by contrast, the shtetl suffers from an *overabundance* of life—the community is too overcrowded and hyperactive to allow for individualism, reflective thought, or productive activity.

Folklore and its relationship to the supposedly faulty values of the tradition therefore remains for Abramovitsh an object of ridicule—whereas for Kane it hardly seems to exist at all—but given the strategic use of folk motifs in Abramovitsh's narratives, folklore continues, because of its persistent vitality, to occupy an ultimately ambivalent position in his writing. This in fact reflects the problematic place of folklore in nineteenth-century European culture generally; the use (and abuse) of folklore in *Dos Vintshfingerl* participates in a larger dialectic within European literary culture during the nineteenth century, at the same time as it internalizes the stigma of Jewish folklore as being outside the pale (because Jews are *inside* the Pale!) of modern European civilization.[39] In *Dos Vintshfingerl*, for example, Mendele relates how the maskil to whom Itsik-Avreyml left his fortune at the end of *Dos Kleyne mentshele* was driven out of Glupsk: "And when he [the maskil] washed the floor of the religious school, the Glupsker Hasidim really saw red: what's the meaning of this? What's the meaning of this! The very idea of doing this in a religious school, the very idea of washing the mud that our holy ancestors left here—only a gentile would think of such!" (*Dos Vintshfingerl*, 7). Here Abramovitsh comically invokes two perennial maskilic themes in one image; the war against the hygienic standards of

Eastern European Jews becomes at one and the same time a war against the accretion of illogical and outdated traditions.

The author, however, extends his parodic critique beyond the supposed excesses of the Hasidim to attack the debilitating influence of fantasy itself. Hence the Litvak chastises Hershele for his belief in a magic ring by saying, "Let's say that Shimen wanted it to be day and Reuben wanted it to be night. Or that Reuben and Shimen wanted to ride together on the same enchanted spirit, and one would tell the spirit to fly to India, the other to the land of Cush! Now you have to understand, Hershele dear, that . . . we'd have to rely on angels, demons, and spirits for everything!" (*Dos Vintshfingerl*, 34). Although Abramovitsh critiques the stock imagery of folklore, he never repudiates it entirely: the magic ring is an inappropriate object of desire because it would upset the natural order of things, it would populate the world with evil spirits and other supernatural beings, it would make its owners slothful and unproductive—but the argument is never made that such fantastic objects don't exist. Though surely Abramovitsh himself—unlike Reb Nakhman—does not believe in the magic of amulets, one senses that he is unwilling to discount the existence of such implements entirely because they are too useful to the fictional world that he, through the traditional, ostensibly folksy Mendele figure, creates. Magic rings may not exist in the real world, but they must exist in Mendele's world, if for no other reason than to give his ostensibly enlightened characters something to complain about!

Both the desire to return Judaism to a "purified" state by removing the accretion of irrational customs, and the critique of magic as unproductive and therefore immoral, resonate with the ethical underpinning of maskilic satire. In this regard, one should consider an incident in *Dos Kleyne mentshele* when Itsik-Avreyml states, "A sin for me meant . . . doubting that Elijah the Prophet visited every house on the first night of Passover for his cup of wine; that dead souls pray in the great synagogue at night; . . . that a ceremonial fur hat [*shtrayml*] is holy, and that even in Egypt the Jews wore such hats and that in the merit of these hats they were redeemed from slavery. . . . These were all I knew of sin, but flattery, hypocrisy, parasitism were all left out of the equation" (Y 98–100; E 211). A sin for Itsik-Avreyml, therefore, is understood as questioning superstition—the point being that in the shtetl, sin, and religion itself, is understood only as a miscellany of irrational beliefs and local customs, rather than, in keeping with Enlightenment principles, a deterrent to immoral behavior, an instrument of social control. By identifying the proper role of religion with the promotion of ethical behavior, rather than doctrines of faith, Abramovitsh affiliates his aspirations for a maskilic Judaism with universal values. Yet by invoking such values inversely, via the "language of Caliban," he reinforces the association of Judaism with irrationality, thus strengthening the ties between superstition and the beliefs of the folk.

By comparison, Linetski also contrasts the concept of morality in the shtetl with the morality of "enlightened" Judaism, and the differences in his observations from Abramovitsh's go a long way toward demonstrating the fundamental distinctions of how these two authors portray their tradition and how they use satire. Thus, Linetski writes at the beginning of *Dos Poylishe yingl*:

> A year before I went to *kheyder* my father had already begun to teach me the commandments—perhaps you think I'm talking about such ordinary commandments as the German Jews teach their little kids, for example—teaching them the verse *toyre tsivo*;[40] kissing papa and mama on the hand before going to bed; thanking God and his parents for everything he has to eat and drink, and similar such commandments? Is that what you think my father taught me? No, no, and a thousand times no! Just the opposite. My father used to teach me constantly how to give my mother the finger, and my mother used to show me how to pull my father by his beard! (10)

Here, the contrast is not between the apparent superstitions of traditional Jews versus the universal morality of enlightened Jews, but between the ostensible savagery of the shtetl versus the civility of Westernized Jews. In such a contrast, the author doesn't assume that modern Jews are more ethical than traditional ones, only more refined—and therefore that their refinement, ultimately, is just as liable to be ridiculed as the primitiveness of the traditional ones.

Moreover, Linetski's protagonist addresses his readers without a mediator such as Mendele, and therefore his narrative retains a greater affinity with oral narration than does Abramovitsh's writing.[41] Indeed, the structure of the novel as a whole resembles nothing so much as a comic routine performed before an audience. The absence of a mediator therefore means that the second-person address is much more intimate in Linetski than in Abramovitsh: the "you" (*ir*) being spoken to here is plural, not formal. Furthermore, Linteski's willingness to conceptualize the difference between tradition and modernity in cultural terms rather than ethical ones indicates that the divide between tradition and modernity is not, even at the outset, so extreme as Abramovitsh or most other maskilim were eager to depict it. Sooner than most, Linetski was willing to write polemics calling for a "united front" between Hasidim and maskilim to serve the Jewish people—thus even in his most extreme maskilic writings, Linetski is implicitly more nationalistic than Abramovitsh. By the same token, the same people whom Linetski praises as the leaders of the Jewish people are also the people whom he ridicules, alternately, as too refined or too coarse: *everything* in Linetski's satiric writings is fair game for ridicule, and this Janus-faced attitude prompts him to write in claustrophobically caustic, parodic terms. Unlike Abramovitsh, Linetski never allows his comic voice the light, or the air, to grow. The relativistic tone in Linetski's satire thus helps demonstrate both the ideological sophistication and the belletristic crudeness of his writing.

To a great extent, Mendele as a *device* prevents Abramovitsh's writing from falling into the narrow monotony that quickly comes to characterize Linetski's work.[42] Mendele's refusal to allow other characters to have the last word prevents his narratives from settling into either stylistic or ideological routine. If Hershele's narrative thus ends with the epiphany that wisdom—understood exclusively as Western learning—is the natural magic ring, Mendele's brief epilogue (*Dos Vintshfingerl*, 40–41) brings the work as a whole to a more materialistic close: his closing paragraph appeals to his reader directly for money, even including a mailing address in transliterated Russian to which contributions can be sent. This conclusion serves both to undermine Hershele's critique of the shtetl by underscoring the supposedly Jewish tendency to seek sustenance through the handout of providence rather than productive labor, while at the same time returning the narrative to the properly "Yiddish," as opposed to the "translated German" of Hershele's manuscript, form of monologue—complete with first-person narration in the present tense, comic patter, and a breaking of the barrier between author and reader by appearing, almost literally, with hat in hand. Through this return to the world of *monologue*, a world Linetski never successfully leaves, Mendele paradoxically establishes a *dialogic* relationship with his protagonist.

The immediate question of providence and material need offers a means for this discussion to return, at long last, to the comparison between Abramovitsh and Kane, and with that comparison, to conclude. Thus, the drastic, self-effacing rejection of traditional African culture—or more accurately, traditional Islam—that *la Grande Royale* advocates is justified by the same discontent that sends Hershele in *Dos Vintshfingerl* off in search of a magic ring: dire economic poverty. As Hershele explains, "In Kabtsansk itself there is no work to be found, unless begging from door to door can be considered a profession. All the sustenance for the town comes from Glupsk: the women go there to sell chickens, eggs, schmaltz, and feathers; the men travel there to hire themselves out as tutors, belfers, mystics, and talmudists; at the High Holy Days they sell themselves to the congregations as prayer leaders; on ordinary days they work as maids or butlers; at Hanukah or Purim they simply go door to door" (*Dos Vintshfingerl*, 12–13). The crucial distinction between these two narratives is the relationship between physical poverty and other forms of poverty. For Mendele, the hyperbolic economic bankruptcy of Kabtsansk, the pauper's town, is representative of its intellectual and spiritual collapse. Hershele's search for a magic ring is indicative of the traditional Jew's escape from reality into fantasy and his reliance on providence from above more than involvement in the natural and social world of the here and now.

For Kane, however, acquiescence to poverty is a value instilled at the Koranic school that is *not* directly challenged in the narrative. As Samba Diallo's father states in the first debate over whether to send him to the colonial school, "We have nothing left—thanks to them—and it is thus that they hold us. . . . The woodcutters and the metalworkers are triumphant everywhere in the world, and their iron holds us under their law. . . . But we are among the last men on earth to possess God as He veritably is in His Oneness . . . " (F 20; E 10). The spiritual value that Kane perceives in the material poverty of the tradition derives from the doctrines of Sufi mysticism in which he was raised and which his novel reflects.[43] Another aspect, however, of greater relevance in this context, is the fact that for Kane in 1961, unlike Abramovitsh in 1865, the modern world that represents colonial power in its technological, intellectual, and cultural aspects is not an abstract concept, but an intimate component of daily life. As Kane writes, "The new [colonial] school shares . . . the characteristics of cannon and of magnet. From the cannon it draws its efficacy as an arm of combat. Better than the cannon, it makes conquest permanent. The cannon compels the body, the school bewitches the soul. . . . From the magnet, the school takes its radiating force. It is bound up with a new order, as a magnetic stone is bound up with a field. The upheaval of the life of man within this new order is similar to the overturn of certain physical laws in a magnetic field" (F 60–61; E 49–50). Poverty thus acquires paradoxical value as an expression of resistance to the materialism of the colonial order.

This linking of the colonial school with the cannon and magnet emphasizes that the modernity introduced to the Diallobé via European education is not only an outside imposition but ultimately a function of imperial domination. Modernity in *L'aventure ambiguë* is not just an alien presence, it is also a system that degrades the traditional culture and disempowers the superseded culture's leaders and adherents. It is possible, however, to understand the relationship between domination and education that generated African modernity as liberating rather than stifling.[44] Such an embrace of modernity tends to produce a *realist* mode of narration at odds with the agonistic and abstracted narrative modes that Kane shares with the French existential writers immediately preceding him. Paradoxically, the oppositional mode of Kane's modernism, like Senghor's before him, is a consequence of his status as an elite: the most eager defenders of African tradition, whether defined in religious or ethnic terms, were those—like the Cheikh, Hamidou Kane—most likely to benefit from the hierarchies instituted by those traditions. Analogously, the authors who situated their negritude on a mastery of French culture, with only an abstracted reference to Africa, were those, like Senghor, who excelled most spectacularly within the limited opportunities that the French regime afforded African students of promise.[45]

By the same token, many early maskilim were also children of relative privilege[46] who, at least in their formative years, enjoyed sufficient economic mobility to afford contact with Western culture, as well as intensive, specialized mastery of Jewish sources. That proponents of these two ideologies therefore express their cultural position in negative terms—dissatisfied both with the cold strangeness of the world beyond their tradition *and* the stagnation of the tradition itself—is an indication of *haskole* and negritude's modernism. As modernist worldviews, these movements are, at the same time, premised on an existential attitude of alienation and despair, but also on Promethean efforts to expand the limits of the possible imposed by the strictures of tradition and the indifference of the new regime. As Sartre describes the underlying pessimism of negritude, with surprising lyricism, "It is from the shock of the white culture that his [the writer's] negritude has passed from immediate existence to the state of reflection. But by the same token he has more or less ceased to live it. In choosing to see that which he is, he has split himself in two, he no longer coincides with himself. And reciprocally, it was because he was already exiled from himself that there was this duty to declare himself. He begins thus by exile; the exile of the body offers a striking example of the exile of his heart" (F XV–XVI; E 18). Indeed, this remark not only provides a rejoinder to Soyinka's oft-quoted remark that "a tiger never has to proclaim his tigertude" but also speaks to the absence of an uninterrupted relationship with Africa, and with the self, that calls negritude into being.

On the level of discourse, Kane's pristinely formal French in *L'aventure ambiguë* reflects his social and historical predicament in a way that can be effectively contrasted with Aksenfeld's broken-down, grotesque Yiddish in *Dos Shterntikhl*; if Aksenfeld's Yiddish suggests the linguistic equivalent of blackface, the performance of an academic French in Kane's novel represents an inversely, though analogously, displaced impersonation of "language as Other." Each linguistic strategy represents an estrangement within the authorial subject predicated on an anxiety toward the language of self. Kane objectifies this anxiety by underscoring the disparity of the lived experience he represents and the language with which he depicts it, as well as by reflecting on the ways in which the French language and civilization inscribe the trauma of colonization on the *évolué*. For Aksenfeld, however, because these anxieties operate exclusively within the native language, they are manifested in the contradictions of his rhetoric, its externalization of difference in the dialogue of his characters. Furthermore, the irremediable otherness of the shtetl inversely matches the irretrievable distance of a romanticized Africa in *L'aventure ambiguë* or Camara's *L'enfant noir*.

With its tragic ending and its persistent tone of elegy, *L'aventure ambiguë* can ultimately be seen as negritude's swan song, even as it offers the most sustained critique of negritude values anywhere in the African novel. As Kane himself writes, "It may be that we shall be captured at the end of our itinerary, vanquished by our adventure itself. It suddenly occurs to us that all along our road, we have not ceased to metamorphose ourselves, and we see ourselves as other than what we were. Sometimes the metamorphosis is not even finished. We have turned ourselves into hybrids, and there we are left" (F 124–125; E 112–113). The novel's resolution in ambivalence and death ultimately suggests the failure of a previous generation's concept of African authenticity—a concept created through an equation of race with culture, an equation inherited, of course, from the nineteenth-century concept of "race" itself. Indeed, in a quest for *authenticity*, what could be more unsettling and discouraging than *ambiguity*? The consequence of this ambiguity is the failure of African culture as such: "I am like a broken balafong, like a musical instrument that has gone dead" (F 163; E 150). Here the balafong, itself a central symbol of negritude, of African authenticity, is rendered defunct, and fallen silent.

Similarly, Mongo Beti, the Cameroonian novelist and more ferocious critic of negritude than Kane, describes his *évolué* (or rather, failed *évolué*) protagonist, in the novel *Mission terminée*, as a sacrifice: "Without being aware of it, I was no more than a sacrifice on the altar of Progress and Civilization. My youth was slipping away, and I was paying a terrible price for—well, for what? Having gone to school, at the decree of my all-powerful father? Having been chained to my books when most children of my age were out playing games?"[47] It should be noted that Kane, the skeptical heir of negritude's mantle, portrays the failure of negritude in more tragic and definitive terms than one of its most openly caustic opponents.

One can contrast the consensus reached by Beti and Kane on the "failure," the unsustainability, of the *évolué*'s contact with modernity to analogous limitations in *haskole*'s modernizing strategies. In 1961, Kane had already been to France and returned—as intimate an exposure to colonial power and its implications as was available to an African of his day. In 1865, Abramovitsh had yet to leave the Czarist Pale of Settlement. His contact with imperial power and the day-to-day culture of modern life was largely abstract; certainly the experience of a Jew attending university in Leipzig was for Abramovitsh as fantastic as anything Hershele could have wished for with a magic ring.[48] Seen through the prism of *L'aventure ambiguë*, the maskilim have not replaced fantasy with reality or unreason with reason. Rather, they have substituted one mystification for another. They have replaced the myth of providence, connected everywhere with traditional religion, with the myth of progress: that is, modernity itself.

Taking this interpretation one step further, one can perceive that Abramovitsh himself is not impervious to the implications of modernity that Kane's argument underscores. For starters, he betrays his anxiety over the simplicity of Hershele's narrative by creating a prologue that is far more interesting and dramatic than Hershele's own story—one, indeed, that ridicules *haskole* ideology by depicting Mendele's own complaint that maskilic books just don't sell! Moreover, the language of the prologue foreshadows and undermines Hershele's naive faith in the power of reason. When Mendele and Senderl recognize one another after their wagons collide, Mendele states, "We both said with great joy that this was providence, that in fact nothing less than the merit of the patriarchs had caused our wagons to collide. . . . Such a wonder is worth telling the world, such a wonder occurs only once in a thousand years" (*Dos Vintshfingerl*, 3). Mendele here speaks in the exaggerated language of faith that Hershele's narrative is meant to refute, and therefore his parodic use of such language serves as an inversion, another mirror, of Hershele's simplistic homily to reason. Significantly, Abramovitsh's decision to omit this prologue from subsequent editions of the novel suggests that he recognizes the problem with Hershele's naive relationship to the modern world. It is as if Mendele were already admitting too much about the pitfalls of modernity, as if he were betraying the optimism of his own protagonist and story.

In a more profound and subtle manner Abramovitsh undermines the straightforward opposition of tradition and modernity, fantasy and realism, poverty and plenty in Hershele's narrative itself. After Hershele has begun his tutorial with the Litvak who will eventually lead him to Germany, he states:

> In half a year's time I read German with complete fluency. Day and night I would sit over a book. When I would become tired and the desire to study would leave me, I would say to myself, "Learn and then you'll have your magic ring." Just like my teacher in *kheyder* used to say to spur me onward, "Learn Hershenyu, learn so the angel will fling you a penny from heaven." Just like the pious Jew compels himself to perform yet another commandment, so that he'll be able to eat a piece of fish from the leviathan, a piece of meat from the heavenly banquet, and to have a seat in paradise—so believes the young boy and the poor, pious, benighted Jew—never understanding the profound intent of the holy words, *skhar mitsve mitsve*: the reward of a good deed is the good deed itself. Our holy wise men further explained the various implications of these words—but this is not the place for this. . . . (*Dos Vintshfingerl*, 36)

Hershele in this free association links himself with two doubles, the traditional student and the pious Jew, and thereby stumbles on the contradictions of his own ideology. Study, he says, and you'll acquire the genuine magic ring. Push yourself like those poor fools, who strive to perform one more commandment without ever understanding that the commandment provides its own reward. But if the commandment provides its own reward, then what reward does the pursuit of secular knowledge provide? A crude material one, like the leviathan and the heavenly feast? If so, is Hershele really better than the Jews he's just condemned? Is his learning of any greater value than theirs? Doesn't Hershele reveal, as the hasty abandonment of his own line of reasoning suggests, that he has merely exchanged one fantasy for another? Or does he cease this argument because by continuing to elaborate on the significance of a rabbinical proverb, he exposes what little distance separates him from the tradition he has supposedly transcended?

By the same token, one can use the supposed moral of *Dos Vintshfingerl* to further interpret *L'aventure ambiguë*. If the value of the tradition can be measured by its poverty, how can it hope to sustain or perpetuate itself?[49] Even the Koranic Teacher admits, "dire poverty is the enemy of God" (F 94; E 82). Indeed, everywhere in this novel, the tradition is equated with night, infirmity, asceticism, and death; by contrast, Europe and modernity are associated with daylight, material plenty, and technology. The observation, noted amid a decisive debate between Samba Diallo's father and the colonial administrator, that "[a]t this moment Lacroix had to fight the temptation to push the electric light switch which was within the reach of his hand" (F 91; E 79), therefore assumes symbolic significance in representing not only the conflict between Africa and the West but also the ambivalence, apparently shared by the author and his personification of colonial authority, toward imposing the material, antispiritual values of the West too suddenly on African culture. The death of Samba Diallo—the character whose life story dramatizes the hazards of "electric light," the sudden, artificial illumination of European culture on the African soul—at the novel's end can thus be interpreted, simultaneously, as the point of epiphany at which his struggle between tradition and modernity can be resolved, but also as a child sacrifice in the tradition's struggle against modernity and, as the novel's title suggests, against ambiguity.

These conflicts therefore prompt the title of this comparison, the rabbinic proverb, attributed to Eleazar ben Azaryah, *eyn kemakh, eyn toyre; eyn toyre, eyn kemakh* (*Pirkey oves*, 3:21): without bread, there is no Torah; without Torah, there is no bread. In this chiasmus, one can observe not only the essence of the mutual critiques between *haskole* and negritude, but also the broader dilemma between tradition and modernity confronting both Yiddish and African culture in the respective time periods under discussion here. For Kane, this dilemma can truly be resolved only in death—at least this is the implication of the literary silence he maintained for nearly thirty-five years after the publication of his first novel.[50] Following Kane, subsequent generations of African writers, in both English and French, have moved beyond the critique of colonialism and the essentialist opposition of Black against white that characterizes negritude. Kane in the era after *L'aventure ambiguë* turned his energies toward building the African state and strengthening its ties with the developed world. Subsequent writers have devoted their energies to critiquing the inability of the African state to provide or recover both physical and spiritual sustenance for the majority of their citizens, a generation after independence.

For Abramovitsh, by contrast, the 1865 edition of *Dos vintshfingerl* was the beginning of a literary career that would take the author and his culture well beyond *haskole* but would compel him to continue struggling with the problems first articulated in this narrative. Over the next forty years, Abramovitsh would produce three subsequent versions of this work, in Yiddish and Hebrew; its final version is ten times larger than the 1865 original. This relentless reworking and revision serves as testimony to the unresolved conflict instituted in the first edition. The subsequent versions and their development are certainly a topic for further study and discussion, but to the extent that this comparison has conveyed both the significance and the complexity of these problems—not just to questions of literary structure but also to broader social and historical concerns—then this discussion will have been a useful first step toward a larger project and a broader dialogue.

Conclusion

By way of conclusion, one should return to the figure of Y. Y. Linetski, the most corrosive satirist of traditional, and especially Hasidic, shtetl life, who nonetheless offers a vision whereby the double-bind of tradition and modernity as systems of power—understood in the Jewish context as Hasidism and *haskole,* respectively—can be elided. Writing in *Kol mevaser* in 1867, he states, "How good it would be, if Jews could support themselves on one foundation, that each one should exert himself to achieve the common goal that both patriots (the Baal-Shem Tov and [Moses] Mendelssohn) had imagined, according to the dictates of his age, until they would be united" (quoted in *Di Yidishe literatur in nayntsntn yorhundert,* 462). That Linetski was not alone at this early date in imagining a Jewish *national* culture that transcended ideology can be seen with respect to a similar editorial written by the editor of *Kol mevaser,* Aleksander Zederbaum, in 1865—the same year that Abramovitsh, having already broken with Zederbaum, published *Dos Vintshfingerl*: "If only Hasidim and the serious among the enlightened could combine their respective virtues, the Hasidic fervor, the enthusiasm, together with educated morality and calmness, then we Jews could once again become one people" (*Di Yidishe literatur in nayntsntn yorhundert,* 463).

Previously, even *Dos Shterntikhl* ends with Mikhl and Sheyntse being married by a Hasidic rebbe (Y 172; E 165), in spite of having expended twenty-four chapters previously railing against the bankruptcy and fraudulence of Hasidic authority! Maskilic ideology, by expressing a fundamental though deterritorialized Jewish nationalism, always imagines an ultimate reconciliation of Jewish factions by appealing to an ethical universal. Indeed, Abramovitsh also appears to have envisioned a synthesis of this sort in the last pages of *Dos Kleyne mentshele*, when Itsik-Avreyml wills his fortune to the maskil Gutman and the local rabbi *jointly* (Y 112–114; E 216). When Mendele indicates in the prologue to *Dos Vintshfingerl* that Gutman has been forced from Glupsk (*Dos Vintshfingerl*, 7), he seems to suggest the limits, at least for the time being, of a partnership between traditionalists and modernizers.

The subsequent reality of Jewish modernity, in fact, would place traditionalist, now "ultra-Orthodox," Jews in a parallel temporality from modern Jews—except, perhaps, in the contemporary State of Israel, where the reality of nation-state politics have created a society far less utopian than what Linetski and Zederbaum had imagined when traditional and modern authorities joined forces. Before this political reality, however, the ideological aspirations of the maskilim themselves would change in response to a disillusionment with the redemptive and transformative capacities of imperial modernity, just as in Africa nationalist intellectuals in the aftermath of independence would become disillusioned with the regimes governing their new nation-states. The manifestation of this disillusionment and discontent, most acutely demonstrated through Abramovitsh's aesthetic and ideological evolution over the 1870s, will provide the subject for the next part of this comparison.

In the meantime, one must return to the fundamental question that began this book. How do the authors in this second section respond to the challenge of Amos Tutuola and Reb Nakhman: to use the tradition as a subversive weapon against modern hegemony? As can be seen both in the cheerfully antitraditional works of Aksenfeld, Dik, Linetski, and Abramovitsh—and in the ambivalently tragic work of Kane and his contemporaries—the response of the writers, none of whom were particularly conscious of their predecessors in the first part, has been not to resolve the conflict between tradition and modernity that history foisted on these peripheral cultures but rather to redefine the problem of individuality itself, to dramatize the no-man's-land between traditional and modern hegemonies. In the following section, a reversal of sorts takes place; the independence and autonomy long sought by African nationalists collapses in the failure of the first independent regimes, whereas *haskole*'s utopian belief in modernity similarly evaporates with the exposure of the actual repression and hostility of the Czarist regime. At this point, ideology must reconfigure itself, with the individual again facing a new world, as before, alone. In the work that emerges from this dystopian dispensation, the lessons learned previously will acquire a new, heretofore unimagined significance. It is to these connotations of individuality and its reflection in narrative form that the next section will turn.

Part Three   *"Thank You (Falettinme Be Mice Elf
Agin); Thank You for Talkin' to Me,
Africa"*

In 1958, two years before Nigeria achieved independence, Amos Tutuola published the novel *The Brave African Huntress*. Like *The Palm-Wine Drinkard*, this book consists of a fearless protagonist's adventures in a forest of demons; in the later work, the heroine enters a fantastic jungle to retrieve her four elder brothers, who have been abducted by pigmies.[1] If anything, this novel returns Tutuola more closely than his debut to the world of Fagunwa and traditional Yoruba folklore: his protagonist's occupation as a "huntress" connects her with the Yoruba tradition's central model for human interaction with the cosmic world.[2] However traditional Tutuola's frame of reference may be, though, his act of *translation* of the traditional worldview into a modern context is of greatest relevance to the contemporary reader.

In this regard, the most significant moment in the novel occurs when the Huntress is captured by the pigmies and brought to what one early reviewer recognized as a concentration camp:[3]

> The wall (rock) of this custody was so high that there was no one who could climb it and escape. Even if one of us attempted to do so in the midnight he or she would be killed by the wild animals and reptiles which were on the only road which led to the town. The houses of these pesters . . . were built a little distance from the rooms of the captives. Uncountable of leather whips, dried long tails of big animals, long big bones of animals, clubs, cudgels, whips, etc., were scattered all over the ground. . . . All these things showed me that there was nothing good in this custody but punishments upon punishments.[4]

Regardless of how much this passage might reflect Tutuola's own experience as a soldier in World War II, one is struck today by the proleptic description this passage provides of Africans in the era of independence imprisoning, torturing, and murdering other Africans.[5]

If, therefore, the definitive literary images of the Francophone African experience during the late 1950s and early 60s—as narrated in the works of Camara, Kane, Oyono, and Mongo Beti—involve a young boy, or teenager, tentatively interacting with colonization and European culture, then Tutuola has here provided, nearly ten years ahead of schedule, a concrete representation of the African experience in the latter half of the 1960s. The vision fostered by negritude and other pan-African ideologies of an independent and modern Africa degenerated, seemingly overnight, into a reality of ethnic and class conflict, political corruption, and the violent repression of the police state.[6] In literary terms, dreams of African liberation had by the mid-1960s given way to the nightmare of history, from which the African writer, like Stephen Dedalus previously, tried to awake.

The process of "awakening," or return to consciousness, requires a representation of the nightmare itself. This obligates the postindependence writer to move from being an opponent of the colonial regime—often expressed, as in the case of Camara and Kane, only obliquely—to an overt antagonist of the neocolonial state, constituted by members of his or her "own" nation.[7] As such, these novels attack both the aesthetic objectives of the previous generation and the political realities of the present one to create a dystopian vision of the African world. The new aesthetic of the postindependence African novel thus deliberately undermines the efforts at synthesis and cultural equilibrium that had defined the aesthetics of the previous generation during the decolonization process. Furthermore, as the bureaucracies of the independence-era governments adopted the same values of mediocrity, indifference, and corruption that the colonial regimes had fostered,[8] the older aesthetic, as a cultural corollary to the independence movement, comes to be seen as a naive exercise in narcissism, a dialogue with colonialism that had excluded the victims of colonialism who in turn would be further persecuted and exploited by the neocolonialist regime. By contrast, the work of the postcolonial novel, in part, involves deflating official fables with a fabulous aesthetic of its own.

In the context of this comparison, one finds the same dismantling of the previous decade's aesthetic and ideological convictions in the Yiddish literature of the 1870s. But just as the literature of the *haskole* and negritude had "met one another coming and going" at the crossroads between universalism and nationalism, the abandonment of these aspirations takes these ideologies in opposite directions. Where Francophone African literature, for example, begins to question the nation-state as a political structure, as well as the commitment to the French language as a cultural vehicle, Yiddish literature in the 1870s attacks the previous decades' strategy of looking to the Czarist government as a catalyst to modernization as well as the negative attitude toward the Yiddish language itself. If the primary condition of African history during the late 1960s is the failure of nationalism, the comparable force in Eastern European Jewish culture of the 1870s is the attenuated valorization of just those nationalist impulses.[9] In linguistic terms, by contrast, writers in both cultures no longer accept the limits imposed ideologically on literary language; language now becomes more responsive to everyday speech, both its highs and lows, even as narratives abandon ostensibly realist, didactic mimesis. The comparison of the two cultures remains relevant, moreover, because a spirit of ideological revision characterizes "third-generation" Yiddish and African literature equally—even when, in the case of Abramovitsh, the author had been a leader of the "second" generation—and because the problem of how a peripheral culture can articulate itself in an era of imperial modernity remains constant.

The comparison in this section will focus mainly on four works: two novels by Sh. Y. Abramovitsh, *Di Klyatshe* ("The Mare," 1873) and *Kitser masoes Benyomin hashlishi* ("The Abridged Travels of Benjamin the Third," 1878); *The Interpreters* (1965), by the Nigerian author Wole Soyinka (b. 1934); and *Les Soleils des indépendances* ("The Suns of Independence," 1968), by the Ivoirian writer Ahmadou Kourouma (1927–2003). The ensuing discussion, divided in two chapters, will focus on two alternating strategies for responding to the failure of the ideologies discussed in the previous part. Chapter 5 will consider the first strategy, as exemplified by *Di Klyatshe* and *The Interpreters*, which examine and parody the role of the intellectual in the newly modern society. The protagonists in both books might have been the ideal agents of modernization from the standpoint of this comparison's previous part, yet here they demonstrate the delusion, despair, and rage engendered by the modernity engulfing them. Conversely, chapter 6, which considers *Masoes Benyomin hashlishi* and *Les Soleils des indépendances*, focuses on the lives of the folk, the persistently nonmodern living amid modernity. These latter novels serve to underscore the prolonged competition between tradition and modernity in the peripheral culture. As such, they alternately ridicule the modern world and expose the consequences of modern regimes that have marginalized the uneducated and powerless.

It should be noted at the outset that although the first two novels discussed in chapter 5, as well as the second pair in chapter 6, all use parody and satire, none of the works considered here are satiric parodies exclusively. Furthermore, the narrative strategies of the respective pairs are not mutually exclusive, as the fact that Abramovitsh employed them both, successively, demonstrates. Finally, in technical terms, both strategies, at least in the examples considered here, focus on modernity and its discontents from an external perspective; that is, in each of the narratives under consideration, the author uses third-person narration—an issue to which the discussion of *Di Klyatshe* must quickly return—and some version of free indirect discourse. This indicates that the author observes the consequences of modernity as an outsider, suggesting that the divide between the author and his native culture, which the ideologies discussed in the previous part were meant to bridge, has only intensified in the interim.

To better understand the role of parody in creating an aesthetic bridge linking the folk culture to the estranged intellectual, as well as the aesthetic continuity between late-nineteenth-century Yiddish and late-twentieth-century African fiction, it is worth invoking the concept of "deformative laughter" discussed by Tyrus Miller.[10] The introduction of deformative laughter—a laughter of negation, madness, or futility[11]—is the crucial formal means by which modernist writers emerging in the late 1920s and 30s distinguish themselves from the High Modernist masters who appeared just before or during World War I. As the ensuing analysis will attempt to demonstrate, Abramovitsh, Soyinka, and Kourouma each introduce deformative laughter, along with motifs of chaos, destruction, and insanity, into their semi-parodic narratives to signal a dissent from the previous decade's conception of artistic decorum as well as from the political assumptions that had fostered the crises of the current moment. One should note that deformative laughter is quite distinct from the "ritual laughter" of the Bakhtinian carnival. Ritual laughter is a means by which a traditional culture makes productive use of its internal contradictions, and as such becomes a crucial defense mechanism in the reconfiguration of the tradition as a counterbalance to modernity. Deformative laughter, by contrast, is a secularizing and dissident gesture; if Tutuola and Reb Nakhman use ritual laughter to rehabilitate the tradition, Abramovitsh, Soyinka, and Kourouma use deformative laughter to undermine the modern order that has displaced the tradition.

There is nonetheless an essential distinction between the peripheral writers under consideration here and the "late modernists" that Miller analyzes: the rupture that the late modernists create separates one group of elite writers at the center of Western civilization from a previous group, equally elite and metropolitan. By contrast, the rupture involving Soyinka and Kourouma, like Abramovitsh before them, severs these writers from the governing ideology of an entire society.[12] As Kwame Appiah has argued, the postcolonial and the postmodern, however similar their aesthetic projections may appear, stem from fundamentally different motivations. The distinction between the postcolonial and the postmodern is both formal and philosophical; the distinction between late modernism and postmodernism—however much this shift reflects changes in the postindustrial global economy—is by comparison largely taxonomic. A consideration of "late modernism" in the context of proto-modernist Yiddish literature in the Realist era or African literature in the postmodern era serves, however, to illustrate the ways in which a "belated" literary culture can actually *anticipate* the literary practices of a metropolitan avant-garde. Moreover, just as Miller distinguishes between "late modernism" and postmodernism as distinct aesthetics that coexist in the era following World War II,[13] so too does periodization in general need to be flexible enough to acknowledge the competition between aesthetic trends, the simultaneous viability of more than one aesthetic strategy, as a fundamental principle of literary dynamics, and itself a catalyst toward new aesthetic possibilities.

These issues ultimately help to explain why either Kourouma or Soyinka and Abramovitsh have more in common with one another than with many of their contemporaries writing in the same language on similar themes. In this regard, one must consider that if Abramovitsh's *Di Klyatshe* looks ahead in its analogical structure and fantastic, transmogrifying imagery to the stream-of-consciousness techniques of *Ulysses*, its tone and ostensibly polemical character look back to such eighteenth-century satires as *Gulliver's Travels* or *Candide*. These paradoxical, "contradictory" aesthetic affinities prompt the question, is Abramovitsh avant-garde or profoundly atavistic in his aesthetic orientation? Does his achievement in fact establish a new synthesis, neither wholly Joyce nor merely Swift, but purely Mendele—that is, thoroughly "minor"?

As indicated previously, one of the main strategies by which the writers in the present discussion distinguish themselves both from their predecessors and from their contemporaries still committed to a programmatic, realist discourse is the return to fantasy. Indeed, as programmatic ideology recedes, both fantasy and the quasi-mythical, cosmological thinking that fantasy represents metaphorically emerge to fill the breach. For both Yiddish and African literature, the wellspring of fantasy is folklore. In the most general sense, this means that Yiddish and African authors in the aftermath of *haskole* and decolonization, respectively, reinvest the traditions that were to have been supplanted by modern ideology with new, if often only symbolic, significance. As Albert Memmi writes, "Now, the young intellectual who . . . ate during Ramadan begins to fast with ostentation. He who considered the rites as inevitable family drudgery, reintroduces them into his social life, gives them a place in his conception of the world. . . . He must bolster his people to affirm his own solidarity with it" (*The Colonizer and the Colonized*, 132–133).[14] Memmi's commentary on the reinvigorated social significance of traditional beliefs finds an aesthetic correlative in the writings of Kourouma, Abramovitsh, and Soyinka; these writers, who remain in personal practice cosmopolitan secularists,[15] nonetheless adopt and adapt their respective traditions as the focal point of an alternative vision, both to the hegemony of unreconstructed religious authority and to a modernity that has failed to deliver its transformative promises of liberation.

Thus, where folklore in maskilic satire, for example, had been an object of ridicule, both folktales themselves and the traditions from which these tales emerged come to represent in Abramovitsh's mature novels a world beyond the reach of a predatory modernity. As Dan Miron describes this transformation of the shtetl in the Yiddish fiction of the late nineteenth century, the act of defining the shtetl as both a "purely" Jewish society and a "natural habitat" for traditional Jewish life signified an investment in the mythological potential of the shtetl over a seemingly more modern commitment to social or historical verisimilitude.[16] Through the depiction of the shtetl, the similarity of Yiddish literature, coming from a diaspora culture, to African literature, coming from a colonized one, becomes comprehensible. However much the historical reality of the shtetl was dystopically "multicultural," its literary representation, an image that shaped and was shaped by the collective self-perception of Eastern European Jews, was of an all-Jewish environment, "a tiny Jewish island in a vast non-Jewish sea" (Miron, "Image," 3).

As such, like the images of African societies in Anglophone or Francophone African literature, the *image* of the shtetl is not only a representation of a traditional society undermined by modernity but also a deceptively homogenous culture conquered by colonialism. The one exception to the depiction of the shtetl as an all-Jewish enclave in the literature considered in this comparison is Katloyke in Dik's utopian manuscript, a shtetl in which Christians and Jews meet in the clubrooms of the Jewish library, and where modern Christians are the role models for "enlightened" Jews struggling to raise themselves to the standards of civilization.[17] Significantly, the difficulties in depicting this singular image of an "integrated" shtetl proved artistically insuperable, and Dik never completed this narrative. By contrast, the mature writings of Abramovitsh under consideration here make manifest a mythical conception of the shtetl that was a latent component of his earlier narratives. That is, mythical references—conveyed through religious institutions, allusions to sacred writings, and the "chronotope" of Jewish holidays—appear throughout the Yiddish literature of the *haskole*; it is only in the aftermath of the *haskole*, however, that Abramovitsh, the one writer in the movement capable of transcending its ideological limitations, develops these mythic or cosmological references to their full artistic potential, as the ensuing discussion will attempt to demonstrate.

Five Mendele's Mare and Soyinka's Interpreters

The discussion itself can at last begin with a consideration of *Di Kly-atshe*. A novel in twenty-four chapters,[1] *Di Klyatshe* describes the fate of Yisrolik, a would-be university student—in this respect it resembles Mongo Beti's *Mission terminée*, which satirizes negritude as *Di Klyatshe* parodies *haskole*—who has been driven to madness by the stress of preparing for his entrance exams. While returning home from a stressful study session, Yisrolik encounters a mare being abused by a band of juvenile delinquents. After Yisrolik rescues her, the mare reveals that she is not a horse after all, but a Jewish prince who has been transmogrified by an evil spell. Promising to help protect the mare, Yisrolik contacts the *tsar baley-khayim*, a Jewish version of the ASPCA. The *tsar baley-khayim*, which is meant to represent the "Society for the Advancement of Enlightenment among the Jews," the same St. Petersburg philanthropical outfit so detrimental to Yisroel Aksenfeld's fate, responds that before they can intervene on the mare's behalf, she must learn to conform to society's expectations for horses. When the mare balks at this, Yisrolik responds that the devil must have gotten into her. In the instant, the demon Ashemdai takes over the narrative and leads Yisrolik on a balloon journey over all of Europe, explaining to him that the technological, political, and cultural apparatuses of the modern world are in fact the devil's tools. As the devil's workshop expands to encompass the entire world, Yisrolik wakes from his nightmare to find his traditional mother, together with a Hasidic *baal-shem* and a Ukrainian faith-healer, keeping   167 watch over him, lamenting his pitiful condition.

In formal terms, the first correlative to the thematic and ideological factors at work in the novel is the problematic status of narrative voice.

As stated at the beginning of this discussion, each of the narratives examined in this section makes use of an external perspective and at least
an attenuated form of free indirect discourse. But how can this be true
of *Di Klyatshe*, which consists of a first-person introduction, written
by Mendele, and the twenty-four chapters of the narrative, written by
Yisrolik himself? In fact, the exact relationship between Mendele, the
"editor" of the novel, and Yisrolik the narrator reveals the presence of
an external consciousness shaping the events of the narrative, mediating
between the protagonist's consciousness and the reader's. As indicated
previously, Mendele is the comic, satirizing alter ego whom Abramovitsh has created to address his Yiddish readership—and eventually his
Hebrew readers, as well—and to connect the modern intellectual with
the still-traditional culture of the shtetl. Mendele as an itinerant book-
peddler is both the point of intersection that links the various *shtetlekh*
and characters with whom he interacts, as well as the agent through
which the world-at-large, as signified by the maskilic pamphlets that he
reluctantly and unprofitably offers for sale, penetrates the traditional
Jewish "habitat."

Thus, in the 1865 edition of *Dos Vintshfingerl* Mendele's prologue and
afterword undercut both the one-dimensional message of Hershele's
narrative and the somewhat pompous seriousness with which he relates
his life story. In *Di Klyatshe*, by comparison, Mendele's shrewd irony
connects rhetorically first with the mare, then with the devil, so that
his role dissipates in the main narrative among the speakers with whom
Yisrolik agonistically relates. Yisrolik is in this respect less the narrator
of the novel than its addressee. Abramovitsh therefore uses madness
as a device to take the narration outside of Yisrolik's perspective—by
portraying him as "out of his head." The structure of successive speakers
taking over the task of narration is of course rooted in the monological
traditions of Yiddish narrative—as exemplified by Linetski's *Dos Poylishe
yingl* and the Mendele prologues throughout Abramovitsh's career—
but *Di Klyatshe* transcends these conventions by using its multiple
speakers to expand the field of vision, as well as the frame of reference,
exponentially. Yisrolik, as much as the reader, is not the producer, but
the *audience* for the rhetorical performances of the narrative's last two-
thirds; the roles of protagonist and reader merge with one another, as

the characters speaking to them reveal themselves to be projections of a single, external, narrating consciousness. Among Abramovitsh's novels, *Di Klyatshe* resembles most closely the pristine model of Deleuze and Guattari's "assemblage." It is indeed fitting that this nightmarish comedy comes the closest of any nineteenth-century Yiddish narrative to Franz Kafka's sensibility.

How, then, did Abramovitsh move from sober, Enlightenment polemic to "Kafkaesque" phantasmagoria, effectively leaping over nineteenth-century realism in the process, during the course of less than a decade? The answer lies at least in part in the ideological transformation that the author underwent at the beginning of the new decade. In the most immediate terms, Abramovitsh changes his formal expectations for Yiddish narrative when he abandons both the didactic functionalism that the maskilim had reserved for writing in Yiddish—"authentically" creative belles-lettres being for them the province of Hebrew literature—as well as *haskole*'s preference for exemplary, potentially larger-than-life young protagonists who would either transform their society or be crippled by its excesses. From the 1860s to the 70s, Abramovitsh exchanges these "typical" protagonists for new characters that, in their very marginality, are able to stand outside their communities, much as the figure of Mendele did, and thus reflect the porousness of the line separating the shtetl from modernity, "the Jew" from "the world," the real from the imaginary.[2]

But this decision to shift the generic burden of his narratives from homiletic "realism" to fantastic comedy is part of a larger ideological progression that ultimately called into question the underlying social and political assumptions of the *haskole*. As Ruth Wisse has explained, Abramovitsh draws attention to his break with *haskole* by advertising *Di Klyatshe* as a sequel to an earlier work, a polemic written in the form of a drama called *Di Takse* ("The Meat-Tax," 1869);[3] in a strategy that mimics *haskole* itself, Abramovitsh broadcasts his abandonment of maskilic convictions by disguising the rupture as a point of continuity. *Di Takse* describes the efforts of Shloyme Veker ("Waker"), to arouse the indignation of his fellow Jews against the exploitation by the shtetl leadership, the *kahal*, of the kosher-meat tax imposed by the Russian government for the ostensible support of Jewish institutions.[4] Wisse writes, "Waker's combination of internal criticism with faith in government was characteristic of the Russian Haskalah that predicated its reformist program on the good will of the regime, especially after the accession of Alexander II. . . . As confirmation of his faith in government, Abramovitsh dedicated the play to 'His Excellency, the Governor of Odessa, True Minister of the Realm, Nikolai Vasilovitsh Novoselsk, as a token of the author's deep esteem and devotion'" ("The Jewish Intellectual and the Jews," 6–7). Despite whatever expectations the author may have entertained about cultivating the favor of the regime, Abramovitsh was forced, like Veker at the end of the play, to flee his base in Barditchev for Zhitomir after angering the Barditchev elite with his caustic portrayal of their corruption.

In his prologue to *Di Klyatshe*, Mendele explains that the new novel is a sequel to the previous work: "I submitted an inquiry to the rabbinical jurors of Glupsk. . . . Because I had promised my audience a second part to the *Takse* without making explicit that this was not a formal oath, was I not essentially bound by my word, according to the current judgment, to publish *Di Klyatshe* as a sequel, and in so doing, would I in fact have fulfilled my oath? They hemmed and hawed, scratching their beards and scratching their heads until at last they said, 'Yes, Reb Mendele, insofar as we have caught here a whiff, a taste, of *Di Takse*, we are releasing you from your obligation.'"⁵ As a parody of rabbinic argumentation, these remarks are typical of Mendele's prologues, which subvert religious authority in order to disguise the modernist implications of the narrative to follow, making it seem more pious than it is, and to level the playing field for the contest between tradition and Abramovitsh's individual talent by undercutting the sanctity of the authorities who would otherwise condemn the ostensible heresy of his writing. The only anomaly, however, is the mention of a sequel to the earlier work. As Wisse makes clear, "[T]here is no obvious connection between *The Meat-Tax* and *The Mare*, written as they are in different genres, different styles, without a single overlapping character [except Mendele]. Abramovitsh evidently introduced this new composition [*Di Klyatshe*] as a sequel to his earlier satire because he wanted readers to make the connection post-facto" ("The Jewish Intellectual and the

Jews," 7). Mendele thus satisfies an oath he never made, producing a sequel that contradicts the premise of the original.

Intervening in the four years that separate *Di Takse* from *Di Klyatshe* was a political crisis affecting Russian Jewry that shook Abramovitsh's faith in *haskole*, and disabused him of the belief that support for Jewish modernizers, or any other Jewish people, would come from the Czarist system. Wisse continues:

> One of the things that occurred between the publication of *The Meat Tax* in 1869 and *The Mare* . . . was the first modern pogrom in the Russian empire. . . . The pogrom raged for four days in May 1871, in Odessa, to whose mayor-governor Abramovitsh had dedicated his satire on the Jews with the assurance that government's benevolence would prove the Jews' salvation. ("The Jewish Intellectual and the Jews," 16)

With this incident, Abramovitsh recognized that rather than calling on the Czar to save Jews from their own community leaders, the paramount obligation of Jewish modernizers was to call attention, as much as censorship allowed, to the exploitation of Jews mandated by the imperial regime. In this regard, fantasy itself becomes a political tool enabling the author to speak against the repressiveness of the social order without being repressed himself. This is the moment at which Abramovitsh can be recognized as a fully modern, fully autonomous writer—waging a war, simultaneously, against the petty tyranny of traditional Jewish leaders, as well as the greater outrages of the modern state. From this moment, the primary focus of his writing is no longer homiletic but existential, as he observes and depicts characters such as Yisrolik alone and defenseless in a hostile world.

As the first chapter of the novel begins, Yisrolik corroborates Abramovitsh's tragicomic conception of the protagonist's essential helplessness. He begins by stating, "Just as Noah long ago in the ark was at the time of the Flood the sole survivor among all the drowned creatures of the world, so I, Yisroel the son of Tsipe, am the last remnant in my shtetl, the solitary bachelor among all my friends, who through the pestilence of the matchmakers have all become young householders before their time, and thus have sunk up to their necks in pitiable poverty and paupery" (Y 19; E 549). This long sentence reaches back to the dawn of history in pursuit of an overarching theme, the poverty of the traditional Jew. Already the evocation of Noah calls attention to the ultimately mythical image of the shtetl that Abramovitsh develops, while also suggesting the proximity of the protagonist with animals. Furthermore, Yisrolik's comparison of his condition with Noah suggests that the life of the shtetl to which he opposes his own ambitions is analogous to the corrupt condition of the world that preceded the Flood. More fundamentally, Mendele presents Yisrolik's "madness" as a consequence of his isolation from humanity, his inability to enter the adult world by forming a conjugal relationship. Nonetheless, by underscoring the hardship and poverty incurred by marrying "before their time," he also indicates that the traditional alternative to Yisrolik's rootlessness is scarcely a preferable option.

But if the shtetl is comparable to the degraded world before the Flood, then Yisrolik soon enough learns the limitations of life aboard the ark. As in the prologue to *Dos Vintshfingerl*, Abramovitsh signals the fundamental distinction between tradition and modernity in textual terms, by discussing the reading lists required in the Russian university curriculum. Thus Yisrolik complains:

> It was most difficult for me to approach history, what they call in their language *slovesnost* [literature]. From memory I had to learn ridiculous stories about wars, how people have from since the world began down to the present day killed one another, brutalized, battered, and beat each others brains out, all recited with precisely the right date, and precisely the right place! . . . On top of that I had to learn all kinds of wild fables, stories about horrible strongmen, notorious drunkards, world-renowned bandits, stories about transmigrations, with witches and warlocks, stories about living and dead waters, golden apples and golden horses. (Y 20–21; E 550)

This passage explicitly ridicules the maskilic valorization of reason and science over fantasy and folklore—Yisrolik claims no difficulty in learning mathematics or science—by calling attention to the significance that contemporary intellectuals, especially in Russia, attached to history, literature, and folklore.

At the same time, however, these remarks underscore the fact that maskilim in the 1870s were beginning the difficult process of engaging with Russian culture and the demands of the Russian higher education system.[6] By contrast, *Di Klyatshe* emphasizes that this effort at engagement with Russian culture was in most instances completely one-sided: not only was there little significant effort at reciprocal engagement with Jewish culture, or most other minority cultures in the empire, by the majority of Russian intellectuals, but even the efforts of Jewish students to participate in the Russian high school or university system were either rebuffed through social ostracism or eventually frustrated by restrictive quotas and other forms of outright discrimination. The root of the problem for Jewish intellectuals in the last third of the nineteenth century, as Abramovitsh suggests, is the futility of their efforts to be acknowledged as equals in contemporary Russian society. No sooner had they abandoned the medieval parochialism of the shtetl, than they encountered the chauvinism of nineteenth-century modernity.

As *Di Klyatshe* continues to develop, Abramovitsh makes the connection between culture and power yet more explicit. In this regard, one of the most significant incidents occurs when Yisrolik finally takes his matriculation exam. Abramovitsh writes:

> The teachers were . . . clothed in uniforms with brass buttons, looking at me with such severity, such malice, as if I were either a thief or a murderer. . . . What is the sense in having teachers, whose very profession obligates them to make from us, their students, rational and compassionate human beings . . . wear uniforms with brass buttons? . . . Can you imagine Socrates, Plato, or Aristotle wearing such buttons, or such sour expressions . . . ? Such was the respect they showed me, such was the expression that the chief examiner wore when he turned to me with a quotation from here, another from there, until at last he arrived at the story of Baba Yaga herself! I was left confused, distraught, up a creek without a paddle! (Y 56; E 581)

One can gauge the ideological distance Abramovitsh has traveled in a single decade by contrasting this scene to Itsik-Avreyml's interview in the *kheyder* in *Dos Kleyne mentshele*. Whereas in the earlier narrative, Itsik-Avreyml was questioned on a verse from the Torah by a benign agent of the modern world—a maskil—in order to expose the deficiencies of traditional Jewish education, thereby advertising the ostensible compatibility between the objectives of the maskilim and "authentic" Jewish piety, here Yisrolik must answer questions on Russian folklore by a militarized pedagogue described as an inquisitor. Moreover, just as *Dos Kleyne mentshele* had shown the maskil as the true champion of the Torah over the benighted *kheyder* teacher, so Yisrolik here identifies himself with the Classical philosophers in his complaint against the debasement of secular knowledge. The stakes for Yisrolik in the fully modern world of the university are nonetheless much higher than for Itsik-Avreyml in the *kheyder*. Abramovitsh here turns an educational interview into a confrontation with ultimate, dehumanizing power.[7]

Into this unequal showdown between the putative maskil and the imperial state enters the mare herself. The horse motif first appears when Yisrolik considers the status of a herd at pasture after an intense study session. Abramovitsh writes, "One of them had a grandfather who was an English stallion that had in bygone days, while traveling through the land of Canaan, married an Arabian filly. Another's grandmother came from a famous family that had in its time smelled its share of gunpowder, while yet another's great-grandmother had received a good education somewhere on a renowned stud farm and was so learned that she gave dance recitals. . . . From all this you can plainly see that among horses lineage plays a significant role, and among themselves they look closely at aristocratic blood, and those with the right pedigree are known as nobility or thoroughbreds" (Y 24; E 553). In the context of the novel as a whole, the association between Yisrolik's impending humiliation at the hands of a rigid, hereditary class system and the fixation on horses' lineage suggests that class and race are as "crazy" as Yisrolik is—that they can only be properly understood through the eyes of a madman.[8]

Furthermore, in terms of *Di Klyatshe*'s transitional place in its author's career, this passage recalls the prologue to *Dos Vintshfingerl*, in which Mendele equates Jews with donkeys, while at the same time it foreshadows the technique developed in *Benyomin hashlishi* in which individual characters or incidents become representative of whole nations or social orders. The novel's eponymous mare extends this function when she narrates her transformation from a noble prince to a harried mare—and indeed, the phrase "unlucky prince, pitiful mare" (Y 82; E 603) captures the fundamental ambiguity of the character and its relationship to the novel, at once male and female, human and animal, tragic and absurd.[9] As the mare/prince herself (himself) relates:

> Once upon a time there was a prince, and a very fine prince he was—intelligent, successful, with every virtue, a rare item indeed. The prince in question traveled in his youth, made long journeys, to see something of the world. . . . Once a king in Egypt, that famous land of gypsies and conjurors, became angry with this prince when he paid the king a visit. He became terrified at the idea that this prince would deal dishonestly with him, and maybe even usurp him from his own throne and land, so he consulted with the best magicians in his realm, and said to them, "Brothers, let's outfox this prince with one of our best numbers."[10] The magicians used the best of their art on the prince to turn him into a beast of burden. . . . And this prince, this schlimazel, stands before you now in the form and appearance of a mare. (Y 30–31; E 558–559)

It may be recalled that at the climax of *Dos Kleyne mentshele*, Itsik-Avreyml explains his lack of scruples by declaring that in his youth "[a] sin for me meant . . . doubting . . . that the sacred soul of a person could be reincarnated as a black cat, a pig, a calf, a rooster. . . . [This was] all I knew of sin, but flattery, hypocrisy, and parasitism were all left out of the equation" (Y 98–100; E 211). In *Di Klyatshe*, however, Abramovitsh revisits the belief in transmogrification, not, as in *Dos Vintshfingerl*, to make the device a vehicle for rationalist homiletics, but to make this belief the dramatic focus of the novel. By using this motif, the author shifts the narrative from the story of an intellectual to the story of a people, reformulated in mythological garb.

Thus, the mare's journey explicitly alludes to the House of Israel's descent from the Land of Canaan to Egypt (Genesis 46:5–27). Having invoked this descent, however, the author nonetheless elides reference to either the Exodus from Egypt or the subsequent establishment of a Kingdom of Israel. Yisrolik is clearly not Moses; in the cosmological chronology of the novel, the redemption of the enslaved Jewish people has yet to occur. The existential forsakenness of the Jews is underscored by the circumstances of the mare's first encounter with Yisrolik. Abramovitsh writes, "I heard from afar a blood-curdling scream, the cries of people and the barking of dogs. . . . Curious, I arose to learn where the voices were coming from and went to a large field overgrown with grass, and there I saw a truly hideous scene: youngsters, hooligans, were chasing on all sides a starving, emaciated mare, stoning her, and siccing a pack of dogs on her" (Y 24; E 553). One can be forgiven for seeing in this scene an allusion to Raskolnikov's dream in Fyodor Dostoyevsky's *Crime and Punishment* (1866), a novel that Abramovitsh—who corresponded with his fiancée in Russian[11]—would surely have been familiar with: in both novels, there is a contrast between healthy stallions and a pitiful old mare; in both works a rowdy mob tortures the mare for the sake of cruelty; in both books this scene connects both thematically and symbolically with the central preoccupations of the narrative as a whole.[12]

It should be noted, however, that whereas in Dostoyevsky, this scene is literally a nightmare, the most grotesque and disturbing anywhere in his writing, in *Di Klyatshe* the scene is integrated into the "waking" reality of the novel, but is nonetheless conveyed much less graphically, in keeping with the parodic nature of the narrative. The scene is thus at once both more and less realistic in Abramovitsh's version than Dostoyevsky's.[13] Furthermore, in Dostoyevsky's version, the ultimate significance of the nightmare is moral and religious; the mare's suffering is invoked, in almost unbearable detail, to recall a Russian readership to Christian ideals of compassion and the sanctity of life[14]—ideals that Raskolnikov, in his waking nihilism, attempts to repress. For Abramovitsh, the metaphor of the tortured mare is primarily political: the persecutors of the mare are not Christians neglecting their duty to other Christians, they are Russians who attack Jews instead of the aristocratic "steeds" who actually rob and oppress them. In the unequal contest between the mare and the ruffians, the Jews and the Russians, Abramovitsh introduces the political argument that the mare, the Jew, should be protected by the rule of law not because of the goodness of Christian society, nor because of the merits of the downtrodden themselves, but because of rights that accrue to the strong and the weak alike. Nonetheless, the ultimate interest of the novel resides not in the allegorical significance of the mare, but rather in the way that fantasy subverts a simple allegorical meaning to the narrative and instead overtakes any rationalist program for improving the world.

When Yisrolik enters the fantastic world of the talking mare, when he responds to the mare as an intellectual and metaphysical equal, the novel ceases to be merely a political fable; like the Endless Forest of *The Palm-Wine Drinkard*, the world of the talking mare in *Di Klyatshe* does not symbolize contemporary Russian society and its relationship to the "Jewish Question." It invokes that world by analogy, using the mare's metempsychosis to remove the crisis facing Russian Jewry from the context of political polemic in order to render it in more fantastic, and therefore metaphysical, terms. Thus, this novel does not extend the polemical character of earlier *haskole* satire so much as it renounces polemic itself[15]—and in so doing, it renounces claims to an absolute, monological monopoly on the truth. As Yisrolik himself states, "It was on this night that I became a wise man, and just as soon as I gained wisdom, it goes without saying, I began to doubt everything, and not only to doubt others—to question if it was at all clear who they were or what they were—but even to doubt who I myself was" (Y 38–39; E 565).

With this self-interrogating doubt comes what might be termed an "anatomization of the self"; just as *Di Klyatshe* represents the projection of an external consciousness onto a first-person narration, so conversely can the novel be seen as the exteriorization of Yisrolik's madness onto the rest of the world. Abramovitsh represents consciousness as such in the novel as a deliberate confusion of exterior and internal perspectives—neither fully first person nor objectively third person, but an assemblage of the two.[16] Seen in this light, Abramovitsh's mare can be identified with what Deleuze and Guattari describe as Kafka's "becoming animals": "To become animal is . . . to find a world where all forms come undone. . . . " (*Toward a Minor Literature*, 13). The concept of the "becoming animal" connects the mare's resistance to Yisrolik's "liberal" efforts to rehabilitate her with his own protest against the efforts of Russian society to turn him into a parrot. Yisrolik's flight from sanity leads him at first into a world of talking horses, a world in which anything can happen, but even here he finds no safe haven, as the mare herself creates another path of escape for herself that leads Yisrolik eventually into another assemblage, one constructed and controlled by the devil himself.[17]

This reflects a further reversal from Abramovitsh's previous maskilic position. For if the mare—who represents the historical experience and the wisdom of the folk—can successfully extricate herself both from the tyranny of the "reactionary" masses and the restrictions that the "progressive" intellectuals of the *tsar baley-khayim* would place on her, why is Yisrolik left, at the novel's climax, still in the devil's clutches?[18] At this point, indeed, the maskilic dichotomy of tradition and the folk, opposed to modernity and the intellectual, collapses. And when this dialectic collapses, everything falls with it, including the individual intellectual's sense of self and his or her place in the world. If the writings of Reb Nakhman or earlier maskilim therefore reflect the sudden intrusion of modernity into the traditional world, the mature narratives of Abramovitsh, like those of Soyinka and Kourouma, grapple with the ultimately more complicated problem of recognizing the *illusion* of concrete, fixed positions of tradition and modernity. As Abramovitsh demonstrates in *Di Klyatshe*, fantasy is the most durable narrative strategy to address this difficulty. And since fantasy has already been identified by *haskole* as a province of the tradition, the reclaiming of fantasy for the modernizing writer entails trespassing the boundary between tradition and modernity in two directions simultaneously; if *L'aventure ambiguë* and *Dos Vintshfingerl* met one another "coming and going" between tradition and modernity, *Di Klyatshe* doesn't know whether it's coming or going. In this newly created no-man's-land, a newly elastic concept of the individual and his or her relationship to the world emerges.

However flexible the categories of internal and external, imaginary and real, may have become for Yisrolik, he nonetheless remains *bound* to the shtetl and the conventional relationships he maintained there. In the absence of a marital relationship like those of his peers, Yisrolik's most meaningful relationship, significantly enough, is with his mother. This fact in itself suggests both the fundamentally unproductive, stunted nature of his personality and of his aspirations, as well as the inability of the Russian maskilim to emerge fully into the modern world. As Yisrolik explains to his mother, "I'm despised in the eyes of my own people, the Jews, and in the eyes of the others, the gentiles.

When one hates me for not being the right kind of Jew, the other hates me for being a Jew like every other Jew. I'm alive and I want to live; I long to escape this confinement to live with people, equal in God's great world, to do whatever is possible, so that Jewishness shouldn't be a liability in my efforts at self-improvement" (Y 52; E 577). The fact that Yisrolik's mother—a traditional Jewish woman incapable of understanding and unwilling to sympathize with his aspirations—is the only human to whom he can confide his frustrations indicates the reflexivity of his aspirations. His efforts to escape the confines of the shtetl thus demonstrate how much he remains trapped there, just as his efforts to join with a larger humanity as part of "God's great world" serve only to underscore his essential and immutable isolation.

A generation later, Abramovitsh's follower Sholem Aleichem (1859–1916) will invert this exchange between Yisrolik and his uncomprehending mother in monologues such as *Dos Tepl*,[19] in which the futility and anguish of a young man giving his life up to study is narrated from the perspective of his still-traditional mother. The distinction between Sholem Aleichem's inverted, indirect strategy and Abramovitsh's ostensibly more straightforward, expository approach stems from Sholem Aleichem's particular talents and inclinations but also underscores, in the broader context of a discussion of gender in *Di Klyatshe*, the almost total absence of fully developed female characters—even in the limited sense of Sholem Aleichem's *yidenes*,[20] who, if not fully three-dimensional according to realist conventions, at least speak for themselves—in Abramovitsh's writing. Yisrolik's mother is the closest exception in Mendele's major works; even the mare reveals herself in fact to be a transmogrified Jewish prince!

Sholem Aleichem, by contrast, excels in creating endless variations on the essentially stereotypical figure of a talkative, domineering, tragicomic Jewish mother in part because for writers of his generation, even more than those in Abramovitsh's heyday, Yiddish had already become associated more closely with the older generation than the younger, despite the fact that Yiddish remained at the turn of the century the dominant language by far for nearly all Russian Jews. Both Abramovitsh's and Sholem Aleichem's *yidenes* invoke a larger symbolic contrast originating in maskilic poetics: between Yiddish, the old-fashioned, primitive, feminine *zhargon*, and Hebrew, the modern, learned, masculine language that brought a distinguished past and a hopeful future together by transcending the limitations of the dismal present.[21]

In this regard, despite the status of Yiddish as the maternal Jewish language par excellence, *dos mame-loshn*, it is significant to note that women play virtually no role in shaping the Yiddish literature of the nineteenth century, beyond the role of consumer designated by Dik's address to the *tayere lezerin* (the "gentle lady reader").[22] Sholem Aleichem, despite the dramatically compelling use to which he puts the *yidene* character type, essentially reiterates the maskilic linguistic dichotomy, which in turn determines his entire literary output; Abramovitsh, at least in *Di Klyatshe*, turns this dialectic on its head by showing the maskil, in spite of his best efforts, captive to the shtetl and capable of speaking only in his mother language—in this regard one should recall his inability to master Russian culture—to his maternal interlocutor. Like the transmogrified mare, Yisrolik is "emasculated" over the course of the novel, linguistically, culturally, and politically.

The issue of gender and its relativity therefore connects explicitly to the reconfiguration of power relations that accompanies Abramovitsh's rejection of conventional maskilic ideology. Just as the scene in which the Russian educational bureaucrats interrogate Yisrolik evokes and inverts the *kheyder* scene in *Dos Kleyne mentshele* to underscore the inequality mandated by the Russian educational system, so too does the novel as a whole ridicule both the possibility of escaping the shtetl and the desirability of such an escape. Modernity in these terms no longer signifies a utopian promise of individual liberation but is instead another institution, another assemblage, that traps the protagonist and frustrates his efforts at self-determination. Although this theme receives its full development only after the devil makes his appearance in the novel, Yisrolik foreshadows this idea when he states, "Perhaps I'm in the hand of another power, which dwells in me, and I'm not the master of my own self, not someone who does everything according to his understanding or will, but this power rules over me and coerces me to do what he wants, so that I should do his bidding and live exactly as he did" (Y 39; E 565). To rebel against the unseen power dwelling within him, Yisrolik can only declare war against himself by abandoning his rationality; insanity, in this context, is a *revolt* against reason—in Yiddish, *seykhl*—and therefore, also *haskole*.

The object of this rebellion comes into focus when the devil makes his appearance in the novel, taking over from the mare, and implicitly Mendele as well, the task of externalizing Yisrolik's fractured consciousness. In the devil's monologue, both the diabolical nature of modernity, and its seamless connection with the *kahal*, the institutional Jewish community—which otherwise appears only implicitly in *Di Klyatshe*, in contrast to its central role in *Di Takse*—becomes explicit. Significantly, the mare herself introduces the demonic dimension of the narrative by offering a review of modern ethical philosophies to justify her rejection of the demands of the modern world, as represented by the *tsar baley-khayim*. As she says to Yisrolik:

> Of course, when the world begins to consider itself, that's when people start to speak about *humanism* . . . about mercy, about compassion; a little later, when the world begins slowly to become more practical, the fashion turns to *utilitarianism*, which means usefulness, the uses to which one can put other people. Only later, when the world receives both reason and fairness, and it better understands the ways of nature and all her creatures, can one begin to speak of *truth*, of *justice*. I don't want to hear any talk about mercy or about usefulness: mercy and usefulness can't sustain the world. I'm the equal of anyone . . . (Y 100–101; E 619–620)

Yisrolik's reaction is to attribute these remarks to the devil, and in the next chapter, the devil appears, taking over the remaining third of the novel. Fantasy thus becomes essential to the structure of the novel by establishing a logic of free association—mention the devil, and he appears through the power of suggestion.

The overall structure of the novel comes at last into focus with the appearance of the devil: in the first eight of the narrative's twenty-four chapters, the emphasis is primarily on Yisrolik as an individual and his failed attempt at matriculation; chapters 9–16 consist of a dialogue between the mare and Yisrolik, and Yisrolik's misguided efforts to engage the *tsar baley-khayim* in the mare's plight; chapters 17–24 are given over to the devil, who expands the perspective from the previous eight chapters' allegory of the mare as representative of the Jewish people to the modern world at large. Each of the three sections is precisely balanced against the other two, so that the novel as a whole develops as a sort of three-movement concerto, though one in which a different soloist dominates each movement.[23] Unlike *Dos Vintshfingerl* (or *L'aventure ambiguë*), this is not a narrative that divides in two; it employs a triadic structure that extends outward, like a gyre, placing the intellectual not as a mediator, on one or the other side of a divide, but at the center of a storm raging between, and thus connecting, tradition and modernity. To schematize this reconfigured relationship, Yisrolik over the course of *Di Klyatshe* comes to see these two polarities as the "superstructure" of Eastern European Jewish life, with the devil providing a cosmological base undergirding them both.

Indeed, it is only the devil, Ashmedai, who makes the connection between the *kahal* and imperial modernity explicit. Explaining his investment in the various institutions that drain the resources of the Jewish community, he asks Yisrolik, "What, then, are those beggars, those idlers? They're people, and a not inconsiderable number at that, who are unable to live otherwise, who would have no existence at all if it weren't for their foolishness. They perform deeds, employ tricks, do whatever they can in order to preserve these foolish customs among you. You *must* preserve their foolishness, because there exist among you such a group of fools; they, a pity, *must* make themselves foolish, because only in this way can they receive their daily bread, their meager comfort in life" (Y 107; E 625). Although Ashmedai appeals to Yisrolik's compassion toward the traditional shtetl, he does so because the traditional Jews who populate the shtetl are too benighted to know any better. The author still portrays the shtetl as an embodiment of human folly, but instead of attacking the irrationality and superstition of traditional Jewish life, he offers a rueful sympathy. The paradox of his "demonic" solidarity with the shtetl provides an ambiguous, dynamic expression of the author's new position—the more humanistic his view of the shtetl becomes, the more complete his ironic dismissal of it is. The closer he identifies with the Jews against the system that limits and oppresses them, the greater his philosophical distance from them becomes apparent. In these paradoxes, the emancipation of the writer from the strictures of both traditional authority and modern hegemony asserts itself.

In this sense, one must emphasize that Ashmedai takes credit for not only the folly of the shtetl but also the excesses of modern, industrial life. Indeed, he defines himself as unmistakably modern when he states, "I'm that person who paves the way to a new world, so that the old should continuallly become new" (Y 103; E 622). One feature of the devil's modernity, surely, is his cosmopolitanism. As Yisrolik describes the panorama that Ashmedai unveils for him, "And immediately I recognize before me whole companies of evil spirits, devils, and all sorts of demons and tormenters, among them magicians, jugglers, tricksters, fortune-tellers of all nations together with water-nymphs, witches, gypsy queens, card-readers of all faiths" (Y 113; E 630). David Roskies explains that this "ecumenical" witches' Sabbath is a later addition inserted at the turn of the century: "The final version, written during the first decade of the twentieth century, had Ashmedai extend his tour to include an apocalyptic landscape of industrial blight and military devastation."[24] Unlike the subsequent revisions of *Dos Vintshfingerl*, however, this later version of *Di Klyatshe* expands the scope of the 1873 original, but it does not alter the plot or revise the underlying rationale of the narrative. The "universality" of this Walpurgisnacht not only extends his parody beyond the confines of the Jewish tradition but also suggests that the "beyond," the cultures outside the Pale, is as demonic, as much in need of ridicule, as the Jewish tradition itself.

In fact, Abramovitsh is just getting warmed up with this inventory of evil spirits and black magicians—an inventory that, in its catholicity, underscores the fact that superstition and fantasy exist in every culture. This insight itself restores to the Jewish tradition an ironic equality with other cultures, including the Western tradition to which the Jewish intellectual was previously expected to elevate himself. As Ashmedai's monologue continues, he takes Yisrolik on a balloon tour of Europe; en route he takes credit for the technological apparatus of modernity:

Look now and you will see smokestacks. From them my thousands of factories spew smoke and manufacture cannons, guns, and every conceivable implement of death; factories that cater to every need; and also factories that make every product you don't need; factories to make devices and machines, to save human labor, to render professions obsolete and deprive workers of their jobs; factories to make every sort

of gadget to save time and shorten distances, and more often than not
to shorten people's lives in the bargain. . . . Simply stated, this is the
smoke of "civilization," as it's known by the likes of you. (Y 122; E 638)

Fully a half-century before Theodor Adorno and Max Horkheimer,
Abramovitsh articulates a dialectic of enlightenment—the same social, technological, and material circumstances that create modernity
and the individual's awareness of the world at large potentially sow the
seeds of civilization's destruction.

Aptly enough, as with the references to Cervantes and Lessing in
the prologue to the 1865 edition of *Dos Vintshfingerl*, Abramovitsh signals a crossing of the threshold between folklore and modernity in textual terms; as Wisse states, "In a thorough study of the demonological
sources of *The Mare*, Shmuel Werses has identified several Hebrew and
European works including Goethe's *Faust*. . . . A more immediate literary source . . . was the Yiddish adaptation that Abramovitsh and his
friend Bienstok had just published of Jules Verne's *Five Weeks in a Balloon*, in which representatives of British civilization observe the dark
continent of Africa from their delightful, precarious balloon-perch"
("The Jewish Intellectual and the Jews," 17). Abramovitsh had apparently translated Verne's adventure story for pedagogical reasons, to edu-
cate his readers about geography and world events through a popular
narrative about the European conquest of Africa. This same narrative,
however, now becomes an object of parody, as Abramovitsh reveals the
real "dark continent" to be Europe itself. The real barbarians are the
perpetrators of a modernity at once industrial and imperial, who have,
as Abramovitsh's allusion to Jules Verne suggests, disrupted and sub-
jected the cultures of Africa and the Pale of Settlement equally.

However implicit the anti-imperialist thrust of Abramovitsh's parody is, though, it is connected explicitly to a critique of the shtetl itself,
and as should be clear, the author's reversal of his previous valorization
of modernity never causes him to romanticize the tradition. Indeed,
Ashmedai seems to take greatest pride in the work of the *baley-toyves*,
the shtetl "philanthropists" who administer the *kahal*:

. . . [T]he kosher meat-tax is absolutely essential to my work. Because
of it a whole troop of *baley-toyves* have emerged to lead all of you by the

nose and leave you without a head on your shoulders. . . . Through the meat-tax you have the clearest sign that with all the expenses which go toward communal necessities you are irrevocably separated from all the other nations of the world; and because of that you will never be able to unite with other people in loyalty to the state, and in turn truly you will always give evil men the excuse to attack you, and your situation will always be hopeless and degraded. (Y 138–139; E 652)

This is in fact the central argument of *Di Takse*, for which *Di Klyatshe* was supposed to be the sequel. Here, though, the devil delivers the arguments that Veker, the maskil, had previously marshaled against the meat-tax. Does this align the devil with the *kahal*, as he claims, or with *haskole*? In fact, here Abramovitsh upends the hope he had expressed at the end of *Dos Kleyne mentshele*, echoed in the polemics of Zederbaum and Linetski, that the best of tradition might join hands with the best of modernity by standing the figure on its head: tradition and modernity have *always* worked together in the devil's foundry, conspiring as complementary hegemonies against the powerless and the deluded.

This paradox, of course, is an inevitable and deliberate consequence of satire as a genre. Satiric discourse emerges when the author refuses to say what he or she *means*—though the refusal to speak straightforwardly can seldom be resolved by interpreting the satiric statement as meaning the diametric opposite of its plain meaning.[25] The devil as a further instance of the "Mendele function" in Abramovitsh's writing therefore is neither a mouthpiece for maskilic critique nor a representation of the *kahal* itself, but a complicated superimposition of two worldviews onto a single, dialogical voice. Abramovitsh foregrounds this complexity when he connects the devil both to the modern institution of the press as an industry, and to the act of writing in general. Thus, Ashmedai describes for Yisrolik a "river of ink": "I created this river that you see, and the woods it runs through, especially for your brothers. As long as the river provides ink and the trees pens, there will be writers to write without rest. Look! From the inkwells flow canals. . . . That canal, number 999,999, which you're considering now, flows directly to the inkwells of the journalists in Dneprovits. I have ink and pens to fill the ocean, and as many writers as grains of sand on the shore!" (Y 137; E 651). The explicit object of Abramovitsh's satire here is the antisemitic press, then inspiring discrimination and pogroms throughout Europe. As such, this passage bears comparison with Kafka's "The Penal Colony," in the sense that writing itself is portrayed as a form of torture, with Yisrolik, the Jew who will bear the blows inspired by the press, as the victim.

At the same time, Abramovitsh implicates himself in this satire, for not only is he at risk of antisemitic abuse to the same extent as his protagonist, but he is also dependent on exactly the same materials as the antisemitic journalists he ridicules. As with "The Penal Colony," the torture that Abramovitsh imagines for Yisrolik becomes, inevitably and deliberately, self-reflexive. And with writing itself implicated as "the devil's work," it is fitting that the novel concludes with Yisrolik's mother, the *baal-shem* (the Hasidic faith-healer), and the Ukrainian folk-healer sitting together, lamenting the protagonist's condition, and condemning the stories that have clouded his mind: "Akh, those stories, those stories!" Yisrolik's mother complains; the *baal-shem* chimes in, "It all comes from them, from them, the evil spirits,[26] I mean." To which the Ukrainian woman adds, in untranslated Ukrainian, "He's right, he is. This is their doing. Goddamn their mothers!" (Y 151; E 663). *Di Klyatshe* concludes with a "minor" strategy that not only works against both Jewish and non-Jewish hegemonies but also places Abramovitsh's reader, as another consumer of the modern stories repudiated by these characters, in an ironically adversarial position to the novel's final speakers.

The last words of *Di Klyatshe* thus belong to the very people whom Abramovitsh in *Dos Vintshfingerl* had castigated as benighted and backward. This scene furthermore shows these characters in a posture of resistance, ultimately, to the forces of modernity and assimilation that have sickened Yisrolik. At the end of the novel, the reader can recognize—better than Yisrolik—an intimate, even surrogate, relationship between the mare and Yisrolik's mother. Each of them rejects, for herself and her son, the role of passive, anonymous beast of burden in the imperial system. In this regard, the mare is able to teach Yisrolik a lesson that his mother was unable to convey or articulate; fantasy has become a means not only of resisting modernity's imperative to be rational and the state's command to be useful, but also of negotiating the cultural and political gap between the generations that in ordinary reality had seemed insurmountable.

Wole Soyinka's 1965 novel *The Interpreters* bears comparison with *Di Klyatshe* not only as a semisatirical critique of the modern intellectual, but also because it shares with Abramovitsh's narrative the view that previous distinctions between tradition and modernity have collapsed. Indeed, the animating idea of this novel, the most devastating portrayal of newly independent Nigeria, is the premise that Nigeria is neither new nor independent; like Faulkner, Soyinka views the past as "not dead, not even past." Thus, the existential crises affecting the novel's multiple protagonists—a group of foreign-educated intellectuals who have returned to Nigeria to build the nation, to "interpret" modernity to their native society—become representative of the failure of the nation-state to create a productive, self-sufficient culture.

The use of a "collective protagonist" is a common strategy in the postcolonial novel for representing the emergence of a new national culture in its various regional and social manifestations.[27] In this regard, it is significant that Soyinka uses this technique to emphasize the *absence* of a unified national culture, the persistent fragmentation, of contemporary Nigeria. The various "late modernist" techniques that Soyinka employs in the novel, and that render a concise synopsis of its action futile,[28] therefore articulate in formal terms a critique of the Nigerian nation-state. The chaos and violence that characterizes the collapse of the African nation-state in the late 1960s is by no means a sealed-off episode in African history, nor is it confined merely to one continent. The multiple protagonists of *The Interpreters*—Sagoe, an alcoholic journalist; Egbo, a diplomatic functionary and heir to a Yoruba kingdom; Bandele, a university professor; Kola, an art instructor and frustrated painter; and Sekoni, an engineer and sculptor—nonetheless create a culturally and historically specific composite portrait of contemporary Nigeria. Rather than showing a single intellectual isolated from human contact, *The Interpreters* depicts a cadre of intellectuals trapped in a net of human entanglements and drowning in a sea of corruption.

Indeed, at precisely the same moment that Soyinka publishes *The Interpreters*, the collapse of Nigeria's First Republic occurs, culminating in the military coup of January 15, 1966. Conducted by the so-called five majors in response to the violent elections of 1964–1965, this coup was an attempt to stamp out "'tribalism, nepotism, and regionalism' and fight the enemies of progress— . . . homosexuals, feudal lords and so on."[29] *The Interpreters* poses an alternate reality to Nigeria's political fate; Soyinka's "interpreters" serve as a mirror to the military cabal then overtaking the nation. It is therefore significant that, like the military conspirators, Soyinka's novel is similarly preoccupied, as are virtually all African novels of the late 60s, with tribalism, nepotism, and regional-ism—but also with feudal lords and, most remarkably, homosexuality. In this respect, the ambiguous character of the American homosexual Joe Golder is significant. Both insider and outsider, predator and vic-tim, destroyer and creator, he is a reflection of the ambiguities of the interpreters themselves, and a stranger even in their alienated circles. But as much as the other characters in the novel, like the coup leaders of 1966, wish to see Golder and the phenomenon he represents (per-haps singularly in African literature of the time) as irrevocably "other," Golder himself resists their efforts to marginalize him: "Do you think I know nothing of your Emirs and their little boys? You forget history is my subject. And what about those exclusive coteries in Lagos?"[30] If anything, Soyinka is making a response in advance to the military's ho-mophobia: homosexuality is neither foreign, nor uniquely modern.

Despite the fact that Soyinka in this novel stresses the continuity be-tween tradition and modernity, the paradoxical oldness of independent Nigeria, he willfully begins the narrative with the shock of the new: "'Metal on concrete jars my drink lobes.' This was Sagoe, grumbling as he stuck fingers in his ears against the mad screech of iron tables. Then his neck was nearly snapped as Dehinwa leapt up and Sagoe's head dan-gled in the void where her lap had been. Bandele's arms never ceased to surprise. At half-span they embraced table and chairs, pushed them deep into the main wall as dancers dodged long chameleon tongues of the cloudburst and the wind leapt at them, visibly malevolent" (*The Interpreters*, 7). The first image of Africa in the novel juxtaposes metal with concrete—an artificial, manufactured image—conflicting with and giving way to the force of nature, the thunderstorm. The scene signifies how precarious urbanization and modernity are in Nigeria, and how dehumanizing their effects are. Sagoe's perspective is skewed both by his quasi-Tutuolan English ("drink lobes") and his position, viewing the chaos from his girlfriend Dehinwa's lap. In personal terms, the dynamics of the situation reinforces the disorientation of the first sentence; Dehinwa, the modern Nigerian woman, abandons Sagoe, rejecting the roles of lover and mother, while Bendele embraces not a dance partner but furniture, as the "movable feast" of the dancehall rushes to escape the punitive fury of the storm.

One may note in this context that both the main narrative of *Di Kly-atshe* and *The Interpreters* open with intimations of a Flood. In schematic terms, though, Abramovitsh's flood is archetypal and metaphorical, whereas Soyinka's is at once apocalyptic and visceral. Moreover, the symbolic trajectories of these two floods diverge into separate sets of association: for Abramovitsh, the Flood foreshadows Yisrolik's connection, like Noah, with the animal kingdom. For Soyinka, the downpour introduces water as the central image in the novel. Indeed, without transition the scene of the nightclub deluge gives way to a flashback in which Egbo returns to the sight of his parents' drowning: "Two paddles clove the still water of the creek, and the canoe trailed behind it a silent groove, between gnarled tears of mangrove; it was dead air, and they came to a spot where an old rusted cannon showed above the water" (*The Interpreters*, 8). Already, the association of the thunderstorm and the creek invest the opening chapter with cosmological, mythological, historical, and psychological resonances. Water signifies the cyclical exchange between heaven and earth, life and death. Water, similarly, is the possession of the Yoruba god Oshun, making the protagonists of *The Interpreters*, like characters in a classical drama, pawns in a game played by the deities. The submerged cannon, as well, connects Egbo to an emblem of Yoruba aristocracy and colonial domination over Nigeria.[31] Finally, the water of the creek serves as a metaphor for the depths of Egbo's anguish and guilt over his parents' death, his conflicted inheritance of their legacy, and the trauma of his interrupted childhood.

At the same time as the nightclub thunderstorm and the visit to the watery grave of Egbo's parents institute a set of circular associations that dominate the novel as a whole, Sagoe's coinage of the term "drink lobes"—itself an image of fluidity—analogously creates a series of linguistic associations covering a spectrum from literary English to Pidgin to occasional phrases of untranslated Yoruba. As Kwame Appiah writes of Soyinka's heteroglossic prose, "Though he writes in a European language, Soyinka is not writing, cannot be writing, with the purposes of English writers of the present. . . . For there is a profound difference between the projects of European and African writers: a difference I shall summarize . . . as the difference between the search for the self and the search for a culture."[32] The diversity of speech habits among the characters in the novel serves to illustrate the range of social types that populate Nigeria, as well as their ambivalent relationship to modernity itself, signified by the mastery of Standard English.

Moreover, the novel's deterritorialization of English can even reflect the unstable status of a single character over the course of the narrative. Thus James Omole describes a scene in which Chief Winsala, one of the corpulent old men who represent the corruption of the First Nigerian Republic, is caught trying to skip out on a bar tab and must rely on Sagoe to bail him out: "Ironically, before this showdown, Winsala has been addressing and threatening the waiter in English. . . . However, the moment he perceives imminent disgrace, he talks quietly to himself in his humble native language, abandoning the language of authority."[33] In fact, the Chief's code-switching serves to underscore the ambiguity of his role as a figure simultaneously modern and traditional, an "urban intellectual"—the member of the editorial board of a newspaper—and a relic of Yorubaland's faded, diminished, corrupted aristocracy. When he speaks English he reflects the contemptuous values of the interpreters at their worst; when he switches to Pidgin, he exposes himself, linguistically and culturally, as a victim of modernity unable to finesse the transition from one hierarchy to another.

A similar gap between languages, social hierarchies, and generations opens up in the second chapter when Dehinwa returns to her apartment with the drunken Sagoe, only to find that her mother and aunt have arrived there from the country. With considerable outrage, Dehinwa's mother says, "Tell me Dehinwa, are good-looking, decent men so hard to find that you must go with a *Gambari*? Don't you know what your name is that you even let yourself be seen with a *Gambari*?" (*The Interpreters*, 37). The untranslated term *Gambari*, a derogatory reference to a Northerner, or a Hausa, points to the resistance to nationalism among the older generation, and further reinforces the burden of the past on the Nigerian present. Such tribalism is at odds with both

Tutuola's seemingly apolitical fantasy and negritude's pan-national romanticism; this exchange thus signifies the failures of African nationalism, the stillborn character of the African nation-state, in a conversation between women of different generations, over the putative father of an as yet *unconceived* child!

Furthermore, Omole emphasizes that this conflict represents not only the ethnic tensions that would soon lead to catastrophic civil war in Nigeria—even though, as it turns out, Sagoe and Dehinwa are both Yoruba—but also the class conflict that would ignite the conflagration: "In spite of all the traditionally persuasive expressions used to convince her, Dehinwa never uses any Yoruba words in her discussion with her mother. Informal and familiar as the situation ought to be, she spoke to her mother in the language of her class throughout" (*The Language of African Literature*, 68). Significantly, this conflict is figured not only generationally, but also linguistically. Soyinka in fact shares this technique with the early *haskole* dramatists, who used Yiddish and German to represent old and young, respectively, and later Yiddish writers such as Sholem Aleichem, who used Yiddish and Russian to the same effect. In each instance, linguistic assimilation serves as a synecdoche for modernization. For Soyinka, this linguistic strategy points to the fundamentally dramatic conception of the narrative, in which a culture finds itself between languages and when literary expression derives from an essentially dramatic, performed conception of language. As such, *The Interpreters*, in spite of its sophisticated pastiche of modernistic techniques, retains an integral connection with performance and oral narrative.

In fact, *The Interpreters*, so unjustly overlooked by most Soyinka commentators in favor of his plays, bears many signs of a dramatist's hand: the protagonists spend much of their time not only together as a group, but in public, social settings—the nightclub, the cocktail party, the formal luncheon or reception—performing before an audience against which they define themselves. Sagoe's antics in particular have a self-conscious, staged quality, as he sets out to play the fool, thus demasking the various corrupt figures of authority with whom he collides. The aspiring prophet Lazarus speaks in sermons or oracles more than in dialogue, and Joe Golder performs monologues in which he advertises his emotional extravagances rather than interacting with other people. Despite the diversity of rhetorical practices, Soyinka's expert use of free indirect discourse subsumes these performances within a larger narrating consciousness so that the set pieces never undermine the overarching narrative structure, and the monological voices never dislodge from the connective fabric of the novel as a whole. Nonetheless, these effects suggest a persistent attraction to the dramatic mode in literatures, such as African or Yiddish literature, that emerge from essentially oral cultures.

To return to the specific drama, or soap opera, of Dehinwa's exchange with her mother, one observes that in addition to the linguistic and generational gaps that Omole notes, Soyinka also uses the geographical differentiation of city and country to depict the fragmentation of contemporary Nigeria. Similarly, when Egbo contemplates the Yoruba kingship to which he is heir, and which his parents had already rejected in favor of Christianity and modernity a generation previously—a decision that contrasts diametrically with the choices Samba Diallo's father, the Knight, had made in *L'aventure ambiguë*—Soyinka describes the royal domain by writing, "The specter of generations rose now above him and Egbo found he would always shrink, although incessantly drawn to the pattern of the dead. And this, waiting near the end of the journey, hesitating on the brink, wincing as he admitted it—was it not exhumation of a better forgotten past?" (*The Interpreters*, 11). The grandfather's kingdom thus resembles the maskilic representations of the shtetl: outside time, cut off from history, and equated with death, as opposed to the dynamic, teeming, overwhelming life of the outside world.

But if Soyinka in these instances sets up a contrast between the immobile, "dead" past of traditional hierarchies and the dynamic, "living" present of the modern city, the contrast itself is by no means static; Soyinka furthermore resists the temptation, the original sin on which nationalism is premised, to impose a reconciliation on these disparities artificially or by fiat. Instead, the novel allows these irreconcilable differences to correspond with one another as a series of thematic, psychic, and metaphysical tensions around which the narrative as a whole is structured. In the author's critical writing, these philosophical tensions are subsumed conceptually within "the chthonic realm"—"the transitional yet inchoate matrix of death and becoming."[34] In the chthonic realm, the contradictions of life and death, which cannot be reconciled in ordinary consciousness, are transcended in a state of perpetual becoming, transformation, and metamorphosis. The chthonic realm, indeed, provides a utopian, metaphysical analogy to the structural principle of the assemblage: like the assemblage, the chthonic realm replaces linear chronology with a circular proliferation of connections, continuities, and returns.

As in James Joyce's *The Dead*, where faintly falling snow, which itself connects associatively with Gabriel Conroy's thickly falling tears, covers both the living and the dead as a metaphor for "chthonic" transcendence, so too in Soyinka's more tropically situated novel, water serves to represent the chthonic realm. Thus in the first chapter, after the high life band flees the nightclub to escape the downpour, it is replaced by an itinerant *apala* band; the thunderstorm washes away the veneer of modernity so that the tradition, otherwise dispossessed and impoverished, can reclaim its space. But it is necessary to stress here that both the modern high life band and the traditional *apala* band, like Reb Nakhman and the maskilim of Uman,[35] share the *same* space. This regrouping of the tradition after the collapse of the city's "sham modernity" parallels the "return of the repressed," the folk traditions and faith healers, of *Di Klyatshe*. In metaphorical terms, the *apala* musicians move in when the high life band leaves because they recognize the chthonic realm for what it is, and are prepared to live in it, whereas the modern world tries continually to deny its existence and escape its effects.

Moreover, with the *apala* band comes a figure, an overweight woman dancing to the traditional music in the rain, who serves both as an embodiment of the chthonic water imagery of the first chapter and as a projection of this cosmology into the lives of the novel's characters and onto the body of a woman: "She had no partner, being wholly self-sufficient. She was immense. She would stand out anywhere, dominating. She filled the floor with her body, dismissing her surroundings with a natural air of superfluity. And she moved slowly, intensely, wrapped in the song and the rhythm of the rain" (*The Interpreters*, 22). This woman quickly becomes an object of fascination for the interpreters, an archetype that evokes "a river swollen on fresh yam hillocks" (*The Interpreters*, 24). At the same time, the woman in the rain connects inversely with another water-woman in the novel, Egbo's girlfriend Simi. As Soyinka narrates the moment when Simi and Egbo first meet, "she has the eyes of a fish, Egbo murmured, and the boys said, Oh, the creek man has found his Mammy Watta" (*The Interpreters*, 52).

The figure with whom Simi is compared, Mami Wata, is indeed a singularly contemporary African deity. As Henry John Drewal writes, "Mami Wata, Pidgin English for 'Mother of Water,' refers to an African water spirit whom Africans regard as foreign in origin. Africans use the pidgin term to acknowledge the spirit's otherness as well as to indicate its incorporation into the African world. The term mediates between Africans and those from overseas and represents Africans' attempts at understanding or constituting meaning from their encounters with overseas strangers."[36] Mami Wata, like Joe Golder, is a figure that connects Africa, however paradoxically, to the outside world; Mami Wata is a consciously imported figure in contemporary African mythology, a specifically African emblem of foreignness that signifies Africa by being *not African*.

Mami Wata, then, is like the characters of the novel, another "interpreter"—hers is a mythology and cosmology for the modern, mobile, materialist Africa—and as such she complements the traditional Yoruba frame of reference, represented by the *apala* band, the dancing woman, and the pantheon of Kola's painting (from which Mami Wata is, of course, excluded), making the monological discourse of authority plural, heteroglossic, contested. Simi's identification with water, and thus with Mami Wata, connects her with the mobility, transience, and potential for transformation that mythologize modernity itself. As such, Simi is the new, urban African woman, and this identity connects her to a series of characters in African literature of the 1950s and 60s[37] who personify the transformation of Africa from a "motherland" to an unfamiliarly alluring and threatening new culture—a culture that is attractive and repellent at the same time.

The first chapter of *The Interpreters* therefore initiates a series of motifs that represent Egbo's ambivalence toward the legacy of his past and the choices that determine his future. At the same time, and this is characteristic of Soyinka's virtuosity, the thunderstorm signifies for the doomed figure Sekoni another set of associations that include his return to Nigeria from England, via boat, and the catastrophe of the power dam project that he undertakes upon his arrival home:

> Once he sat on a tall water spout high above the tallest trees and beyond low clouds. Across his sight in endless mammoth rolls, columns of rock, petrifications of divine droppings from eternity. If the mountain won't come . . . then let us to the mountains now, in the name of Mohammed. . . . And the logic of nature's growth was bettered by the cabalistic equations of the sprouting derrick, chaos of snakes and other forest threads by parallels of railtracks, road extravagances and a nervous electronic core. Sekoni rushed down the gangway, sought the hand of kindred spirits for the flare of electricity, but it slipped with grease and pointed to his desk. "I'm here. Let me know if there is anything else you need. That is a bell for the messenger". . . . "Bicycle advance . . . let me see now, that should be File C/S 429. I'll check among the B.U.s in the S.M.E.K.'s office. (*The Interpreters*, 26–27)

Sekoni's "maskilic" dream of modernity—bringing electrical power to the new nation, taming its wilderness, elevating civilization above nature's "chaos"—gives way, like Yisrolik's educational ambitions, to the reality of office bureaucracy, petty corruption, and the alienation of the worker from his or her labor. If Egbo is therefore an emblem of the past that refuses to die, Sekoni represents the future unable to be born. Both are thus tragic figures, redeemed by the circularity and cosmological continuity of water itself. If *L'aventure ambiguë* is a tragedy for its African characters and a comedy for its French ones, *The Interpreters* is by curious analogy a tragedy for its human characters and a comedy for the cosmological powers that undergird it. Like Wallace Stevens in "The Auroras of Autumn," Soyinka writes here of "An unhappy people in a happy world."

Moreover, Soyinka uses this cosmological perspective to suggest a critique of the personal limitations of his protagonists, as well as the myth of modernity they would ostensibly embrace. This is especially true of Sekoni, who in many respects is the most attractive character in the novel. As Mark Kinkead-Weekes writes, "[I]f we really look at Sekoni's dream, are there not several worrying features? The godlike power is to be exercised by the individual with suspicious ease, and in a world in which human beings are conspicuously absent. . . . Is it an accident that Soyinka makes him short-sighted, eventually fatally so?"[38] In this context, one can begin to differentiate the use to which Soyinka puts the polyphonic discourse of the novel from the more consciously ritualistic character of his dramas; Soyinka here uses the heteroglossia inherent in the novel form to ironize characters that would, at least in a tragic context, be sacralized in drama.

It is precisely as a heteroglossic and satirizing presence—as well as a vocal critic of the ideologies of African modernity—that Soyinka employs Sagoe. Indeed, his coinage of the term "drink lobes" is part of a quasi-nativist parodic ideology that seems explicitly to attack negritude; when riding home from the nightclub with Dehinwa in the second chapter, he complains of her driving, "You are jarring my drink lobes. . . . I should have stuck to beer. Those whiskies burnt out all my negritude" (The Interpreters, 34). Just as Sagoe here ridicules negritude explicitly, he implicitly invokes the philosophy elsewhere in his "Book of Voidancy," which along with "drink lobes," counts as the most noteworthy neologism in the novel. This book, a journal of his most memorable trips to the toilet, makes literal the negritude rhetoric of Africa's proximity to the earth, nature, and the body: "And silence is to the Voidante as the fumes of opium are to the mystics of the Orient. The silence of the lavatory in an English suburban house when the household and the neighbours have departed to their daily toil, and the guest voidates alone. That is a silence you can touch. In France, of course, the myth of sophistication is nothing but shallow and awkward posturing. . . . There I sought the fumes of silence in vain, till in the end, to escape the soul-debasing state of the hostel lavatories I would retire with a book and shovel into the nearby woods" (The Interpreters, 96).

Like Senghor and Cesaire, Sagoe creates his philosophy of "Voidancy" in Europe, and indeed, when resorting to his book-and-shovel retreats in France, he evokes through "Voidancy" negritude's idyllic aspirations:

> [H]ere I founded a little arbour where I contemplated regularly, read or merely listened to the descant of Gallic birds. It was, I confess, cramped Voidancy. . . . Worse still, the feel of a sudden wet blade of grass in the midst of my devotion made me leap in fear that a snake was trying to lick my balls. But the wet, heavy, bird-interpolated si-

lence was a mystical experience, it made the risk of emasculation a minor thing. And now, my friends, I must tell you a shameful episode. Two hiking students followed me one day, curious to find where the daily combination of book and shovel led. . . . Against their vision of virginal nature and arborial voidatory, my warnings of the snake menace proved ineffectual. It was gratifying to sow the seeds of Voidancy on the continent of Europe, but in a way, it was a small defeat, for I was powerless against their damned regression. (*The Interpreters*, 96–97)

Sagoe in the French woods becomes Adam in a solitary Garden of Eden, complete with an imaginary but menacing serpent. Voidancy, though a parody of artistic creation, nonetheless entails a form of creativity—and as such is as imprisoned by the expectations of its European audience as any other African "cultural production"! These images of an African Adam trapped by European modernity resurface at the end of the novel's first part, when the interpreters gather at a pretentious cocktail party hosted by an absurdly Europeanized couple, the Oguazors. At this party, Sagoe lights upon a fruit bowl, exclaiming, "To hell with patriotism, Bandele, there is no fruit in the world to beat the European apple" (*The Interpreters*, 140). Sagoe's disillusionment with this archetypally forbidden fruit is instantaneous, however, when he discovers that it, like everything else at the party, is a plastic imitation. "What on earth," he states, "does anyone in the country want with plastic fruits. . . . I feel let loose in the Petrified Forest. . . . Have they petrified brains to match?" (*The Interpreters*, 140). Sagoe's clowning thus grows out of a romantic impulse; he would like to be in paradise, but modernity *always* intervenes.

However comic Sagoe's philosophical horseplay is, therefore, he is at the same time able to offer a serious critique of contemporary Africa, and to participate in the same cosmic drama as the rest of the interpreters. For example, the "Voidancy" philosophy gives Sagoe this insight into modern Nigeria:

Next to death . . . shit is the most vernacular atmosphere of our beloved country. It was hardly a month since Mathias gave him some news he could hardly credit. . . . Mathias had passed the sight coming to work in the morning as his bus made a sudden, near disastrous

swerve to avoid the spot. Round the corner of the Renascent High
School it lay, some yards from the first bus stop entering Abule Ije-
sha. . . . Over twenty yards were spread huge pottage mounds, twenty
yards of solid and running, plebian and politician, indigenous and foreign shit. (*The Interpreters*, 108)

One should note that the seemingly naturalistic location of the monstrous pile of excrement around the corner from the Renascent High
School is a detail that at once offers a scatological assessment of the
Nigerian educational system, and alludes to the same chthonic process
that preoccupies Egbo and Sekoni.

Indeed, one can contrast Sagoe's credo—"in release is birth" (*The
Interpreters*, 71)—with Egbo's complaint against Kola's painting of the
Yoruba pantheon: "I cannot accept this view of life. He has made the
beginning itself a resurrection. This is an optimist's delusion of continuity" (*The Interpreters*, 233). Sagoe's philosophy of Voidancy, though
clearly parodic of modern ideology generally and negritude specifically, nonetheless connects on a deeper analogical level to the cyclical
correspondence among life, death, and rebirth that recurs throughout
the novel, on all levels of association. If Voidancy does not provide the
reader with a valid philosophy of living, it may nonetheless offer instructive clues toward a philosophy of reading this novel.

In order to understand the chthonic implications of Sagoe's Voidante
philosophy as it relates to the development of the novel as a whole, it is
worth considering the overall structure of the narrative, and the systematic correspondences—parallels and inversions—between its characters.
There is thus a deliberate proximity between Egbo's reflections on the
connections between past and present and the distillation of Sekoni's
thoughts on the same subject. Soyinka describes Egbo's fantasy of returning to his grandfather's realm as an

illicit pleasure at the thought that a kingdom awaited him whenever
he wanted it. . . . And this was not now a question of conscience but
the progress of wisdom, and for a man himself, merely a question of
drowning . . . like the darkness of the grove and then . . . the water
of the suspension bridge, seeing for a fleeting moment water indeed
suspended, a bridge of clear water suspensions. And he only plunged

again into the ancient, psychic life of still sediment, muttering, how
long will the jealous dead remain among us! (*The Interpreters*, 120)

Egbo's kingdom becomes here the kingdom of the afterlife, where he
experiences death and rebirth at the same time. This kingdom therefore seems to derive from a traditional Yoruba conception of the afterlife, *orun*, as a "cool watery environment beneath the sea . . . going
to the home of the God of the Sea (Olokun) is the same as going to
orun."[39] Sekoni articulates an inverse ontology, his speech impediment
notwithstanding: "In the dddome of the cosmos, th-there is complete
unity of Lllife. Llife is like the g-g-godhead, the p-p-plurality of its
mmmanifestations is only an illusion. Th-the g-g-godhead is one. So
is life, or d-d-death, b-b-both are c-c-contained in the . . . d-d-dome of
ex . . . istence" (*The Interpreters*, 122).

For Egbo, however, it is precisely the isolation of his inherited kingdom that appeals to him; the idea of a dome of existence linking the living and the dead, the present and the past, terrifies and immobilizes him:
"Egbo cried, 'Is it so impossible to seal off the past and let it alone? Let
it stay in its harmless anachronistic unit so we can dip into it at will and
leave it without commitment, without impositions!'" (*The Interpreters*,
121). It is in this moment of existential panic that Egbo's philosophical
ambivalence begins to resemble Sagoe's, and the dichotomy between
the sacred and the secular begins to break down. For Egbo's burden of
the past contrasts with a similarly fraught relationship that Sagoe maintains with the ghost of his employer, Sir Derinola. As Soyinka describes
Sagoe's encounter with this ghost, in Dehinwa's bedroom, "The wind
and the weight of Dehinwa's dressing-gown won in the end. The hat-
box stayed in place but the wardrobe door pressed outwards, very very
slowly, and the good knight himself came out, naked except for a pair
of Dehinwa's brassieres over his chest. Sagoe felt suddenly very prudish
and he outbawled the rain. 'Sir Derin, what do you want? You look in-
decent!'" (*The Interpreters*, 64). As with the "Book of Voidancy," Sagoe's
carnivalistic fantasy here serves to render the rhetoric of a monological
philosophy *literal*—in this instance, he turns the idea of a past that refuses to die into an absurd and obscene joke.

As with all of Sagoe's jokes, however, there is much serious psychic and philosophical work being conducted in this scene. Indeed, Sir Derinola compares with Egbo's grandfather in the sense that each of these old men stands as a surrogate father for the two interpreters. It is therefore significant for both of these surrogate relationships that Sagoe performs a "double castration" on his dead employer, first by imagining him clothed in nothing but a brassiere, second by replacing his penis—as Sir Derinola states in the subsequent paragraph—with a graveyard worm. The worm in particular is a carnival image, conveying the superimposition of the charnel on the carnal, thereby suggesting parasitism, impotence, and death *without* rebirth. The dialogue between these two characters resembles the phantasmagoria of the "Circe" episode in Joyce's *Ulysses*, as well as the conversations of the protagonist with his murdered father in Shakespeare's *Hamlet*, a point of reference *The Interpreters* shares with *Ulysses*.

Phantasmagoria is not the only characteristic that *The Interpreters* shares with *Ulysses*, and without arguing for a specific derivation of Soyinka's novel from Joyce's, anymore than Joyce's novel derives specifically from *Hamlet*, considering their similarities helps clarify Soyinka's relationship to Modernism in general.[40] Even if *Ulysses* is not a conscious model for Soyinka's novel, the analogy is helpful in one crucial respect: both novels describe urban, modernist trajectories in mock-epic terms that are dependent on an epic subtext—for Joyce, the *Odyssey*, for Soyinka, the Yoruba pantheon—for their coherence and narrative force.[41] It is worth noting, moreover, that Soyinka succeeded in writing the perfect (Anglophone) Yoruba tragedy, *Death and the King's Horseman*,[42] only after he completed an adaptation of Euripides' *The Bacchae*.[43] It is therefore essential to a proper understanding of his creativity to examine the plurality of his inspirations, his location in cosmopolitan modernity as well as local traditions.

When such an examination is undertaken critically, it becomes clear that although an epic subtext connects *The Interpreters* to *Ulysses*, and therefore to High Modernism in general, Soyinka's use of ritual and sacrifice as complementary motifs to myth differentiates his writing from European Modernism and indicates how far indeed postcolonial literature, at least in Africa, is from the aesthetic and metaphysical assumptions of a contemporaneous metropolitan postmodernism. It is with this in mind that one should consider Soyinka's description of Kola's nearly completed pantheon:

> And of these floods of the beginning, of the fevered fogs of the begin-
> ning, of the first messenger, the thimble of earth, a fowl and an ear of
> corn, seeking the spot where a scratch would become a peopled island;
> of the first apostate rolling the boulder down the back of the unsus-
> pecting deity . . . and shattering him in fragments, which were picked
> up and pieced together with devotion; shell of the tortoise around
> divine breath; of the endless chain for the summons of the god and the
> phallus of unorigin pointed at the sky-hole past divination; of the lover
> of purity, the unblemished one whose large compassion embraced the
> cripples and the dumb, the dwarf, the epileptic—and why not, indeed,
> for they were creations of his drunken hand and what does it avail,
> the eternal penance of favoritism and abstinence? (*The Interpreters*,
> 224–225)

One notes again the Joycean mix of alliteration and repetition—"floods of the beginning," "the fevered fogs of the beginning"—in this passage, which simultaneously provides an account of the Yoruba myth(s) of creation and a representation of Kola's own artistic creativity. This parallel between artistic creation and cosmic origins is a quintessential Modernist device that represents the transubstantiation of religious mythology in the work of art.

But precisely at this point Kola's painting fails to meet the Modernist expectations for Modernist art. For not only is his pantheon *not* a displacement or substitute for a fallen mythology—as Kola himself admits, "You must know by now that I am not really an artist" (*The Interpreters*, 227)—but the religious tradition reasserts itself in the consecration of Kola's painting when Egbo brings a black ram to sacrifice at the opening of Kola's exhibition. This sacrifice threatens to overwhelm the power of Kola's painting for the interpreters, in turn violating the decorum of the art show for the other patrons, but it serves as an expiation and a reminder of Egbo's previous "sacrifice," his seduction and impregnation of an unnamed virgin. More generally, Kola's artistic efforts cannot take the place of sacrifice because his painting, unlike that of European artists, is situated in a society where religious sacrifices are performed every day; modern artists such as Kola cannot occupy the space once held by traditional religion, because the traditional religion has yet to vacate that space. Unlike the cultures of the metropolis, postcolonial Africa remains a society in which modernity and tradition continue to compete with and inform one another in intimate contact.

Soyinka both acknowledges and ironizes this point in his own critical writing when he begins the lectures collected as *Myth, Literature, and the African World* by stating, "I shall begin by commemorating the gods for their self-sacrifice on the altar of literature" (1). In his novel, by contrast, the gods refuse to sacrifice themselves on the altar of modern art, either because the artist in question, Kola, lacks the necessary mastery to command this sacrifice, or because in modern Nigeria, unlike the halls of Cambridge University where Soyinka delivered his talks on African literature—significantly, in the Department of Social Anthropology—the gods continue to exert their authority too profoundly to be neutralized by aesthetics. In this respect, the tradition participates in the formulation of what modernity is in modern Nigeria, just as the modern art of its constituent cultures derives its meaning from the rituals and metaphysical assumptions of these traditions. As a general principle, neither Yoruba nor Yiddish art can be fully secular, cosmopolitan, or assimilated. And just as Soyinka here focuses on the crises affecting modern intellectuals in Africa, so could another novelist—such as Kourouma in *Les Soleils des indépendances*, as will soon be demonstrated—focus with equal intensity on the trauma affecting still-traditional Africans who continue to practice the rituals of the native religions.

With native religions thus participating in the creation of African modernity, *The Interpreters* resembles a "late modernist" novel most closely in that it reflects the failure of modernity to supplant the tradition. As much as Egbo evokes the presence of Ogun—"the explorer, warrior, creative god" (*The Interpreters*, 259)—he ultimately cannot *be* Ogun,[44] anymore than Yisrolik can serve as a modern Moses leading the mares and Jews of Eastern Europe to their redemption. There is therefore a tragic disparity between the mythical ideal and fallible, human reality. This is a gap that can only be bridged by sacrifice,[45] but "sacrifices" in the modern, corrupt, and degraded world of the novel are either never forthcoming or, with the exception of Egbo's ram, fail to serve their intended function. It should furthermore be considered that most of Soyinka's justly celebrated polemical remarks regarding Ogun as a model for the creative artist pertain explicitly to drama and its relationship with ritual; Soyinka's essay "The Fourth Stage"[46] refers to a theatrical space as much as a cosmological one. The significance of Ogun as a theological role model is thus deliberately attenuated in a narrative that lacks a sacrificial component and cannot function as a ritual. *The Interpreters* is a novel about performance, ritual, and religion, but it is narrated from the modern, secular perspective of free indirect discourse, and this technique is the fundamental distinction between Soyinka's prose and his dramas.

It is with a sense of the failure of sacrifice in this novel—as opposed to its centrality in Soyinka's conception of tragedy—that one should approach its central "sacrificial" incident, which occurs at the beginning of the second part: "The rains of May become in July slit arteries of the sacrificial bull, a million bleeding punctures of the sky-bull hidden in convulsive cloud humps, black, overfed for this one event, nourished on horizon tops of endless choice grazing, distant beyond giraffe reach" (*The Interpreters*, 155). This passage thus connects the water imagery that structures the novel with the blood flowing from sacrifice, thereby connecting the organic with the inorganic, the lower realm of earth with the upper realm of heaven, nature with ritual, the physical with the metaphysical. These connective contrasts in turn make explicit the purpose of the book's water imagery, which is to illustrate the *fluidity* of existence, the cyclical progression of birth, death, and rebirth. In this passage the novel's metaphysics are conveyed in the style of an oracle—hence the rains *become*, in the continuous tense of prophecy or epic, rather than *became*, the tense of modern, realist narrative. This visionary intonation renders all the more poignant the revelation that the sacrificial bull invoked in this passage is none other than the novel's own metaphysician, Sekoni, killed in a traffic accident; the bathetic contrast between tragic divination and everyday misfortune parallels the sensory disorientation at the start of the novel, restating the same sense of loss and confusion in a rhetoric that undermines the sequestration of elevated, religious discourse from the degraded naturalism of urban catastrophe.

Once again, even Sagoe's characteristically parodic reaction both satirizes and underscores the philosophical implications of the main narrative action. In this instance, he retreats, grief-stricken, from the news of Sekoni's death to "beer and vomit" and his "Book of Voidancy," from which he obligates Dehinwa to recite: " . . . I remember at this period of my childhood, and the door of our huge sprawling guaranteed eternal dug-out, a portrait in colour of a pair of supra-human beings, ethereal, other-existential in crown and jewels, in wide fur-borders, gold, velvet, and ermine, with orbs and sceptres and behind them, golden thrones. . . . [I]n my child's eye, these two figures could be no less than angels, or God and his wife. . . . [I]t became an obsession with me, the limitations on this delicate, unreal pair. Did they, or didn't they? . . . In one session of a purely Voidante nature, I realised finally the attitudinal division within this human function" (*The Interpreters*, 155–156). The "Book of Voidancy" here again parallels the action of the novel; his speculation over whether or not the Windsor monarchs use the bathroom reinscribes in colonial terms the metaphysical disparity between high and low, between noble language and sordid, mundane reality.

Since it is the metaphysical purpose of carnival, parody, and satire to traverse the boundaries of high and low, it is important to consider Sagoe's role in the narrative when evaluating the at times "oracular" manner in which the novel's structure, and particularly the relationship between its two parts, can be understood. In fact, as Sekoni would argue, there is a dome of continuity connecting the two parts. In this light, mythical implications are present from the very beginning, and are implicit in the thunderstorm at the beginning of Part One, just as they are in the floods of Part Two, but at no point in the novel do these resonances coalesce as a final, monological voice of authority for the narrative.

Moreover, just as tragedy is not the uncontested mode of the second part, so too is even Sekoni's death not left as a definitive metaphysical condition. It is in this context that one can understand the continuity between Sekoni's death and the introduction of Lazarus, the charismatic preacher and albino who claims to have risen from the dead: "I fall dead in the streets of a strange village. The kind people bury me the following day, only, as they are lowering the coffin into the grave, I wake up and begin to knock on the lid. . . . I do not know what I was before I died, or where I came from, but what really frightened the villagers is that before they put me in the coffin, I was like you, like all your friends, black. When I woke up, I have become like this" (*The Interpreters*, 160–161). Just as Sekoni leaves the stage—to invoke theater as a metaphor, *not* a formal designation—Lazarus enters, thereby connecting Sekoni's sacrifice with rebirth and resurrection, and making manifest Sekoni's meditations on the dome of existence that subsumes both birth and death into a single existential condition. In this respect, it is important to emphasize that Sekoni is the novel's one observant Muslim, and Lazarus the most sincere Christian; both "world religions" thus become subsumed within Soyinka's own interpretation of Yoruba metaphysics.

Moreover, Lazarus not only is representative of a reconfigured, African Christianity but also is the most fully developed "organic intellectual" in a novel about foreign-educated, "institutional intellectuals." As such, his voice stands as a rejoinder—much like the *baal-shem*, the folk-healer, and Yisrolik's mother at the end of *Di Klyatshe*—to the modernity of the novel's protagonists. In this respect, Lazarus's preaching style exemplifies the power of "ordinary" Africans to reconfigure Christianity and the English language in their own image: "[B]efore I was born, long before our great great great grandfathers were born, the Lord Jesus Christ defeated death. . . . He wrestled with death and he knocked him down. Death said, let us try *gidigbo* [wrestling] and Christ held him by the neck, he squeezed that neck until Death bleated for mercy. But Death never learns his lesson, he went and brought boxing gloves. When Christ gave him an uppercut like Dick Tiger all his teeth were scattered from Kaduna to Aiyetoro" (*The Interpreters*, 165). Here the reader witnesses the "return" of Tutuola's syncretism, mixing, more freely than Tutuola himself, English with Yoruba, as well as the Christian belief in Jesus's defeat of death and Yoruba folklore where Death is personified as a trickster figure.[47] Lazarus's mixture of references is furthermore both synchronic and diachronic, in that the confrontation between Jesus and Death is portrayed both along lines suggested by traditional Yoruba folklore and as a contemporary boxing match.[48]

The context of Lazarus's sermon makes his connection to the broader cosmology of the novel, as well as his contrast with the book's protagonists, all the more explicit; the interpreters visit his church on a day when the death of an older congregant, Ezra, is commemorated, and when a new "apostle," Noah, is admitted. Just as Lazarus becomes a focal character in the narrative only after Sekoni's death, so is Noah, at least according to Lazarus's perspective, meant to supplant the loss of Ezra. And because this ceremony as a whole invokes the chthonic cycle on which the novel is premised, one should not at all be surprised that it similarly provokes the interpreters' ambivalence, both toward the "folk" who constitute Lazarus's church, and toward the metaphysics they affirm: "There are bells ringing wildly and the white-robed women who appear to have no hand at all in the running of the church come into their own at last, running up and down with handbells, going everywhere. The result is a Witches' Sabbath, clangorous and weird" (*The Interpreters*, 174). The perspective in this episode shifts abruptly from the dramatic present—and indeed, the church service itself forms a ritualistic drama within the narrative—to the anthropological present.

Soyinka therefore sets up a contrast between presenting the service from the viewpoint of participants to showing it from the viewpoint of the interpreters, as well as the reader. Just as the anthropological description of the church service estranges the reader from a romanticized valorization of the "primitive" Christianity of the congregants, so too does it ironize the position of the interpreters, who as "sophisticated" modern intellectuals are unable to see their more traditional countrymen and women as anything other than witches. As such, the episode articulates the lack of a common social language through which these two groups could communicate. Once again, this novel participates in the same critique of modernity initiated by *Di Klyatshe*—with its own antinostalgic view of shtetl "primitivism" and prominent use of a witches' Sabbath. The congregants, reconfigured as witches when seen from the interpreters' perspective, thus become, like the monsters in Tutuola's forest, a metaphor simultaneously for the persistence of tradition, as well as the transmogrification of the modern world.

Nonetheless, when seen from Egbo's perspective—the one character most thoroughly riven by the conflict between the Yoruba tradition and secular modernity—the problem with the ritual performance at Lazarus's church is not too much estrangement, but too much familiarity: "Egbo left before the others; he had seen too much like her [a woman speaking in tongues] and could never like it. *Esu. Sango.* Similar throes of a scotched boa. At such times Egbo longed for the other possession, the triumph of serene joys and sublimated passions. The young maid of *Ela.* The transfigured wrinkles of *Orisa-nla*" (*The Interpreters*, 176). From Egbo's perspective, the "problem" of Lazarus's church service re- volves not around the conflict between the temporal polarities of tradi- tion and modernity, but between two spiritual extremes. As everywhere in this novel, the conflicts in this scene resonate on various levels: at once both social *and* metaphysical, novel *and* myth.

As one should by now expect, these tensions never resolve them- selves in this novel, but continue to proliferate, in keeping with the principle of the assemblage, until the very end. Thus, the relationship between Lazarus and Noah does not replicate the quasi-paternal "apos- tleship" of Lazarus and Ezra, but instead becomes a symbolic and struc- tural struggle between the elements of fire and water. As Kola says when surveying the ruins brought about by the flooding of Lazarus's lagoon- side church, "So ends the reign of Noah as the sunshine saint" (*The Interpreters*, 220). Noah was to have been the sunrise, the new dawn- ing of the church, but instead the church itself becomes reclaimed by the waters of the flood—and indeed, the name taken by this "apostate apostle" should have served to warn Lazarus that this would happen. But as much as Lazarus would like to make Noah, the supposedly re- habilitated thief, into the harbinger of the dawn, when he proposes to test Noah's faith in a trial by fire, Noah in fact runs away to his eventual doom at the hands of an unwitting culprit, Joe Golder.

Noah in this episode establishes a link between Lazarus and Joe Golder, who become connected symbolically, like the opposition in Noah's failed trial of fire and water, with respect to the polarities of Blackness and whiteness, as Soyinka narrates Sagoe's complaints to Golder: "'It is this cult of black beauty which sickens me. Are albinos supposed to go and drown themselves, for instance?' Until then, he had completely forgotten Lazarus. His mind went to him now and it made him suddenly restless" (*The Interpreters*, 196). Golder, an African Amer- ican of mixed (and perhaps partly Jewish) origin, indeed, is a seem- ingly white man—at least in the eyes of Africans such as Sagoe—who attempts to will himself into Blackness. Lazarus, similarly, is an African "reborn" with white skin; both figures therefore expose the untenability of essentialist conceptions of race, and the fact that their connection is first revealed through Sagoe's consciousness makes clear that their presence in the novel further undermines the ideological and existential assumptions of negritude.

Just as the novel depicts the breakdown of a stable, supercessionist relationship between modernity and tradition, so too does it attack the essentialist definition of race—much as *Di Klyatshe*'s mare suggests a proto-modernist parody of gender essentialism—that itself forms one of the governing myths of Western modernity. In this respect, Golder is central to the novel's structure, nearly a lynchpin. Not only is he catalytic to the plot, but his presence represents simultaneously the outer limits of Blackness and the ultimate interconnectedness of the Black Atlantic world. Nothing indicates his integral place in the novel more clearly than the contempt that the other characters, particularly Egbo, feel toward him; he is the scapegoat's scapegoat, the figure that exposes the limits of the other characters' modernity and humanism.

With this in mind, one should further consider the encounter between Joe Golder and Sagoe as a parodic philosophical dialogue between negritude and Voidancy, a Menippean satire as well as an ideological polemic on the meaning of Blackness: "'Black is something I like to be, that I have every right to be. There is no reason at all why I shouldn't have been born jet black.' 'You would have died of over-masturbation, I am sure.' 'You enjoy being vulgar?' 'A genteel British reproof. It is amazing how much English did get into you. Perhaps that's why you are constantly attacking. Look, the truth is that I get rather sick of self-love'" (*The Interpreters*, 195). Sagoe's bracingly virulent attack on Black narcissism is not the only objective of this exchange; it is the clash of exaggeratedly opposed worldviews that exposes the ultimate relativity of the concept of race.

Moreover, Golder himself participates as fully as Sagoe in the cosmological and mythological drama that lays the foundation for Soyinka's dialogical novel. Thus, Joe Golder, the homosexual American mulatto—or, to use racist terminology yet more precisely, "quadroon"—the character most seemingly estranged from African "authenticity," is the character who at the book's end has the last word, or at least the last performance in this dramatist's novel of set pieces. The last instance of conscious creativity that sets the stage for the narrative's conclusion is in fact not spoken, but sung, the African American spiritual "Sometimes I Feel Like a Motherless Child," which itself indicates that the homeless condition of the novel's protagonists is universal, extending to the most attenuated periphery of the African diaspora. This performance signifies at the same time that estrangement and orphanhood, rather than a racialized essence, are the conditions that characterize contemporary African society. Joe Golder thus closes a circle of associations beginning with Sagoe's displacement from Dehinwa's lap.

The last chapter therefore concludes the novel with an irreconcilable generation gap, figured by the absent figure of the girl whom Egbo has impregnated, known only as "the new woman of my generation" (*The Interpreters*, 235). Soyinka describes this woman's pregnancy from Egbo's perspective, as a rebirth for the interpreters and for Africa: "But the clouds held the water, though he longed for the rain to fall, to break, even if the sky held firm, to break at least the earth beneath his feet into loose sands, liberate his skin from the fevered tingling into the running freedom of skin clarity, bared quartz in quick runnels, hearing his racing heart pound now slow but strong against staggered flagstones of threaded granite . . . but the rain stayed dry above him and the earth was mere wet clods against his futile kicks" (*The Interpreters*, 245–246). The kicks Egbo feels are at once the baby's kicks against its mother's womb, and his own frustrated rebellion against the limits of a corrupted modernity. The final images of the novel are ones of orphanhood, illegitimacy, and estrangement, between Bandele and the other interpreters, between Egbo and Simi, between old and young. The narrative suggests, however, that despite its despair, a new generation can be born when the corruption of the past is washed away. This ambivalence toward modernity and the temporality of past and future finds a precedent, of all places, in Abramovitsh's *Benyomin hashlishi*, the first focus of this comparison's next chapter.

If, as was argued in the second part of this book, *Dos Kleyne mentshele*
and *Dos Vintshfingerl* are by virtue of their antithetical protagonists a
study in contrasts, a further instance of the mirror structure that characterizes and divides Abramovitsh's conception of *haskole*, then an
analogous relationship exists between *Masoes Benyomin hashlishi* and
Di Klyatshe. Yisrolik, like Hershele in *Dos Vintshfingerl*, is the maskil
aspiring toward assimilation of modern values and contact with the
non-Jewish world. By contrast, the Benyomin (Benjamin) of *Benyomin hashlishi*, like Itsik-Avreyml in *Dos Kleyne mentshele*, is a reflection
of the isolation, closed-mindedness, and claustrophobic relations of
traditional society. But whereas Itsik-Avreyml and Hershele are "typical" shtetl figures whose life stories encompass a range of representative
experiences, both Yisrolik and Benyomin are presented, parodically, as
extraordinary, "heroic" characters; the return to fantasy in these later
narratives thus signifies a return to larger-than-life situations, which
paradoxically illustrate the reality of technological and political upheaval in the latter half of the nineteenth century much more effectively
than the more "realist," pseudo-autobiographical style of Abramovitsh's
previous writing.

Moreover, Mendele's role, having grown in the decade separating *Di
Klyatshe* from *Dos Kleyne mentshele*, similarly differs diametrically in the
two later novels: in *Di Klyatshe*, the role of Mendele—as master ironist,
voice of reason, and protagonist's tormentor—is taken over, consecu-
tively, by the mare herself (himself) and Ashmedai. In *Benyomin hashlishi*, by contrast, it is Mendele who takes over, from Benyomin, the task
of narration. In both novels, however, the "Mendele function" is un-

210

stable, somewhere between narrator and interacting character, and his presence reflects both Abramovitsh's restlessness with respect to novelistic form and the unsettled relationship of Yiddish literature to narrative conventions. These conventions were, of course, less established in Yiddish culture than in the metropolitan cultures of Europe during the golden age of literary realism. It is therefore necessary both to note the role of satire in Abramovitsh's writing and to consider how uncharacteristic a genre satire as a distinct discourse was for most European novelists during the latter half of the nineteenth century.

In this respect, *Di Klyatshe* and *Masoes Benyomin hashlishi* are complementary political satires—though each transcends the formal and ideological limits of parody—to a much greater degree than Abramovitsh's previous narratives. Of the two, it is *Benyomin hashlishi* that has sealed Abramovitsh's reputation as a political humorist. This narrative describes the misadventures of two traditional Jews at the time of the Crimean War (1854–1856), Benyomin and Senderl, who under the influence of medieval Jewish legends set out from their native shtetl Tuneyadevke ("the town of the idlers")[1] in search of the "Red Jews," remnants of the Ten Tribes lost to Judaism when the Northern Kingdom of Israel was conquered by Assyria (Second Kings 17:1–18:12), who live on the far side of the impassable Sambatyon River. Their journey, which if successful would initiate the "ingathering of the exiles" necessary to herald the coming of the messiah, takes them as far afield as the shtetl of Teterevke, the small city of Glupsk (the "Fool's Town"), and the larger city of Dneprovits, where they are impressed into the Russian army. The momentum of the novel thus takes the protagonists from the shtetl to the city, and from the realm of medieval Jewish fantasy to modern, imperial reality. Fantasy and the tradition with which it is identified reassert themselves at the novel's end, however, when Benyomin and Senderl desert their army post with impunity, and again resume their utopian wandering.

The ostensible motivation for Benyomin's messianic quest is the appearance in Tuneyadevke of a single date:

> It happened by chance once that someone brought a date into the
> shtetl, and you should have seen how they ran and looked at the won-

der, how they brought a Pentateuch and showed that *tomer*, the date, is written about in the Torah! That is, the date, this very date, was brought from the land of Israel! When looking at the date, it seemed as if the land of Israel itself stood before their eyes, that there flowed the Jordan, there stood the cave of the patriarchs, there the grave of the matriarch Rachel. . . . "At that time," writes Benyomin, "all of Tuney-adevke, however large she is, was in the Land of Israel. We spoke at length about the Messiah, saying that God's great Sabbath was near at hand."[2]

The appearance of this date unleashes a collective fantasy of Zion that in turn inspires Benyomin's even more fantastic ambition, thus grounding the novel mythologically in the condition of diaspora and a longing for return. But at the same time, Benyomin's description of Tuney-adevke as *in* the Land of Israel links the shtetl metonymically with the displaced homeland itself. As Miron writes, "The shtetl was Jerusalem in her fallen state, and yet it was still Jerusalem—the Jewish polity par excellence" ("Image," 33).

This motif of the shtetl as a Jewish universe juxtaposed against the outer world is perhaps *the* organizing principle of nineteenth-century Yiddish literature, examples of which can be found in Reb Nakhman's "Story of a Sophisticate and a Simpleton," Aksenfeld's *Dos Shterntikhl*, Abramovitsh's *Dos Kleyne mentshele*, and Dik's unfinished utopia, among countless others. This principle achieves its most complex development in the mature writings of Abramovitsh, primarily *Benyomin hashlishi*, but also *Fishke der krumer* ("Fishke the Lame") and the revised editions of *Dos Vintshfingerl*. As much as an indication of his developing talent, this motif offers a measure of Abramovitsh's growing distance from the generic straitjacket of maskilic satire. In the later phase of Abramovitsh's career, the shtetl can serve simultaneously as a stand-in for the Garden of Eden, Jerusalem, and Egypt: that is, Paradise, Promised Land, and Diaspora, at once. The ambiguity of this symbolism signifies not only the psychological function of the shtetl's image and its mythological underpinning—to reconcile contradictions that are neither surmountable nor expressible in rational terms—but also articulates the role of the shtetl in the imagination of the urbanized, modern intellectual, as both a paradise lost and a forsaken house of bondage. Such images, though envisioned through different cultural associations, apply equally well to the traditional communities depicted in *The Interpreters* and *Les Soleils des indépendances*.

Although the shtetl Tuneyadevke is the comic half of a Janus-faced "archetype," life there is not entirely bucolic, as can be surmised by the fact that Benyomin and Senderl leave home on their wanderings. Indeed, Benyomin explains in his description of the date how the talk of *Erets yisroel* was motivated by the antisemitism of the new constable (*pristav*): "The new constable . . . led the town most despotically. He slapped the yarmulkes off a couple of Jews, and even cut the side lock off one; others he caught, unfortunately, late at night on a side street without a passport, and from yet another he confiscated a goat that had eaten up a newly thatched roof" (Y 168; E 184). The "messianic fervor" inspired by the constable in turn leads Benyomin in search of the Red Jews—a search itself connected to both the fact of the Diaspora and the hope for redemption and reconciliation of the Jewish people to one another, their land, and God. However "paltry" the pretext for these messianic longings may be, the fact of the constable's presence—as a synecdoche for the outside world, and one of the few non-Jewish figures to appear in the shtetl anywhere in Abramovitsh's writing—connects Tuneyadevke not only to the political autocracy of the Russian Empire, but in an attenuated sense to the geopolitical realities of the Crimean War.

In keeping with the parodic and idyllic aspects of the novel, these political motifs find their echo in the social life of the shtetl itself, which is organized around a parliamentary system, complete with a lower house that meets behind the stove of the synagogue, and an upper house that meets on the benches of the steam bath. The "political work" of this comical parliament, of course, only serves to underscore the powerlessness and isolation of the shtetl, and the cheerful incompatibility of traditional Jews with the distasteful business of warfare, political dealmaking, and imperial conquest. As Miron and Norich state, "Instead of political action Tuneyadevke takes to political daydreaming. Benjamin, whose urge to become a voyager was aroused on this occasion, is therefore both the extension and the negation of his hometown. . . . If Tuneyadevke is a mock Britannia, Benjamin then is a mock Disraeli" ("The Politics of Benjamin III," 54).

The alignment of Tuneyadevke's Benyomin with Benjamin Disraeli of course takes the narrative far afield from the narrow parodic aims of previous maskilic satires. Before investigating the way in which this identification ultimately serves to articulate a sophisticated critique of contemporary imperialism, it is necessary to consider the motivations and literary antecedents of the novel's parody of the shtetl itself. As a parody, the ostensible targets of Abramovitsh's satire in this narrative are the medieval works of fantasy and folklore that even in the late nineteenth century continued to be repackaged as Yiddish chapbooks, and sold by peddlers like Mendele; along these lines, one might expect that the narrative follows the precedent of *Dos Vintshfingerl* of using Yiddish folklore to disparage the intellectual limitations and moral shortcomings of the Jewish folk. The ultimate source for this sort of parody is Cervantes' *Don Quixote*, and the two protagonists of *Benyomin hashlishi*, Benyomin and Senderl, are clearly meant to correspond to Don Quixote and Sancho Panza, respectively. Indeed, Nakhman Mayzl notes, "In 1885, *Masoes Benyomin hashlishi* was translated into Polish under the title 'The Jewish Don Quixote'"[3] (Y 157).

Thus, Abramovitsh's invocation of *Don Quixote*, itself a parody of medieval romance, is an instance of double-voiced parody on a "metatextual" level: the author is fully aware, as he indicates satirically in the prologue to the 1865 edition of *Dos Vintshfingerl*, of *Don Quixote*'s status as a foundational novel in modern European literature. *Benyomin hashlishi* is therefore a further ironization of Cervantes' narrative; however absurd the senile protagonist of the earlier novel is, he at least comes from a culture in which heroism and chivalry were once possible. Benyomin's supposedly heroic adventures are still more absurd than Don Quixote's, because in his culture even the possibility of "noble deeds" or historical achievement is moot.[4] At the same time as the comparison between early modern Spain and the contemporary Jewish shtetl is meant to extend the comic bathos of the latter novel, it is meant to call attention to the author's attack on the same type of literature that Cervantes attacks—the fantastic medieval romance that has fogged the mind and blinded the eye toward historical reality. This polemically motivated generic attack is of course indicative of a more significant historical critique of the fundamentally medieval character of Jewish shtetl society, amid the rapidly emerging modernity of the rest of Eastern Europe.

One early incident in the novel that illustrates, simultaneously, the absurdity of a heroic character emerging from the shtetl, the medieval isolation of traditional Jewish life, and the psychological depiction of Tuneyadevke as a Jewish "homeland" occurs when, before embarking on his journey, Benyomin one day finds himself lost outside the limits of his town. Panicking after having spent a night in the woods, he encounters a Ukrainian peasant: "*Dobri-Dien*, Benyomin abruptly said approaching the peasant, in a strange voice that conveyed several meanings at once—crying, begging, saying, 'Here, here, do with me what you wish,' but also pleading, 'Help, have mercy on me, on my wife and children, pity!'" (Y 174; E 191). At this point, the reader can conclude that the Ukrainian greeting *dobri-dien* is meant to convey just about anything, except its literal meaning, "good morning"! Language in this passage, and in the subsequent, comically uncomprehending dialogue that follows, ceases to serve as a vehicle of communication but is instead a sign of irreconcilable cultural difference. This is in fact the first of several instances of linguistic confusion between Jews and non-Jews in the novel. Where diglossia in maskilic drama had therefore focused on the similarity, the "narcissism of the small difference," between the Yiddish spoken by provincial, old-fashioned Jews and the German, or *daytsh-merish*, spoken by modern, urban Jews, here the emphasis is placed on the irreconcilable difference between Jewish and non-Jewish languages.

This type of confusion between languages is of course a pointed literary exaggeration that overlooks the genuinely multilingual texture of everyday life in Eastern Europe: not every Jew spoke Ukrainian or the other coterritorial languages of Eastern Europe, nor did every non-Jew speak Yiddish, but enough of both did to make commerce and communication possible. Benyomin's inability to speak Ukrainian, which distinguishes and diminishes him both in comparison with the women of the marketplace—who find Benyomin sprawled amid the produce that the peasant has brought with him into town—and his traveling companion Senderl,[5] is a further representation of the shtetl as an imagined, ahistorical Jewish microcosm. Benyomin cannot speak Ukrainian, because he lives only in the world of the shtetl, where diglossia consists neither of Yiddish and German nor Yiddish and Ukrainian, but Yiddish and *Loshn-koydesh*. His mentality is thus shaped not by contact with other people, or peoples, but with Jewish *texts*, and as such the fruitlessness of his efforts to communicate with the non-Jews around him is representative of a shtetl that exists only in texts, belletristic ones, and that is imagined as wholly Jewish. The shtetl in this context emerges not only as a "Jewish polity," in Miron's phrasing, but also as a Jewish *interior space*, both socially and psychologically, and is contrasted, especially in the encounter between Benyomin and the peasant, with an outside world depicted as non-Jewish, foreign, hostile, and menacing—but also productive, practical, and organic.

At the same time, Abramovitsh's depiction of the traditional worlds of the peasant countryside and the Jewish shtetl as being unable to communicate with one another becomes a means for the author and his readers to differentiate themselves from the tradition and to use their modernity to mediate between Jewish and non-Jewish cultures. In the ensuing dialogue between Benyomin and the peasant, the author quotes the Ukrainian without translation, either expecting his audience to be more fluent and cosmopolitan than Benyomin is, or else expecting greater fluency in Ukrainian than *Loshn-koydesh*, phrases of which *are* typically translated into Yiddish.[6] Alternately, he allows the presence of these Slavic exchanges to exert the same disorienting effect on the unfamiliar reader as they do on Benyomin. The fact that Abramovitsh and most of his readers *can* understand both the peasant and Benyomin, however, places the Jewish reader, for once, in a position of power, as a reader of *modern* literature, over the static, "tribal" hegemonies of rural and semirural Eastern Europe, even though it should be recalled that neither Benyomin nor the peasant is in fact empowered or in a position of hegemony.

Furthermore, the decision to depict this imagined unintelligibility offers paradoxical evidence of a newfound openness in Yiddish literature toward outside languages and modes of being; as Mikhail Bakhtin explains, "This verbal-ideological decentering [heteroglossia's tendency to relativize and decenter literary and linguistic consciousness] will occur only when a national culture loses its sealed-off and self-sufficient character, when it becomes conscious of itself as only one among *other* cultures and languages."[7] For several reasons, therefore, an encounter between Benyomin and the peasant would have been inconceivable in Abramovitsh's writings of the 1860s: fundamentally, there are no non-Jews to speak of in these earlier narratives. Similarly, whatever non-Jewish expressions are spoken in these works are mediated through Yiddish, and thereby neutralized of their foreignness for a Jewish audience. But more significantly, the idea of the outside world as an unfamiliar, forbidding, incomprehensible space—though in historical terms more characteristic of an earlier age than of the 1870s—would work against *haskole* ideology, which sought to reform Jewish life by importing outside ideas in foreign languages, and therefore tended to minimize the strangeness and the distance of the world beyond the shtetl.

For these reasons, the world outside the shtetl in Abramovitsh's early fiction can only be invoked through figures like Lessing and Cervantes; it can't be depicted through encounters with peasants or army officers.[8] As Yisrolik demonstrates in advance of Benyomin, it's only when the maskil drops his pretensions to rationality and control of his surroundings that the outside world, with all its discontents, can truly come rushing into his shtetl. It is therefore necessary to recall that Hershele's eventual migration to Leipzig is invoked in *Dos Vintshfingerl*, but never depicted. Within the frame of their respective narratives, Benyomin is by far a more experienced traveler—with the panic and discomfort over an encounter with the unfamiliar to prove it. Moreover, one can better understand Bakhtin's comments regarding the heteroglossia of a *national* culture by reading these remarks against *Benyomin hashlishi*. A shtetl such as Kabtsansk in Abramovitsh's maskilic fiction is, as Bakhtin would characterize it, sealed-off from other cultures, but it is hardly conceived of as self-sufficient. By contrast, Benyomin's Tuneyadevke gains a sense of autonomy and a mythic resonance with Jewish nationhood precisely when seen against a backdrop not only of "primitive" Slavic culture, but also the machinations of the industrial, imperial world. Neither Benyomin's Tuneyadevke nor Hershele's Kabtsansk is national in Bakhtin's sense of the term, or any other definition of nationalism, and this fact underscores the usefulness of recognizing Yiddish literature—in its classic period more than ever—as a deterritorialized literature.

Moreover, the fact of this uncomprehending exchange between Benyomin and the peasant places *Benyomin hashlishi* far away from the language of realism and the decorum of the nineteenth-century novel.[9] In this context, it is significant that when Benyomin asks Senderl to negotiate with the captain of a barge to take the two of them across the Piatignilevke River outside of Glupsk, Senderl is literally reduced to gesturing with his hands: "'Tell him, Senderl' Benyomin shouted, 'you should explain to him about the mountain. Make him understand however you can.' Senderl raised his hands together high to depict the hills, shouting all the while *het, het visoko*! [very, very high]" (Y 232; E 245). At this point, Abramovitsh engages in a radical deformation of language more characteristic of "late modernism" than either contemporaneous realism or the polemics of *haskole*.

Thus, however much the premise and pretext of *Benyomin hashlishi* extends the maskilic critique of the shtetl that Abramovitsh articulated in his first two Yiddish narratives, both the historical circumstances in which the author found himself during the 1870s, as well as the content of the novel itself, have deepened and complicated both its satire and its ideological message. The potential for such a multivalent, "post-maskilic" critique becomes apparent from the first page of Mendele's prologue, when he asks, "How is it that a Jew, a Polish Jew, without weapons, without machines, but armed only with a sack on his shoulders and a *talis* and *tfillin* bag under his arm, should come to rest in such places, where even famous English explorers have yet to arrive at! It can't be otherwise than that all this occurred through a superhuman power, such a power which human rationality is entirely unable to comprehend—that is, human rationality is just as powerless as this particular power is irrational" (Y 161; E 179–180). The essence of the novel's ideological critique, offered here ostensibly in the voice of the "English and German gazettes" (Y 161; E 179), is stated explicitly in this passage. Fundamentally, the Yiddish novelist "translates" the words from cosmopolitan sources "back" into Yiddish, thus placing Yiddish words in the mouths of the German and English journalists, as if they spoke like Jews from the shtetl. This initiates another contrast in the novel, between the shtetl and the modern world—an opposition that, over the course of the novel, will collapse as one perspective becomes superimposed on the other, and the two worldviews collide.

In this regard, Mendele's contrast of the Jewish begging sack with weapons and machines extends the critique of modernity initiated by *Di Klyatshe*; the poverty and debasement of traditional Jewish life remain objects of ridicule, but the destructive, mechanized world of the West now no longer stands as an object of desire, or even a valid alternative. Moreover, the remark that Benyomin travels to lands where even English explorers were unable to reach identifies the Eastern European shtetl, the milieu in which he remains throughout his "adventures," as beyond the pale, literally, of contemporary Western imperialism, and creates at the same time an association between the shtetl and the lands then being colonized by the Western superpower. Finally, the chiasmus "reason lacks power, just as this particular power lacks reason" suggests a contrast that undermines the fundamental assumptions of *haskole*, that the power of imperial modernity was a function of superior reasoning—as well as morality, social organization, cultural aesthetics—and that reason as such was validated by technical, economic, and political might.

Abramovitsh accomplishes the superimposition of the shtetl onto the modern world, and vice versa, by subsuming the shtetl perspective of Benyomin as well as the cosmopolitan perspective of the European journalists—both of which are, of course, products of his own imagination—by means of the Mendele persona. The Mendele figure therefore functions in a mediating role as a kind of ethnographer of modernity for the shtetl, and of the shtetl for his modern readers. This establishes a further connection between Abramovitsh and Kourouma, for Mendele is surely no less an anthropologist in his "editorship" of *Benyomin hashlishi* than Kourouma, as will soon be seen, is in *Les Soleils des indépendances*. Both, in fact, serve as mocking "native informants" to an ostensibly uninitiated reader. Furthermore, imperialist ethnography of the nineteenth century is as much a target of his satire here as the absurdity of shtetl life.[10] More specifically, it seems clear that Mendele uses the rhetoric of nineteenth-century ethnography, fully aware of its racist and colonialist assumptions, as a means of articulating a parody simultaneously of the shtetl and the modern world that would supplant it. The use of ethnography thus enacts a classic parodic strategy—defamiliarizing the ordinary—that would also serve as a fundamental principle for High Modernism, and which recurs in *The Interpreters* and *Les Soleils des indépendances*.

Moreover, this "ethnographic perspective" both reflects and facilitates a broader significance to Benyomin's adventures. As Miron and Norich explain, Benyomin in Abramovitsh's novel is the "third" in a line of "great" Jewish explorers; the first was Benjamin of Tudela, who lived in twelfth-century Spain and traveled throughout the Mediterranean, through Palestine, across the Persian Gulf, and as far afield as India, Ceylon, and perhaps China;[11] Benjamin "the Second" was "Israel Joseph Benjamin . . . born in 1818 in a small Moldavian shtetl and who, by 1845, was on his way to India . . . by 1851 left for North Africa . . . in 1859 crossed the Atlantic to New York, in 1860 crossed the Isthmus of Panama and arrived by ship to California, then crossed the entire continent back to New York. . . . He published various travelogues in French and German, was encouraged by such eminent scholars as Alexander von Humboldt, and was even awarded decorations by the kings of Sweden and Hanover a short time before his death in 1864" ("The Politics of Benjamin III," 26). By 1878, however, this "Benjamin the Second" was virtually a forgotten figure, and the invocation of his memory calls to mind that other, more significant Benjamin—Benjamin Disraeli.

With Abramovitsh's Benjamin the Third stalking the "real" Benjamin,[12] the ultimate significance of Benyomin's recurring dream of meeting Alexander the Great comes into focus, as does the narrative's critical relationship to the contemporary political realities of Russian Jewry: "Alexander the Great, who is desperate to meet Benjamin, is used here as a reference to another Alexander (at the time of the writing of *Masoes Benyomin hashlishi* the Russian Czar was Alexander II), and the meeting resulting in the crushing of the stinking bed bug [Y 237; E 250] is an almost obscene reference to the relationship between the Jews and the Czarist government. . . . " ("The Politics of Benjamin III," 97). Connected with the political symbolism of the ostensibly liberal Czar Alexander II "shaking hands" with the ostensibly Jewish Benjamin Disraeli is the (ahistorical) occasion of their interaction, the Crimean War, a conflict that Alexander had in fact inherited from his father Nicholas, which concluded more than a decade before Disraeli first became prime minister. These details notwithstanding, the war is essential to the novel because it too had a Jewish subtext, insofar as one of its motivations was Russia's challenge to Turkey's imperial control over Palestine and its holy sites.[13]

The Crimean War was at once a struggle between the leading imperial powers of European modernity and a rehashing—history repeated as a farce for the rulers, a tragedy for the combatants—of the quintessential conflict of the medieval world, the Crusades. As such, this conflict is a particularly acute setting for dramatizing the emergence of a backward, provincial Eastern European Jewry from the slumber of the Middle Ages into the dawn of modernity.[14] Moreover, Benyomin's parody of the leading personality of this era, Disraeli, superimposes a medieval Jewish mentality over the "ultimate" modern Jew—so modern that he worshiped in the Church of England[15]—but in so doing, this parody calls to mind the medieval entanglements that continue to characterize this modern Jew and the imperial culture he led.

Just as the Crimean War recapitulates in modern garb fundamentally medieval rivalries among the monarchs of Europe and "the Orient," so too does Abramovitsh contextualize this conflict within the shtetl world not once but twice. Thus Mendele describes the debates in the Tuneyadevke house of study by stating, "To that place . . . all discussions lead themselves eventually, whether regarding the secrets of domestic life, or the politics of Istanbul, whether the Turkish Sultan or the Austrian Kaiser, whether high finance and the fortunes of Rothschild . . . whether the contemporary persecutions or the Red Jews, etc." (Y 165–166; E 182). In this setting, geopolitical events involving the Rothschilds and the crowns of Europe are seen alternately in the intimate terms of domestic gossip and the legendary terms of the Red Jews. But the reader encounters these historical figures again when Benyomin and Senderl present themselves to the house of study in Teterevke:

> Because Khaykl the Brainiac was so head-over-heels with Vicki [Queen Victoria], Itsik the Simpleton, Khaykl's life-long critic in every matter,

attached himself to Aunt Rosie [Russia] and supported her with all his might. . . . Khaykl stood shoulder to shoulder for a time with Shmulik Carob, the president of Uncle Ishmael's fan club, and had nearly gone in 50–50 with Berl the Frenchman, Napoleon's biggest fan, when Itsik made a racket and attracted Tuvye Mok, the Kaiser's man, and then rumors started pouring in from all sides, with each launching his own rockets, overturning the world and rocking the synagogue to its foundation. (Y 207; E 221)[16]

Just as with the European journalists who herald Benyomin in the discourse of shtetl Jews, here too Abramovitsh superimposes the monarchs of Europe onto the small-town chatterboxes of the synagogue to make each group a reflection of the other. For if the Tuneyadevke steam bath can be seen as a House of Lords "without pants," can't the House of Lords be seen as a kind of "steam bath *with* pants"? The parodic epic here simultaneously inflates the Jewish bathhouse and deflates imperial England, precisely as similar mock-epic motifs function in *The Interpreters* or *Ulysses*.

It is structurally significant that the arrival of Benyomin and Senderl at the Teterevke house of study occurs exactly at the halfway point of this novel, in the beginning of Chapter Seven. Here, unlike either *Dos Vintshfingerl* or *L'aventure ambiguë*, one encounters a binary narrative that nonetheless doesn't undermine itself dialectically, but instead plays out like a theme with variations, a repetition with signal differences.[17] *Benyomin hashlishi* as a narrative, and the shtetl world it describes as a social system, thus form a proliferating assemblage in which the constituent parts no longer cancel each other out, but reflect one another in a potentially infinite series of duplication that conceivably could carry the shtetl, or the wandering protagonists emerging from it, beyond the Pale of Settlement to the capitals of Europe, or the empires these capitals begin to command, by remote control, over the course of the nineteenth century. Abramovitsh therefore doesn't come to the conclusion that modernity, as constituted by the imperial state—whether, in this context, Russia or Great Britain—is bankrupt; he discovers this fact by working out the logic of the satirical mock epic. The genre and form of the novel here, more clearly than elsewhere, determines its ideological content.

Abramovitsh establishes the parodic correspondence between the

world of the shtetl and the world of imperial modernity—thus collaps-
ing the difference between these worlds that had structured his maskilic
narratives—through the comic wanderings of Benyomin and Senderl.
To this pair, Abramovitsh adds two pairs of "city folk" who parallel and
mirror the novel's protagonists. For example, when the wanderers from
Tuneyadevke first enter the large, commercial shtetl of Glupsk, they are
depicted through the eyes of two servant women there, Dobrish and
Khaye-Beyle: "'What's going on over there with all those people running? Something must be burning somewhere. It's the second fire already today. By nightfall there'll be many more fires.' 'There's no alarm,
though, Dobrish. If there was a fire we'd have heard the fire bell.' 'Hush,
now, there goes the broker's wife, I'll ask her. Sime-Dvosye, Sime-Dvosye! Where's everybody going? . . . ' [Another woman, Nakhme-Gise,
answers] 'I should know? Something about the Red Jews'" (Y 222; E
235–236). As Miron states ("Image," 16–18), fires in shtetl literature are
a constant motif that serves to invoke the destruction of the First and
Second Temples in Jerusalem, thereby connecting the shtetl ambivalently to Zion and the Diaspora at one and the same time. In this instance, however, the fire turns out to be a false alarm, because what
arrives in town is not a tragic reminder of the Destruction, but a comic,
parodic foreshadowing of the Redemption.

Indeed, Benyomin and Senderl are referred to in this scene as "the
Red Jews," thereby becoming, metonymically, the object of their own
quest; in the "modern city" of Glupsk—more modern and more urban,
at least, than Tuneyadevke—the two protagonists become exotics because they, like the mythical Red Jews, have been cut off from history.
And yet, amid the crowd of women that join Dobrish and Khaye-Beyle
is a second pair, Toltse and Trayne, "two of a certain sort of *yidenes*, kosher souls the both of them, who used to, as was well known, pass every
evening clothed in Sabbath finery, in silk jackets and ornamented head-
bands, strolling in the city streets ready to greet the Messiah" (Y 222;
E 236). These women are a perfect inversion of Benyomin and Senderl:
anachronistic Glupsker women who encounter the Tuneyadevke couple
in search of exactly the same redemption as themselves. Like Harry Potter's Mirror of Erised,[18] these characters reflect not only the protagonists
of the novel but also their deepest, potentially most delusional desires.

If Dobrish and Khaye-Beyle, and Toltse and Trayne, reflect, respectively, the benighted chatter and the naive messianism of Benyomin and Senderl, it is significant that the parallel should serve, like the mare's transmogrification in *Di Klyatshe*, to call into question the fixity of gender roles in a changing Jewish social order. Indeed, Benyomin and Senderl are androgynous figures, and Senderl is even known in Tuney-advke as "Senderl the *yidene*"; Senderl as an unknowing fool, a *tam*, is a generic convention in Yiddish satire, but Senderl as a nearly transvestite *tam* is a seemingly unique literary creation, one that relates as much to Reb Nakhman's *bas-keyser*—who disguises herself as a man and whom the narrator refers to with masculine pronouns—in his second story as the *tam* in "The Tale of the Sophisticate and the Simpleton." In morphological terms, he is the character who connects this novel to the transmogrified world of *Di Klyatshe*, in which the representative of the Jewish past is, simultaneously, a prince and a mare.

Moreover, in parodic terms, the relationship between Benyomin and Senderl is explicitly homoerotic. Although Benyomin himself is unaware of this aspect of his relationship with Senderl, he nonetheless makes their implications clear when, discussing travel plans with his companion, he exclaims, "Senderl. . . . We're a match made in heaven; with you worrying about our physical needs regarding food and drink on our journey, and me worrying about the spiritual aspects, we're like a body and a soul" (Y 194; E 209).[19] The parodic language of love notwithstanding, what is most revealing in this passage is Benyomin's designation of Senderl as the body and himself as the soul—neither of them is a fully complete or individuated person—which is not only Abramovitsh's critical point, but also the role that Mendele, the only adult presence in the novel, takes upon himself to fulfill. In Freudian terms, therefore, one can venture to suggest that the three characters Senderl, Benyomin, and Mendele divide among themselves the function of id, ego, and superego, respectively. The analogy is imperfect, but the comparison helps schematize how Senderl's concentration on material needs, to the exclusion of any higher aspirations, contrasts with Benyomin's preoccupation with personal aggrandizement and superhuman achievement (he is the ego in the negative sense), to the exclusion of practical concerns. Mendele intervenes between these two underdeveloped psyches, supplying a "reality principle" that they both lack, and in the process he commandeers the work of narration that neither character would be able to fulfill.

More obviously, Benyomin is, in parodic terms, "larger than life," whereas Senderl is "smaller than life"; Mendele fills in the breach, the real life missing from their experience. As such, Mendele is the only "real" psyche in the narrative, and his psychological independence is achieved, significantly, through his ability to stand outside of, cut off from, the *shtetlekh* that (de)form the other characters' perception of reality. At the same time, one should note that in contrast to earlier "psycho-linguistic" dynamics in the *haskole*, such as has been identified in Yosef Perl's trilingual polemics—where Yiddish stood for the "id," German for the "superego," and maskilic Hebrew for the "ego"—here these psychological functions are dispersed among characters, each of whom "live" in a Yiddish environment. Although shtetl life is still inadequate to the task of generating fully psychologized characters, at least the Yiddish language is no longer identified as a culprit in this syndrome.

Part of the reason for emancipating Yiddish from the role of scapegoat for the evils of traditional Ashkenazic life is Abramovitsh's developing sophistication toward the language and its aesthetic resources. This development is connected to his efforts in the mid-1870s to translate the Book of Psalms into modern Yiddish and thereby provide Yiddish with a classical model for poetry, an inconceivable ambition for most, though certainly not all, maskilim of an earlier generation.[20] Connected to this developing aesthetic attitude, and indeed superseding it, is a deepening recognition that just as Yiddish is no less intrinsically worthy a language than German or Hebrew, so too can one no longer conclude that the traditional life of Eastern European Jews is inherently worse than any other culture in the world. In fact, the opposition of the shtetl to the world collapses definitively in *Benyomin hashlishi*, as it had in *Di Klyatshe*, when Benyomin and Senderl arrive in Dneprovits, and fall almost immediately into the clutches of a pair of ostensibly observant Jews who promptly sell the two out to the Russian army. Significantly, Abramovitsh allows Benyomin and Senderl to enjoy one contented day on the road before their betrayal: "With joy and gladness our heroes left the city one afternoon to play together, to look each other in the eyes, simply to enjoy one another's company. They resembled a loving couple, just after the wedding" (Y 234; E 247). This "consummation" of Benyomin and Senderl's parodic marriage turns out to be the moment of bliss, of paradise lost, before they fall, literally, into the hands of the *khapers* (abductors).

In historical terms, the role of the *khapers*, though it led to a devastating crisis in moral authority within the traditional Jewish community, originated in Czarist military policy itself.[21] The *khaper* episode therefore begins with a conventional maskilic satire of the *kahal* (the organized community) and expands associatively to a critique of warfare and the modern, militarized Russian state. In this way Abramovitsh establishes his independence, as in *Di Klyatshe*, from both the traditional community and the modern hegemony. The two *khapers*, like the Devil with his "10 Commandments" at the end of *Di Klyatshe*—a not accidental association—therefore represent both the worst of provincial Jewish chauvinism and the most exploitative aspects of the imperial system. As Mendele conveys the conversation in which they dupe Benyomin and Senderl, the *khapers* ask rhetorically, "What can't Jews do? All the innovations of the world, whether the telegraph, the railroad, or whatever other contraption, were already well known long before among the Jews. But all that is just a trifle. The real point is something else— that little spark, the Jewish soul, that's what really matters" (Y 240; E 253). Two affluent Jews thus extol the familiarity of Jews with telegraphs and railroads to two poor Jews who have seen neither; two community representatives sing the praises of a "racial" Jewish essence while they plot to sell two indigent strangers to the Russian army, in the name of the community itself.

The site of Benyomin and Senderl's betrayal, fittingly, is a bathhouse—where previously the "House of Lords" in Tuneyadevke had sat, and where the simultaneous parody of the shtetl and the modern, imperial world receives its most intimate juxtaposition. Abramovitsh continues his satire of the "body politic" with this motif when he writes, "A Jew comes to the bathhouse as if to his fatherland, as if in a free land, where everyone's opinion is treated equally, where everyone can achieve, just like the well-born, the summit of the topmost bench"

(Y 241; E 254). As Miron and Norich make clear, "[W]alking to what they may regard as the equivalent of political freedom, a fatherland and democracy, they are about to be plummeted into bondage of the harshest and most rigidly hierarchical army in the world" ("The Politics of Benjamin III," 99). Benyomin and Senderl's ultimately harmless fate is of course far less severe than that of the actual recruits, who suffered the full brunt of the Russian Empire's efforts to convert the Jews and assimilate them completely into Russian society. But because of this harmlessness, Abramovitsh's narrative fulfills one of the psychic functions of comedy: to replay the trauma of real life for laughs, to neutralize the pain inflicted by history on a downtrodden folk.

Significantly, one of the ways in which Abramovitsh shrugs off the trauma of history is through the language of folklore. As Mendele relates the clueless reactions of the pair to their predicament: "It seemed as if they were in an enchanted castle, like in old-wive's tales or 'A Thousand and One Nights,' and soon the princesses, the king's daughters, would receive them and they would dwell there and live the Life of Reilly. But instead of king's daughters, a soldier wearing medallions came to them and asked them to undress" (Y 242; E 255). Here Abramovitsh returns to the realm of Reb Nakhman's *mayse aleph*, though in this instance the dangers that remain subliminal in the earlier story are made manifest with the appearance of the Russian soldier, and with him the apparatus of modern warfare and the imperial state. Yet it is worth noting that in both Reb Nakhman's and Abramovitsh's narratives, the fairy-tale image of a mysterious, conspicuously non-Jewish castle provides the setting for the characters' confrontation—collision—with the outside, modern world. Seen through the perspective of *Benyomin hashlishi*, therefore, *mayse aleph* can be regarded as a parody of the fairy tale motifs that Reb Nakhman appropriates from folklore, just as Abramovitsh's later satire parodies the ostensibly secular tradition of Yiddish storytelling that has clouded Benyomin's thinking and set him on his journey.

When confronted with a choice between Benyomin's impossible fantasies, and the grim realities of imperial warfare, Abramovitsh invests his sympathies with the former, thus turning his back on the pragmatic, positivist agenda of the *haskole*:

Akh, Benyomin and Senderl never realized that it wasn't only in the desert that travelers had to fear the wild lizards, scorpions, dragons, and evil beasts, but that here in these parts lays the greatest danger! For the time when our heroes took off on their journey was also the difficult, dark, bitter time when one Jew sought another to catch . . . and betray for a sacrifice in place of his children, or even someone else's! Akh, our pitiful protagonists had no idea that they were already lost in the wilderness, among wild beasts and predators, and the two fine, upstanding Jews were the worst dragons of them all! (Y 244; E 256–257)

It is only in the context of *Di Klyatshe* that the denouement of *Benyomin hashlishi* can be understood as heroic, that the incompatibility of the two shtetl protagonists with modern, imperial, military culture can be seen as salutary. By creating two protagonists that the reader can appreciate as both laudable and ludicrous—"*un*conscientious" (indeed, barely conscious) objectors—Abramovitsh, as a modern writer, creates a path of escape from the nihilistic point at which *Di Klyatshe* literally goes to the devil. *Di Klyatshe* thus politicizes *Benyomin hashlishi*; *Benyomin hashlishi* completes *Di Klyatshe*. The two works are connected via the Mendele figure, the cog that links each of Abramovitsh's deterritorialized, bilingual writings.

Indeed, having invested his sympathies finally with Benyomin over the modern world, Abramovitsh allows his protagonist two singular moments of moral and political clarity when he decides to abandon the army and resume his journey. As he explains to Senderl, "What good are we to them, and why do they have to have us here. . . . On the contrary, Senderl, tell me honestly, if the enemy, God forbid, were to come, would two such as us be able to stand up against them? And if you were to tell him a thousand times, 'get away from here, or else I'll make with the pow, pow,' do you think he'll hear you? Just the opposite—he'll capture you, and you'll have your lucky stars to thank if you escape with your life" (Y 246; E 259). Similarly, when the two are caught trying to escape, Benyomin breaks character from the cowardly and tongue-tied dreamer he has played throughout the novel to tell the military tribunal at his court-martial, "Kidnapping people in broad daylight and selling them like chickens at the market, that's allowed, but when these pitiful victims try to escape, that you call a crime! If that's the case, then there's no morality in the world, and I don't even begin to know the meaning of the words 'permitted' and 'forbidden'" (Y 251; E 263).

Although the outlandish appearance that Benyomin makes on the military tribunal convinces them to release him from his obligations, rather than the eloquence of his arguments—which are of course eloquent only in Yiddish, since neither Benyomin nor Senderl can speak Russian—this fact makes Benyomin's absurdity itself into a survival strategy and defense mechanism.[22] Moreover, it underscores the contrast between the harmless surrealism of Benyomin's worldview and the destructive, nihilistic pointlessness of warfare itself. Thus, when after being captured during his escape from the army, Senderl finally manages to fall asleep in the stockade, he dreams of his grandfather, who had brought him as a child a bow and arrow to play with at the holiday of *Simkhes toyre*, a dreydl at Hanukah, and a noisemaker at Purim (Y 250; E 262). The bow-and-arrow as a child's diversion during the long celebrations around the Torah at *Simkhes toyre* connects the celebrations of the other two holidays, which commemorate military victories of the Jews over their persecutors, with Senderl's degraded condition as a soldier and prisoner of the Czar, a persecutor of the Jews if ever there was one. This contrast at once suggests the long historical decline of Jewish power, and the infantilization or emasculation of the Jewish man, but it also implies that the proper realm for warfare is the harmless world of childhood. In this light, glorifying warfare and the military as such can be seen as ultimately, ridiculously childish.

Senderl therefore emerges—like the mare in *Di Klyatshe*, who proves herself to be cleverer and freer than Yisrolik—as the central focus of the last chapters of the novel. As in Reb Nakhman's "Story of a Sophisticate and a Simpleton," the *tam*, not the supposed *hokhem*, is valorized at the end of *Benyomin hashlishi*; it is *his* commedia, at the end, *his* happy ending, that is celebrated. And so, when he acquiesces to escape with Benyomin, as he gives in to each of Benyomin's impulses, he offers, at last, his own justification for their journey: "I think . . . that a formal farewell here is unnecessary. . . . After all, when we left our home a year ago, we didn't even say 'go to hell' to anybody, not even our wives and kids!" (Y 247; E 260). Here Senderl reveals, almost unwittingly, that

the ultimate purpose of his journey with Benyomin is escape itself—
first from their "traditional" responsibilities to wife, children, and the
community, and finally from the imperial state.

It is therefore appropriate that a novel about escape should never
reach a final resolution; at the end, Benyomin and Senderl are still on
the lam, eternally.[23] But then, doesn't Mendele himself make a similar
escape simply by traveling from shtetl to shtetl, participating in the
life of the community just long enough to absorb the local stories and
move on, evading the emotional entanglements of his family? Like
Benyomin and Senderl, Mendele is always one step ahead of the burdens of daily life, and even of a modern economic order that by the end
of Abramovitsh's career had rendered the itinerant book peddler almost
completely obsolete. In this vein, Benyomin and Senderl are, at this
late stage of their adventures, "reborn" out of the womb of the colonizing mother country, as the first adolescent—preceding, in fact, the
introduction of the term[24]—antiheroes of modernist fiction: 12 years
before Knut Hamsun's *Hunger*, 38 years before James Joyce's *Portrait
of the Artist as a Young Man*, and, more crucially still, 14 years before
the debut of Sholem Aleichem's Menakhem-Mendl, Yiddish literature's
most significant perpetual adolescent character. Abramovitsh's characters anticipate all of these later figures, and surpass them in their pursuit
of a utopian freedom that serves as its own form of redemption.

If Abramovitsh's *Benyomin hashlishi* becomes, in the final analysis, a
story of eternal escape and the joy of trespassing the official lines that
separate, estrange, and exclude the people marginalized by modernity,
Ahmadou Kourouma's novel *Les Soleils des indépendances* is correspondingly a narrative about characters with nowhere to run, whose life and
death are circumscribed by borders and boundaries that divide communities against themselves and differentiate the modern from the traditional, rich from poor, elite from dispossessed, men from women,
the written from the oral. Nonetheless, folklore and the language of
the folk—particularly the Africanized French of the postcolonial metropolis, which receives in this book its first literary representation in
the Francophone novel[25]—serve, if not as a means of evading these lines
of demarcation, at least as a force that demasks social realities, and thus

forms a *discourse of resistance* against the hegemony that dominates the lives of the novel's protagonists and the various groups they represent. This effort to break out of the class strictures that have previously demarcated the African novel clearly distinguishes Kourouma's novel from Soyinka's, which focuses almost exclusively on an educated but alienated elite, but links it to the ironic populism of Abramovitsh's *Benyomin hashlishi*.

Opening in an unnamed African city—one closely resembling Abidjan, the capital of the Ivory Coast—*Les Soleils des indépendances* alternates its focus between Fama, an illiterate and dispossessed Mande aristocrat, and his wife Salimata, with whom he lives in unconcealed estrangement. Like *Di Klyatshe*, *Les Soleils* divides into three parts: the first describes Fama and Salimata's life in the city; the second narrates Fama's return to his native village, Togobala (in Guinea), where he reclaims his ancestral title and takes a young bride whom he mistakenly believes will provide him the heir that Salimata has been unable to conceive; the third part relates Fama's return to the city, where he is arrested for unwittingly associating with a putative conspirator in a plot to overthrow the government. When in a gesture of feigned magnanimity the country's ruler pardons Fama along with the rest of the "coup leaders," Fama rejects the leader's ostensible generosity and attempts to return to his home community. By now, however, the borders of the postcolonial nations separating the city from Fama's home have been sealed, an apparent reference to the guarded borders dividing Sekou Touré's Guinea from Félix Houphouët-Boigny's Ivory Coast, and Fama is killed trying to swim the river between the two countries.[26]

The plot of *Les Soleils* therefore resembles *Benyomin hashlishi* both in its connection to historical events and in the obliviousness of the still-traditional protagonists whose lives are disrupted by the events themselves. At the same time, Kourouma's writing resembles Abramovitsh's in that it offers a simultaneous parody and vindication of the traditional worldview that continues to define and constrain his protagonists. This *return* to the tradition as a discourse that shapes the language in which the narrative is written is paradoxically the essence of Kourouma's radical break with the Francophone literature that precedes him. Although the linguistic practice of *Les Soleils* closely resembles Tutuola's writing from the 1950s, Kourouma belongs to the third generation of Francophone African writers—after Senghor, then Camara and Kane—whereas Tutuola is part of the first generation of Anglophone writers; Kourouma's writing belongs explicitly to the era of the postcolonial nation-state, rather than the colonial era or the time of the independence movement. It is thus only at the end of the 1960s that Francophone and Anglophone African literatures share common formal, ideological, and linguistic features, and these intersections derive explicitly from a common condition of political crisis.

The formal similarity between Kourouma's debut and Tutuola's asserts itself from the first page of *Les Soleils*: "One week had passed since Koné Ibrahima, of the Mande race, had met his end in the capital city, or to put it in Mande: he'd been defeated by a mere cold."[27] Like *The Palm-Wine Drinkard*, *Les Soleils* opens with a death, and the rest of the novel transpires in its shadow, casting the events in cosmological terms on the border between life and death, the one border the characters are able to negotiate without a passport or government permission. The novel thus reverses the pseudo-autobiographical strategy of the postnegritude novel by beginning with old age and death instead of childhood or the awakening of perception. This in turn serves to reassert the past as a tangible, even cancerous presence in the brave new world of independence, as signified by the identification of Koné not as a citizen of a nation-state, but as a member of "the Mande race," a deterritorialized designation, like the Diallobé in *L'aventure ambiguë*, at once smaller than the nation and transcendent of it. Moreover, the opening of the narrative calls attention to the discontinuities and incompatibilities of traditional funeral customs in the ostensibly modern life of the city; this in turn ironizes the novel as a whole, which employs a structure and a cosmology derived from the Mande tradition, but grafts these traditions onto the modern, malleable form of the Francophone novel.

The protagonist Fama further reflects these indeterminacies when he makes his appearance in the novel. As Kourouma writes, Fama enters the narrative from "the far end of the bridge linking the white men's town with the African quarter, and it was time for second prayer; the ceremony had begun. . . . What a miserable misbegotten time of year it was here, between seasons, mingling sunshine and rain" (F 11; E 5).

Fama therefore makes his first appearance in a liminal space, on a bridge between the Black and white parts of town, at a liminal time of year, running late for Koné Ibrahima's ceremony of transition between life and death! Moreover, the author here underscores the relationship between the urban setting and Fama's sense of entrapment and his loss of control over his circumstances. At the same time as *Les Soleils* advertises a "neotraditional" aesthetic by incorporating Mande folklore into the discourse of the novel, it is also one of the first significant depictions of modern, urban life in Francophone African literature. Whereas before the era of independence there is scarcely a description of the African metropolis to be found in Francophone fiction, Kourouma writes here of "horns hooting, motors racing, tires flapping, passers-by and drivers shouting" (F 11; E 5). This scene deliberately contrasts with the tranquility of *L'enfant noir*, the isolation of characters in *L'aventure ambiguë*, and the cordoning off of African characters from most of the apparatuses of modernity in *Une Vie de boy*.

It is of course from Fama's perspective that the modern city appears so strange, cacophonous, and hostile; Fama is the "last legitimate Dumbaya," and as a nobleman within the Mande caste system, he has been dispossessed by modernity and independence. With the arrival of individual autonomy comes the loss of guaranteed prestige to those born to positions of rank in the tradition. The tradition reasserts itself, nonetheless, ironically and at Fama's expense, through the narrator's discourse. Thus, when the narrator describes Koné Ibrahima's journey after death back to his native village, he adds, "You seem skeptical" (F 9; E 3). This second-person plural address, though seeming to acknowledge modern doubts engendered toward traditional cosmology, is in fact a reassertion of orality in the written form of the novel. It is a dialogical strategy for depicting the conflict between the natural and the supernatural, realism and fantasy, modernity and tradition, the West and Africa, French and Mande. This phrase, and the traditional belief of the spirit's journey after death that it comments on, split the difference between tradition and modernity. Although this juxtaposition contributes to the author's portrayal of these anomalies, it should be recalled that the assimilation of new, even averse, circumstances to a pattern of continuity is what tradition does—to a real extent, what it *is*—and therefore this passage represents a process observable everywhere in contemporary Africa.

The incorporation of an oral narrative style of direct appeal to the reader additionally underscores the perception—in both *The Interpreters* and *Les Soleils des indépendances*, like the Abramovitsh novels discussed in this section—that the language of realism, both in the sense of standard English or French, and in the sense of narrative decorum, interior psychology, linear chronology, and so forth, has failed. This signals both the failure of a superficially assimilated modern rationalism, and the failure of a new society, the nation-state, that was to have been created along these modern, rational, essentially Western lines. Indeed, the failed nation-state, the most catastrophic collision of power with desire, is perhaps the ultimate assemblage, as these satirical critiques reveal; in these novels, the use of multiple perspectives, though representative of the collectivizing logic of the modern nation, in fact indicates the inability of the nation itself to coalesce, to integrate itself either into a single consciousness or a unified representation.

Similarly, the linguistic character of *Les Soleils* is an important aesthetic component in the author's rejection of the nation-state, because the *Francophonie* of negritude, the faith in the French language's ability to transcend religious, ethnic, and class differences, was essential to the hopes of creating a national consciousness and the modern nation-state in West Africa.[28] Negritude similarly invests in the French language a quest for universalism, and a means of bringing Africa to the banquet table of modern civilization—what Aliounne Diop referred to as "a *dialogue of cultures* . . . A full-fledged, civilized community must know how to appreciate . . . the wealth and the meaning of that which it borrows from other civilizations. . . . Particularly in the Black world, the dialogue must first take place within each of the nations, between the people and their Westernized elite—in order to preserve . . . the creative vitality of our global civilization."[29] That the journal *Présence Africaine* formed the fruits of Diop's premise is an indication of how explicitly negritude's dialogue between cultures depended on French as its vehicle.

The investment in French as the linguistic vehicle for a universal Black civilization contrasts with the status of English in the Anglophone African world.[30] In addition to the contrast in colonial policy between the French and the English, the doctrine of Francophone assimilation served to repress the reality of French as it was spoken in West Africa. Bakhtin theorizes this point: "What inevitably happens [in instances of literary heteroglossia] is a decay and collapse of the religious, political, and ideological authority connected with that language. It is during this process of decay that the decentered language consciousness of prose art ripens, finding its support in the social heteroglossia of national languages that are actually spoken" (*The Dialogic Imagination*, 370). Although Bakhtin has in mind the breakdown of medieval, Church-dominated Latin into the literary vernaculars of the Renaissance, the same process repeats itself when colonial French collapses along with the neocolonial nation-state. And here's where *Les Soleils des indépendances* comes in, where the national language, French, is the Other's language, the literary language that at once unites and estranges its respective postcolonial and metropolitan audiences.

At this point in the development of Francophone literature, Kourouma's characters can speak the Mande-inflected French of the Ivoirean cities, rather than having their language, as in *L'aventure ambiguë*, invoked in the consciously stylized, pristine, and alienated French of the *Académie française*. As Kourouma himself described the process of writing the novel, "I thought it in Mande and wrote in French, taking liberties that I consider natural with the classical language. . . . I therefore translated the Mande into French, breaking the French in order to find and restore the African rhythm."[31] In fact, the Madagascan poet and political leader Jacques Rabemananjara (1913–2005) had already acknowledged, and romanticized, this phenomenon in terms characteristic of negritude ideology: "The truth is that the imperatives of our drama force us to speak Madagascan, Arabic, Wolof, and Bantu in the language of our masters. Because our language is the same, even if we do not use the same language, we manage to understand each other perfectly from Tantare to Kingston, from Pointe-à-Pitre to Zomba."[32] The circumstances that both Rabemananjara and Kourouma describe are common to all writers using deterritorialized, global languages, but few postcolonial writers have made the lines of correspondence between the maternal language below and the vehicular language above so explicitly a part of their discourse as Kourouma has in *Les Soleils des indépendances*.

Nonetheless, Mande-inflected French is not identical to writing in Mande, and at the same time that Kourouma reshapes the structure of French grammar and syntax to accommodate Mande idioms, he also underscores, perhaps unwittingly, the absence of the Mande language itself in his narrative. The absence of Mande in *Les Soleils* in this regard differs little from the invoked languages of *Une Vie de boy* (Ewondo), *L'aventure ambiguë* (its African sections, in Peul), or *Mission terminée* (one of the Beti languages of South-Central Cameroon). Indeed, most African literature of the 1950s and 60s, whether written in English[33] or French, is the translation of an original that never existed. And as such, the phantom evoked by the African novel is inevitably the reflection of an African language conceived of by its author as a fundamentally *oral* language that refuses to be *reduced* to writing.

In this situation, the act of writing is a struggle against the oral tradition, against the modern hegemony of colonial literacy, and against the fixed divide between writing and speech. Just as Reb Nakhman's stories anticipate, surpass, and frustrate the interpretive strategies employed to streamline their complexities, so too does the African novel exemplify and resist the poststructuralist strategies developed in the following generation for understanding the relationship between speaking and writing. African novels emerge from a recognition of the fundamental disjuncture between speech and writing, but they politicize these problems in a way that transcends the philosophical paradoxes that characterize purely "textual" analyses. *Les Soleils* is nonetheless significant for bringing this conflict between orality and literacy, between Mande and French, into the discourse of the novel itself. Following Bakhtin, the distinction between Kourouma's writing and the (post-) negritude narratives that precede it reflects nothing less than two stylistic lines of development for the novel as a literary form. As Bakhtin defines the first stylistic line of development, "Its primary characteristic is the fact that it knows only a single language and a single style . . . heteroglossia remains *outside* the novel" (*The Dialogic Imagination,* 375). Because heteroglossia is an integrated presence within the discourse of *Les Soleils*, it is an example of the "second line," which in the history of the novel, as much as in the parades of the New Orleans Mardi Gras, is where the counterhegemonic cross-rhythms of the dispossessed work against the grain of official discourse, insistently marching to the beat of their drums.

Les Soleils is the most important instance of this antihegemonic de-territorialization in French, but it is by no means an isolated case. As Manthia Diawara relates of a conversation with Williams Sassine (1944–1997) in which Sassine uses the term *autonomous sadness*: "The phrase he actually used was *indépendant triste*, a play on words characteristic of Afro-pessimist writers such as himself, Henry Lopez [*sic*], Ahmadou Kourouma, and Sony Labou Tansi.³⁴ These writers liked to 'deform' the meaning of French words by playing on their pronunciations (for example, *indépendantiste* and *indépendant triste*), by literally translating African imagery into French, or by connecting specific words to local events like coups d'etat and economic crises."³⁵ Thus a collective effort emerges among this generation of Francophone writers for the first time to "Africanize" French in the manner that Tutuola had "African-ized" English two decades previously. Considering Bakhtin's remarks on the significance of such deterritorialization for the development of novelistic discourse, French and English once again become, like Yid-dish, *fusion languages*, recognizable as such for the first time since the Middle Ages, in the work of African writers.

At the same time that Kourouma injects traditional African dis-course—specifically the idioms and belief system of the Mande—into the modern form of the French novel, he also depicts the transforma-tion of the Mande tradition in the modern era; as much as he depicts the "return of the repressed" in the modern African metropolis, he also pushes the tradition he reclaims *forward* into a new historical and ex-istential context. With this in mind, one can consider Adrien Huan-nou's characterization of the narrative technique in *Les Soleils*: "This process is similar to the dream technique used in film. . . . [T]he past and the present, dream and reality, are intimately mingled in the narra-tive, which at times achieves the status of an epic" ("La technique du récit," 32). Huannou's suggestion that Kourouma's narrative techniques derive as much from film as from traditional griotic narrative points to a significant formal characteristic of modern African literature—the convergence of Western High Modernist, or postmodernist, and tradi-tional oral aesthetics.

Thus just as Kourouma represents the city, as seen from Fama's perspective, through the static bustle, the "changing same" of the traffic jam, he also uses Fama's relationship to the urban terrain to locate this character in temporal terms, as well as social ones, between his current predicament and his previous aspirations: "After the market, the central avenue led to the cemetery and beyond that to the lagoon, which could be glimpsed at the end under heavy rain. Fama knew this central avenue as well as he knew his wife Salimata's body; it reminded him both of trade and anti-colonialist activities" (F 24; E 13). This description of the central avenue, associated with Salimata's body, makes her, in turn, equally suggestive of commerce and a territorial struggle over possession and domination. The avenue itself, however, provides a metaphorical itinerary of Fama's life, leading inexorably to the cemetery—just as the narrative as a whole opens in the terminal situation of a funeral— but beyond death lies the lagoon and the heavy rain, an aquatic image of release and regeneration that is itself indicative of the cyclical redemption that water signifies in Sufi mysticism. The central avenue in this description becomes an urbanized, anthropomorphic image of Africa, contrasted with the more "classical" figure of Africa as "his wife's body," and as such combines Fama's traditional role as a Mande trader with his ostensibly national, modern role as an anticolonial fighter.

Fama's (unspecified) background as a participant in the independence struggle likewise refutes the association of Fama's traditional status with political conservatism, and throws his discontent with the "suns of independence," the rising stars of the neocolonial state, into sharper relief, marking him as another figure of resistance against European and African hegemonies. As Kourouma writes:

> Fama burned with remorse because he had hated the French and opposed their presence, rather like the blade of grass that complained because the tall tree was taking all the sunlight; once the tree was felled, it had its share of the sun, but also of the wind, which crushed it. Let no one take Fama for a colonialist, mind. For he had seen the colonial era, had known the French administrators who meant many things and many troubles: forced labor in the wood-cutting camps, on the roads and bridges; taxes and more taxes, and fifty other levies such as every conqueror demands, not to forget the lash of the whip and other torments. (F 22; E 12–13)

This cataloguing of colonial abuses is both a corollary and a corrective to the disillusionment with independence. Without it, the reader might think that Kourouma, or at least his protagonist, is nostalgic for colonialism. Rather, the failure of independence signifies, in addition to the accretion of further miseries on an oppressed and degraded society, the failure of the dialectic that sets Blacks against whites and tradition against modernity. In the aftermath of independence, the postcolonial subject is truly alone—both free of previous constraints, and bereft of support from any previously stable culture or social identity.

However much Fama's predicament is rooted in the neocolonial moment, Kourouma's discourse in describing it is rooted in the Mande tradition, which is itself a mode of resistance against the nation-state. Even the ambiguities of Fama's position with respect to tradition and modernity receive a "traditionalist" gloss, as when Kourouma writes, "Mande are full of duplicity because deep down inside they are blacker than their skin, while the words they speak are whiter than their teeth. Are they fetish-worshippers or Muslims? A Muslim heeds the Koran, a fetish-worshipper follows the Koma; but in Togobala, everyone publicly proclaims himself a devout Muslim, but everyone privately fears the fetish. Neither lizard nor swallow!" (F 105; E 72). Thus even before the era of independence, the Mande had distinguished themselves ethnically and cosmologically through their liminal status between African animism and orthodox Islam. Ultimately, these identifications with either fetishism or Islam are exposed as masks that the individual can change as circumstance demands—just as the narrator's own strategies derive from oral sources in order to conceal, and reconfigure, his dependence on literacy itself for the production of his story.

The ambivalence toward Islam in *Les Soleils* contrasts both with the syncretic harmony projected between Islam and African animism in *L'enfant noir*—another, earlier product of Mande culture—and with the austere orthodoxy of *L'aventure ambiguë*. Seen from the perspective of Yiddish literature, however, *Les Soleils* is more genuinely an "Islamic" novel to the extent that Islam enters the novel's discourse as a "living thing," a part of daily life to be interrogated and integrated into ordinary experience as much as any other cultural reference. It is with this in mind that one can understand Salimata's interior monologue in which she contemplates her incessant supplications for a child: "[S]he was praying that she might be unfaithful, commit adultery. Allah, beneficent provider, forgive the blasphemy! Had she sinned? No! Salimata was not an impious sinner; her marriage bound together a sterile husband and a faithful wife. . . . She smiled slightly, but quickly repressed it: never smile while on the prayer mat of Allah" (F 44; E 27–28). In fact, religious discourse in this novel generally consists of smiling not only on the prayer mat, but also at its expense.

What is therefore significant about this passage—not only in terms of Islam specifically, but the novel's relationship to authority in general—is not Salimata's repression of her smile, but the smile's refusal to be repressed. Here, as in Abramovitsh's narratives, the tradition is no longer a sacred relic, but a living entity to be at turns laughed at for its superstitions and rigid caste system, at other times to be indicted for the needless suffering and abuse of characters such as Salimata, and still other times to be mobilized as a force of resistance against the neocolonial order. Therefore, just as Kane sets up a dichotomy whereby Samba Diallo's story can be seen either as a comedy from a modern, European perspective or a tragedy from a traditional, Islamic-African one, Kourouma establishes an analogous divergence of perspective between Fama and Salimata, between men and women.

These roles reverse, however, when Fama goes to prison; then, his life becomes a tragedy,[36] and Salimata's a *commedia*.[37] But whereas Samba Diallo's story can be, at least until its conclusion, either comic or tragic, Fama and Salimata are the objects of the author's satire and empathy, respectively. Moreover, the dialectic between the comic and the tragic, the Western and the African, the novel and the epic, the male and the female corresponds to a deeper structure that aligns men with the centrifugal dynamics of modernity and women with the pacified embodiment of tradition and Africa. If anything, however, the structure intensifies the irony of Fama's position, which is as much the antithesis of dynamic male vigor as it is anti-Western and antimodern.

Kourouma's focus on gender and his willingness to challenge the metaphorical and political associations of traditional gender roles takes on greater significance when one considers the near-total absence in his generation of female writers in Francophone Africa. As Christopher

Miller writes, "*Les Soleils des indépendances* comes in the middle of a long silence, the 'silence' of women's exclusion from black African literary francophonie. It is only in the mid-1970s that the first novels by women are published, making the first generation of women writers a greatly belated one" (*Theories of Africans*, 225). The voicelessness of women in the Francophone tradition, like the avoidance of Africanized usages in the colonial language, contrasts with the Anglophone tradition, where female writers such as Flora Nwapa, Efua T. Sutherland (1924–1996), and Ama Ata Aidoo (b. 1942) had been active from the mid-60s. And yet this time lag is no different from the near-total absence of published women writers in modern Yiddish before the twentieth century. These absences are all the more telling when one considers the status of Yiddish as *dos mame-loshn* and the centrality of Africa as "the motherland" in the iconography of negritude. In both instances the symbolic visibility of women conceals their silence and participates in their suppression. As with his representation of traditional characters struggling with modernity, Kourouma's focus on the plight of women, laboring under dual burdens of neocolonial poverty and traditional oppression, is a step toward expanding the representation of women in African literature.

Conclusion

As significant as Kourouma's representation of Salimata in *Les Soleils* is to the status of women in Francophone African fiction, it is no substitute for the transformation of this tradition that begins when women begin to write their own narratives; similarly, his representation of Mande-inflected French cannot be confused with the growth of native African-language writing that begins with Ngugi wa Thiong'o's theater work in Gikuyu in the 1970s. To the extent that this comparison has focused primarily on formal questions of literary structure and narrative voice, an equally significant transition occurs—in both Yiddish and African literature—in the subsequent generation when authors turn from the depiction of traditional characters through an external narrator, and create first-person narratives for such traditional characters. This development signals a reinscription of oral narrative and folkloric themes that further differentiate these peripheral literatures from the dominant trends of metropolitan cultures. At the same time, the willingness of modern writers to depict folk traditions, and the folk themselves, from the internal perspective of first-person narration, rather than the external, ethnographic technique of indirect discourse signals a decisive turn in the ethics of the imagination and the politics of identification.

In this regard, the essential difference between Mendele's *Benyomin hashlishi* or Kourouma's *Les Soleils des indépendances* and Sholem Aleichem's *Tevye der milkhiker* ("Tevye the Dairyman," published serially from 1894 until 1916) or *Sozaboy: A Novel in Rotten English* (1985) by the Nigerian author Ken Saro-Wiwa (1941–1996) is the use in the first two works of free indirect discourse (or the Yiddish equivalent, the mediating and manipulating presence of the Mendele figure),[1] as opposed to the presentation of an ostensibly unmediated folkloric, oral consciousness in the latter. With respect to Yiddish literature, it is noteworthy that Abramovitsh's use of third-person narration occurs most successfully in *Benyomin hashlishi*; his earlier maskilic "monologic" narratives are by contrast narrated in the first person. Sholem Aleichem is, paradoxically, never more dialogical than when using the monologue form.

At stake in Abramovitsh's move from first-person to third-person narration is the traditional status of Yiddish as a primarily oral language. What is significant about the author's transition from quasi-oral confessional narrative forms to more "writerly" indirect discourse is his *inability* to break completely with oral conventions—however attenuated, there remains in *Benyomin hashlishi* a speaking protagonist's voice, to which Mendele adds commentary. Rather than supplanting the oral narrator with authorial omniscience, Abramovitsh creates a structure of competing testimonies: Mendele's versus Benyomin's. A generation later, Sholem Aleichem reverses this process; in the Tevye stories, as in his other monologues, the folk character speaks, and the interlocutor—usually Sholem Aleichem himself, who is no less an artistic construct than Abramovitsh's Mendele is[2]—relates the story without interruption. Tevye and Sholem Aleichem thus represent a diametric inversion of the relationship between Benyomin and Mendele.

The Sozaboy ("soldier boy") in Saro-Wiwa's novel about the Biafran Civil War similarly speaks directly to the reader, in contrast to Kourouma's characters. This strategy provides a narrative corollary to the broader emergence of neotraditional aesthetics in the African culture of the 1980s and 90s. As Kwame Appiah writes, "Despite the overwhelming reality of economic decline; despite unimaginable poverty; despite wars, malnutrition, disease and political instability, African cultural productivity grows apace: popular literatures, oral narrative and poetry, dance, drama, music, and visual art all thrive. The contemporary cultural production of many African societies . . . is an antidote to the dark vision of the postcolonial novelist" (*In My Father's House*, 157). The fact that popular arts in Africa "speak" in so different a voice from the established norms of postcolonial belles-lettres helps to explain their validity as aesthetic models, and of the people who create and consume these cultural productions as subjects for the postcolonial writer. These representations of a transformed traditional culture were precisely the aspects of African culture that were marginalized by the creation of a modern nation-state.[3] The failure of the nation-state therefore suggests these representatives of an alternative identity as a new path of escape for the postcolonial author.

It is to this effort toward valorization of the transformed tradition that the next generation of African narratives orients itself in the ongoing elaboration of a peripheral aesthetic and worldview. The formal mediation by which African authors achieve this represented reconciliation with the voices of the modernized African folk would require a separate study. For the time being, the present discussion can conclude, having connected African and Yiddish literature to one another, to a broader phenomenon of "minor" literatures, and to the continuing efforts of dissident writers to validate their traditions for a better future.

Conclusion *At the Limits of the Periphery*
The Future of the "Minor" in Minority Literatures

In 1978, my parents mistakenly wandered into a cinema where the Cheech and Chong comedy *Up in Smoke* was playing. As far removed from the marijuana-infused counterculture of the 1970s as any other middle-aged, middle-class couple in Alexandria, Louisiana, most of the film's humor went over—or under—their head. One scene, however, amused them tremendously, and subsequently entered the proverbial wisdom of family lore: when Tommy Chong's character first joins Cheech Marin's rock band, he responds to a fellow musician's suggestion that the group wear uniforms by saying, "If we're gonna wear uniforms, man, ya know, let's everybody wear something different." Cheech promptly responds, " . . . Yeah, we want something where everyone wears something different, but the same, ya know?" (It should be noted at this point that my family's business sells uniforms to city agencies in Alexandria.)

Peripheral literatures share with Cheech and Chong's post-hippie humor an affirmation of difference in the midst of conformity; to the canon of modern, Western literature, the peripheral proposes a parallel countercanon, a fugal polyphony, at once different, and the same, as the hegemony it resists. At the heart of peripheral literature, like the Cheech and Chong movie—which, similar to its distant generic cousin *Benyomin hashlishi*, is ultimately as much about utopian friendship as it is the specifics of scoring and smoking dope—is an affirmation of a community that is at once both collective and private. The particular   245 phenomenon of experiencing a peripheral culture is increasingly familiar to more and more people around the world, even in the United States, despite its role in creating much of the world's popular culture and its hegemony over the world's political and economic agenda.[1] By considering how the aesthetics of peripherality have shaped the literary cultures of nineteenth-century Jewish Eastern Europe and twentieth-century West Africa, this comparison has sought to suggest strategies for understanding the mechanism of resistance in minority cultures undergoing the process of modernization. These strategies, in turn, offer possibilities for new modes of resistance, at the same time radical and rooted in a tradition, for the future.

The Yiddish component of this book concludes historically around the turn of the twentieth century; Yiddish literature of course continues to appear thereafter—even in the present day—but Yiddish as an automatic expression of Ashkenazic Jewish peripherality essentially comes to an end in the decade prior to World War I. As Benyomin Moss writes, "The 1905 Revolution demonstrated the symbolic importance of Yiddish in the political struggle for Jewish rights and also cleared the way legally for a massive expansion of the Yiddish press and print market. . . . The flourishing of Yiddish print culture in general and Yiddish literature in particular during and after 1905 stood in stark contrast to a sudden and shocking crisis in the material conditions of Hebrew literature."[2] Although Moss points out that the cultural primacy of Yiddish was ultimately short-lived due both to a resurgence of political repression in Czarist Russia, and to the eventual establishment of a Hebrew-language cultural center in Palestine, the year 1905 stands effectively as the marker separating the Yiddish literature of the nineteenth century from that of the twentieth.

In 1908, the Czernowitz language conference declared Yiddish "a national language of the Jewish people";[3] prior to this revolutionary valorization of Yiddish as a cultural expression of Jewish nationalism, Hebrew writers had begun an ultimately successful campaign against Yiddish in favor of an autonomous spoken, read, and written modern Hebrew. With these parallel movements toward linguistic nationalism and autonomy, Yiddish loses its symbiosis with *Loshn-koydesh*, and it ceases to signify the peripheral status of Jewish vernacularity vis-à-vis either metropolitan modernity or hegemonic tradition. After the Czernowitz conference, and particularly the efforts of Y. L. Peretz (1852–

1915) to create a modern, aesthetic Yiddish literature emancipated from oral techniques of monologue and burlesque, Yiddish writers, like their Hebrew counterparts, could participate in an unreconstructed fashion in the leading trends of modern literature. Thus Dovid Bergelson (1884–1952), for example, employs the same techniques of psychological introspection and indirect discourse as Henry James, Anton Chekhov, or Thomas Mann. Bergelson's contemporary Y. Y. Singer (1893–1944, I. B. Singer's older brother) similarly devotes his career primarily to "major" genres of novelistic realism such as the family saga and the historical novel. At the same time as these prose writers begin their career in Europe, the first major Yiddish poetic movement, *Di Yunge* ("the Young Ones"), emerges in the United States and makes of Yiddish a truly international literature.

In the interwar era, Yiddish would create within itself "functional" literatures—for example, the serialized, propagandistic literatures of political parties such as the communists, socialist-Yiddishist Bundists, and the Orthodox *Agudes yisroyl* or the *shund* ("trashy") novels of the popular press—and in this context "minority" could become an artistic strategy to be deployed to resist either ideological or economic imperatives of the literary marketplace. In this regard, one can recognize the early, symbolist fiction of Der Nister (1884–1950) as "minor," but not his later, socialist realist prose. Similarly, the monologue stories of I. B. Singer[+] (circa 1904–1991) are "minor," but not his novels; likewise, the prose of Avrom Sutzkever (1913–2010), but not his poetry.[5] These developments, which reached their apex in Poland, the Soviet Union, and the United States during the 1930s, neither anticipate nor mimic trends in metropolitan literature but rather contribute to the formulation of an international Modernist literature.

And then came the Holocaust.

After World War II, Yiddish writing consolidated primarily into a literature of commemoration—though in the work of writers such as Sutzkever and Singer, the task of commemoration evoked an extraordinary range and depth of artistry, seldom equaled by Holocaust literature in other languages. A few authors of significant talent emerged in Yiddish after the war—such as the prose writers Yosl Birstein (1920–2004) and Chava Rosenfarb (1923–2011), and the poets H. Benyomin (b. 1928) and

Rukhl Fishman (1935–1984)—but the ability of Yiddish to speak for a modern collective, other than a spectral one, becomes more limited with each year. In its accumulating absence, Jewish literature today comes to be characterized along three lines: essentially, the last sixty years have seen the emergence of a Hebrew literature in Israel that has developed as a national literature; an Anglophone literature in North America that ultimately resembles other American "ethnic" literatures more than it resembles its counterpart in Israel; and splitting the difference between these two dominant Jewish communities is a memoiristic literature in most of the European languages that saw Jewish communities affected by the Holocaust.[6] Thus, though the cultures of Judaism continue to distinguish themselves as cosmopolitan, nomadic, and borderless, both with respect to coterritorial cultures and to other Jewish communities, the belletristic literature of contemporary Jews comes increasingly to be defined and contained within linguistic and national limits.

The division of current Jewish literature along national and functional lines therefore poses the question of whether it is possible to speak of a single, unified concept of Jewish literature at all. It should thus come as no surprise that a number of studies have emerged recently dedicated to the idea of either a national or an international canon of Jewish literature.[7] In this regard, Ruth Wisse's study of modern Jewish literature is revealing in its methodology; Wisse's list of authors excluded from the survey, and presumably from the Jewish canon—including canonical Modernists such as Gertrude Stein, Bruno Schulz, and Paul Celan (*The Modern Jewish Canon*, 18)—serves to indicate the limitations of "Jewish literature" as an all-encompassing concept. Equally significant is the decision to confine her focus to the twentieth century. Indeed, it would be difficult to imagine what a "major" Jewish literary tradition originating in the nineteenth century might consist of. True, maskilim such as Naphtali Herz Wessely, Avraham Mapu, and Peretz Smolenskin devoted themselves to the formation of just such a literature—but who reads these authors today? Nonetheless, if Wisse's intention is to provide modern Jewish culture with a "major" canon, then her examples, of Franz Kafka and Isaac Babel alongside Sholem Aleichem and Sh. Y. Agnon, are telling: these authors are central to the

Jewish cultural canon precisely because they articulate the *peripherality* of Jews in relation to the experience of Western modernity.

The essential dilemma of this peripherality hinges on the question of how to participate in the modern world without having to negate identification, along renegotiated terms, with the Jewish tradition. This challenge engages precisely the questions of language, temporality, and national identity that have determined the readings in this comparison. Indeed, the structural character of this problem seems to have evolved little from the terms in which it was first expressed during the nineteenth century, although the choices available to Jews, at least in liberal societies, have increased greatly. In this context, it is revealing to consider, again, how Jewish intellectuals first began to formulate the negotiation between tradition and modernity in relative terms, rather than dialectical ones. As Immanuel Etkes writes, "It was Eliezer Tsevi Zweifel (1815–88) who first broke with the Haskalah's traditional hostility to hasidism. In his *Shalom al yisra'el* (1868), Zweifel described hasidism as a legitimate phenomenon, alongside the Talmud and kabbalah."[8] Although Zweifel was the first to make this argument formally in the only vehicle that other maskilim would validate—a schematic polemic written in Hebrew—Yiddish writers such as Y. Y. Linetski and Aleksander Zederbaum had, in less systematic terms, articulated similar expressions of guarded respect for the Hasidic movement, if only in its earlier generations, as early as 1865.

Indeed, soon enough the historical legitimation of Hasidism would become a virtual cliché in Jewish intellectual circles; in this regard, Zweifel is a precursor to the turn-of-the-century adoption, by writers as diverse as Y. L. Peretz and Martin Buber, of the early Hasidic masters as neoromantic heroes. He moreover anticipates the historical bias, initiated by Simon Dubnow but persisting today, of regarding the genuinely innovative and creative period of the Hasidic movement as ending definitively in the first two decades of the nineteenth century—that is, scarcely after the movement had begun to penetrate the daily life and social structures of nearly all of Eastern European Judaism. It should be stressed that both the historical and literary interest in Hasidism has proceeded over the past century with hardly the slightest effort at rapprochement or engagement with living Hasidim. This, too, follows the precedent of Zweifel and the other proto-nationalist maskilic "apologists" for the Hasidic movement. Moreover, the ability to praise the Hasidim as an abstraction of charismatic Jewish mysticism, while avoiding or ignoring the presence of real-life Hasidim, offers evidence of the actual process of modernization: Hasidim, as conscious embodiments of traditional culture, no longer have to be seen as a threat to modernity if they no longer share the same space, or compete for the same cultural capital, as the maskilim or their more completely modern successors.

The essential conflict in Ashkenazic modernity between Hasidism and *haskole* remains constant today: modern Jews continue to see a dialectic between the modern world and Jewishness that, however much many of them seek to mediate by creating a hybrid, Jewish ("minor") modernity, nonetheless seems to pull the majority of Jews in each generation in a centrifugal direction. This book itself is a product of maskilic sensibilities, ones expressed as early as 1867 in Linetski's polemic calling for reconciliation between the "best" of modernity and the "best" of *khsides*—a reconciliation that Jewish culture still awaits, more than 140 years later. Similarly, Hasidic culture, though never holding a monopoly on traditional Jewish observance—consider, for example, "Lithuanian" *misnagdes*, German neo-Orthodoxy, "oriental" Judaism of the Ottoman Empire and beyond—has exerted a remarkable monopoly on the imagination and representation of traditional Judaism, among both modern and observant Jews (and every shade in between!). Thus, the questions posed at the outset of this study by maskilim such as the young Sh. Y. Abramovitsh, and even earlier by the (also young) *khosid* Reb Nakhman, remain relevant to contemporary Jewish culture, even as the Yiddish language in which these questions were conceptualized has ceased to provide a common language in which answers might be debated among the factions that constitute Jewish life today.

It is precisely because these questions were first thought about and discussed in Yiddish that makes the study of Yiddish culture and literature so relevant for modern Jews today. And yet Yiddish, even among the modern Orthodox, remains an undervalued and unappreciated cultural resource, eclipsed by the engagement with modern culture primarily in English—even, often, in Israel—and the study of traditional Judaism in *Loshn-koydesh* (which most modern Jews are unable or unwilling to differentiate from modern Hebrew). The eclipse of Yiddish in the present generation is both consistent with and a consequence of a profound amnesia affecting the immigrant generations of American Jews. The trauma internalized from previous generations of coming to America, and to modernity, engendered a tremendous forgetfulness, such that for many contemporary Jews, to use a wildly inapt analogy, Jewishness is as much imagined as Africa is for many African Americans. Nonetheless, for contemporary Jews, forgotten Jewish traditions differ from the repressed African traditions from which African Americans were torn by slavery in the sense that Jewish traditions have been recorded in writing and as such can be replicated more fully in a new context than primarily oral African traditions that of necessity have been transformed and adapted in the New World. But as Haym Soloveitchik notes, the text-based reconstitution of the Jewish tradition created by contemporary Orthodox Jews is often quite different, in the form and extent of its preoccupations, from the tradition it ostensibly returns to.[9]

In more philosophical terms, one must recognize that memory is by definition conservative; forgetfulness is liberal.[10] It is forgetfulness that enables Russian and American scientists to work together in the aftermath of the Cold War. Forgetfulness enables middle-class African Americans to return to the Deep South. Forgetfulness, similarly, will be a likely prerequisite to any solution to the ongoing conflict between Israelis and Palestinians. The question posed to (and by) multiculturalism and other varieties of liberal humanism is the challenge of using memory as a progressive force—beating out a counterrhythm, like the second-line dancers at the Mardi Gras parades so crucial to the development of jazz, to the long victory march of modernity. Ralph Ellison identifies this type of memory with the Blues: "The blues is an impulse to keep the painful details and episodes of a brutal experience alive in one's aching consciousness, to finger its jagged grain, and to transcend it, not by the consolation of philosophy but by squeezing from it a near-tragic, near-comic lyricism."[11] Such pain, as Friedrich Nietzsche recognizes in *The Genealogy of Morals*, serves a mnemonic function. In this respect, I propose that a memory of Yiddish culture—a critical

engagement and confrontation with its literature—offers the most sophisticated and complex example of a peripheral ("Blues") sensibility at
once modern, humane, and uniquely Jewish.

The moment of rupture between Hebrew and Yiddish at the beginning
of the twentieth century is relevant to the comparison between Yiddish and African literature because at the beginning of the twenty-first
century, one of the central questions confronting African culture—*as
culture*—is the question of language. Indeed, this question, conceived
along the "quadratic" division of labor among maternal, vehicular, referential, and mythological components, has been the definitive formulation of "minor" literature throughout this discussion. At the dawn of
the twenty-first century, African literature defines itself in part through a
choice of competing "peripheralities": Should African authors continue
to write in colonial languages, thus marginalizing themselves from the
day-to-day culture of their native communities, which continue to be
conducted primarily in maternal languages, or should they participate
in the creation of a native-language modern literature that would inevitably lead to a marginalization, even more acute than that of the present
moment, of African literature vis-à-vis the metropolitan literatures of
Europe and the Americas?

To a certain degree, the relationship between specific languages and
modernity is moot. Hence Benedict Anderson writes, "Nothing suggests that Ghanaian nationalism is any less real than Indonesian simply
because its national language is English rather than Ashanti. It is always
a mistake to treat languages . . . as emblems of nation-ness, like flags,
costumes, folk-dances, and the rest. . . . Print language is what invents
nationalism, not *a* particular language per se."[12] Yet at the same time,
the linguistic question posed to African writers is quite different from
that posed to Jewish ones. Whereas the choice, typically, for Ashkenazic
writers historically has been between a national or imperial language
and one of two Jewish ones—Yiddish or Hebrew—shared in theory
by everyone in his or her community, for Africans the choice lies between the global, formerly colonial language, and one of approximately
a thousand languages,[13] many of which are spoken by comparatively
small groups of mostly nonliterate people.[14]

Nonetheless, the attraction to writing in native African languages has been a constant in postcolonial African polemics, from the era of decolonization to the present day. Albert Memmi in 1957 thus anticipated Ngugi wa Thiong'o's native-language activism by more than twenty years when he wrote, "colonized literature in European languages appears condemned to die young."[15] Such reports, needless to say, are premature. And yet, the statistical evidence of linguistic affiliation, at least in Anglophone—or ostensibly Anglophone—Africa, is difficult to untangle, as Eyamba Bokamba indicates:

> It is estimated . . . that no more than 10 percent of the population of any African country speaks the official language . . . except in the English-settled nations of Liberia, South Africa, and Zimbabwe. . . . Admittedly, the number of English speakers in Africa will increase steadily as the use of English as a compulsory school subject expands. . . . In education, for example . . . 47.1 percent of primary school students and 96.9 percent of those in secondary schools throughout Africa are enrolled in English classes. These are the highest percentages on any continent. . . . African speakers learn English at school and use it for very specific functions: education, official business . . . international diplomacy, and broadcasting. (*The Other Tongue*, 140–141)

At the very least, these figures point to the persistence of the distinction between vehicular and maternal languages, which from the outset has been the defining characteristic of a "minor" culture. Which of these two language choices, though, is best suited to contemporary Africa's confrontation with modernity?

Oyekan Owomoyela begins to answer this question by calling attention to the apparent exceptionality of the fact that the language of African literature is a political question in the first place: "Whereas elsewhere language in literature attracts attention and debate only in terms of the artistic effectiveness of its use, in Africa the major point of contention is in what language or languages the literatures may legitimately be expressed."[16] By the same token, though, what is the "legitimate" language for Jewish literature—a literature that, like African literature, is multilingual and multinational; what is the appropriate language for Africans, or Jews, to communicate with one another when they never in their history, or in the case of Jewish history, never in the last 2,500 years—have *spoken* a single language? Indeed, the advocacy of linguistic nationalism in the case of "minor" cultures such as Africans and Jews exposes the paradoxes of nationalism, for if the aim of cultural nationalism is to unify a group of people within a single language, then does the advocacy of linguistic nationalism underscore the inability of Jews or Africans to speak in a single language, a single voice? This would seem to be a paradox that Ngugi, at least, is aware of. Hence one can begin to identify in his linguistic nationalism a genuine "minor" sensibility: an act of protest against the hegemony of monolingualism and univocalism in the neocolonial nation-state.

And yet, there are clearly pitfalls—to invoke a metaphor from Fanon—to the use of native languages that either Ngugi or other language activists seem reluctant to acknowledge. In part, this can be demonstrated through the semantic problems with the term "national language" itself: English *is* the national language in Nigeria. Yoruba is not, or at least not in the same sense; Yoruba is the language of a particular ethnic group that has never defined itself as a nation in the modern, *European* sense of the term. Nigeria as a confederation was meant to mediate between ethnic groups and create a national identity that transcends tribal affinities. Returning to Yoruba, or any other local language, thus flies in the face of nationalism as it has been constituted in Africa—which considering the condition of the nation-state in much of the continent may not be such a bad thing after all.

On the other hand, the ideological loyalty to a local language might add an additional source of conflict to African societies already overburdened by conflicts based on religion, caste, and clan. Thus Owomoyela's reference to Canadian language activism as a model for Africa seems particularly ill-considered: "[T]he French-speaking Canadian province of Quebec has rekindled the old smoldering fire of their campaign to make French the only legitimate language in the province, and thus *to ensure that the French character of the province . . .* is reflected in the language it uses, permits, or privileges" (*A History of Twentieth Century African Literatures*, 363–364, emphasis added). And there's the rub: What do efforts to ensure the ethnic character of a particular place mean for people unable or unwilling to conform to the designated ethnic profile?

Is Francophone nationalism in Quebec an act of resistance to English hegemony, or an act of repression against the increasing multicultural-ism of urban Canadian society? It could, of course, be both, but the flight of Anglophone Canadians, including a conspicuous number of Jews not necessarily invested in the cultural supremacy of either En-glish or French, does not recommend the particular example of Quebec as a model for African linguistic "nationalism"—especially in countries such as Nigeria, Rwanda, Sierra Leone, or Sudan, where such ethnic conflicts, unlike those in Canada, have resulted in violence and even genocide.

Although nobody would argue that the choice of language is a de-cision worth dying or killing for, native languages clearly have a role to play in the articulation of a minority culture's experience of moder-nity. In this regard, the case of Sh. An-ski (1863–1920), easily the most important bilingual Russian-Yiddish author, underscores the fraught relationship between language and culture. As Mikhail Krutikov de-scribes the circuitous evolution of An-ski's play *Der Dibek*—probably the greatest Yiddish drama—from a manuscript in Russian to its osten-sibly final form in Yiddish: "The Russian version of *The Dybbuk* shows clearly how difficult it was for An-Ski to express kabalistic and Hasidic concepts. At times his translations [into Russian] are simply unintel-ligible without the Yiddish text, while at other times they sound too foreign to a Yiddish ear, because the entire 'spiritual' vocabulary in Rus-sian derives from Christianity. . . . Of course, in the Yiddish version, no hint of these difficulties remains."[17] The challenge of translating a foreign symbol system into a new language is one of the characteristic problems of "minor" writing in global languages. At the same time, however, as Amos Tutuola demonstrates, the incongruity of expressing one worldview in the language of another is precisely the attraction that peripheral literature offers to its readers. Moreover, it is this refusal to "coincide," whether linguistically or ideologically, that defines the char-acter of peripheral literature.

Thus, just as Jewish culture today is left with the same struggle first represented by the choice between Hasidism and *haskole*, so too in the African context one can recognize that the debate over negritude in-volving the representation of native culture in the colonial language, or the representation of imperial modernity in the native one, has only been transmogrified, not resolved. The various conflicts over language, as well as religion, ethnicity, and nationhood, which currently affect the whole continent of Africa, are variations of the dilemma among universalism and Blackness, modernity and tradition, first confronted by Senghor and Césaire in Paris during the 1930s. Can a dialogical examination of the respective conflicts involving African and Jewish modernity shed light on them both? Are solutions applicable to one culture transferable to the other?

The dilemma of African and Jewish writers caught between traditional hegemony and imperial modernity suggests that individual autonomy as such is perhaps always embattled, provisional, and tentative. Each individual is pressured by larger social forces to conform; what's more, many people choose to live significant segments of their lives—and most people choose to live as such at least occasionally—affiliated with larger, "anonymous" structures. But there is a distinction between modern individuals choosing the affiliation with larger communities, and individuals whose fates are determined in advance by an immutable label of tribe, caste, and class. As much as African and Jewish cultures are connected by commonalities of narrative form, they are equally connected by the historical fact of catastrophic suffering. If literary form cannot redeem this suffering, and it can't, it can perhaps reassert the dignity of the sufferers and commemorate those whom the impersonal forces of catastrophe would efface from history. In this regard, the words of Albert Memmi—a theorist, like Jacques Derrida invoked at the beginning of this comparison, who is both Jewish and African—are instructive:

> In order that his [the colonized] liberation may be complete, he must free himself from those inevitable conditions of his struggle. A nationalist, because he had to fight for the emergence and dignity of his nation, he must conquer himself and be free in relation to that nation. He can, of course, assert himself as a nationalist. But it is indispensable that he have a free choice and not that he exist only through his nation. He must conquer himself and be free in relation to the religion of his group, which he can retain or reject, but he must stop existing only through it. (*The Colonizer and the Colonized*, 152)

The fact that individuals from "minor" cultures must confront these challenges as a condition of their modernity indicates that their experience offers valuable lessons for people in the luxurious position of being able to take their modernity for granted. Peripheral literature can help the metropolitan culture become aware of itself and the demands it places on others. The key, therefore, to the perennial scholarly and political debates surrounding issues of canon and culture—debates into which this comparison has inserted itself—is not the dismantling or promotion of the Western canon per se, but rather a fostering of fundamental antihegemonic values: freedom; tolerance; curiosity about the world; respect for dissent; and a critical stance toward received traditions, particularly when these traditions result in the misery of whole societies, as well as skepticism toward the demands of modernity or any sort of "universalism."

Seen in this light, this book records, like a satellite signal in outer space, the distant echoes and fading half-life of the Enlightenment itself. This comparison has sought to identify the blindnesses of the Enlightenment by tracing the impact of its ideas, with all their paradoxes, on two cultures, African and Jewish, that were examples for most Enlightenment thinkers of inassimilable exceptions to the forward march of reason, truth, and history. When writers from Black and Jewish cultures belatedly gain access to this discourse, they expose the contradictions both of the Enlightenment itself and their own predicament. But in so doing, they began a process that confers on the Enlightenment a more genuine innovative and liberational potential than its original formulators could have envisioned, or perhaps would have tolerated.

In this context, the bracing critique of Achille Mbembe offers an unexpected insight: reviewing the problems of applying Western notions of modernity to Africa, he writes, "I have sought neither to discover traces of European modernity in Africa nor to sketch dubious comparisons between historical trajectories. . . . As with the Jews in a recent period, many African thinkers, moved by determination to rebuild a history of the 'black nation,' have in effect devoted their work to offering Africans a view of their historical destiny that is dense with meaning."[18] In the space of less than a paragraph, Mbembe disavows a comparison between African and European modernity, but then invokes just such a comparison—between modern African and Jewish cultures! One may argue that such a comparison is not dubious at all, but is in fact justified by the analogous relationship that African and Jewish modernity maintains with Western hegemonies, and by an analogous place, or placelessness, that peripheral modernity occupies in the imagination of the West. But having recognized in one another a comparable displacement—a final mirroring of one another—African and Yiddish literature may now contribute to a new conception of cultural space: one big enough, open enough, and hospitable enough for everyone, after so long a journey, to find a home.

Marc Caplan

April 28, 2009 / 4 Iyyar 5769

Notes

Introduction

1. I am grateful to my friend Professor Esther Goodman for identifying Professor Ortiz to me.

2. See Gilles Deleuze and Félix Guattari, *Kafka: Toward a Minor Literature,* trans. Dana Polan (Minneapolis: University of Minnesota Press, 1975; 1994).

3. Even the most original, least "European" of African novelists in English, Amos Tutuola, displays this familiarity on the level of analogy: the monsters in his phantasmogoric picaresques roll "on the ground as if a thousand petrol drums were pushing along a hard road" (205); a protagonist's dead cousin establishes a METHODIST CHURCH OF THE BUSH OF GHOSTS, complete with a missionary hospital and bureaucratic "Director of Medical Services" (146, 149); a hero returns to his hometown via the magical powers of a "Television-handed Ghostess" (161) (see Amos Tutuola, *The Palm-Wine Drinkard and My Life in the Bush of Ghosts* [New York: Grove Press, 1994]). In each of these images, modern and traditional reference systems meet one another coming and going.

4. Yiddish of course remains the spoken language of the *beys-medresh* ("study house") in Ashkenazic precincts of the ultra-Orthodox world. It goes nearly without saying, however, that academic researchers on Yiddish almost never come out of these locales.

5. For an autobiographical account of this return to Gikuyu, as well as a manifesto for its emulation by other African writers, see Ngugi wa Thiong'o, *Decolonising the Mind: The Politics of Language in African Literature* (London: James Currey, 1986; 1988).

6. Jacques Derrida, *Monolingualism of the Other or the Prosthesis of Origin,* trans. Patrick Mensah (Stanford, CA: Stanford University Press, 1996; 1998), 2. I am grateful to my colleague Professor Katrin Pahl for introducing this essay to me.   259

7. *Monolingualism of the Other* is representative of postcolonial theory's circulation from periphery to center and back: though Derrida writes in this essay explicitly as an Algerian Jew, he published the work in Paris, after having delivered

it as an address in the United States—fittingly enough, for the purposes of this analysis, in my home state of Louisiana, my mother's hometown of Baton Rouge, and my parents' alma mater of Louisiana State University. *Geaux* Tigers!

8. The declaration that monolingual Jewish cultures exist today only in English or Hebrew might prompt the question of Jews living in nations such as France, Argentina, or Hungary, where the language of daily life is neither English nor Hebrew. Jews of course live in these nations, and many others as well, but nearly always they live, unlike the majority of Jews in the United States or Israel, in more than one language.

9. Benjamin Harshav, "Chagall: Postmodernism and Fictional Worlds in Painting," in *Marc Chagall and the Jewish Theater* (New York: Guggenheim Museum, 1992), 18, emphasis in original.

10. In this latter regard, Isaac Bashevis Singer notes of the stylistic difficulties that young Yiddish readers encountered in the work of Y. L. Peretz: "Often the son would ask his father for an explanation of this or the other expression. The father considered Peretz a heretic, but he was pleased that the son had to appeal to him for the explanation of a Talmudic saying." See Yitzkhak Varshavski, *"A Naye oysgabe fun peretses verk"* ("A New Edition of Peretz's Work"), *Forverts*, July 5, 1947, 2, quoted in Ruth R. Wisse, *I. L. Peretz and the Making of Modern Jewish Culture* (Seattle: University of Washington Press, 1991), 114n27.

11. A charming example of this frame of reference—all the more representative for the randomness of its source—occurs in the children's song *Di Grine katshke* ("The Green Duck"), currently a favorite on my daughter's hit parade, written by the bohemian Yiddish artist Zuni Maud. Its last stanza states, *Geyt di grine katshke / Geyt arum un trakht / Vil zi davnen minkhe / Falt shoyn tsu di nakht* ("There goes the green duck / She walks around and thinks / She wants to say afternoon prayers / But it's already too late"). Here, one of the most valuable commodities in the shtetl marketplace, a duck, wants to participate in the sanctified ritual of the synagogue—only to be excluded for arriving too late to make a *minyan*! All this, in a children's song written in New York by a secular intellectual who, but for an accident in geography, might otherwise be known as a Yiddish Dadaist. See *Di Grine Katshke / The Green Duck: A Menagerie of Yiddish Animal-Songs for Children* (Living Traditions CD LTD 1801), 1997. For more on Maud, see my friend Eddy Portnoy's "Do You Know What Time It Isn't," *Pakn-Treger* (Fall 2007): 14–21, http://www.yiddishbookcenter.org/pdf/pt/55/zunimaud.pdf. Accessed February 14, 2011.

12. Note that the appearance of Fernandez de Lizardi's foundational text of postcolonial nationalism appears only one year after the first autonomously imagined collection of stories to appear in modern Yiddish (and Hebrew), Reb Nakhman of Breslov's *Seyfer sipurey mayses* ("The Holy Book of Stories"); although the first Yiddish novel, Yisroel Aksenfeld's *Dos Shterntikhl* ("The Headband"), only appears in print in 1861, it was certainly written decades before, probably in the 1820s or 30s.

13. Bendict Anderson, *Imagined Communities: Reflections on the Origin and Spread of Nationalism* (London: Verso, 1983; 1991), 30.

14. My colleagues specializing in other national traditions have also pointed out to me that the term "Modernism" at least as a global category in literary criticism is almost exclusively a preoccupation of Anglo-American academia, seldom encountered, for example, in French or German literary criticism and even less so in Eastern European literatures. I nonetheless consider the term fundamental to my analysis in a radically reconsidered way: not as an aesthetic taxonomy forcing together a variety of artistic, philosophical, and political positions (Brecht and Borges? Ibsen and Ionesco? Mallarmé and Mann?), but as a historical phenomenon through which the psychological, social, and technological transformations of modernization are simultaneously internalized and critiqued. For the purposes of this analysis, it is necessary to note the semantic distinction between "modernism" (lower-case "m"), the historical phenomenon I'm attempting to analyze, and "Modernism" (upper-case "M"), the periodization of early twentieth-century avant-garde European high culture that my comparison proposes to critique.

15. One effective example of the steady traffic between secularizing politics and traditional rhetoric is the title of Dovid Bergelson's 1929 novel, *Mides ha-din* (roughly, "Strict Justice"). Although the subject of the novel is the imposition of Soviet authority on the Ukrainian Pale of Settlement, and the author's ideological commitments are unmistakably Marxist—if not yet didactically communist—the novel's name refers explicitly, and only half-ironically, to the theological concept of God's capacity to judge humanity.

16. Max Horkheimer and Theodor W. Adorno, *Dialektik der Aufklärung: Philosophische Fragmente* (Frankfurt am Main: Fischer Taschenbuch Verlag. 1988; 2003); the English translation is *Dialectic of Enlightenment: Philosophical Fragments,* trans. Edmund Jephcott and ed. Gunzelin Schmid Noerr (Stanford, CA: Stanford University Press, 2002).

17. See Henry Louis Gates Jr., *The Signifying Monkey: A Theory of African-American Literary Criticism* (New York: Oxford University Press, 1988; 1989), Chapter 4, "The Trope of the Talking Book," 127–169.

18. The most vivid description of the Koran's linguistic, cultural, and metaphysical status in West Africa occurs in Cheikh Hamidou Kane's novel *L'aventure ambiguë* ("Ambiguous Adventure").

19. Moreover, in the case of missionary Protestantism, throughout Africa, efforts to attract converts provided the paradoxical origins of a vernacular literature in native African languages; the first modern book to be produced in any number of African languages was typically a translation of the Christian Bible. As such, rather than providing the mythopoetic foundation for resistance to a hegemonical racism—as the King James Bible served in slave narratives—the Bible in this context served as an extension of colonial authority. For more on the politics of Bible translation in the colonial era, and its implications for subsequent vernacular

literature, see Moradewun Adejunmobi, "Major and Minor Discourses of the Vernacular: Discrepant African Histories," in *Minor Transnationalism*, ed. Françoise Lionnet and Shu-mei Shih (Durham, NC: Duke University Press, 2005), 179–197. I am grateful to my colleague Professor Gabrielle Spiegel for introducing this extraordinary collection to me.

20. This fact is crucial to Gates's connection, in the first chapter of *The Signifying Monkey*, of the African American trope of signification to the precedent of Yoruba trickster figures and divination rituals. See "A Myth of Origins: Esu-Elegbara and the Signifying Monkey," 3–43.

21. On the concept and function of obsolescent language, see Uriel Weinreich, *Languages in Contact* (The Hague: Mouton, 1963).

Part 1

1. In this study, the terms "minor literature" and "the peripheral" will necessarily be used *almost* interchangeably. I nonetheless prefer the term "peripheral" over "minor" not only in response to the legitimate critiques of Deleuze and Guattari's model for the "minor," but also because peripherality suggests a process of circulation between the margins and the center, whereas "minority" implies a hierarchy in which the "minor" is, inevitably, subordinated to the "major." For a compelling summary of peripherality's conceptual potential, see Sara Nadal, "Introduction: Around . . . Peripheries/Propositions," in *Around: Planning the Periphery* (Barcelona: Editorial Gustavo Gili, 2002).

2. Abdul R. JanMohamed and David Lloyd, "Introduction: Toward a Theory of Minority Discourse: What Is to Be Done?" in *The Nature and Context of Minority Discourse*, ed. Abdul R. JanMohamed and David Lloyd (New York: Oxford University Press, 1990), 1. In the twenty years since this essay was published, it has become foundational to the field of "Minor" Studies nearly to the extent of the Deluze and Guattari monograph that prompted it. If Deleuze and Guattari created a discourse, JanMohamed and Lloyd in turn have created a discipline. Consider, for example, the exceptional collection *Minor Transnationalism*, ed. Françoise Lionnet and Shu-mei Shih (Durham, NC: Duke University Press, 2005); although many of the essays included in this volume take issue with aspects of JanMohamed and Lloyd's argument, they nonetheless cite it and adopt its terminology to their purposes.

3. Gilles Deleuze and Félix Guattari, *Kafka: Toward a Minor Literature*, trans. Dana Polan (Minneapolis: University of Minnesota Press, 1975; 1994). (Subsequent references incorporated in text as *Toward a Minor Literature*.)

4. It may be noted that Deleuze and Guattari in this instance are merely paraphrasing what Franz Kafka himself had said about Yiddish literature in a public address that provides Deleuze and Guattari with the point of departure for their theory. But Kafka, of course, knew little more about Yiddish literature than Deleuze or Guattari.

5. Because Yiddish is written in the Hebrew alphabet, transliteration varies from source to source; thus with the spelling of Reb Nakhman's name, for example, one encounters, variously, "Reb Nachman," "R. Nahman," etc. Transliteration from Yiddish (and where relevant, Hebrew as well) in this book will rely, for the most part, on the system instituted by the *Yidisher visnshaftlekher institut* (YIVO Institute for Jewish Research)—hence, Reb Nakhman. With respect to the transcription of Reb Nakhman's town of residence, the Yiddish linguist Dr. Mordkhe Schaechter counted no less than eleven variants. See his *Laytish mame-loshn* ("Authentic Yiddish," New York: League for Yiddish, 1986), 26–27. I have chosen the spelling "Breslov" because this is the version preferred by contemporary Breslover Hasidim. According to these Hasidim, the vocalization "Breslov" can be found in Hasidic publications dating from the time of Reb Nakhman. See *Rabbi Nachman's Wisdom*, trans. and ann. Rabbi Aryeh Kaplan (Brooklyn, NY: Breslov Research Institute, 1973), 455–456.

6. *Seyfer sipurey mayses* is published by the Breslover Hasidim in a bilingual edition, with the premodern fusion language of Hebrew and Aramaic, *Loshn-koydesh* (the "language of holiness"), on the upper half of the page, and Yiddish below—an arrangement that will prompt extensive commentary in this discussion. The edition I will be using for this comparison was published in Jerusalem by *Makhon "Toyres haNetsakh" Breslov* in 1991—elsewhere referred to as "Y." There are two primary translations of the complete stories in English: the translation, with invaluable commentary, published by the Breslover Hasidim themselves is *Rabbi Nachman's Stories*, trans. Rabbi Aryeh Kaplan (New York: Breslov Research Institute, 1983); a more straightforward edition is *Nahman of Bratslav: The Tales*, trans. Arnold J. Band (New York: Paulist Press, 1978). Although I will translate citations myself from the Yiddish, page numbers will be provided from the Kaplan translation, elsewhere referred to as "E," unless otherwise stated.

7. Amos Tutuola, *The Palm-Wine Drinkard and His Dead Palm-Wine Tapster in the Dead's Town*, collected in *The Palm-Wine Drinkard and My Life in the Bush of Ghosts* (New York: Grove Press, 1954; 1984). Subsequent references incorporated in text as "*PWD*."

8. Charles R. Larson, *The Emergence of African Fiction* (Bloomington: Indiana University Press, 1971; 1972), 3–4. One should add to Larson's list Peter Abrahams's surprisingly good-natured 1946 social-protest novel, *Mine Boy* (1946), billed in the 1989 edition published by Heinemann as "the first modern novel of Black South Africa."

9. For an illuminating comparison of Fagunwa with Tutuola, see "D. O. Fagunwa as Compound of Spells," in Olakunle George's *Relocating Agency: Modernity and African Letters* (Albany: State University of New York Press, 2003), 134–138.

10. See Chone Shmeruk, *Di altyidishe literatur: onheybn, meglekhkaytn, kontaktn* ("The Old-Yiddish Literature: Beginnings, Possibilites, Contacts"), in *Prokim fun*

der yidisher literatur-geshikhte ("Yiddish Literature: Aspects of Its History," Tel Aviv: I. L. Peretz Publishing House, 1988), 11–49.

11. See Max Weinreich, *Geshikhte fun der yidisher shprakh: Bagrifn, faktn, metodn* ("The History of the Yiddish Language: Concepts, Facts, Methods," New York: YIVO Institute for Jewish Research, 1973), 1:3–7.

12. In addition to the various examples of narrative adaptations cited in this context, there is one genre popular in seventeenth-century Yiddish literature that can be termed original—the widespread production of topical ballads, typically commemorating local atrocities, which were produced throughout the premodern Ashkenazic world. On this subject, see Jean Baumgarten, *Introduction to Old Yiddish Literature*, ed. and trans. Jerold C. Frakes (New York: Oxford University Press, 2005), 328–341. Though this genre complicates the categorical distinction between premodern and modern Yiddish literature upon which this entire comparison rests, unlike the development of modern prose fiction at issue here, these ballads were written in verse and they recorded, in however stylized a manner, true events; they were neither prose nor fiction. They therefore were not a precedent for the works under discussion in this comparison, and in fact they had been essentially forgotten by the beginning of the nineteenth century.

13. As David Stern writes, "There is nothing in the history of [Jewish] literature comparable to the discerned narrative tradition in Western or European literature, where it is possible to speak of a continuum passing more or less directly from the epic to romance to novel. . . . Most fictional narratives in rabbinic and medieval Hebrew literature appeared in their earliest contexts within the framework of other literary forms: the legal code, the commentary, or the sermon." See David Stern, "Introduction," in *Rabbinic Fantasies: Imaginative Narratives from Classical Hebrew Literature*, ed. David Stern and Mark Jay Mirsky (New Haven: Yale University Press, 1990), 3.

14. Max Erik, *Vegn altyidshn roman un novele, fertsenter-zektsenter yorhundert* ("On Old-Yiddish Novels and Novellas, 14th–16th Century") (Kowel: Der veg tsum visn, 1926), 22–23. Though most of the details of Erik's scholarship in this book have been challenged by subsequent research, the general conclusion he draws on the essentially *derivative* character of premodern Yiddish literature has not.

15. For information on the romantic appropriation of Hasidism generally at the beginning of the twentieth century, see Paul Mendes-Flohr, "Fin-de-Siecle Orientalism, the *Ostjuden* and the Aesthetics of Jewish Self-Affirmation," in *Divided Passions: Jewish Intellectuals and the Experience of Modernity* (Detroit: Wayne State University, 1991), 77–132. The most famous instance of this appropriation is Martin Buber's reworking of Reb Nakhman's stories, his first foray into Hasidic culture; see Buber, *The Tales of Rabbi Nachman,* trans. M. Friedman (Bloomington: University of Indiana Press, 1906; 1956). For a Yiddish version of the secular-romantic

Reb Nakhman "gestalt," see Y. L. Peretz, *"Reb Nakhmankes mayses"* (1904), in *Ale verk fun Y. L. Peretz*, vol. 4 (New York: "CYCO" Bicher-Farlag, 1947), 187–201.

16. Ora Wiskind-Elper, *Tradition and Fantasy in the Tales of Reb Nahman of Bratslav* (Albany: State University of New York Press, 1998), 7.

17. Ato Quayson, *Strategic Transformations in Nigerian Writing: Orality & History in the Work of Rev. Samuel Johnson, Amos Tutuola, Wole Soyinka & Ben Okri* (Bloomington: Indiana University Press) 1997, 36. Quayson's source for this quote is the *Lagos Observer*, October 27 and November 3, 1888.

Chapter 1

1. Michel de Certeau, *The Practice of Everyday Life*, trans. Steven Rendall (Berkeley: University of California Press, 1984; 1988), 168.

2. Brian Stock, *Listening for the Text: On the Uses of the Past* (Philadelphia: University of Pennsylvania Press, 1990; 1996), 19. I am grateful to my teacher Timothy Reiss for recommending this book to me.

3. Moving beyond the question of literary convention—as if anything existed beyond literature!—one can further understand the medieval character of eighteenth-century Eastern Europe in socioeconomic terms by considering Gershon Hundert's remark, "The birth of the Polish bourgeoisie came only at the end of the eighteenth century." (See Gershon David Hundert, *Jews in Poland-Lithuania in the Eighteenth Century: A Genealogy of Modernity* [Berkeley: University of California Press, 2004], 47.) This process of belated modernization and embourgeoisement proved to be crucial to the emergence of Eastern European Jewish society as a peripheral culture.

4. With respect to this distinction, it is useful to consider a further remark by Stock: "Modernity did not come to a 'traditional' society [like the Western Middle Ages] from the outside, like British government to Mughal India. It came from medieval society itself" (*Listening for the Text*, 167). This observation makes clear precisely how Stock's schematization of the dialogical tensions between tradition and modernity in Western Europe differs from a discussion of the same tensions in Eastern European Yiddish and postcolonial African cultures. Modernity in these latter contexts *was* introduced from the outside, in similar fashion to the arrival of British imperialism in India.

5. As Margaret Drewal writes of Yoruba culture in this connection, "Anthropologists have often associated . . . change with modernization, beginning with the colonial period, or before, through to the present. . . . [Such scholars] pit modernizing movements against ritual—movements which themselves incorporate ritual—and modernity against ritual action, that is, the changing versus the unchanging. It seems equally plausible, however, that these [modernizing] movements attempt to purge ritual precisely because its generative force runs counter to the one that the movement is attempting to set into action. In that case, the

conflict is not between movement and stasis, but . . . the established ritual and the establishing movement." See Margaret Thompson Drewal, *Yoruba Ritual: Performers, Play, Agency* (Bloomington: University of Indiana Press, 1992), 8–9. Drewal's remarks, though seemingly marginalized to the endnotes of this book, will nonetheless animate the central arguments of this book.

6. Abiola Irele takes note of this fact when he writes: "In no other area of Africa is the current along which this elaboration in literature of a continuous stream of the collective consciousness, from the traditional to the modern, so clearly evident and so well marked out, as in Yorubaland. . . . In Yorubaland we have the extraordinary situation where the vast folk literature, alive and vigorously contemporary, remains available to provide a constant support for new forms . . . to provide a source for the new literature in English." See "Tradition and the Yoruba Writer: D. O. Fagunwa, Amos Tutuola, and Wole Soyinka" [1969], in his collection *The African Experience in Literature and Ideology* (Bloomington: Indiana University Press, 1975; 1990), 174–175.

7. Meir Wiener, *Di rol fun shablonisher frazeologye in der literatur fun der haskole* ["The role of clichéd phraseology in *haskole* literature," 1940], in *Di Yidishe literatur in nayntsentn yorhundert: Zamlung fun yidisher literatur-forshung un kritik in ratn farband* ["Yiddish Literature in the 19th Century: A Collection of Yiddish Literature-Research and Criticism in Soviet Union"], ed. Chava Turniansky (Jerusalem: Magnes Press, 1993), 96. The translation is my own.

8. Wiener was, however, the most sensitive scholarly reader of the *sipurey mayses* of his day. Although intrigued by these stories' mixture of traditional Jewish imagery with international folk motifs, and aware of their potential for political critique—the highest literary criterion for a Soviet critic—Wiener nonetheless concludes that Reb Nakhman's style remains "*unnatural* and inorganic" (his emphasis) and his "strange book, with its folkloric, worldly, and to a certain extent heretical elements . . . served not to lighten the disposition of the masses, but rather to darken it further by its poeticizing of medieval concepts." See Wiener's *Tsu der geshikhte fun der yidisher literatur in 19tn yorhundert: Ershter band* ("On the History of Yiddish Literature in the 19th Century: Volume One") (New York: YKUF, 1945), 35, 38. The translation is my own.

9. Lest the thought of a "joyous Reb Nakhman" strike the reader as excessive, it is worth recalling that the last story in the *sipurey mayses*, the "Tale of the Seven Beggars," begins with the epigraph, "I will tell you how it once was to be joyous" (Y 405; E 354).

10. What I am referring to here as "intrinsic" and "extrinsic" forms of deterritorialization might also be understood in more conventional linguistic terms as two different sorts of diglossia—a traditional, complementary type (*Loshn-koydesh* with Yiddish) and a modern, supercessionist one (English against Yoruba). I owe this clarification to a lecture given by the sociolinguist Joshua A. Fishman on September 15, 2003, in Bloomington, Indiana.

11. As David Roskies writes: "Among the many traditions that Bratslav Hasidism exploited to its advantage [when publishing the *sipurey mayses*] was the standard division of labor between Hebrew and Yiddish. . . . [F]or the first time, the scribe felt mandated to preserve the *spokenness* of Nahman's original . . . ; and since Hebrew had been used solely as a high literary language, Nathan [Reb Noson of Nemirov, the original editor of Reb Nakhman's writings] had to invent a hybrid Hebrew style that would capture Nahman's spoken Yiddish. . . . Nathan did not try to compensate for the loss of vitality by making his Hebrew version resonate with scriptural and other learned echoes. Instead, it was Yiddish syntax and vocabulary that echoed throughout, often deviating from the grammar of rabbinic Hebrew—and from the elevated style of rabbinic speech." See David G. Roskies, *A Bridge of Longing: The Lost Art of Yiddish Storytelling* (Cambridge, MA: Harvard University Press, 1995), 30–31.

12. One can further contextualize this theoretical assertion with reference to Emmanuel Obiechina's observation that "[t]o the West African living in one of the ex-British colonies, English is the national, administrative, legal, and (along with the vernaculars), literary language. The writer using the English language is therefore bilingual and expected to be 'at home' both in English and in his own language." Emmanuel N. Obiechina, *Language and Theme: Essays on African Literature* (Washington, DC: Howard University Press, 1990), 53.

13. In the first story alone, one finds, for example, such singular constructions as *mekhavev zayn, meshasheye zayn zikh, meakev zayn, misgaber zayn, madkhe zayn,* and *meshakhed zayn.*

14. See Roskies, *Bridge of Longing,* 20–55; and Shmeruk, *Yiddish Literature,* 211–263. Moreover, in the first half of the twentieth century, sympathetic, if ultimately superficial, acknowledgments of Reb Nakhman's role in the development of modern Yiddish literature could be found in the writings of Zalman Reyzn, Meir Wiener, Sh. Niger, and Hillel Zeitlin. See Reyzn, *Fun Mendelssohn biz Mendele* ("From Mendelssohn to Mendele") (Warsaw: Farlag Kultur-Lige, 1923), 107–124; Wiener, *Tsu der geshikhte fun der yidisher literatur in 19tn yorhundert* ("To the History of Yiddish Literature in the 19th Century") (New York: YKUF, 1945), 33–38; Niger, *Dertseylers un romanistn* ("Storytellers and Novelists") (New York: Tsiko farlag, 1946), 20–24; Zeitlin, *Reb Nakhman Braslaver: Der zeyr fun padolye* ("Reb Nakhman of Braslav: The Seer of Padolia") (New York: Matones), 1952, 224–239.

15. For a full listing of these "other commentators," far beyond what can be mentioned or acknowledged in this study, see David Assaf, *Breslav bibliografyah mu'eret: R. Nahman mi-breslov, toldatav u'morashto hasifrutit* ("Breslov Annotated Bibliography: Reb Nakhman of Breslov, His History and Literary Legacy") (Jerusalem: Zalman Shazar Center, 2000).

16. Arnold J. Band, "The Text and Translation," in *Nahman of Bratslav: The Tales* (New York: Paulist Press, 1978), 47. To a certain extent, the bias against the Yiddish versions of Reb Nakhman's bilingual stories persists in the scholarship

of later bilingual Jewish writers. David Aberbach, for example, in his study of Mendele Moykher-Sforim's Hebrew writings states, "His Yiddish stories may be read easily, as straightforward, highly colloquial literature, whereas the Hebrew reworkings demand close study as they allude constantly to biblical, rabbinic, and medieval sources. . . . Mendele's most enduring achievement . . . was to give modern Hebrew literary prose the breath of life via Yiddish." This, of the greatest nineteenth-century Yiddish writer! See Aberbach, *Realism, Caricature, and Bias: The Fiction of Mendele Mocher Sefarim* (London: Littman Library of Jewish Civilization, 1993), 11.

17. Because modern Hebrew, more or less as it is used in Israel today, dates at the earliest from the 1850s, with the publication of writers such as the novelist Abraham Mapu (1808–1867), Reb Nakhman's stories are seldom included in discussions of modern Hebrew literature; moreover, whenever his work is presented outside the circles of the Breslover Hasidim, his Hebrew is modernized—or, as is said in Yiddish, *farshenert un farbesert* ("beautified and improved upon")! Because most commentators ignore the Yiddish versions of his stories, his importance to modern Yiddish literature tends similarly, though more unfairly, to be minimized.

18. A. Afolayan, "Language and Sources of Amos Tutuola," in *Critical Perspectives on Amos Tutuola*, ed. Bernth Lindfors (Boulder, CO: Three Continents Press, 1975), 194–195. Subsequent references to this indispensable collection incorporated in text as *Critical Perspectives*.

19. Bernth Lindfors quotes from an August 27, 1951, letter that Tutuola sent to his publishers, Faber & Faber, requesting their permission to translate the novel, in response to a request from the (colonial) deputy director of education for a Yoruba-literature course book in Nigerian schools; Faber & Faber enthusiastically granted permission on October 3 of that year. See Lindfors, "Amos Tutuola's Search for a Publisher," in *The Blind Men and the Elephant and Other Essays in Biographical Criticism* (Trenton, NJ: Africa World Press, 1999), 109–133 (esp. 121–123). In an August 20, 2000, e-mail Lindfors informed me that Tutuola did prepare a Yoruba translation of the novel, but the Nigerian Education Department "expressed no interest in publishing it (before or after independence)." Tutuola next arranged for Abiola Irele to publish his translation with New Horn Press in Ibadan, Nigeria, but Irele left for the United States shortly thereafter, "and nothing came of the venture." According to Lindfors, the exact whereabouts of the translation today is unknown, though "a quantity of Yoruba materials" is archived in the Humanities Research Center of the University of Texas at Austin. In an October 31, 2000, e-mail, however, Irele stated that he was "not aware that Tutuola translated *The Palm-Wine Drinkard* into Yoruba. He did translate his last novel published in English [presumably *Pauper, Brawler, Slanderer*] and when I was running New Horn Press, I came across the manuscript and sent it to an outside editor to prepare it for press. He never delivered the manuscript and I have no idea where he is today. We must therefore consider the manuscript lost."

20. Chris Dunton suggests that this "rationalizing" gesture lies at the heart of Tutuola's discontent with Kola Ogunmola's 1962 Yoruba-language stage adaptation of *The Palm-Wine Drinkard*, which transferred the narrative action from "a story that happened" to "a fantasia that is staged." After the fact, Tutuola came to credit Ogunmola with doing "no more than translating the play into Yoruba" and "came to feel that the . . . adaptation had been hijacked by Ogunmola and that his own role—his ownership of the work—had been brushed aside." See Dunton's "Pupils, Witch Doctor, Vengeance: Amos Tutuola as Playwright," *Research in African Literatures* 37, no. 4 (Winter 2006): 3.

21. Obiechina elaborates on this problem in more general terms when he writes, "The situation whereby no more than one-quarter of the people is developing a literary 'minority' culture, based on the use of the English language . . . is obviously unhealthy. When creative writers, members of the 'minority' culture, attempt, as they are constantly doing, to interpret the largely emasculated 'majority' culture, sensitive people are bound to show some uneasiness. . . . [T]here is always a sneaking suspicion that the writer is doing something opportunistic, like cashing in on an infirmity" (*Language and Theme*, 66).

22. Thus Robert Philipson contextualizes a remark by the late Frederick Karl: "As Frederick Karl observes . . . Chaucer, Dante, and the Provençal troubadours . . . needed to break with Latin . . . as a way of expressing their present day sensibilities. 'We have, then, a constant: the use of language as a way of separating modern from antiquity, as a form of divisiveness and definition. . . . That shift in languages is connected to slow shifts in modes of perceptions, really cultural earthquakes.'" Robert Philipson, *The Identity Question: Blacks and Jews in Europe and America* (Jackson: University Press of Mississippi, 2000), 41. Philipson quotes from Frederick Karl, *Modern and Modernism: The Sovereignty of the Artist 1885–1925* (New York: Atheneum, 1985), 7. A similar remark on the relationship of Tutuola's English to the colonial language of Imperial London emerges directly from the historical moment that Karl analyzes, in Samuel Beckett's spirited defense of James Joyce's (then incomplete) *Finnegans Wake*: "If English is not yet so definitely a polite necessity as Latin was in the Middle Ages, at least one is justified in declaring that its position in relation to other European languages is to a great extent that of medieval Latin to the Italian dialects." If English assumed such a status vis-à-vis the sovereign languages of Europe, how much more so its status vis-à-vis the languages and cultures that England was then colonizing! See Samuel Beckett, "Dante . . . Bruno . Vico . . Joyce," in *Our Exagmination Round His Factification for Incamination of Work in Progress* (republished and fortunately retitled as *James Joyce/Finnegans Wake: A Symposium* [New York: New Directions, 1929; 1972], 18).

23. For Roskies' account of this crisis and how it resulted in Reb Nakhman's decision to tell stories, see *A Bridge of Longing*, 26: "The events leading up to the summer of 1806 formed a three-act drama. The first was a period of frenetic activity, as Reb Nahman threw himself into the cause of universal redemption. . . . In

the second act, the revolution failed. The mission of the disciples to proclaim the messianic era received no support . . . the hasidic establishment openly attacked Reb Nahman . . . the inner ranks of his disciples began to thin. . . . What was needed in the third act was a return to something elemental. . . . Were it not for the present crisis that forced Reb Nahman to rechannel his redemptive faith into a more potent . . . medium, he would never have gone back to so primitive a form [as storytelling]."

24. Glenn Dynner thus quotes Reb Nakhman as complaining, "In this land [i.e., Eastern Europe], for example, *ba'alei shem* [Jewish faith healers, prototypes of the Hasidic rebbe] are esteemed. And in truth, there have been some authentic *ba'alei shem* and *tsadikim*. But nowadays fraudulent *ba'alei shem* have proliferated. And as a rule, anyone who wishes and desires to go into it . . . succeeds even if he is a fraud and really knows nothing except that it is based on his rapture: how he bestirs himself and revels in it." See "The Hasidic Conquest of Small-Town Central Poland, 1754–1818," in *Polin: Studies in Polish Jewry*, vol. 17, *The Shtetl: Myth and Reality*, ed. Antony Polonsky (Oxford: Littman Library of Jewish Civilization, 2004), 56. Dynner's source is a posthumous collection of Reb Nakhman's informal remarks, *Sikhes ha"Ran*. For a (somewhat bowdlerized) translation, see *Rabbi Nachman's Wisdom*, 171–172.

25. As Hundert notes, however, a process of modernization had already begun in Poland immediately prior to the partition period: "In the last years of the eighteenth century, the beginnings of a secular trend of disintegration of the 'feudal' system were intensified by the partitions of Poland. Jews . . . experienced displacement and dislocation because of the economic changes that developed at a growing pace in the nineteenth century. Before the end of the eighteenth century, however, the signs of the coming disintegration were discernible" (*Jews in Poland-Lithuania in the Eighteenth Century*, 56).

26. With respect to this process of industrialization, Michael Stanislawski writes, "During the first half of the nineteenth century, Jewish businessmen . . . began to invest quite extensively in two fields of manufacturing that were growing in the Russian empire at this time, textiles and beet sugar." Nonetheless, the role that Jews played in the development of industrial capitalism was, at best, peripheral; Stanislawski continues, "These were the two least 'capitalistic' of industries, both developed by landlords on their estates primarily with the use of serf laborers." See Michael Stanislawski, *Tsar Nicholas I and the Jews: The Transformation of Jewish Society in Russia, 1825–1855* (Philadelphia: Jewish Publication Society of America, 1983), 177. These facts notwithstanding, the presence of Jews within the merchant class was economically and demographically significant. As Hundert writes, "The role of Jews in commerce [during the eighteenth century], and particularly in the domestic market, was crucial. In some towns, as many as 80 or 90 percent of all merchants were Jewish. . . . Generally speaking . . . 50 to 60 percent

of domestic trade was in the hands of Jewish traders" (*Jews in Poland-Lithuania in the Eighteenth-Century*, 33–34).

27. As Max Weinreich describes the role that itinerant merchants played in "importing" modern sensibilities to Eastern Europe, "One can consider the merchants who traveled to the Leipzig fairs at the beginning of the 19th century to be the predecessors of secular Jewish culture." See Max Weinreich, *Geshikhte fun der yidisher shprakh*, 1:247. Hundert supports the significance of the Leipzig fairs to Jewish modernity—at least in economic terms—by writing, "Even in foreign trade, Jewish numbers were quite significant, especially during the last quarter of the [eighteenth] century. At the time, for every Christian merchant from Poland at the fairs in Leipzig, there were seven Jewish merchants" (*Jews in Poland-Lithuania in the Eighteenth Century*, 34).

28. Nonetheless, from a purely institutional perspective—as opposed to, for example, a theological or metaphysical one—Adam Teller's analysis of Hasidism's emergence is particularly compelling. As he states, Hasidism emerged during a moment of crisis affecting previous communal organizations: "The Jewish communities, which generally served as part of Poland's administrative apparatus, also suffered from severe dysfunction during this period [of partition, 1772–1795]. As in the rest of the state apparatus, the communities' problems seem to have been caused by the transfer of authority from the communal institutions to the magnates or to the individuals and groups who had their support." See his "Hasidism and the Challenge of Geography: The Polish Background to the Spread of the Hasidic Movement," *AJS Review* 30, no. 1 (2006): 13.

29. Hasidism as a cohesive movement first emerged in the Ukrainian town of Miedzybóz among the disciples of Israel ben Eliezer (c. 1700–1760), known as the Baal Shem Tov ("Master of the Good Name"), a ritual healer, mystic, and charismatic preacher. The Baal Shem Tov, or BeSh"T, was Reb Nakhman's maternal great-grandfather.

30. Moshe J. Rosman, "Social Conflicts in Miedzybóz in the Generation of the Besht," in *Hasidism Reappraised*, ed. Ada Rapoport-Albert (London: Littman Library of Jewish Civilization, 1997), 58–59.

31. Indeed, Teller states explicitly, "part of the Hasidic movement's success in winning so many adherents may be attributed to the fact that at the turn of the eighteenth and nineteenth centuries—a time when the partitioning powers were putting a great deal of pressure on the Jewish communities as part of their policy of centralization—Hasidism offered a flexible system for self-government outside the communities that enabled Jewish society to preserve its internal integrity" ("Hasidism and the Challenge of Geography," 29).

32. Moreover, as Hundert notes, Hasidism is only one of several revivalist movements—Quietism, Jansenism, the Great Awakening, the Old Believers, etc.—emerging globally in the latter half of the eighteenth century. Although one should not look too closely for cultural or political overlaps between discrete

movements within disparate religious traditions, Hundert identifies a common modernity to all of them: "None of these [revivalist] movements, including Hasidism, should be seen ab initio as a reaction to the Enlightenment. Rather they were coextensive with the Enlightenment. What the spiritual movements and the Enlightenment shared was, most particularly, the emboldening of the individual to independence in matters of thought and spirit" (*Jews in Poland-Lithuania in the Eighteenth Century*, 177). Although this statement equivocates on the status of the individual in terms of the dynamic between the Hasidic rebbe and his Hasidim, it helps to identify a general historical moment in which Reb Nakhman's radicalism becomes comprehensible.

33. John Klier, "Polish Shtetls under Russian Rule, 1772–1914," *Polin: Studies in Polish Jewry* 17 (2004): 104.

34. Max Weinreich, *Bilder fun der yidisher literaturgeshikhte: fun di onheybn biz Mendele Moykher-Sforim* ("Studies in the History of Yiddish Literature: From Its Beginnings to Mendele Moykher-Sforim") (Vilna: Farlag "Tomor," 1928), 273–274. The translation is my own.

35. In addition to Rosman's previously cited essay, see Gershon David Hundert, "The Conditions in Jewish Society in the Polish-Lithuanian Commonwealth in the Middle Decades of the Eighteenth Century," *Hasidism Reappraised*, 45–50; and Shmuel Ettinger, "Hasidism and *Kahal* [Jewish community administration] in Eastern Europe," *Hasidism Reappraised*, 63–75.

36. As Yehezkl Lifschutz writes on the replacement of the *marshalik*, or wedding jester, with the *badkhn*, or wedding preacher in Ashkenazic society: "The 17th century saw the flowering of a moralistic literature in Yiddish. . . . After the Khmielnicki massacres the Jews of Poland became eager consumers of moralistic literature. The masses sought consolation for their great misfortunes and were led to believe that they had not been sufficiently pious. . . . " E. Lifschutz, "Merrymakers and Jesters among Jews (Materials for a Lexicon)," *YIVO Annual of Jewish Social Science* 7 (1952): 48–49.

37. The *seyfer Shivkhey HaBeSh"T* was first published in *Loshn-koydesh* in 1814—four years after Reb Nakhman's death—and in a somewhat different Yiddish version in 1815; nonetheless many of these *shvokhim* (hagiographical stories) would have been familiar to Reb Nakhman, given his geographical and genealogical proximity to the Baal Shem Tov's inner circle. An exhaustive, if overly literal, translation of *Shivkhey HaBeSh"T* (the *Loshn-koydesh* version) is titled *In Praise of the Baal Shem Tov*, trans. and ed. Dan Ben-Amos and Jerome R. Mintz (Northvale, NJ: Jason Aronson, 1970; 1993. A modern edition in (atrocious) Yiddish was also published in Brooklyn by one A. Weinstock in 1988.

38. For a discussion of how Hasidic culture defined its social innovations around the figure of the rebbe, and indeed disguised them in the language of tradition, see Mendel Piekarz's "Hasidism as a Socio-religious Movement on the Evidence of *Devekut*," in *Hasidism Reappraised*, 225–248.

39. See Simon Dubnow, *Geshikhte fun khasidizm*, translated from Hebrew into Yiddish by Zelig Kalmanovitch under the supervision of the author (Vilna: Farlag fun B. Kletskin, 1930), 1:6. The translation from Yiddish is my own. More recently, Nathaniel Deutsch has argued similarly, "The implicit tension between [Reb] Nahman and the Besht hints at a widespread concern within Hasidism at the end of the eighteenth and beginning of the nineteenth centuries, namely, how to achieve a transition from a group of founding fathers . . . to a widespread movement. . . . The creation of an oral biographical tradition and eventually the development of Hasidic hagiography . . . helped to achieve this transition. The Besht, the Maggid of Mezeritch [1710–1772, the BeSh"T's "successor"], and other early figures continued to 'live' in the tales told and written about them." See Nathaniel Deutsch, "Rabbi Nahman of Bratslav: The Zaddik as Androgyne," in *God's Voice from the Void: Old and New Studies in Bratslav Hasidism*, ed. Shaul Magid (Albany: State University of New York Press, 2002), 193.

40. Although the convening of this legislature, like virtually every development in the troubled political history of Nigeria, did not occur without contention, the main fault lines at this point separated north from south, rather than Yoruba and Igbo. See Eghosa E. Osaghae, *Crippled Giant: Nigeria since Independence* (Bloomington: Indiana University Press, 1998), 6.

41. Emmanuel Obiechina's bibliography of market literature published between 1946 and 1966 indicates that approximately 40 of the 270 or so titles address explicitly political themes, typically in the form of biographical polemics on current African leaders—Nnamdi Azikwe, Patrice Lumumba, Julius Nyerere, etc.— but also including such figures as John F. Kennedy and, to make a distinction, Adolf Hitler. See Obiechina's *An African Popular Literature: A Study of Onitsha Market Pamphlets* (New York: Cambridge University Press, 1973), 237–244. Given the conspicuous attention this market literature accords modernizing discourses such as history, politics, social obligation, and financial success, one can draw an additional analogy between these publications and the values of the *haskole*. Stylistically speaking, market literature's closest affinities are with Tutuola, and by extension in this context Reb Nakhman; ideologically these works are the country cousins of (Igbo-origin) Nigerian realists such as Chinua Achebe or Cyprian Ekwensi. Such affinities and discontinuities between style and ideology in fact animate all literary discourse, but peripheral literatures bear the strain of these tensions in an especially conspicuous way. The similarities between Onitsha Market literature and the Yiddish *haskole*, particularly their respective attraction to dramatic form and domestic comedy, will be the subject of a separate article I am now preparing for publication.

42. Mark Slobin, *Tenement Songs: The Popular Music of Jewish Immigrants* (Urbana: University of Illinois Press, 1982; 1996), 106.

43. Deleuze and Guattari's model for the literary assemblage is, of course, Kafka, whose writing assembles, in their parlance, into a single "machine" consist-

ing of the "cogs" created by interconnected and radically incomplete forms such as the novel, the stories, letters, and diaries. Their discussion of Kafka finds an echo in Theodor Adorno's monograph on Gustav Mahler; while discussing Mahler's "renunciation of fixed themes," Adorno declares that "[a]ll of Mahler's works communicate subterraneanly, like Kafka's through the passages of his Burrow." See Theodor W. Adorno, *Mahler: A Musical Physiognomy*, trans. Edmund Jephcott (Chicago: University of Chicago Press, 1971; 1992), 50; 53.

44. See Amos Tutuola, *The Wild Hunter in the Bush of Ghosts*, ed. Bernth Lindfors (Washington, DC: Three Continents Press, 1948; 1982; 1989), 36–43.

45. The ultimate interrelationship among Tutuola's entire body of work underscores the unfortunate fact that virtually all critical commentary on Tutuola considers *The Palm-Wine Drinkard* to the exclusion of his eight other remarkable, often equally worthy novels. This discussion will follow this unhappy trend only because the presumably accidental structural and motivic correspondences between this novel and Reb Nakhman's stories—each of them originary works in the modern literatures of their respective cultures—make for a stronger and more thorough comparison than his later writing.

46. Walter Ong, *Orality and Literacy: The Technologizing of the Word* (London: Routledge, 1982; 1995), 144. Ong's model of the differences between oral and written cultures is not without its critics, particularly in African studies. See, for example, Emevwo Biakolo, "On the Theoretical Foundations of Orality and Literacy," *Research in African Literatures* 30, no. 2 (Summer 1999): 42–65. By way of rejoinder, it is useful to consider the following from Ong: "Paradoxically, Plato could formulate his . . . preference for orality over writing, clearly and effectively only because he could write. Plato's phonocentrism is textually contrived and textually defended" (*Orality and Literacy,* 168). Similarly, Biakolo's critique of Ong could only be conceived, and could only appear, in the written context of an academic journal.

47. Consider, in this respect, the remarks of the Francophone author Camara Laye, who was accused of imitating Kafka's *The Castle* in his 1956 novel *Le regard du roi*: "When they say, for example, that I'm copying Kafka. . . . No, on the contrary, maybe it's Kafka who's copying us? Kafka is copying Africa without knowing it. . . . " Quoted in Christopher L. Miller, *Theories of Africans: Francophone Literature and Anthropology in Africa* (Chicago: University of Chicago Press, 1990), 175. For a convincing alternative interpretation to the accusations against *Le regard du roi*, see Kenneth W. Harrow, "Camara Laye, Cheikh Hamidou Kane, and Tayeb Salih: Three Sufi Authors," in *Faces of Islam in African Literature*, ed. Kenneth W. Harrow (Portsmouth, NH: Heinemann, 1991), 261–297.

48. *Until the Mashiach*, a biography authorized by the Breslover themselves, lists five categories of unpublished manuscripts—out of twelve categories of his writings—including "hidden books," a "burned book," "manuscripts," and uncollected parables, stories, and anecdotes. See Rabbi Dovid Shapiro, ed., *Until the*

Mashiach: The Life of Rabbi Nachman, trans. Rabbi Aryeh Kaplan (Far Rockaway, NY: Breslov Research Institute, 1985), 287–295. One such "hidden" or esoteric manuscript has recently been published by Professor Zvi Mark as *The Scroll of Secrets: The Hidden Messianic Vision of R. Nachman of Breslav*, trans. Naftali Moses (Brighton, MA: Academic Studies Press, 2010).

49. Consider, for example, "*[T]he experience of the absence of God, or man's inability to experience God directly, must be taken seriously.* Man lives in a world where God cannot be 'seen'; given this reality, doubt is an inevitable part of the life of every religious human being . . . " [emphasis in original]. See Arthur Green, *Tormented Master: The Life and Spiritual Quest of Rabbi Nahman of Bratslav* (Woodstock, VT: Jewish Lights Publishing, 1979; 1992), 291.

50. Michel Foucault, "What Is an Author?" in *Textual Strategies: Perspectives in Post-Structuralist Criticism*, ed. Josue V. Harari (Ithaca, NY: Cornell University Press, 1979; 1986), 141–160.

51. Antonio Gramsci, "The Intellectuals," in *Selections from the Prison Notebooks*, ed. and trans. Quintin Hoare and Geoffrey Nowell Smith (New York: International Publishers, 1971; 1995), 5–23.

52. To a certain extent, the nineteenth-century conflict between maskilim and Hasidim also recapitulates the conflict of institutional and organic intellectuals; as Raphael Mahler writes, "In the ranks of the Maskilim we must . . . include the Jewish professional intelligentsia, consisting largely of teachers, employed in the close to a hundred German-Jewish schools and . . . in private homes. . . . Included among the professional intelligentsia were also the court versifiers, and other penmen that were maintained or aided by wealthy Jewish patrons." See Raphael Mahler, "The Social and Political Aspects of the Haskalah in Galicia," *YIVO Annual of Jewish Social Science* 1 (1946): 67. Moreover, despite the comparatively small size of the traditional shtetl, in the context of early-modern Eastern Europe the Jewish population, whether maskilic or Hasidic, was almost uniformly urban. Thus Hundert writes, "It should be stressed that not only was the Jewish population essentially urban, but that it lived in the midst of a society that was overwhelmingly rural and agricultural. The consequence of this was that half of the urban population, and in large parts of the country more than half, was Jewish" (*Jews in Poland-Lithuania in the Eighteenth Century*, 29).

53. Adam Teller proposes "a definition of the shtetl (in the conditions of the eighteenth century) as a small settlement of less than 300 houses, which dealt mostly in agricultural produce, and at least 40 per cent of whose total urban population was Jewish." See his article "The Shtetl as an Arena for Polish-Jewish Integration in the Eighteenth Century," in *Polin: Studies in Polish Jewry*, vol. 17, *The Shtetl: Myth and Reality*, ed. Antony Polonsky (Oxford: Littman Library of Jewish Civilization, 2004), 39.

54. Simon Dubnow, *Geshikhte fun khasidizm* ("The History of Hasidism"), vol. 2, translated from Hebrew into Yiddish by Zelig Kalmanovitch under the supervi-

sion of the author (Buenos Aires: Alveltlekher Yidisher Kultur-Kongres, Argentiner Opteyl, 1930; 1957), 245.

55. See Dubnow, *Ob izuchenii istorii russkikh evreev i uchrezhdenii Istoricheskogo obschevstva, Voskhod* 4–9 (1891): 57. Quoted in my colleague Elissa Bemporad's "From Literature of the People to History of the People: Simon Dubnow and the Origins of Russian Jewish Historiography," 14; published in Italian as "Da letteratura del popolo a storia del popolo: Simon Dubnow e l'origine della storiografia russo-ebraica," in *Annali di Storia dell'Esegesi*, Universita' degli Studi di Bologna 18, no. 2 (2001): 533–557. I wish to thank Professor David Roskies for making the English version of this essay available to me.

56. See Paul Neumarkt, "Amos Tutuola: Emerging African Literature," *American Imago* 28 (1971): 129–145. This "diagnosis" of Tutuola does not improve appreciably over the course of the article.

57. Quoted in *Critical Perspectives*, 31.

Chapter 2

1. *Hot zikh im aroysgekhapt a vort der nisht-guter zol dikh aveknemen.* For emphasis, the *Loshn-koydesh* version of the story also interpolates this line from the Yiddish. In Yiddish, the term *"der nisht-guter"* is one of the innumerable synonyms and euphemisms for the devil. As before, the source for these stories is Reb Nakhman of Breslov, *Seyfer sipurey mayses* (Jerusalem: Makhon "Toyres haNetsakh" Breslov, 1991), trans. Rabbi Aryeh Kaplan in *Rabbi Nachman's Stories* (New York: Breslov Research Institute, 1983). Subsequent references incorporated in text as "Y" and "E," respectively."

2. A fruitful comparison could also be made between the "Complete Gentleman" episode and Edgar Allan Poe's story "The Man That Was Used Up: A Tale of the Late Bugaboo and Kickapoo Campaign." Like the episode in Tutuola's novel, Poe's story is a satire of modernity, technology, and imperialism in which the erstwhile commander of a military campaign against American Indians—a man distinguished in public by the "supreme excellence of his bodily endowments"—orders his Black slave to affix prosthetics to replace the various limbs he has lost in battle. See Edgar Allan Poe, *Complete Tales & Poems* (New York: Vintage Books, 1938; 1975), 405–412.

3. Thus, Vladimir Propp writes, "[I]t would be possible to satisfy ourselves that all of the tales given can be morphologically deduced from the tales about the kidnapping of a princess by a dragon. . . . " See his *Morphology of the Folktale*, trans. Laurence Scott, 2nd ed., rev. and ed. Louis A. Wagner (Austin: University of Texas Press, 1968; 1994), 114.

4. It must obviously be reiterated, however, that in the case of Reb Nakhman, unlike Tutuola, the original circumstance of this story's appearance *was* oral performance, and part of the reason for publishing his stories, unlike his other writ-

ings, in Yiddish is to capture, as faithfully as possible, the oral quality of his narration (*A Bridge of Longing*, 31). The distinction between oral and written in this comparison therefore refers primarily to the consciousness of the author, his freedom in adapting the tale structure to new purposes, rather than to the phenomenological difference between speaking and writing.

5. See *Critical Perspectives*, 245.

6. For a more intensive use of Propp's model to analyze Reb Nakhman's *mayse aleph*, see Yoav Elstein's study *Pa-amei bat melekh* ("In the Footsteps of a Lost Princess: A Structural Analysis of the First Tale by Rabbi Nachman of Braslav") (Ramat-Gan: Bar-Ilan University, 1984). Elstein divides the story into 108 "moves" (123–129), organized into 11 "episodes" (160–161), the eleventh of which—*geulat bat hamelekh* ("the redemption of the *bas-meylekh*")—remains unnarrated in the story itself.

7. In fact, the stereotype of an antisemitic, decadent, sexually predatory Polish nobleman (*porets*) is a stock character in Yiddish and Hebrew literature throughout the nineteenth and even early twentieth centuries. For more on this figure, see Israel Bartal, "Non-Jews and Gentile Society in East European Hebrew and Yiddish Literature 1856–1914," in *Studies from Polin: From Shtetl to Socialism*, ed. Antony Polansky (London: Littman Library of Jewish Civilization, 1993), 134–150.

8. Thus Raphael Mahler writes, "The newly risen class of big businessmen supplied the spokesmen as well as the patrons of the Galician Haskalah. . . . The Maskilim themselves were aware of the close social relationship between the rise of the big business in these Galician border cities and the Haskalah. . . . Nachman Krochmal [an important early maskilic philosopher] . . . describes [the Galician city] Brody as a city 'where wisdom and wealth, Torah and understanding, commerce and faith are united'" ("The Social and Political Aspects of the Haskalah in Galicia," 65).

9. Also referred to as *Mayse mizayin betlers*; the Hebrew letter zayin represents the number seven in *Loshn-koydesh*.

10. For an illuminating discussion of the "tale of the heart and the spring," and its significance to Reb Nakhman's teachings as a whole, see *Tradition and Fantasy in the Tales of Reb Nahman*, 209–219. Similarly, Joseph Weiss, in his posthumous study of Reb Nakhman's thought, writes of this episode, "Whatever the precise meaning may be of the well and of the heart and of the mountain, etc., the allegory is for the allegorist not merely vain talk, but rather as precise a tool as a concept for a philosopher. Here is expressed the metaphysical melancholy of modern man, with respect to the psychological impossibility of experiencing holiness in complete spiritual elation. Seldom in the history of religion has the feeling of religious longing, bound up with a feeling of powerlessness, been given so forceful an expression as in this image. The foundation of this longing is the painful and unmitigated awareness of the complete impossibility to take even one step toward the fulfillment of this longing. . . . This image is the supreme expression of

the spiritual fact about which Reb Nakhman protests unremittingly: the terrible heaviness that overcomes him when he rouses himself to perform an act of holiness." See Joseph Weiss, "*Koakh-hamoshekh shel hagvul*," *Mekhkarim bekhasidut breslov* ("The Attraction of the Extreme"), in *Studies in Braslav Hassidism* [Jerusalem: Bialik Institute, 1974], 97). One's attention is captivated by Weiss's characteristically paradoxical formulation regarding the power of Reb Nakhman's expression of powerlessness. By way of commentary it should be stated that the triangular relationship among the heart, the well, and the mountain is not an allegory, but rather a structure of irreconcilable tensions that finds analogy in various guises throughout Reb Nakhman's tales. Many thanks to my wife Brukhe for her help with translating this passage.

11. Theodor Adorno makes a similar observation in his fragmentary study of Reb Nakhman's contemporary Ludwig van Beethoven, regarding the *Missa Solemnis*: "Something in his [Beethoven's] genius, probably the deepest thing, refused to reconcile in the image what is unreconciled in reality." See his *Beethoven: The Philosophy of Music*, trans. Edmund Jephcott. (Stanford, CA: Stanford University Press, 1998), 152.

12. A further parallel between *mayse aleph* and *mayse yud-giml* occurs on the sixth day of the "Tale of the Seven Beggars," the last completed portion of the narrative. On the sixth day, the sixth beggar describes a king who has abducted a princess (a *bas-malke*, rather than a king's daughter, a *bas-melekh*, as in *mayse aleph*). Escaping from the clutches of this evil king, the princess flees to an underwater castle, where her life is saved by the sixth beggar himself (Y 479–484; E 422–434). In schematic terms, despite the revision or inversion of certain details, this episode seems to retell the basic premise of *mayse aleph*—from the perspective of the *nisht-guter*. Just as the first tale describes a triangular relationship among the Viceroy, the King, and the King's Daughter, here as well there is a triangular relationship among the Sixth Beggar, the Evil King, and the Princess. Understood as a parallel to *mayse aleph*, this incident indicates that Satan, the evil king, is like everyone else ultimately a victim of his own desires. The Israeli scholar Joseph Dan, in his groundbreaking study of Hasidic literature, similarly observes a relationship between these two stories: "The connection between the 'Tale of the Seven Beggars' and the 'Tale of a Lost Princess' is most explicit in the story of the sixth beggar, with which Reb Nakhman ends the tale; in this story he makes apparent the connection to the first tale, the ending of which he likewise chose not to reveal. Reb Nakhman returns in this sixth story to the kabalistic and folkloristic symbolism that he had used in the 'Tale of the Lost Princess,' but in a more detailed and profound way." See Yosef Dan, *Hasippur hahasidi* ("The Hasidic Story") (Jerusalem: Keter Publishing House, 1975), 167. For help with translating this reference I am grateful to my wife Brukhe.

13. See, for example, *Tradition and Fantasy in the Tales of Reb Nahman*, 104–105; and *A Bridge of Longing*, 33.

14. This reflexive construction is, in fact, absent from the *Loshn-koydesh* version: *eylekh v'anase*.

15. Quoted in Benzion Dinur, "The Origins of Hasidism and Its Social and Messianic Foundations," in *Essential Papers on Hasidism: Origins to the Present*, ed. Gershon David Hundert (New York: New York University Press, 1991), 153.

16. Indeed, the second introduction to *Seyfer sipurey mayses* (1850), presumably written by Reb Noson, cites a story in *Toldes yankev-yoysef* about a merchant and his wife at sea, and repeats Reb Yankev-Yoysef's explanation that "a God-fearing woman is the congregation of Israel" [*al hakdome zoy sh'isha yiras hashem hi keneses yisroyl*] (Y viii; E 15).

17. See Gershom G. Scholem, *Major Trends in Jewish Mysticism* (New York: Schocken Books, 1941; 1974), 273–278. In Scholem's view, the Hasidic movement as a whole constitutes an effort at popularizing Luria's esoteric doctrines among the Jewish masses (*Major Trends in Jewish Mysticism*, 327–328). Gershon Hundert, however, notes that a popular kabalistic literature had already emerged in Eastern Europe immediately prior to the establishment of Hasidism (see *Jews in Poland-Lithuania*, 119–130). One can therefore suggest that although the Hasidic movement did not, as Scholem suggests, merely popularize kabalistic ideas, this movement did concentrate these newly popular ideas, and provided a context through which they could achieve collective expression. Nonetheless, as Hundert cautions, "The very concepts of 'social movement' or 'religious movement' would have been distinctly foreign to the worldview of the Ba'al Shem Tov" (*Jews in Poland-Lithuania*, 161).

18. *In veg hob ikh dertseylt a mayse. vos ver es hot zi gehert hot gehat a hirhur tshuve un dos iz di mayse* (Y 1). I should note that it was only when I attempted to retell this story to a friend that I realized that each of the tests to which the Viceroy submits himself resembles, of course, an act of penance; it is significant that he apparently fails in each instance.

19. The only exception is the very brief fifth story; even here, however, one can see that the strategic use of periphrastic verbs such as *mispalel zayn* (to pray) and *modiye zayn* (to inform) serves an analogous function in a social, collective context, to the inherently private, introspective verb *myashev zayn zikh*.

20. See, for example, *A Bridge of Longing*, 27; 29 for a comparison of Reb Nakhman with the Brothers Grimm. For a more extended discussion, see Wiskind-Elper, "The Romantic Drama," 75–114. Arthur Green, similarly, invokes William Blake in discussing Reb Nakhman's reaction to the encroaching industrialization of the nineteenth century; see *Tormented Master*, 343.

21. For example, Margaret Drewal notes, "Divination verses tell of the journeys of ancient diviners and of deities and witches, 'when they were coming from heaven to earth'. . . . The journey . . . is an important organizing metaphor in Yoruba thought. . . . More than simply a movement forward, the act of traveling implies a transformation in the process, a progression" (*Yoruba Ritual*, 32–33).

22. As Quayson states, this narrative strategy signifies that the ultimate focus of this episode is not the Lady's relationship with the Complete Gentleman, but with the Palm-Wine Drinkard: "[W]e can say that Tutuola's changes to the tale [of the Complete Gentleman] lead to a change in its function in relation to the consequences that derive from it for the rest of the narrative. Though the young girl does learn a lesson, the significant consequence for the rest of the narrative is that the hero acquires a bride and not merely that the young girl learns a harsh lesson. . . . [T]he functions of the 'complete gentleman' tale are multiplied by being placed within the context of a larger story which exerts different thematic pulls by virtue of being a weave of different folktale segments" (*Strategic Transformations*, 49).

23. As Chinua Achebe notes, "Although the Drinkard may not know or acknowledge it, this child is like a distorting mirror reflecting his father's image in even less flattering proportions. . . . He has the same insatiable appetite, the same lack of self-control and moderation, the same readiness to victimize and enslave others. He is of course an altogether nastier person than his father, but the essential ingredients of character are the same." Chinua Achebe, "Work and Play in Tutuola's The Palm-Wine Drinkard" (1977), in *Hopes and Impediments: Selected Essays* (New York: Anchor, 1989), 108–109. Achebe's essay remains to date the best analysis of Tutuola's writing. Nonetheless, Paul Edwards in "The Farm and the Wilderness in Tutuola's The Palm-Wine Drinkard" (1974) makes virtually the same point: "The baby both parodies and parallels the Drinkard's own parasitism in the opening part of the novel; its vast appetite . . . recalls the Drinkard's gigantic capacity for palm-wine. . . . " See *Critical Perspectives*, 257.

24. See Terence Ranger, "The Invention of Tradition in Colonial Africa," in *The Invention of Tradition*, ed. Eric Hobsbawm and Terence Ranger (Cambridge, UK: Cambridge University Press, 1997), 214: "It was not the invented traditions of European workers and peasants, but those of gentlemen . . . which were most important to whites in Africa, and which had the greatest impact upon blacks."

25. See Bernth Lindfors, "Amos Tutuola, Oral Tradition, and the Motif-Index," in *African Textualities: Texts, Pre-Texts, and Contexts of African Literature* (Trenton, NJ: Africa World Press, 1997), 101. In a footnote, Charles Larson offers yet other versions of the Complete Gentleman motif in African narrative: "For two other variants see Melville J. and Frances S. Herskovits, *Dahomean Narrative* (Evanston, IL: Northwestern University Press, 1958), 243–245. The Herskovitses have titled their version, 'The Chosen Suitor.' Timothy M. Aluko, who is Yoruba, like Tutuola, has recorded the same basic story in his novel, *One Man, One Matchet* (London: Heinemann, 1964), 20–24." See *The Emergence of African Fiction*, 98–99. In a previous essay, "Amos Tutuola: Debts and Assets" (1970), Lindfors lists sources for a dozen additional variants of the Complete Gentleman motif among the Yoruba and coterritorial ethnic groups. See *Critical Perspectives*, 286–288.

26. On the role of the marketplace as a transition point between tradition and modernity, Africa and the outside world, the economic and the metaphysical, consider Manthia Diawara's statement that "Everything—from computers and fax machines to brandname shoes and gold jewelry—can be found, covered with dust, in the marketplace. . . . Markets occupy an important place in the collective unconscious of West Africans. . . . West African folklore abounds with market stories in which human beings conduct transactions during the daytime and the spirits take over at night." Manthia Diawara, *In Search of Africa* (Cambridge, MA: Harvard University Press, 1998), 143. Significantly, the Complete Gentleman's transformation into the Skull begins at closing time, at twilight (*PWD*, 202).

Part 1 Conclusion

1. See Wole Soyinka, "A Dance of the Forests," *Collected Plays, Vol. 1* (Oxford, UK: Oxford University Press, 1973; 1986), 1–77. It is essential to recall in this context that this extraordinary play premiered as part of the Nigerian Independence Celebrations in October 1960.

Part 2

1. Reb Nakhman of Breslov, *Seyfer sipurey mayses* (Jerusalem: Makhon "Toyres haNetsakh" Breslov, 1991), 136. English translation published as *Rabbi Nachman's Stories*, trans. Rabbi Aryeh Kaplan (New York: Breslov Research Institute, 1983), 167. Subsequent references incorporated in text as "Y" and "E," respectively.

2. He also uses the verb once with reference to the king's decision to appoint the Simpleton as governor of the province (Y 156; E 180–181). The pejorative or negative connotation of the verb with respect to the *hokhem* is unique in the *sipurey mayses*, and it prompts a series of questions, well beyond the scope of these cursory remarks, regarding the identification of this verb with the work of Reb Nakhman himself.

3. Christopher L. Miller, *Theories of Africans: Francophone Literature and Anthropology in Africa* (Chicago: University of Chicago Press, 1990), 47. Miller's source for these remarks is Fanon's essay "On National Culture"; see *The Wretched of the Earth*, trans. Constance Farrington (New York: Grove Press, 1961; 1963), 221–223.

4. Nokhem Oyslender, *Mendeles mitgeyer in di 60er–70er yorn* ("Mendele's contemporaries in the 60s and 70s" [1940]), in *Di Yidishe literatur in nayntsntn yorhundert: zamlung fun yidisher literatur-forshung un kritik in ratn-farband* ("Yiddish Literature in the Nineteenth Century: A Collection of Literary Research and Criticism from the Soviet Union"), ed. Chava Turniansky (Jerusalem: Magnes Press, 1993), 452–453. The translation, such as it is, is my own. Subsequent references to this extraordinary collection will be incorporated in text as *Di Yidishe literatur in nayntsntn yorhundert*.

5. Cheikh Hamidou Kane, *L'aventure ambiguë* (Paris: Éditions 10/18, 1961; 1998), 155–156. Subsequent references incorporated in text as "F." Translated as *Ambiguous Adventure* by Katherine Woods (Oxford: Heinemann, 1963; 1972), 142–143. Subsequent references incorporated in text as "E," although my translations will occasionally depart from the published version.

6. Quoted in Michael Stanislawski, *For Whom Do I Toil? Judah Leib Gordon and the Crisis of Russian Jewry* (New York: Oxford University Press, 1988), 17–18. For more on the eighteenth- and nineteenth-century image of Russian culture as the Western bridgehead of Asia, and as such outside the orbit of European civilization, see Dale E. Peterson, *Up from Bondage: The Literatures of Russian and African American Soul* (Durham, NC: Duke University Press, 2000), 1–14. For more on the Jewish self-perception as "Asiatic," and its implications for Eastern European Jewry's relationship with modernity and Western Jews, see Steven E. Ascheim, *Brothers and Strangers: The East European Jew in German and German Jewish Consciousness, 1800–1923* (Madison: University of Wisconsin Press, 1982), 3–31.

Chapter 3

1. As Robert Alter writes, "[B]y the late eighteenth century European Jewry was launching . . . that process of radical historical transformation we call modernization, and what was at issue now in the act of writing Hebrew was not just an aesthetic pursuit but a programmatic renegotiation of the terms of Jewish collective identity. It is surely not a coincidence that Christian Wilhelm von Dohm brought out his essay 'Concerning the Amelioration of the Civil Status of the Jews' in 1781, that Joseph II of Austria issued his Edict of Toleration in 1782, and that the founding journal of Haskalah . . . the quarterly *HaMe'asef*, began publication in Koenigsberg in 1783." See Alter, *The Invention of Hebrew Prose: Modern Fiction and the Language of Realism* (Seattle: University of Washington Press, 1988), 3–4.

2. For example, Jay Harris summarizes the efforts of the Austrian Emperor Josef II to *coerce* the Jews of his realm to modernize: "In an effort to change the Jewish economic profile, Jews in villages were forbidden to engage in trade; the so-called 'Edict of Toleration' of 1789 banished Jews from these villages unless they engaged in handicrafts or agriculture. . . . A special tax on ritual slaughtering was introduced in 1784 and tripled over the next thirty-two years. In 1797, a candle tax was imposed, in which every married Jewish woman had to pay a tax on two candles whether she had money to buy the candles or not. . . . Parallel to this economic exploitation. . . . were the flagrant attempts by the Austrian government to Germanize its Jews. Jewish children were prohibited from studying Talmud in a school until they had completed a course of study in a government school. Any voter in *kehillah* [Jewish community] elections was required to demonstrate fluency in German, and Jews were prohibited from marrying until they had demonstrated such fluency." See Jay M. Harris, *Nachman Krochmal:*

Guiding the Perplexed of the Modern Age (New York: New York University Press, 1991), 3–4.

3. Thus Israel Bartal writes of the Russian effort to "mandate" modernity: "The imperial project to enlighten and reeducate the Jews in the spirit of the autocratic Russian state was to be implemented through the establishment of a system of Jewish schools, with instruction in Russian. The actions of the authorities in the days of the affair of 'government-sponsored enlightenment' were similar to those taken by colonial regimes that sought to disseminate European culture among the natives in their overseas colonies." See Israel Bartal, *The Jews of Eastern Europe, 1772–1881*, trans. Chaya Naor (Philadelphia: University of Pennsylvania Press, 2002; 2005), 66.

4. As Michael Stanislawski characterizes the modernity of *haskole*: "The radical innovation of this movement [*haskole*] was not its recourse to German, natural science, or rationalist philosophy per se, but a new intellectual and social ideology: an acceptance of the authority of non-Jewish thought and mores as at least equal to traditional Jewish teachings and behavior, and a concomitant commitment to a fundamental reform of Jewish life according to 'European' dictates and standards." See Michael Stanislawski, *Tsar Nicolas I and the Jews*, 49.

5. As Adam Teller notes, "The claim that hasidic practices were based on non-Jewish customs was used quite systematically by maskilim during the nineteenth century as a means of discrediting the new movement." See his article "Hasidism and the Challenge of Geography: The Polish Background to the Spread of the Hasidic Movement," *AJS Review* 30, no. 1 (2006): 21n85. This persistent maskilic attack against Hasidism indicates that each movement saw itself as a defender of "authentic" Jewish values opposed to the upstarts in the rival camp; seizing the mantle of tradition as an ideological position, ultimately, indicates the newness of both movements, formed as a response to the external modernity that encroached upon the previously autonomous Jewish society as a whole.

6. As Shmuel Feiner writes of one nineteenth-century maskil, "Shalom Hacohen, who made a lone attempt to renew *Hame'asef* in the first decade of the nineteenth century when the Haskalah in Germany was already declining both as an ideology and as the focus of a social circle, warned against misrepresenting the term *Aufklärung* by identifying it with Deistic interpretations, rapprochement with Christians, or abrogation of Jewish law. According to Hacohen, the correct meaning of *Aufklärung* in the Jewish context was the cultivation of Hebrew language and literature, especially Hebrew poetry. See Shmuel Feiner, "Toward a Historical Definition of the Haskalah," in *New Perspectives on the Haskalah*, ed. Shmuel Feiner and David Sorkin (London: Littman Library of Jewish Civilization, 2001), 194. Although Feiner states that Hacohen's definition, offered in an 1807 polemic, was both defensive and retrograde—social integration and philosophical deism having already led to a diminishment of religious observance among German-Jewish intellectuals—this definition nonetheless continues to characterize maskilic culture

in Eastern Europe for the next half-century. The intimate, essential connection of *haskole* and Hebrew literature in particular becomes a central preoccupation of Eastern European maskilim, at a time when most German-Jewish intellectuals, even religiously observant ones, had already adopted the national language for their writing. To use Hebrew in modern literary and philosophical contexts represented for Eastern European maskilim a way to be both modern and Jewish; it defined the "revolutionary traditionalism" of Eastern European *haskole*.

7. As Steven Zipperstein explains, "In Russia, the virtual nonexistence of a bourgeoisie espousing a secular *Weltanschauung* that might be emulated by Jews, the absence (except for brief periods) of the prospect of emancipation, and the weakness of Russia's primary and secondary school system, coupled with the lack of practical incentives for pursuing a secular education, all reinforced traditional standards, with the result that Haskalah was seen as the primary agent of Jewish adaptation to modernity." See Zipperstein, *The Jews of Odessa: A Cultural History, 1794–1881* (Stanford, CA: Stanford University Press, 1986), 13.

8. The rise of *haskole* is coincident, however, with a reappraisal of Enlightenment philosophers, particularly the French *philosophes*, that occurs in Western Europe during the mid-nineteenth century. See Owen Chadwick, "Voltaire in the Nineteenth Century," in *The Secularization of the European Mind in the 19th Century* (Cambridge, UK: Cambridge University Press, 1975; 1995), 143–160. It should be noted, though, that Chadwick's focus in this essay is England and France, and the essential opposition that motivates the renewed popularity of Voltaire and his contemporaries involves religion and science—an apparent consequence of the philosophical upheaval initiated by Darwin's publication of *The Origin of Species* in 1859—rather than universal values and national ones.

9. As Johnson states, by 1915, the inhabitants of these "four communes," known as *originaires*, "could vote in French elections, stand for public office, travel freely within the French empire and in France, but in matters of marriage, inheritance, and certain family arrangements they could, if they chose, follow customary law. . . . They were in fact full French citizens . . . whereas relatives or friends born outside of the communes or living in the Protectorate . . . were simply . . . subjects without status and with limited rights under the French colonial regime. . . . Only those families who could show parents born in the communes, or long association with the cities, were eligible." See G. Wesley Johnson Jr., "The Senegalese Urban Elite, 1900–1945," in *Africa & the West: Intellectual Responses to European Culture*, ed. Philip Curtin (Madison: University of Wisconsin Press, 1972), 141.

10. Consider in this regard Léopold Senghor's ode "To New York": "New York! I say New York, let black blood flow into your blood. / Let it wash the rust from your steel joints, like an oil of life / Let it give your bridges the curve of hips and supple vines" «New York! Je dis New York, laisse affleur le sang noir dans ton sang / Qu'il dérouille tes articulations d'acier, comme une huile de vie / Qu'il donne à tes ponts la courbe des croupes et la souplesse des lianes.»). *Ethiopiques*

(1956) in *Léopold Sédar Senghor: The Collected Poetry*, trans. Melvin Dixon (Charlottesville: University Press of Virginia, 1991), 88; 371.

11. Zionism's relationship with "the folk," ideologically unaffiliated Jews, was and is of course ambivalent, like almost any issue having to do with Zionism: at times contemptuous, at others patronizing, and at still others valorizing—depending on the specifics of the ideological orientation of the Zionists in question with respect to class, the land, and language. In a sense this ambivalence is a legacy of *haskole*, but to the extent that Zionism as a national movement is dependent on a mass following in a way that *haskole* never was, it sees the Jewish masses as an object of at least ultimate or eventual cultivation, rather than an impediment to enlightenment, as often seems the case in maskilic literature.

12. See Dan Miron, "A Language as Caliban," in *A Traveler Disguised: The Rise of Modern Yiddish Fiction in the Nineteenth Century* (Syracuse, NY: Syracuse University Press, 1973; 1996), 34–42.

13. This maskilic "pseudo-critique" of Yiddish brings to mind a remark of Michel-Rolph Trouillot, comparing colonialist assumptions of non-Western attitudes toward history with non-Western languages: "Because these [colonialist] observers did not find grammar books or dictionaries among the so-called savages, because they could not understand or apply the grammatical rules that governed these languages, they promptly concluded that such rules did not exist." See his *Silencing the Past: Power and the Production of History* (Boston: Beacon Press, 1995), 7. In both cases, of course, the "enlightened" modern observer connects the alleged disorder of the subaltern language to a metaphysical *absence* of order in the culture as a whole.

14. Shmuel Werses, "*Tsvishn dray shprakhn: Vegn yoysef perls yidishe ksovim in likht fun naye materialn*" ("Between Three Languages: Yosef Perl's Yiddish Writings in the Light of New Materials"), *Di Goldene keyt* 89 (1976): 156. The translation is my own.

15. By extension, as David Roskies has suggested to me, Hebrew figures in this "psycholinguistic dynamic" as the ego: the desired, completed self, the collective Jewish past, present, and future reconciled in a single cultural formulation.

16. As Sander Gilman writes, "Toleration draws the line at language difference. The German Enlightenment demanded that the Jews accept the majority's language of economic and social intercourse and abandon their language of deception [Yiddish]. This is not far from the demands of the seventeenth-century writers who saw in the linguistic unification of the Germans a substitute for political chaos. But by the mid-eighteenth century this view had become completely confused with the essence rather than the politics of German self-determination." See Sander L. Gilman, *Jewish Self-Hatred: Anti-Semitism and the Hidden Language of the Jews* (Baltimore: Johns Hopkins University Press, 1986), 85.

17. The one exception to the blackout of maskilic literature in Yiddish during this era is the author Isaac Meyer Dik, who began publishing in Yiddish during

the 1850s, and thereafter never wanted for a publisher or an audience. For more on his publishing history, see David G. Roskies, "An Annotated Bibliography of Ayzik-Meyer Dik," in *The Field of Yiddish: Fourth Collection*, ed. Marvin I. Herzog, Barbara Kirshenblatt-Gimblett, Dan Miron, and Ruth Wisse (Philadelphia: Institute for the Study of Human Issues, 1980), 117–184. Dik's exceptionality stems from two significant factors: based in Vilna, in the "Lithuanian" sector of the Jewish Pale of Settlement, he was out of reach of the Hasidic power base that constituted the most formidable opposition to *haskole* within Jewish society; moreover, his version of *haskole* was mild and accommodating enough to escape the censure of the local religious establishment. This discussion will soon return to Dik, an important writer who, despite the mildness of his ideology, is in many ways representative of *haskole* as it played out in Yiddish literature.

18. See Chone Shmeruk, *Tsvishn khsides un haskole*, in his *Prokim fun der yidisher literatur-geshikhte* ("Between *khsides* and *haskole*," in "Yiddish Literature: Aspects of Its History") (Tel Aviv: I. L. Peretz Publishing House, 1988), 263–289.

19. See Dr. Yisroyl Tsinberg, *Di Geshikhte fun der literatur ba yidn* ("The History of the Jewish Literature"), vol. 8, book 2 (Vilna: "Tomor" Publishing, 1937), 190.

20. See *A Traveler Disguised*, 263.

21. For information on these two publishing centers, and their relationship with *haskole*, see David G. Roskies, *A Bridge of Longing: The Lost Art of Yiddish Storytelling* (Cambridge, MA: Harvard University Press, 1995), 63.

22. Also referred to in the scholarly literature as the *khevre mefitsey haskole*.

23. For a full account of Aksenfeld's travails, see *Prokim fun der yidisher literatur-geshikhte*, 272–275; see as well the "biographical notes" by Shmuel Rozhanski in Yisroyl Aksenfeld, *Dos Shtern-tikhl un Der Ershter yidisher rekrut*, vol. 47 of the *Musterverk* library of Yiddish literature (Buenos Aires: Ateneo Literario en el IWO, 1971), 6–8.

24. Caliban: "You taught me language; and my profit on't / Is, I know how to curse. The red plague rid you / For learning me your language!" (*The Tempest*, Act I, scene ii, ll 363–365).

25. See Sh. Niger, *A Maskils utopye* ("A Maskil's Utopia"), *YIVO-Bleter* 36 (1952): 136–190. Subsequent references incorporated in text as "*A Maskils utopye.*" Translations will be my own. Roskies hypothesizes that the manuscript was written in the early 1870s; see *The Field of Yiddish*, 4:171.

26. In fact, among Dik's activities on behalf of *haskole* in Vilna was a brief involvement in a breakaway "reformed" congregation during the 1840s; on this point, see Roskies, *A Bridge of Longing*, 66.

27. Dik's voluminous writings are extremely difficult to find in their original versions; the best source for his most famous stories is a volume of *Geklibene verk* ("Selected Works"), ed. Sh. Niger and published in New York by the Congress for Jewish Culture (1954). Even this collection, however, is a "corrected" edition,

with many of Dik's signature *daytshmerismen* and Slavicisms replaced with a later generation's conception of "proper" literary Yiddish.

28. By way of comparison, it is revealing to consider Dan Miron's summary of Aksenfeld's novelistic style: "*Dos Shterntikhl* . . . in large parts is nothing but camouflaged drama, a series of scenic episodes cemented by a narrator and structured, to a very large extent, along the lines of comic melodrama" (*A Traveler Disguised*, 251).

29. As Mikhail Bakhtin remarks, "The novel, when torn out of authentic linguistic speech diversity, emerges in most cases as a 'closet drama,' with detailed, fully developed and 'artistically worked out' stage directions (it is, of course, bad drama). In such a novel, divested of its language diversity, authorial language inevitably ends up in the awkward and absurd position of the language of stage directions in plays." See M. M. Bakhtin, *The Dialogic Imagination: Four Essays*, trans. Caryl Emerson and Michael Holquist (Austin: University of Texas Press, 1981; 1987), 327. Bakhtin's comments compare with the remarks of Meir Wiener specifically pertaining to the maskilic writings of Shloyme Ettinger (c. 1803–1856): "However stylistically practiced Ettinger is in creating negative figures that are overly verbose, when he attempts to articulate a modern idea, his language becomes quite limited. Later in the development of Yiddish literature there occur similar relapses into aphasia; that is, a retreat to the German language . . . or to the awkward Germanisms and macaronic expressions found in nearly every work by I. M. Dik." See Wiener, *Di Rol fun shablonisher frazeologiye in der literatur fun der haskole* ("The Role of Clichéd Phraseology in the Literature of the *Haskole*," 1928), in *Di Yidishe literatur in nayntsntn yorhundert*, 97. One should consider how similar in tone and conclusion Wiener's words are to Bakhtin's; Wiener's essay appeared in the Soviet Union at least six years before Bakhtin's. Who gets translated, though?

30. In July 1843, Dik himself, along with a group of other Vilna maskilim, petitioned the deputy minister of education under the czar to outlaw traditional Jewish clothing—though by the time he probably wrote this manuscript, Dik had reportedly reverted to wearing a traditional gaberdine coat and yarmulke. See *A Bridge of Longing*, 66; 68.

31. Thus, the enlightened rabbi of Katloyke refers to the late Czar Alexander I with the honorific *zikhroyne levrokhe* (*A Maskils utopye*, 184), "may his memory be a blessing," a term usually reserved only for a great religious leader or a close family member. Most modern Jews would probably suggest as an alternative term for a Russian czar *yemakh shemoy*, "may his name be blotted out"!

32. For a historical survey of attitudes among Yiddish linguists toward *daytshmerism*, see Christopher Hutton, "Normativism and the Notion of Authenticity in Yiddish Linguistics," in *The Field of Yiddish: Studies in Language, Folklore, and Literature, Fifth Collection*, ed. David Goldberg (Evanston, IL: Northwestern University Press, 1993), 11–57 (esp. 14–28).

33. Houston A. Baker Jr., *Modernism and the Harlem Renaissance* (Chicago: University of Chicago Press, 1987; 1989), 80.

34. In this regard, it is worthwhile to point out that *daytshmerism* is a central preoccupation of most twentieth-century Yiddish linguists determined to raise the status of Yiddish and create an autonomous language. Thus my late teacher Dr. Mordkhe Schaechter, one of the chief polemicists against *daytshmerism* in the last half-century, noted many pejorative descriptions for *daytshmerism* (itself a pejorative term), including *dizn-dazn loshn*, *berditchever daytsh*, and *makhe-teyse daytsh*. See his *Laytish mame-loshn* ("Authentic Yiddish") (New York: League for Yiddish, 1986), 61–67. Moreover, just as Yiddish linguists have campaigned against German-inflected Yiddish (*daytshmerism*), there is also a campaign against Yiddish-inflected German (*mauscheln* or *jüdeln*)—a campaign that Sander Gilman persuasively connects to the rise of modern German antisemitism. See his *Jewish Self-Hatred*, 139–148. The difference between the Yiddishist campaign against *daytshmerism* and the German campaign against *mauscheln*, of course, is the difference between a "minor" culture's effort to achieve autonomy and a "major" culture's attempt to preserve hegemony.

35. It later spread like a virus in the early twentieth century because of its ubiquity in the early-twentieth-century popular press—hence the association of *daytshmerism* with low literary standards—both in Europe and the United States. As Leo Wiener writes of Dik in the first serious study of modern Yiddish literature, "Dick [*sic*] looked upon Judeo-German only as a means to lead his people to German culture, and his stories are written in a curious mixture in which German at times predominates. This evil practice, which in Dick may be excused on the ground that it served him only as a means to an end, has come to be a mannerism in writers of the lower kind. . . . The scribblers of that class have not only corrupted the literature but also the language of the Jews." See Wiener, *The History of Yiddish Literature in the Nineteenth Century* (New York: Charles Scribner's, 1899), 22.

36. Indeed, the linguistic policies of the Austrian empire effectively circumscribed the production of Yiddish literature there because of the quick and successful assimilation of German by most Austrian Jews. By the time modern Jewish literature became a significant cultural undertaking, in the mid-nineteenth century, most Austrian Jewish writers did not resort to *daytshmerism* because they and their readers were already completely comfortable with *daytsh*, i.e., proper German. Yiddish nonetheless perseveres in the Austrian Empire as a spoken language among Jews in Galicia, Jews on the Russian border, rural Jews, and the religiously orthodox. Thus the German novelist and journalist Joseph Roth (1894–1939) grew up in the Galician city Brody speaking both German and Yiddish; the religiously observant Nobel laureate Sh. Y. Agnon (1888–1970) began his literary career in Buczacz writing in Yiddish before switching as a young adult to Hebrew; Rokhl Korn (1898–1982), one of the most important female writers in Yiddish, hailed from the rural area around Podliski, where because of its isolation Yiddish remained the primary language for Jews. Of equal significance, Moyshe-Leyb

Halpern (1886–1932), the most talented American poet in Yiddish, began his career as a German poet after traveling from Zlotshev, in Galicia, to Vienna, but he switched to Yiddish in the United States because the literary market for Yiddish there was much more extensive at the time than for German.

37. Benedict Anderson, *Imagined Communities: Reflections on the Origin and Spread of Nationalism* (London: Verso, 1983; 1994), 196.

38. Pascale Casanova, *The World Republic of Letters*, trans. M. B. DeBevoise (Cambridge, MA: Harvard University Press, 2004), 18–19.

39. The Yiddish version of *Dos Shterntikhl* consulted in this discussion was prepared by Meir Wiener (Moscow: Emes, 1938); subsequent references incorporated in text as "Y." Many thanks to my friend Professor Dov-Ber Kerler for making a .pdf file of this rare edition available to me. An English translation of the novel can be found in Joachim Neugroschel's anthology *The Shtetl* (Woodstock, NY: Overlook Press, 1979; 1989), 49–172; subsequent references incorporated in text as "E." As indicated previously, the first edition of the novel appeared in Leipzig in 1861, though it was probably written about two or three decades earlier.

40. For an excellent selection and analysis of early-modern Yiddish farce, see my friends Joel Berkowitz and Jeremy Dauber's collection *Landmark Yiddish Plays: A Critical Anthology* (Albany: State University of New York Press, 2006).

41. As Wiener explains, Mendele's *nusekh* (style) "eventually becomes Abramovitsh's *nusekh*" (*Di Yidishe literatur in nayntsntn yorhundert*, 79): the author, Abramovitsh, over time internalizes the voice of his literary persona, using quasi-folkloric discourse not merely as a vehicle for ridiculing the tradition but also to express the complexity of his own ambivalence toward modernity. This internalization of what *haskole* had originally set out to mock is the best illustration of how post-maskilic satire—Yiddish fiction in its classic stage—uses the discourse of tradition as a means of criticizing the failures of modernization for Eastern European Jews. What Wiener refers to as *nusekh* becomes the rhetorical foundation of Yiddish Modernism, akin to the way minstrelsy a century later transforms into rock 'n' roll when the voice of the Other becomes internalized as a vehicle for self-expression—as Bob Dylan acknowledges by titling one of his best albums *"Love and Theft"* (New York: Columbia Records, 2001, CK 86076), after the definitive study of American minstrelsy, Eric Lott's *Love & Theft: Blackface Minstrelsy and the American Working Class* (New York: Oxford University Press, 1995).

42. For a celebrated recent collection of American Jewish minstrelsy, consider the rock critic Jody Rosen's musical compilation *Jewface* (Reboot Stereophonic, 2006, RSR 006). This album features a selection of early-twentieth-century, English-language comedy records on Jewish themes, the majority of which are performed by Jewish entertainers. The purpose of these performances seems simultaneously to assure Jewish listeners of how far they have come from the greenhorn antics and broken English of newly arrived immigrants, while fixing the greenhorn stereotype as an absurd and impotent caricature for the amusement of

non-Jewish audiences. The stereotype thus signifies progress and upward mobility for Jews rejecting and projecting this image onto more newly arrived Jewish immigrants, and the indelible antithesis of these aspirations for non-Jews who would believe that this stereotype betrays an essential feature of an unchanging Jewish character. The performances preserve an image of the Jew as Other that gives both Jews and antisemites something to laugh about: an ideal formula for commercial success!

43. Periphrastic verbs are, of course, a standard and characteristic feature of Yiddish grammar. There is nonetheless no figure in modern Yiddish literature who used them as extensively or productively as Reb Nakhman did.

44. Aksenfeld's complacent description of the Napoleonic Wars as a nice money-making opportunity for enterprising Jews able to learn a little Russian conforms with Steven Zipperstein's comment that "the Napoleonic wars . . . made little impression (on the values, at least) of the cloistered Lithuanian Jews, with whom the French came into direct contact. . . . By contrast, the war conducted in the remote Crimea four decades later apparently evoked considerable interest" (*The Jews of Odessa*, 17).

45. For more on the image of non-Jews in modern literature in Jewish languages generally, see Israel Bartal, "Non-Jews and Gentile Society in East European Hebrew and Yiddish Literature 1856–1914," in *Studies from Polin: From* Shtetl *to Socialism*, ed. Antony Polansky (London: Littman Library of Jewish Civilization, 1993), 134–150.

46. In this respect, Jay Harris writes of the maskilic philosopher Nachman Krochmal (1785–1840), "While Krochmal was probably the most 'acculturated' of his colleagues [in the Galician *haskole*] in the sense that he was fully at home in the world of German culture, the fact is that he did not live within this cultural sphere. He lived in a society in which the surrounding culture was Polish, and there is no evidence of familiarity with it. The cultural world he knew did not overlay with his immediate social environment at all" (*Nachman Krochmal*, 313).

47. Bennetta Jules-Rosette, "Conjugating Cultural Realities: *Présence Africaine*," in *The Surreptitious Speech*: Présence Africaine *and the Politics of Otherness, 1947–1987*, ed. V. Y. Mudimbe. (Chicago: University of Chicago Press, 1992), 33. Jules-Rosette's characterization refers specifically to Leopold Senghor's essay "L'esprit de la civilisation ou les lois de la culture Négro-Africaine" (1956), a central manifesto of negritude in Africa.

48. For an excellent discussion of the intellectual atmosphere out of which nineteenth-century pan-Africanism emerged, see Kwame Anthony Appiah's *In My Father's House: Africa in the Philosophy of Culture* (New York: Oxford University Press, 1992; 1993), particularly the first two chapters. For the best discussion of the culture this ideology produced, see Leo Spitzer's "The Sierra Leone Creoles, 1870–1900," in *Africa & the West: Intellectual Responses to European Culture*, ed. Philip D. Curtin (Madison: University of Wisconsin Press, 1972), 99–138. Al-

though a thorough comparison of *haskole* with contemporaneous developments in Black thought would be very illuminating, it should be noted from the outset that nineteenth-century pan-Africanism differs from *haskole* not only with respect to language—the language of pan-Africanist polemic is unambiguously English in a way that no single language could contain or convey the contradictions of *haskole*—but also because most of the leading figures in the early pan-African movement were transplanted intellectuals born in the African diaspora, the Caribbean or the United States, who resided in "Black" settler colonies such as Liberia or Sierra Leone. Although pan-Africanism thus produced ambivalence and contradictions of an equal magnitude to *haskole*, it nonetheless occupies a fundamentally different temporality, while sharing the same historical moment.

49. As Maryse Condé has written, "From the end of the nineteenth century, all of anglophone West Africa was the site of an intense intellectual activity which simply did not choose literature as its field" (quoted in *Theories of Africans*, 196).

50. Quoted in Lilyan Kesteloot, *Black Writers in French: A Literary History of Negritude*, trans. Ellen Conroy Kennedy (Washington, DC: Howard University Press, 1963; 1991), xxiii–xxiv.

51. Quoted by his widow, Christiane Yandé Diop, in *The Surreptitious Speech*, xvi.

52. V. Y. Mudimbe, *L'autre face du royaume: une introduction à la critique des langages en folie* ("The Other Side of the Kingdom: An Introduction to the Critique of the Languages of Madness") (Paris: L'age d'homme, 1973), 99–100. The translation is my own.

53. Enda Duffy, *The Subaltern Ulysses* (Minneapolis: University of Minnesota Press, 1994), 45.

54. As Abiola Irele states, "In its origins, modern nationalism in Africa . . . was primarily a reaction to the colonial situation, and only secondarily an advocacy of the rights of particular African peoples to self-determination." See Abiola Irele, "Pan-Africanism and African Nationalism" (1971), *The African Experience in Literature and Ideology* (Bloomington: Indiana University Press, 1975; 1990), 119–120.

55. The split between Caribbean and African articulations of negritude can be compared with the legacy of *haskole* in Germany as opposed to Eastern Europe: by the early nineteenth century *haskole* had given way in Germany to "deistic" convictions, social integration between Jewish and non-Jewish elites, and a monolingual German culture. *Haskole* in Eastern Europe maintains its autonomous commitment to Jewish languages, particularly Hebrew, as well as the structures of Jewish communal life and general adherence to ritual law, primarily because the Eastern European shtetl lacked the same attractions of contact with non-Jewish elites available in the West. Similarly, Caribbean negritude's embrace of communism and surrealism demonstrate the enticements and requirements of a vanguard movement in a more fully modern context than was available in Africa. The fact that Senghor's poetics are more pristine and his politics are more conservative than Caribbean counterparts such as Aimé Césaire (1913–2008) indicates the extent to

which Africa occupied a different temporality from the Caribbean during the colonial era.

56. Elaborating on this view, Senghor writes, "In Black Africa, any work of art is at the same time a magic operation. The aim is to enclose a vital force in a tangible casing, and, at the appropriate moment, release this force by means of dance or prayer." Quoted in Wole Soyinka, *The Burden of Memory, The Muse of Forgiveness* (New York: Oxford University Press, 1999; 2000), 119–120.

57. In this regard, Christopher Miller writes, "UNESCO statistics on francophone countries show literacy rates ranging from less than 1% in Niger to 6% in Senegal (in 1961), 19% in Cameroon (in 1962), and 30% in Zaïre (in 1962). Literacy in all these cases means literacy in French; illiteracy is defined by UNESCO in these terms: 'A person is illiterate who cannot with understanding both read and write a short simple sentence on his everyday life'. . . . On the other hand, in certain small areas of certain countries, the rate of enrollment in school and therefore of literacy is significantly higher: of children 7 to 12 years old in the Ivory Coast, fifty percent are estimated to be in school" (*Theories of Africans*, 69–70n3). One can only add that however low literacy rates were in the era of independence invoked in this citation, they were lower during the colonial era, when Senghor formulated his negritude polemics.

58. One could argue at this point that the maskilic rejection of Yiddish in favor of German (or Hebrew) is ultimately no different than Senghor's use of French. Nonetheless, there is an ethical difference between the rejection of Yiddish—the one language all Eastern European Jews shared—in favor of languages that almost no Eastern European Jews understood, as opposed to the adoption of French by an international cadre of Black intellectuals who otherwise lacked a language in common. Moreover, although most negritude ideologues never took seriously the prospect of writing in native Black languages, none of them, as far as I know, attacked their mother tongue in the manner of maskilic polemics against Yiddish.

59. Probably the best available appreciation, at least in English, of Senghor as a *thinker* is V. Y. Mudimbe's *The Invention of Africa: Gnosis, Philosophy, and the Order of Knowledge* (Bloomington: Indiana University Press, 1988), 92–97. See as well Janet G. Vaillant, *Black, French, and African: A Life of Léopld Sédar Senghor* (Cambridge, MA: Harvard University Press, 1990).

60. The reference is to Sartre's encomium to negritude, *Orphée noir*, the preface to the *Anthologie de la nouvelle poèsie nègre et malagache de langue française* ("Anthology of the New Black and Malagacy Poetry in French"), ed. Léopold Sédar Senghor (Paris: Presses Universitaires de France, 1948; 1997. As Olakunle George has suggested, the history of postcolonial African literature as an object of academic study really begins with the publication of this collection; see Olakunle George, *Relocating Agency: Modernity and African Letters* (Albany: State University of New York Press, 2003), 196.

61. The efforts of negritude writers to establish an African "authenticity" while

writing in French, thus creating a cultural space neither traditionally African nor imitatively French, call to mind the "invented traditions" of the Creoles of Sierra Leone and Liberia during the nineteenth century. As Leo Spitzer writes of the Sierra Leone Creoles, "In defining elements of the black personality as they saw fit—far enough removed from up-country realities so that no confusion would arise—they were able both to have their cake and to eat it: they could believe that they were no longer wholesale imitators of the Europeans and were shaping their culture more in keeping with their 'racial destiny,' without, at the same time, being frightened that they were in any way reverting to the ways of up-country 'barbarian aborigines.'" See *Africa & the West*, 116.

62. In this regard Eric Hobsbawm writes that "[w]hile . . . national liberation movements in the Third World were in theory modeled on the nationalism of the west, in practice the states they attempted to construct were . . . generally the opposite of the ethnically and linguistically homogenous entities which came to be seen as the standard form of 'nation-state' in the west." See his *Nations and Nationalism since 1780: Programme, Myth, Reality* (Cambridge, UK: Cambridge University Press, 1990; 1997), 169.

63. As Miller states, "The inventors of negritude ideology . . . were educated in the French colonial system and were more accustomed to expressing themselves in French than in Martinican Creole or Senegalese Wolof. The birthplace of black francophone literature is more Paris than Fort-de-France or Dakar, and it is now easy to recognize in negritude . . . the signs of alienation from the author's native past: nostalgia, so to speak, the desire to coincide again, to bring the past back" (*Theories of Africans*, 16).

64. Quoted in Ngugi wa Thiong'o's *Decolonising the Mind: The Politics of Language in African Literature* (London: James Currey, 1986; 1988), 19. Ngugi's source is the *postface* to Senghor's 1956 collection of poems, *Ethiopiques*. For the original, see Senghor's *Liberté 1: Négritude et Humanisme* (Paris: Éditions du Seuil, 1964), 225–226. I am very grateful to my friend Manuel Bronstein, of blessed memory, for presenting me with this volume.

65. Jean-Paul Sartre, *Orphée Noir*, XI. Translated as "Black Orpheus" by S. W. Allen (Paris: *Présence Africaine*, n.d.), 11. Subsequent references incorporated in text as "F" and "E" respectively.

66. On the subject of authenticity, it is revealing to consider Sartre's yardstick: "A Jew, white among white men, can deny that he is a Jew, can declare himself a man among men. The Negro cannot deny that he is Negro or claim for himself this abstract uncolored humanity. He is black. Thus he is held to authenticity" (F XIV; E 15). Of course, for both the antisemites of the Enlightenment and the proponents of *haskole*, the badge of incriminating "authenticity" was not skin color, but language—a badge that "colored" Jews as indelibly as skin color did colonized Blacks. For more on the stigmatizing "authenticity" of Jewish speech and its role in modern antisemitism, see Sander Gilman's *Jewish Self-Hatred*.

67. Hence Mudimbe writes in *L'autre face du royaume*, "The product of a singular moment in European history, more particularly in French thought, it [negritude] carries these marks. Nonetheless, the fact that its promoters had appealed to a Western 'technician,' J. P. Sartre, to establish it theoretically according to a distinguished and rigorous philosophical tradition, provides evidence for the existence of a quite particular intellectual line of descent" (*L'autre face du royaume*, 101). Note, of course, that Mudimbe sees negritude as the African response to a particular moment in French thought—not African culture.

68. In the book *Rereading Camara Laye* (Lincoln: University of Nebraska Press, 2002), Adele King has raised serious allegations regarding the authenticity of Camara's writing and his role in producing the works that bear his name. Nonetheless, as Abiola Irele states persuasively in his review of these charges, "despite the assertive tone of her book, the case King endeavors to make against Laye remains unproven, and must be considered ultimately unconvincing." See F. Abiola Irele, "In Search of Camara Laye," *Research in African Literatures* 37, no. 1 (Spring 2006): 111.

69. Among the negative assessments of *L'enfant noir* that Miller recounts in his definitive study of the narrative, one by the Marxist critic Nicole Medjigbodo is typical: she accuses Camara of "a deliberate will to mask the sad and negative aspects in the village, to give the reader an image of order and beauty . . . an illusion of immobility . . . a myth of static and happy societies." To this critique Miller himself adds, "No French colonial administrators interfere in the Mande world of *L'Enfant noir*; the tension comes not from overt resistance to colonialism but from a feeling of *falling away* from traditional culture" (see *Theories of Africans*, 123–124). By contrast, the remarks that follow here agree with a more contemporary approach toward the narrative, to see it "as a work of subtly *sublimated*, rather than *repressed* politics" (*Theories of Africans*, 124).

70. Camara Laye, *L'enfant noir* (Paris: Librairie Plon, 1954, 1998), 84. Subsequent references incorporated in text as "F." Translated as *The Dark Child* by James Kirkup and Ernest Jones (New York: Noonday Press, 1954; 1994), 79–80. Subsequent references incorporated in text as "E."

71. Michel Foucault, *Discipline & Punish: The Birth of the Prison*, trans. Alan Sheridan (New York: Vintage Books, 1975; 1995), 201. The distance separating Foucault's "panopticon" from Deleuze and Guattari's "assemblage"—the former an image of total domination, the latter of eternal escape—is, at once, just around the corner and halfway around the world (a phenomenon familiar to anyone in New York who has ever walked from Broadway to West End Avenue).

72. It is moreover significant that this alignment of the griot with Islam appears only in the French original. As Eric Sellin concludes, "The English translation . . . makes no mention of Allah, omitting the last two lines of dialogue [between Kouyaté and his father] altogether, which . . . is an egregious omission, for the matter-of-fact acceptance of that oath tells us how completely and unselfcon-

sciously Islam has been integrated into the truth system in the world described by Camara Laye in his novel." See Sellin, "Islamic Elements in Camara Laye's *L'enfant noir*," in *Faces of Islam in African Literature*, ed. Kenneth W. Harrow (Portsmouth, NH: Heinemann, 1991), 234.

73. For more on the relationship between the author, his father, and the griot, see *Theories of Africans*, 162–171.

74. As Mildred Mortimer writes, "In oral tradition, the griot, mediator between tale and audience, relates the exploits of others; he dares not tell his own story. When Camara Laye composed his autobiographical novel . . . he turned to his African heritage for his subject matter, but to European literature for literary techniques." See Mildred Mortimer, *Journeys through the French African Novel* (Portsmouth, NH: Heinemann, 1990), 41.

75. With respect to this paradox, Miller quotes the Cameroonian philosopher Marcien Towa, "In order to affirm and assure itself, the self must expressly aim to become like the other, similar to the other, and thereby uncolonizable by the other" (*Theories of Africans*, 38). The consequence of this, as Miller himself makes explicit, collapses the distance between the polarities of identity that negritude was formulated to valorize. As Miller states, "Without equivocation, Towa sees what this suggests: that the African become just like the European" (*Theories of Africans*, 38).

76. Hence George Lang writes of Senghor's *Les fondements de l'africanité, ou negritude et arabité*, "It is hardly surprising that Senghor's *Fondements* was conceived as an address delivered in the presence of Gamal Abdel Nasser, or that as the Catholic president of a nation over 90 percent Muslim, Senghor found good reasons of his own to attribute an important role for Islam in his Universal Synthesis of cultures." See George Lang, "Through a Prism Darkly: 'Orientalism' in European-Language African Writing," in *Faces of Islam in African Literature*, 306.

77. On the "manufacture" of ritual within traditional African societies, see Terence Ranger, "The Invention of Tradition in Colonial Africa," in *The Invention of Tradition*, ed. Eric Hobsbawm and Terence Ranger (Cambridge, UK: Cambridge University Press, 1983; 1997), 211–262, particularly the subheading "African Manipulation of Invented Custom," 252–254.

78. In this context it is illuminating to read the historical background that Olakunle George cites to Wole Soyinka's great tragedy, *Death and the King's Horseman*: "the King of Oyo, Alaafin Siyenbola Ladigbolu, whose death set the play's events in motion, reigned for thirty-three years (1911–44) and was legendary for his collusion with British authorities" (see *Relocating Agency*, 166).

79. As Terence Ranger states of British colonialism, "Since so few connections could be made between British and African political, social, and legal systems, British administrators set about inventing African traditions for Africans. Their own respect for 'tradition' disposed them to look with favor upon what they took to be traditional in Africa. They set about to codify and promulgate these tradi-

tions, thereby transforming flexible custom into hard prescription" (*The Invention of Tradition*, 212).

80. Indeed, David Murphy states explicitly, "Negritude was for a long time a 'reformist' movement that sought a compromise with colonialism; Senghor and his acolytes did not envisage or even desire the possibility of independence until the 1950s." See his article "Birth of a Nation? The Origins of Senegalese Literature in French," *Research in African Literatures* 39, no. 1 (2008): 62. This ambivalence toward independence, which found confirmation in the close coordination of Senegalese economic and foreign policy with France under Senghor's presidency, corresponds directly to the simultaneous loyalty to the Czar and the Jewish "nation"—the "non-nationalist nationalism"—of maskilim such as Isaac Meyer Dik.

81. As Anderson further notes, "There seems to have been nothing similar in British West Africa [to the William Ponty school], whether because the British colonies were non-contiguous, or because London was wealthy and liberal enough to start secondary schools almost simultaneously in the major territories, or because of the localism of rival Protestant missionary organizations" (*Imagined Communities*, 124n16).

Chapter 4

1. *Dos Vintshfingerl* was first published as a 42–page pamphlet in Warsaw in 1865 by Yoysef Lebnzon. Although a translation of an expanded version of the novel begun in 1888 and revised repeatedly over the next two decades was prepared by Michael Wex and published by Syracuse University Press in 2003, this version differs so completely from the original under consideration here that reference to the English version is impossible. Translations in this discussion, therefore, will be my own. For the publishing history of *Dos Vintshfingerl*, see Max Weinreich, "*Mendeles onheyb*," in *Bilder fun der yidisher literaturgeshikhte: fun di onheybn biz Mendele Moykher-Sforim* ("Mendele's Beginnings," "Studies in the History of Yiddish Literature from Its Origins until Mendele Moykher-Sforim") (Vilna: Farlag "Tomor," 1928), 342–351.

2. As Sh. Niger states, "If the *yidish-frage* were not for Abramovitsh an *ikh-frage* . . . he would never have preoccupied himself to such an extent with Yiddish." Quoted in Yudl Mark, *Mendeles loshn* ("The Language of Mendele Moykher-Sforim"), *Yidishe Shprakh* ("The Yiddish Language") 27, no. 1 (June 1967): 3. The translation, needless to say, is my own. Niger's appraisal of Abramovitsh plays on the two meanings of the term *yidish-frage*—"Yiddish question" and "Jewish question"—and thus offers the psychological insight that creating a literary language in Yiddish was for Abramovitsh not only a means of creating a cultural vocabulary for newly modern Jews, but also a means of creating an individual identity for himself.

3. To the extent that maskilic satires in Yiddish received any circulation at all in

the first half of the nineteenth century, they did so privately through the exchange of manuscripts among like-minded correspondents. The practice of circulating hand-copied manuscripts to create an underground discourse of dissent finds its primary counterpart in the activities of Russian intellectuals during the reign of Czar Nicholas I; on this practice, see *Up from Bondage*, 18.

4. On Berditchev as the model for "Glupsk," see the essay "Sh. Y. Abramovitsh and His 'Mendele,'" in Dan Miron's collection *The Image of the Shtetl and Other Studies of Modern Jewish Literary Imagination* (Syracuse, NY: Syracuse University Press, 1996; 2000), 108–113.

5. Indeed, the mirror, which is a standard trope of premodern Yiddish ethical literature, can prove to be an apt structure not only for discussing the relationship between characters, or between authors and their material, but even between characters and their audience; hence, the editors of Y. Y. Linetski's novel *Dos Poylishe yingl* ("The Polish Lad") (Odessa: *Hameylits*, 1869) credit the book's popularity— second only to Abramovitsh's *Dos Kleyne mentshele* in its day—to "the naturalness with which the author has described the life of Polish [i.e., Eastern European] Jewry. . . . Each reader can find here *a genuine mirror of his own childhood*, and even those readers who themselves never experienced such events have seen them happen to their friends" (*Dos Poylishe yingl*, 3, emphasis added). The translation, inevitably, is my own; I'm grateful to Dr. David Goldberg for making his extremely rare copy of the original edition of this novel available to me.

6. Marcus Mosley, *Being for Myself Alone: Origins of Jewish Autobiography* (Stanford, CA: Stanford University Press, 2006), 7. The phrase "new biographical model" is Philippe Lejeune's.

7. For a stimulating discussion of Maimon's autobiography, taken in comparison with the slave narrative of Olaudah Equiano, see Robert Philipson, *The Identity Question: Blacks and Jews in Europe and America* (Jackson: University of Mississippi Press, 2000), 30–73. Maimon's book is available in English as *Solomon Maimon: An Autobiography*, trans. J. Clark Murray (Urbana: University of Illinois Press, 2001). Although a fascinating work in its own right, which dramatizes many of the tensions between *Aufklärung* and *haskole*, the fact that it is written in German and provides explanations of basic Jewish concepts indicates that it is addressed primarily to a non-Jewish readership, unlike the subsequent Hebrew and Yiddish narratives it inspired.

8. A similar structure divides Samba Diallo's story in two nearly equal parts, between Africa and France, in *L'aventure ambiguë*. For more on the structure of *L'aventure ambiguë*, see William S. Shiver, "A Summary of Interior Monologue in Cheikh Hamidou Kane's 'Ambiguous Adventure,'" *Présence Africaine* 101/102 (1977): 212–215.

9. In a different context, one could make a revealing comparison between *L'aventure ambiguë* and Henry Roth's 1934 novel *Call It Sleep*. Like *L'aventure ambiguë*, *Call It Sleep* invokes a juxtaposition of initiation and education, death and

resurrection (or in Kane's instance, communication beyond the grave). Although such a comparison would yield much interpretative fruit, in a morphological sense Roth is out of place here because his Anglophone High Modernist portrayal of immigrant life follows seventy years of literary representations of Jewish childhood, commencing with Abramovitsh's first narratives, as well as a half-century of Jewish American immigrant literature, for which his novel serves not as an introduction but a culmination, whereas Kane's depiction of African childhood, though analogously marking an endpoint in negritude aesthetics, is nonetheless part of a pioneering moment in the formation of the Francophone African novel.

10. Emmanuel N. Obiechina, "Perceptions of Colonialism in West African Literature," in *Language and Theme: Essays on African Literature* (Washington, DC: Howard University Press, 1974; 1990), 82.

11. Christopher L. Miller lists five sub-Saharan African narratives published in French during the 1920s in his book *Nationalists and Nomads: Essays on Francophone African Literature and Culture* (Chicago: University of Chicago Press, 1998), 20–21. These works are Ahmadou Mapaté Diagne's *Les Trois Volontés de Malic* (1920), Massyla Diop's *Le Réprouvé* (1925), Bakary Diallo's *Force-Bonté* (1926), Lamine Senghor's *La Violation d'un pays* (1927), and Félix Couchero's *L'Esclave* (1929). The one work in this group that shares an affinity with *L'aventure ambiguë* is *Force-Bonté*; as Vincent Monteil notes, "Cheikh Kane's hero is 'dislocated,' and his death resembles a suicide. Already, after the First World War, another Senegalese author, Bacari Diallo (in his book *Force-Bonté*) examines a similar subject" ("Préface," *L'aventure ambiguë*, 8; the translation is my own). Abiola Irele has noted, however, that *Force-Bonté* in both its politics and the mechanics of its composition is more a collaboration between Bakary Diallo and Lucie Cousturier than the work of an autonomous author. This collaboration, or more accurately "cooptation," accounts for the work's uneven linguistic character, between academic French and the demotic *Petit nègre* (reflected in its title), as well as its contradictory politics, between praise of colonialism's "civilizing" mission and protest against France's capricious treatment of its Black subjects. See Irele's "In Search of Camara Laye," 113. For more on the history of Francophone writing in the colonial era, and particularly on Bakary Diallo, see David Murphy's "Birth of a Nation?" 48–69. In this context, it is also worth acknowledging René Maran's *Batouala*, the first French novel by a Black author (born in Martinique) set in Africa, and the recipient of the 1921 Prix Goncourt. Nonetheless, as Kesteloot states, "Having lived in France . . . René Maran lost his Negro characteristics and acquired a French style, without effort, without self-alienation [?]. . . . [I]n spite of his sympathy for his racial brothers, he regretfully confessed [to Kesteloot] he was too Westernized fully to understand them" (*Black Writers in French*, 106–107). However significant these works are as prehistory, the history of the Francophone African novel as a postcolonial literary expression begins in earnest with *L'enfant noir* in 1953.

12. In this respect, one should note that the narrator refers to Samba Dial-

lo's father exclusively as "the knight" (*le chevalier*) after the colonial official Jean Lacroix—whose name (*la croix!*) suggests that the conflict in this book between Africa and the West extends symbolically back to the medieval struggle between Islam and Christianity—describes him as such. Through this perspective, the narrator tells Samba Diallo's story from a Western perspective. One can see the adoption of a white man's description of a Black character as the author's acknowledgment that most of his readers will view this book, given that it was published in France, through the eyes of white people.

13. In this regard, Nouréini Tidjani-Serpos comments on the ideological ambiguity of the novel by writing, "In a novel such as *L'aventure ambiguë*, why does one assume that Kane agrees more with the ideas of the Chief [of the Diallobé] than with those of *La Grande Royale*, or those of Demba, or those of the Marxist Lucienne? All of these characters are vehicles of insight that are not identical with one another, but confront and oppose each other." Nouréini Tidjani-Serpos, *De l'école coranique à l'école étrangère ou le passage tragique de l'Ancien au Nouveau dans "L'Aventure ambiguë" de Cheikh Hamidou Kane* ("From the Koranic School to the Foreign School, or the tragic transition from ancient to modern in Cheikh Hamidou Kane's *L'aventure ambiguë*"), *Préscence Africaine* 101/102 (1977): 205. The translations from this article are, for better or worse, my own.

14. This motif in *Dos Vintshfingerl* echoes a similar aspiration recounted in Solomon Maimon's autobiography; see *Solomon Maimon*, 101–103.

15. As Victor Aire states, Samba Diallo's anxieties toward adulthood provide a metaphor for the Diallobé's anxiety toward modernity: "Here [in the Night of the Koran] Kane sings the swan song not only for his protagonist's childhood but also for an era in the history of his people." See Victor O. Aire, «Mort et devenir: Lecture thanato-sociologique de *L'Aventure ambiguë*,» *French Review*, 55, no. 6 (May 1982): 756.

16. In commenting on the ending of the novel, Kane himself, though not contradicting the interpretation of Samba Diallo's death as a sacrifice to the struggle between Africa and the West, emphasizes its spiritual significance over politics. He states, "In my view this is not a hopeless ending. The death of Samba Diallo is only the proof that there is a real conflict. You understand, if there had not been the initial civilization in which Samba was rooted, there would have been no problem when he was introduced to Western civilization; he would have thrived in it. On the contrary, he dies because of it. Why? . . . It means: 1) That we do have permanent values . . . and we therefore must nurture them. . . . 2) By not recognizing that, we reach the point of negating ourselves and our specific values; this will destroy us. . . . Western values inculcated indiscriminately can lead to the destruction of the African who is unable to assimilate them." Quoted in *Journeys through the African Novel*, 64.

17. Mildred Mortimer explains this historical context by writing, "Among the Toucouleur of Senegal, Kane's ethnic group, Islamization took place in the

eighteenth century; the *torodbe* (religious aristocracy) drove out the animist Peul dynasty in 1776. In the past two centuries, the Toucouleur have felt themselves to be the carriers of Muslim civilization and from the time of their conversion began to launch holy wars on neighboring groups. . . . For Kane, Islam is a powerful spiritual force that must be used in the struggle to resist Western materialism" (*Journeys through the African Novel*, 54).

18. See D. T. Niane, *Soundjata, ou l'Epopée Mandingue* (Paris: Présence Africaine, 1960). English translation is *Sundiata: An Epic of Old Mali,* trans. G. D. Pickett (Harlow, UK: Longman Group, 1965; 1994).

19. For an illuminating discussion of this description, see Miller's *Theories of Africans*, 9–10

20. See *Africa & the West*, 235–238.

21. Abramovitsh recycles this comic episode for the opening of his classic novel, *Fishke der krumer* ("Fishke the Lame," 1869; 1888; 1907). For the standard version, see Mendele Moykher-Sforim, *Geklibene verk, band* 3 (Selected Works, vol. 3) (New York: Ikuf, 1947), 13–161. The only acceptable translation in English to date is by Gerald Stillman in *Selected Works of Mendele Moykher-Sforim*, ed. Marvin Zuckerman, Gerald Stillman, and Marion Herbst (Malibu, CA: Pangloss Press, 1991), 171–312.

22. The actual name of the language is Peul in Francophone Africa, Fula in Anglophone areas.

23. The definitive study of this early Russian-Jewish culture is Benjamin Nathans' *Beyond the Pale: The Jewish Encounter with Late Imperial Russia* (Berkeley: University of California Press, 2004).

24. This is a point that Joanna Sullivan makes explicit in the context of colonial and independence-era Nigeria: "Nigerian authors who hoped to publish via the wealthy British houses were forced to write in English. While Nigerian publishing houses have existed in abundance, the poor quality of their typesetting and the lack of financial support to advertise, promote internationally, or even pay the author, further encouraged authors to look abroad for help." See her article "The Question of a National Literature for Nigeria," *Research in African Literatures* 32, no. 3 (Fall 2001): 75.

25. Ferdinand Oyono, *Une Vie de boy* (Paris: Pocket, 1956; 1998). Translated as *Houseboy* by John Reed (Oxford: Heinemann, 1966; 1990). Subsequent references incorporated in text as "F" and "E," respectively. On the subject of translation and mistranslation, by the way, it is curious to note that on the inside front cover of the French text, the publisher lists under the heading *Du même auteur* Camara Laye's *L'enfant noir*!

26. For reasons known only to the translator, Oyono's «un gros peigne indigène en ébène» is rendered "a large native comb made of ivory."

27. In this context, it is worth considering an anecdote related by Christopher Miller: "Many African languages have been heavily penetrated by European

words. As a prestige-linked speech pattern, the use of French words in Bambara, for example, is so frequent in the Malian capital of Bamako that a radio personality has a contest once a year to see if anyone can speak Bambara for a few minutes without using a single French word" (*Theories of Africans*, 70n4).

28. In a broader sense, one can observe the inherent double-voiced tension between German (a hegemonical language in terms of modern culture, if not always a directly imperial language for most Eastern European Jews) and Yiddish in the situation, familiar to most Yiddish speakers, of conversing with a German speaker: when the Yiddish speaker wishes, he or she can manipulate the language to make it virtually identical to (a "dialect" of) German; in an instant, however, the Yiddish speaker can introduce a Slavic or *Loshn-koydesh* element from *within* Yiddish to make the language entirely foreign to a German speaker. The German speaker, by contrast, and by virtue of the vehicular and referential nature of German as a language of *modern culture*, is always open, exposed, linguistically, to the Yiddish speaker. In many moments of cultural contact, this was the only sense in which the Yiddish speaker could exert power, from a subordinate, therefore subversive, position, over the German. During the Holocaust, of course, this disparity could become a survival strategy for Yiddish speakers.

29. When Mendele refers to a *daytsh*, a German, he means a Jew dressed in modern, "German" (i.e., Western) clothes—a *maskil*. One finds the same terminology and associations in Reb Nakhman's bizarrely satirical second story. See Reb Nakhman (Y 36; E 73).

30. See, for example, the essays collected in *Nation and Narration*, ed. Homi K. Bhabha (London: Routledge, 1990; 1995).

31. Indeed, when Abramovitsh's literary disciple Sholem Aleichem (1859–1916) published a highly revised version of *Dos Vintshfingerl* in his collection, *Yidishe folks-bibliotek* (1888), he asked Abramovitsh to delete this fantastic "digression"; Abramovitsh, writing with affectionate irony as Mendele, categorically refused Sholem Aleichem's suggestion, and the anecdote remains, in this and in all other versions of the narrative. For Abramovitsh's letter to Sholem Aleichem, see Nokehm Shtif, ed., *Mendele Moykher-Sforim's briv* ("The Letters of Mendele Moykher-Sforim), in *Shriftn*, vol. 1 (Kiev: Farlag Kultur-Lige, 1928), 254–256.

32. The motif of illustrious figures from Jewish antiquity returning to earth, particularly the patriarchs and Elijah the Prophet, is a perennial one in Jewish folklore. To cite one example from *Dos mayse-bukh* (1602), the most important premodern Yiddish folktale collection, consider story No. 163, in which a young bridegroom, and future son-in-law of the illustrious Reb Judah the Pietist, is forced to take refuge in the mountains one Sabbath en route to his wedding; in his shelter he celebrates the Sabbath with Elijah, the patriarchs, Moses, Aaron, and the prophet Jeremiah, among other luminaries. See the bilingual French-Yiddish edition prepared by Astrid Starck, *Un beau livre d'histoires: Eyn shön Mayse bukh* (Basel: Schwabe Verlag, 2004), 2:420–435. For an English version, see *Ma'aseh*

Book, trans. Moses Gaster (Philadelphia: Jewish Publication Society of America, 1934; 1981), 341–353.

33. Dan Miron alleges that the conception of Reb Shmelke's wife is far from immaculate: "He [Abramovitsh] makes abundantly clear that the supposed legendary guests, whom the Rebbe of Shpole himself had given permission to appear in his territory . . . were simply thieves, and that one of them seduced his wife." See *Batrakhtungen vegn klasishn imazh fun shtetl in der yidisher beletristik* in his *Der Imazh fun shtetl: Dray literarishe shtudyes* ("Considerations on the Classic Image of the Shtetl in Yiddish Belles Lettres," "The Shtetl Image: Three Literary Studies") (Tel Aviv: I. L. Peretz Publishing House, 1981), 53. See also *The Image of the Shtetl*, 42.

34. As Miron has discussed, this strategy of using folklore to undermine superstition and the Hasidic "folk religion" is a characteristic strategy for maskilic fiction. See Dan Miron, "Folklore and Antifolklore in the Yiddish Fiction of the Haskala," in *The Image of the Shtetl*, 49–80.

35. The first (1864) edition of *Dos Kleyne mentshele* has been published in an invaluable scholarly edition by the Literature Department of the University of Haifa (Israel), 1994, prepared by Shalom Luria. An English translation of this edition appears in Joachim Neugroschel's *No Star Too Beautiful: An Anthology of Yiddish Stories from 1382 to the Present* (New York: W. W. Norton, 2002), 189–218; the translations here will nevertheless be my own.

36. See Vincent Monteil, "Préface" to *L'aventure ambiguë*, 6: "Within his family Cheikh Kane is known as 'Samba,' which is the name of rank for a second son." The translation is my own.

37. For more on this maskilic critique, see Dan Miron, "Rediscovering Haskalah Poetry," *Prooftexts: A Journal of Jewish Literary History* 1, no. 3 (September 1981): 292–305.

38. Bakhtin's remarks appear to betray a Russian Orthodox "blind spot" in his writing; at the same time, however, one can perceive in them a humanist's anguish over the increasingly stultifying effect of a totalitarian regime on the dialogic life so essential to him. The target of Bakhtin's complaint here is as much Stalin as the Patriarch of the Orthodox Church.

39. As Paul Zumthor writes, "Until sometime around 1900, in scholarly discourses, all non-European literature was relegated to the status of folklore. Conversely, the nineteenth-century discovery of folklore and what were called, tellingly, oral literatures flew in the face of the Institution [of literary scholarship] at the very moment that Literature undertook its quest for identity, assembling for its purposes philosophy, history, and linguistics." See Paul Zumthor, *Oral Poetry: An Introduction*, trans. Kathryn Murphy-Judy (Minneapolis: University of Minnesota Press, 1990), 16.

40. The verse *toyre tsivo lonu moyshe morosho khiles yankev* ("The Torah that Mo-

ses commanded us is the heritage of the congregation of Jacob," Deuteronomy 33:4) is among the verses that are said immediately upon rising in the traditional Jewish liturgy, and therefore is among the first verses a Jewish child would be expected to learn, traditionally, as Linetski implies, by the age of three.

41. Later in his career, Abramovitsh himself would adopt the monologue form in a series of stories narrated by Mendele and resembling theatrical pieces in which, as Miron writes, Mendele "stands near the footlights, halfway between the audience and the fictional action" (*A Traveler Disguised*, 200). The crucial distinction between Abramovitsh's later monologues and Linetski's novel is the length of the narratives in question: Abramovitsh has chosen a tale form that can easily accommodate the monologue style; Linetski has chosen a more extended form that cannot.

42. As Miron writes, "[B]y standing . . . *outside* the immediate sphere of the story, by becoming by degrees its editor and manipulator, [Mendele] slowly develops the presence of the epic raconteur. He becomes *the first narrating consciousness* of modern Yiddish literature, and he frees this literature from the limitations of parody and from the staccato rhythm of comic dialogue." See Dan Miron, "The Discovery of Mendele Moykher-Sforim and the Beginnings of Modern Yiddish Literature," *YIVO Annual* 15 (1974): 81 (emphasis in original).

43. On Kane's incorporation of Sufi principles in *L'aventure amibiguë*, see Kenneth W. Harrow, "Camara Laye, Cheikh Hamidou Kane, and Tayeb Sali: Three Sufi Authors," in *Faces of Islam in African Literature*, 261–297.

44. As Manthia Diawara notes, "Writers such as Sembene Ousmane and Ngugi wa Thiong'o link the rise of national consciousness in Africa to World War II, in which Africans fought alongside white people to resist fascism, xenophobia, and racism. In *O pays, mon beau peuple*, one of Sembene's characters argues that the war was more important for Africans than education, because it demystified white men for black people, who traveled to Europe and learned that whites were normal human beings, capable of evil and good, cowardice and courage." See Manthia Diawara, *In Search of Africa* (Cambridge, MA: Harvard University Press, 1998), 142.

45. In this respect, G. Wesley Johnson notes that Senghor was the first African to earn an *agrégé* (state certification for *Lycée* teachers) in France, and was indeed "still better known in France than in Senegal when he became the grammarian of the French Constituent Assembly in 1945–46." See *Africa & the West*, 178.

46. Nonetheless, Michael Stanislawski writes, "Wealthier Jews could, of course, better afford the luxury of heresy than those who were dependent on the community for sustenance, but most wealthy Jews did not accept the new notions or bear their consequences. From the beginning, the Haskalah gained adherents from all segments of Jewish society, and for most maskilim there was no economic aspect to their ideology. On the contrary, their break with the mainstream often led to their impoverishment. [Isaac Ber] Levinsohn . . . was symptomatic; though

his family's economic position may have facilitated his original enlightenment, his acceptance of the goals and values of the Haskalah condemned him to a life of poverty" (*Tsar Nicolas I*, 56–57).

47. Mongo Beti, *Mission Terminée* (Paris: Buchet/Chastel, 1957; 1999), 94. Translated as *Mission to Kala* by Peter Green (Portsmouth, NH: Heinemann, 1964), 63.

48. Similarly, Jay Harris writes of Nachman Krochmal, "[In Galicia] [t]here was no outside world into which one could hope to assimilate, despite the fact that some maskilim wrote as if there were. Certainly, for Krochmal himself, the outside world in which he participated intellectually was German and not Polish; he admitted though that this world was not for him a living reality. . . . He was a recipient of German culture, but . . . could harbor no hope of participation in its shaping. Thus, his underestimation of the transformative character of modernity may be due to the fact that he experienced it from a distance and in a strictly theoretical way" (*Nachman Krochmal*, 31).

49. Abramovitsh's critique of the "cult of poverty" not only cuts against Kane's asceticism, but also an overly simplistic equation of poverty with goodness in the first version of *Dos Kleyne mentshele*, in which the protagonist tells his rabbi, "You, rabbi, are a righteous person, an honest man: I know this because you are such a great pauper" (Y 112; E 216); later he writes, "Let the whole world know that wealth won't make you happy" (Y 114; E 217). True, but as my grandmother often said, "it can make misery so much more enjoyable!"

50. Though Kane's literary reputation rests primarily on *L'aventure amgbiguë*, he has also written a second novel, *Les Gardiens du temple* (Paris: Roman Editions Stock, 1995; 1997). A synopsis of the novel on the back cover states: "Five years after its independence, an African country (which strongly resembles Senegal) is divided between tradition and progress, self-assertion and Western influence. It is not by chance, therefore, that a revolt breaks out in the community that most fervently defends its ancestral customs, the Sessene. The Sessene don't bury their dead, they cover them in a thin layer of clay before placing them, upright, in a hollow baobab tree. The government decides to punish their 'reactionary' behavior, but it loses control of the situation and soon a general strike is declared and the entire country is consumed by insurrection" (my translation). To which one could add, in more than one sense, *plus sa change, plus c'est la même chose*!!

Part 3

1. Tutuola's casting of Pygmies, a Central African ethnicity, in the villainous role played by the Complete Gentleman/Skull in *The Palm-Wine Drinkard*, can perhaps be understood with respect to the anthropological categories of the Fang, an ethnic group more-or-less coterritorial with the Yoruba in West Africa. According to James Fernandez, until the 1920s, the Fang grouped Pygmies together with gorillas and chimpanzees in the hierarchy of humans and animals—that is, as a

classification somewhere between the "fully human" and the "animal world." By the 1920s, however, gorillas and chimpanzees are recognized as animals, and Pygmies as fully human, a reclassification that Fernandez attributes to contact with white missionaries. See James W. Fernandez, "Fang Representations under Acculturation," in *Africa & the West: Intellectual Responses to European Culture*, ed. Philip D. Curtin (Madison: University of Wisconsin Press, 1972), 40–42. If Tutuola, who would have had no direct contact with Pygmy culture, draws on a mythologizing attitude of the precolonial era toward Pygmies, then his decision to place them so prominently in this novel aptly serves to express the liminal status among animal, human, and spirit worlds that the jungle signifies generally in his work.

2. As Abiola Irele writes, "There is a real sense in which the hunter can be said to be a 'given' hero in the Yoruba imagination. . . . " See his "Tradition and the Yoruba Writer: D. O. Fagunwa, Amos Tutuola, and Wole Soyinka" [1975], in *The African Experience in Literature and Ideology* (Bloomington: Indiana University Press, 1990), 180.

3. See Harold R. Collins, "Founding a New National Literature: The Ghost Novels of Amos Tutuola" [1961], in *Critical Perspectives on Amos Tutuola*, ed. Bernth Lindfors (Boulder, CO: Three Continents Press), 1975, 65.

4. Amos Tutuola, *The Brave African Huntress* (New York: Grove Press, 1958; 1970), 86–87.

5. Compare Tutuola's description of the Pygmy concentration camp with Wole Soyinka's reflections on being taken into custody by the Nigerian police: "The moment when the key was turned in the locks often comes back to me . . . and it occurred to me . . . that we were all black, that Mallam D. [Soyinka's interrogator] another black man had given the order and fled, that I was not a 'convict' in a chain-gang in South Alabama or Johannesburg but that this human antithesis had its enactment in the modern office of a modern skyscraper in cosmopolitan Lagos in the year 1967." See *The Man Died: Prison Notes of Wole Soyinka* (New York: Farrar, Straus, and Giroux, 1972; 1988), 39.

6. Indeed, as Emmanuel N. Obiechina notes, "Between 1960 and 1968 alone, there were twenty-five unconstitutional changes of government in Africa, of which eighteen were military coups and others were military-inspired." See his "Post-Independence Disillusionment" [1976], in *Language and Theme: Essays on African Literature* (Washington, DC: Howard University Press, 1990), 121.

7. Of course, in the context of the Biafran civil war described in Soyinka's prison memoir, or in more recent depredations such as those of Darfur, Rwanda, or Zimbabwe, just who or what constitutes a nation is precisely at issue, and the answers to this question can have life or death consequences.

8. With respect to the low moral and cultural standards of the colonial regime, consider the words of Albert Memmi: "[O]ne generally finds only men of small stature beyond the pomp or simple pride of the petty colonizer. With practically no knowledge of history, politicians given the task of shaping history are always

taken by surprise or incapable of forecasting events. Specialists responsible for the technical future of a country turn out to be technicians who are behind the time because they are spared from all competition. As far as administrators are concerned, the negligence and indigence of colonial management are well known." See *The Colonizer and the Colonized*, trans. Howard Greenfield (Boston: Beacon Press, 1957; 1965; 1991), 49. Nearly fifty years later, Achille Mbembe elaborates on Memmi's observations by writing, "The lack of justice of the means, and the lack of legitimacy of the ends, conspired to allow an arbitrariness and intrinsic unconditionality that may be said to have been the distinctive feature of colonial sovereignty. Postcolonial state forms have inherited this unconditionality and the regime of impunity that was its corollary." See *On the Postcolony* (Berkeley: University of California Press, 2001), 26.

9. Thus Shmuel Feiner states, "In the 1870s more and more of its [*haskole*'s] central beliefs, such as the hopes pinned on benevolent absolutist regimes and faith in history's progress towards a brighter future, were being destroyed by radical and nationalist maskilim. In an attempt to rewrite Jewish history for the modern age, [the Hebrew novelist and polemicist Peretz] Smolenskin called upon maskilim to change their order of priorities and give preference to the struggle against all forms of anti-nationalist assimilation." See "Towards a Historical Definition of the Haskalah," in *New Perspectives on the Haskalah*, ed. Shmuel Feiner and David Sorkin (London: Littman Library of Jewish Civilization, 2001), 202.

10. Tyrus Miller, *Late Modernism: Politics, Fiction, and the Arts between the World Wars* (Berkeley: University of California Press, 1999).

11. See, for example, *Late Modernism*, 19–20: "In their struggle against what they perceived as the apotheosis of form in earlier [high] modernism, late modernist writers conjured the disruptive, deforming spell of laughter. . . . Within the late modernist novel, the formal 'lapses' bound to laughter allowed expression of those negative forces of the age that could not be coaxed into any admirable design of words: its violence, madness, absurd contingencies, and sudden deaths."

12. Ato Quayson makes this point more eloquently when, dedicating an essay to the recently murdered Nigerian author Ken Saro-Wiwa, he writes, "With people like him [Saro-Wiwa] and Wole Soyinka, we know that the context of African literature is fraught with choices that are not solely literary. They are about life, and quite often about death itself." See his "Wole Soyinka and Autobiography as Political Unconscious," *Journal of Commonwealth Literature* 31, no. 2 (1996): 19.

13. Miller cites in this context the architectural historian Charles Jencks; see *Late Modernism*, 9.

14. When Memmi wrote these remarks, in the mid-50s, he was profiling an anticolonial revolutionary; today, his description would refer to what is now referred to as an "Islamic fundamentalist." It is therefore worth considering the role of neocolonialism and the enduring cultural hegemony of the West in the rise of antimodern Islamic ideologies. In this context, the French sociologist Farhad

Khosrokhavar has referred to a class of disaffected, French-born Arabs as "the new martyrs. . . . Islam is the only plausible identity they can endorse. . . . To accept their identity as French might mean accepting the inferiority they feel in their daily life as a second-rate citizen. The inevitable result is a hatred for France, and, by extension, for the West." Quoted in Seymour M. Hersh, "The Twentieth Man," *The New Yorker*, September 30, 2002, 72. By the same token, one is tempted to argue that the literature under consideration in this chapter articulates a significant challenge to both the hegemony of the West and the totalitarian politicization of religious orthodoxy—if only these books were better known!

15. Nonetheless, toward the end of his life, Abramovitsh reportedly returned to the traditional religious observance of his youth; probably throughout his life he was at least nominally observant of traditional Jewish dietary and Sabbath laws. On these points, see David Aberbach, *Realism, Caricature, and Bias: The Fiction of Mendele Mocher Sefarim* (London: Littman Library of Jewish Civilization, 1993), 33.

16. See Dan Miron, "The Literary Image of the Shtetl" (1995), in *The Image of the Shtetl and Other Studies of Modern Jewish Literary Imagination* (Syracuse, NY: Syracuse University Press, 2000), 45–46. Subsequent references incorporated in text as "Image."

17. A similarly decorous image of Jews and Christians intermingling in a civil space occurs in *Dos Shterntikhl* when Aksenfeld describes the protagonist's transformative journey to the theaters and beer gardens of Breslau. It should be noted, however, that Breslau—then a German city—is explicitly figured not as a "perfected" shtetl, but as the political, linguistic, and temporal antithesis of contemporaneous Jewish life. Aksenfeld's location of modernity beyond the Pale of Settlement indicates some of the distinctions between his "radical" *haskole* and Dik's "reformist" version, and also underscores how fatally fantastic Dik's utopia was, since to achieve Dik's vision, the shtetl would have to cease being a shtetl!

Chapter 5

1. The original 1873 edition of *Di Klyatshe* was published in sixteen chapters, but like most of Abramovitsh's major works, it was reworked over the remainder of his career. The version under consideration here is based on the "Jubilee edition" of the author's writings, published from 1911 to 1913; the expanded edition of the novel was first serialized in the Warsaw Yiddish newspaper *Der Yid* in 1902. See Dan Miron, *A Traveler Disguised: The Rise of Modern Yiddish Literature in the Nineteenth Century* (Syracuse, NY: Syracuse University Press, 1973; 1996), 316–317.

2. As Dan Miron and Anita Norich write, "In the 1870s Abramovitsh's allegiance to the average sensual man was at an end. For the entire decade he shifted his belletristic interests from the usual to the peculiar, from the normal to the abnormal. What made Yisrolik the madman, the hero of *Di klyatshe*, the true herald

of this decade in Abramovitsh's writing was precisely the fact of his abnormality." See Dan Miron and Anita Norich, "The Politics of Benjamin III: Intellectual Significance and Its Formal Correlatives in Sh. Y. Abramovitsh's *Masoes Benyomin Hashlishi*," in *The Field of Yiddish: Studies in Language, Folklore, and Literature*, Fourth Collection, ed. Marvin I. Herzog, Barbara Kirshenblatt-Gimblett, Dan Miron, and Ruth Wisse (Philadelphia: Institute for the Study of Human Issues, 1980), 11–12. Subsequent references to this monograph incorporated in text as "The Politics of Benjamin III." Elsewhere Miron explains that Abramovitsh's original intention for *Di Klyatshe* was to make it the first in a series of works narrated by "Yisrolik the madman," a figure who was to have eventually superseded Mendele in order to enable the author to introduce a more modern perspective into his belletristic writing without having to hide behind the "folksiness" of the Mendele mask. See *A Traveler Disguised*, 238, particularly Miron's comment, "That the plan remained for the most part unrealized is, however, also significant."

3. *Di Takse* is collected in Mendele Moykher-Sforim, *Geklibene verk, Band 1* ("Selected Works," vol. 1) (New York: YKUF, 1946), 155–250.

4. As Wisse states, "The meat-tax or Korobka was a tax on kosher meat, controlled by the Russian government, ostensibly for the maintenance of Jewish communal institutions such as the ritual bath, the cemetery, the school for indigent children, and so forth. It was administered locally by tax warders, an elected group of prominent, wealthy Jews who paid out a designated sum to the government in return for which they collected a self-determined percentage of tax from the sale of kosher meat and candles." See Ruth R. Wisse, "The Jewish Intellectual and the Jews: The Case of *Di Klyatshe* (The Mare) by Mendele Mocher Sforim," Daniel E. Koshland Memorial Lecture of the Congregation Emanu-El, San Francisco (uncollected), March 24, 1992, 5–6.

5. Mendele Moykher-Sforim, *Di Klyatshe*, in *Geklibene verk, Band 2* ("The Mare," in "Selected Works," vol. 2) (New York: YKUF, 1946), 16. Translated as *The Mare* in *The Great Works of Jewish Fantasy and Occult*, comp., trans., and introduction by Joachim Neugroschel (Woodstock, NY: Overlook Press, 1976; 1986), 547–548. Subsequent references incorporated in text as "Y" and "E," respectively, though translations, as here, will be my own.

6. As Michael Stanislawski writes, "The fact that the latter [maskilim] read more Russian books and adopted more Russian attitudes was a consequence of the substantial transformation of the Russian intelligentsia itself . . . on the one hand, the turning inward to Russian sources and the Russian nation; on the other, the dissemination of the intelligentsia's new views from the rarefied preserve of the capitals' salons to broad segments of society in the provinces." See his *Tsar Nicolas I and the Jews: The Transformation of Jewish Society in Russia 1825–1855* (Philadelphia: Jewish Publication Society of America, 1983), 118.

7. It should be understood that however much Abramovitsh exploits the symbolic association of knowledge and power in this scene, the educational system,

like all aspects of the Czarist bureaucracy, *was* intimately connected with, and organized along the lines of, the military hierarchy.

8. It should be noted that the talking, or more precisely *writing*, dogs in Nikolai Gogol's story "Diary of a Madman" (1834) similarly function as a parallel and parody of the rigid, dehumanizing class system that drives the narrator of that story insane; indeed, Gogol's influence on the development of nineteenth-century Yiddish literature was enormous. This points to a noteworthy instance of correspondence between a "major" literary tradition and a "minor" one; of all the great Russian writers, however, Gogol—born in the Ukraine—is the most "minor." Indeed, Gogol is, like Kafka, an author *and* a bureaucrat whose unfinishable novel and interconnected short stories bear fruitful comparison to the various types of assemblage that Deleuze and Guattari describe.

9. The same underlying, alternating structure of an unhappy prince and a pitiful mare refers to Yisrolik, thus making the mare a mirror for Yisrolik. In this regard consider that Yisrolik refers to himself by saying, "An orphan you are Yisroel, and a bridegroom too! A bridegroom, which is compared to a king, and an orphan—a worm, trod underfoot; that's like mixing honey with gall" (Y 77; E 599). In psychological terms, Yisrolik's unstable political and social status accounts for his lack of a stable identity or conception of reality. Similarly, this alternating structure orders the rhythm by which the narrative as a whole vacillates between fantasy and verisimilitude.

10. In the original, Abramovitsh writes first in *Loshn-koydesh*, then in translation, "Come on, let us deal wisely with them" (Exodus 1:10), the words Pharaoh says when he enslaves the Israelites.

11. See *Mendele Moykher-Sforims briv* ("Mendele Moykher-Sforim's letters"), collected by Nokhem Shtif in *Shriftn: Ershter band* ("Writings, Volume 1") (Kiev: Kultur-Lige, 1928), 221–233.

12. David Aberbach discusses additional parallels between *Di Klyatshe* and Ivan Turgenev's *Fathers and Sons*, a novel on which Abramovitsh modeled his first Hebrew novel *Ha'avot vehabanim* ("The Fathers and the Sons," 1862; 1868). See *Realism, Caricature, and Bias*, 80–81.

13. Whether or not Dostoyevsky's novel was an explicit source of inspiration for Abramovitsh, the author's own account of the novel's genesis was, as may be expected, much more fantastic and folkloric. According to Sholem Aleichem's memoir *Fir zenen mir gezesn* ("We Four Sat Together," 1908), Abramovitsh related that the specific impetus for *Di Klyatshe* occurred while on holiday. Outside his cabin, he observed "an exhausted and overheated Jew . . . standing and flogging a poor, exhausted, overheated mare with a scarred hide, hitched to a fully loaded wagon with bricks, damning to hell himself, the mare, and the world at large. . . . And she, the mare, turned her wasted, blackened chin to the Jew, and, it seemed to me, said, 'Idiot! You're calling me an old mare? You're the mare!'" (Quoted in Nakhman Mayzl's introduction to the YKUF edition of *Di Klyatshe*, 7–8.) It

should be stressed that Sholem Aleichem, who actively colluded with Abramovitsh in creating the "Mendele myth," connects *Di Klyatshe* to a source fully as literary as *Crime and Punishment*—the story of Balaam's donkey (Numbers 15:21–35). That archetypal donkey, like Abramovitsh's mare, protests her master's gratuitously cruel treatment of her, suggesting that he, not she, is the real ass.

14. In this respect, the moral center of the episode occurs when an old man shouts at the peasant mistreating the mare, "How come there's a cross on you? You're no Christian, you're a devil!" See *Crime and Punishment*, trans. Sidney Monas (New York: Signet Classic, 1968), 64.

15. It is characteristic of Abramovitsh's satirical motivations that *Di Klyatshe* concludes on an explicitly polemical note, in which the author offers a revision of the Ten Commandments for the rehabilitation of shtetl life. Appropriately, Yisroylik—again, no Moses at Mount Sinai—receives these new commandments from Lucifer; polemic as such is ceded in the novel, along with the rest of modernity, to the devil himself! (See Y 142–144; E 655–657.)

16. In this sense, Wisse is perhaps too hasty (cf. "The Jewish Intellectual and the Jews," 11) to dismiss the importance of gender to the novel's structuring metaphors. Thus Yisrolik remarks, "If the mare, a female, is a prince, am I, a male, in fact a princess? If souls should happen to wander among various incarnations, this too is entirely possible" (Y 39; E 566). Gender is therefore not only a political device for expressing the powerlessness of Jews, male or female, but also an index of ultimate relativity, suggesting that any fixed, "essentialist" identity—with the possible, and revealing, exception of Jewishness—is either a consequence of social perceptions, or a kind of cosmic masquerade.

17. Both the mare's "path of escape" and Yisroylik's "flight from sanity" connect these characters to Mendele himself, the itinerant bookseller always in motion, between *shtetlekh*. In fact, the Mendele figure is not a character possessing mimetic verisimilitude, but an assemblage of narrative functions.

18. Of course, the mare does return to the novel at the climax of Yisrolik's encounter with the devil (Y 147–148; E 659–660), but even here she stands primarily as a figure of *resistance*, challenging the devil who would again make of her a beast of burden, and encouraging Yisrolik similarly to resist the devil's efforts to make of him another parasitic agent of the organized community. The mare in her essence resists all authority—whether reactionary, progressive, or demonic.

19. See the collection *Monologen* ("Monologues") in *Ale verk fun Sholem-Aleichem*, vol. 25 (New York: Morgen-Frayhayt Edition, 1937), 7–25. *Dos Tepl* (1901) appears as "The Little Pot" in *Collected Stories of Sholom Aleichem*, trans. Frances Butwin (New York: Crown, 1949), 180–191.

20. The term *yidene* is a usually pejorative term for an old-fashioned Jewish woman.

21. For more on the attribution of gender to Jewish languages by maskilim and other modern intellectuals, see Naomi Seidman, *A Marriage Made in Heaven:*

The Sexual Politics of Hebrew and Yiddish (Berkeley: University of California Press, 1997). It should be recalled in this context that *Di Klyatshe*, like all of Abramovitsh's major Yiddish works, also exists in a Hebrew version, *Susati*, which appeared in its final form in 1911.

22. On the female readership of nineteenth-century Jewish literature, see Iris Parush, *Reading Jewish Women: Marginality and Modernization in Nineteenth-Century Eastern European Jewish Society*, trans. Saadya Sternberg (Waltham, MA: Brandeis University Press, 2004).

23. Readers finding this analogy too whimsical should consider the example of Alban Berg's Chamber Concerto for piano, violin, and thirteen wind instruments, in which the piano dominates the first movement, the violin in the second (which is a palindrome), and the third, a reconfiguration of the musical material in the two movements, consists of a *tutti* for the entire ensemble.

24. David G. Roskies, *Against the Apocalypse: Responses to Catastrophe in Modern Jewish Culture* (Cambridge, MA: Harvard University Press, 1984), 64–65.

25. This is also the characteristic condition for what Henry Louis Gates Jr. describes as "Signifyin[g]." As he writes, "This mode of Signifyin(g) is commonly practiced by Afro-American adults. It is functionally equivalent to one of its embedded tropes, often called louding or loud-talking, which . . . connotes exactly the opposite of that which it denotes: one successfully loud-talks by speaking to a second person remarks in fact directed to a third person, at a level just audible to the third person. A sign of the success of this practice is an indignant 'What?' from the third person, to which the speaker responds, 'I wasn't talking to you.' Of course, the speaker was, yet simultaneously was not." See *The Signifying Monkey: A Theory of African-American Literary Criticism* (New York: Oxford University Press, 1988; 1989), 82.

26. Aptly enough, the phrase *gute layt*, which in this context clearly refers to evil spirits, could either be a euphemism, like *a gut oyg* (a good eye) for "the evil eye," or a literal reference to well-positioned people. Though on the literal level Yisrolik's mother and her friends confirm the fantastic nature of Yisrolik's adventures, metaphorically, they speak like radical maskilim or proto-revolutionaries in their condemnation of the bourgeoisie!

27. This technique is particularly common in novels depicting wars of national liberation: consider, for example, S. Yizhar's *Yamey Tsiklag* ("The Days of Ziklag") (Israel, 1958); Assia Djebar's *Les Enfants du nouveau monde* (Algeria, 1962—notable for creating a collective female protagonist); Pepetela's *Mayombe* (Angola, 1980); or Shimmer Chinodya's *Harvest of Thorns* (Zimbabwe, 1989).

28. Abdulrazak Gurnah nonetheless makes an effort at synopsis that makes clear how little is conveyed by a simple summary of the narrative action: "Part One begins at the night-club, takes us to eat with the Faseyis and introduces us to Simi as an image of female sensuality. This is followed by the long chapter which deals with the corruption of the big men. We see Sekoni and Kola at work. There is a

funeral. We witness the chase of Noah. We see the 'sacrifice' of the girl at Egbo's 'shrine' and we attend the Oguazor party. Part Two also begins at the night-club. We meet Lazarus and hear his story. . . . We meet Joe Golder, an image of another kind of sensuality. We eat with the Faseyis again. We witness another chase, again involving Noah. There is a second funeral, this time of Sekoni. We see Kola at work on his canvas. There is another sacrifice, the death of the boy Noah, and the novel ends with a confrontation with the Oguazors again." See Abdulrazak Gurnah, "The Fiction of Wole Soyinka," in *Wole Soyinka: An Appraisal*, ed. Adewale Maja-Pearce (Oxford: Heinemann, 1994), 80n5.

29. See Eghosa E. Osaghae, *Crippled Giant: Nigeria since Independence* (Bloomington: Indiana University Press, 1998), 56.

30. Wole Soyinka, *The Interpreters* (Portsmouth, NH: Heinemann, 1965; 1986), 199.

31. The cannon might also connect Egbo's family to the slave trade. As Flora Nwapa (1931–1993) writes in *Efuru*, the first important Nigerian novel by a woman author, the firing of a cannon at the death of the protagonist's father signifies for the traditional Igbo community in which the novel is set "the departure of a great son, the last of the generation that had direct contact with the white people who exchanged their cannons, hot drinks and cheap ornaments for black slaves." See *Efuru* (London: Heinemann, 1966; 1986), 203.

32. Kwame Anthony Appiah, *In My Father's House: Africa in the Philosophy of Culture* (New York: Oxford University Press, 1992; 1993), 74.

33. James O. Omole, "Code-Switching in Soyinka's *The Interpreters*," in *The Language of African Literature*, ed. Edmund L. Epstein and Robert Kole (Trenton, NJ: Africa World Press, 1998), 67. For this episode, see *The Interpreters*, 83–87; 89–93.

34. Wole Soyinka, *Myth, Literature, and the African World* (Cambridge, UK: Cambridge University Press, 1976; 1992), 142.

35. See on this subject the fascinating article by Khaim Liberman, "Rabbi Nakhman Bratslaver and the Maskilim of Uman," in *YIVO Annual of Jewish Social Science*, vol. 6, ed. Koppel S. Pinson (New York: Yiddish Scientific Institute—YIVO, 1951), 287–301.

36. Henry John Drewal, "Performing the Other: Mami Wata Worship in Africa," *Drama Review* 32, no. 2 (Summer 1988): 160.

37. One thinks immediately of Niam's unnamed wife, whose absence both motivates and parallels the hero's odyssey in Mongo Beti's *Mission terminée* (1957), the eponymous protagonist of Cyprian Ekwensi's *Jagua Nana* (1961), the unfaithful Elsie in Chinua Achebe's *A Man of the People* (1966), as well as countless tragicomic heroines from the pamphlets of the Onitsha markets.

38. Mark Kinkead-Weekes, "*The Interpreters*—A Form of Criticism," in *Critical Perspectives on Wole Soyinka*, ed. James Gibbs (Washington, DC: Three Continents Press, 1980), 221–222.

39. Margaret Thompson Drewal, *Yoruba Ritual: Performers, Play, Agency* (Bloomington: Indiana University Press, 1992), 207n13.

40. The idea of comparing *The Interpreters* to *Ulysses* was first suggested to me by my late professor Michael Cooke, who in his 1987 course on the African novel in English described the opening sentence of Soyinka's novel as an instance of "Joycean synesthesia."

41. Another, more unfortunate, similarity that Joyce and Soyinka share is the gratuitous charge of obscurantism that has been leveled against both writers. See on this score Bernth Lindfors's polemic, "Wole Soyinka, When Are You Coming Home?" in his collection *The Blind Man and the Elephant* (Trenton, NJ: Africa World Press, 1999), 51–65. More notoriously, consider Chinweizu, Onwuchekwa Jemie, and Ihechukwu Madubuike's book-length rant, *Toward the Decolonization of African Literature*, vol. 1 (Washington, DC: Howard University Press, 1983).

42. Wole Soyinka, *Death and the King's Horseman* (New York: Noonday Press, 1975; 1991).

43. Wole Soyinka, *The Bacchae of Euripides: A Communion Rite, Collected Plays*, vol. 1 (Oxford: Oxford University Press, 1973; 1986), 233–307.

44. Abdulrazak Gurnah makes this point both in terms of Egbo's modeling for Kola's portrait of Ogun, and his relationship with the other characters in the novel: "What Egbo had demanded of Kola's depiction of Ogun [which is also a depiction of Egbo], that he should not have ignored the poetic possibilities of Ogun's contradictions, he is unable to achieve himself in his response to Joe Golder. In this instance, Egbo fails by any standards of human compassion, but he also fails because he is shown to be inadequate to the creative contradictions that characterize the gods" ("The Fiction of Wole Soyinka," 71).

45. As Soyinka writes, "Tragic feeling in Yoruba drama stems from sympathetic knowledge of the protagonist's foray into this psychic abyss of the re-creative energies. . . . The gulf is what must constantly be diminished . . . by sacrifices, rituals, ceremonies of appeasement to the cosmic powers which lie guardian to the gulf" (*Myth, Literature, and the African World*, 30–31).

46. Ibid., 140–160.

47. As when Death appears in *The Palm-Wine Drinkard* in the second trial confronting the protagonist before his encounter with the "Complete Gentleman." See *PWD*, 195–199.

48. The dynamic and innovative aspects of Lazarus's sermon are completely lost on James Omole, who writes that Soyinka "wants to ridicule the idea of Christ's victory over death." See "Code-Switching in Soyinka's *The Interpreters*," in *The Language of African Literature*, 68–69. In fact, this victory, particularly when expressed in the syncretic terms of Lazarus's sermon, offers a marvelously dramatic—which is to say, novelistic—illustration of Soyinka's "chthonic" cosmology.

Chapter 6

1. Tuneyadevke is also the name of the shtetl where Shloyme Veker had lived before moving to Glupsk in *Di Takse*, but as Miron explains, Abramovitsh has significantly altered both the character and the symbolic function of the town between the earlier, maskilic drama and the later novel: "It's entirely possible that the model for Tuneyadevke in 1869 was in fact not a small town, but more likely the city Kremenets-Podolsk, where Abramovitsh . . . had spent several years before he arrived in Berditchev-Glupsk. The real Tuneyadevke was another place entirely. If this shtetl had any model whatsoever, it would have to be Abramovitsh's own hometown Kapulye, in its idealized aspects." See Dan Miron, *Batrakhtungen vegn klasishn imazh fun shtetl in der yidisher beletristik, Der Imazh fun shtetl: dray literarishe shtudyes* ("Considerations on the Classic Image of the Shtetl in Yiddish Belles Lettres," "The Shtetl Image: Three Literary Studies") (Tel Aviv: I. L. Peretz Publishing House, 1981), 68. The translation from the Yiddish is my own. Subsequent references to this version of the "Literary Image of the Shtetl" essay, which really is distinct enough to merit a separate title, will be incorporated in text as *Imazh*. Considered in this light, it's possible that just as Hershele's pilgrimage to the Litvak's home in *Dos Vintshfingerl* parallels and inverts Abramovitsh's southward journey to Berditchev, so too does Benyomin's emergence from the shtetl at the time of the Crimean War parallel the author's wanderings after leaving the yeshiva and the traditional world following the death of his father, also in the early 1850s.

2. Mendele Moicher Sforim, *Geklibene verk, Band II* (Selected Works, vol. 2) (New York: YKUF, 1946), 167–168. Subsequent references incorporated in text as "Y." More than any other work by Abramovitsh, *Benyomin hashlishi* exists in several English translations. For an English version, see Joachim Neugroschel's *The Shtetl: A Creative Anthology of Jewish Life in Eastern Europe* (Woodstock, NY: Overlook Press, 1979; 1989), 184. Subsequent references incorporated in text as "E."

3. It's worth noting here that Abramovitsh was probably the first Yiddish writer whose work was professionally translated into a coterritorial language—a notable index both of the growing stature of Yiddish literature, and Abramovitsh's canonical place in it.

4. As Ruth Wisse writes in an early study, "[W]hereas Quixote is clearly an aristocratic dreamer, Benjamin is a beggar, a pauper representing the whole society of paupers. . . . The Spanish echo makes the satire at one and the same time more familiar and more formidable, not unlike the ambiguous effect of Ulysses dwarfing Bloom." See Ruth R. Wisse, *The Schlemiel as Modern Hero* (Chicago: University of Chicago Press, 1971), 32. One may note that Abramovitsh's parody of *Don Quixote* parallels a contemporaneous "Shakespearean" motif in Russian literature, as exemplified by Turgenev's "A Hamlet of the Shchigry District" and Nikolai Leskov's "Lady Macbeth of Mtsensk." Hugh McLean comments on this trend, writing, "The point of such titles is to juxtapose a Shakespearean archetype

at a high level of psychological universalization with a specific, local, utterly Russian, and contemporary milieu. The effect on a Russian reader of that time was almost oxymoronic: how could there be a 'Lady Macbeth,' especially nowadays, in such a mudhole as Mtsensk?" Quoted in David McDuff's Introduction to Nikolai Leskov, *Lady Macbeth of Mtsensk and Other Stories* (New York: Penguin Books, 1987), 17.

5. Thus Benyomin says to Senderl on their departure, "Here in the diaspora [*khuts l'arets*] you'll do better than I at having it out with the peasants in their vulgar language" (Y 195; E 209). Though *khuts l'arets* literally means "outside the Holy Land," in this context it's unclear if Benyomin is referring to the land of Israel to which he thinks he's headed, or the shtetl from which he's just departed—and this ambiguity is yet another instance of the interpenetration between myth and reality, Zion and the diaspora, in the poetics of this novel.

6. In the Hebrew version of *Benyomin hashlishi*, however, Abramovitsh does provide a translation of the peasant's Ukrainian. See *Kol Kitvey Mendele Mokher Sforim, Seyfer shlishi* ("The Complete Writings of Mendele Moykher-Sforim," vol. 3) (Berlin: "Moriah" Publishers, 1922), 106–107.

7. M. M. Bakhtin, *The Dialogic Imagination: Four Essays*, trans. Caryl Emerson and Michael Holquist (Austin: University of Texas Press, 1981; 1987), 370.

8. By contrast, of course, Aksenfeld's *Dos Shterntikhl* does depict an encounter with Russian army officers and foot soldiers, but in this narrative, as with the conflict between maskilim and Hasidim, the portrayal is as symbolic as the use of Lessing and Cervantes in the prologue to *Dos Vintshfingerl*; non-Jewish characters in Aksenfeld's novel serve as stereotypes that extend its masquerade and its ideological contrasts, without complicating or even distracting from the essential dramatic situation involving the Jewish characters exclusively.

9. Consider, for example, the opening dialogue in Tolstoy's *War and Peace*, which takes place in French. In keeping with the intended irony of depicting a Russian aristocracy thoroughly immersed in French culture preparing for war against Napoleon, the author presumes not only his aristocratic characters' fluency in both Russian and French, but his readers' as well. Abramovitsh by contrast capitalizes on his characters' respective ignorance of one another's language.

10. In this regard the author kills two birds with one stone by offering a parodic anthropology of the shtetl Glupsk's origins: "The archeologists [*khoykrey kadmoynyes*], who in their great wisdom can make a heap of nutmeg out of nothing, have taken the local legends and made a complete interpretation, deriving a thousand points from them, as is their custom, and thus uncovering the truth from these tales. The evidence they marshal is as follows—first, the grotesque and outlandish style of the houses are wildly out of date, as if they were made a thousand years ago, from the time when people still lived in tents. . . . Second, the customs of the residents are apparently preserved from the heathens. Writing and

arithmetic, for example, are seldom to be encountered, such that all communal and social affairs are conducted without recordkeeping. . . . " (Y 226–227; E 240).

11. For an English edition of Benjamin "the First's" travel writings, along with many other works alluded to in *Benyomin hashlishi*, see *Jewish Travelers in the Middle Ages: 19 Firsthand Accounts*, ed. Elkan Nathan Adler (New York: Dover, 1930; 1987).

12. When Abramovitsh translates *Benyomin hashlishi* into Hebrew, nearly twenty years after he first wrote it, the protagonist stands in for yet another Jewish Benjamin at work on the world stage, as Miron and Norich explain: "In 1896, Abramovitsh published his Hebrew adaptation of *Masoes Benyomin hashlishi*, which in the meantime assumed a renewed political topicality—this being the year of Theodor Herzl's hectic Zionist activity which culminated in the First Zionist Congress. Herzl, whose Hebrew name was Binyamin Ze'ev, went to the Middle East, met with Turkish dignitaries and the sultan himself, and his activities certainly freshened the entire political sense of *Masoes Benyomin hashlishi*" ("The Politics of Benjamin III," 104–105). For a detailed discussion of the Hebrew version's political significance vis-à-vis contemporaneous (and contemporary) Zionism, see Sidra DeKoven Ezrahi's *Booking Passage: Exile and Homecoming in the Modern Jewish Imagination* (Berkeley: University of California Press, 2000), 52–80.

13. For more on the geopolitical significance of the Crimean War, see "The Politics of Benjamin III," 72–73.

14. For quite a different treatment in Yiddish literature of the conflict between Christian Europe and Muslim Turkey, see Sh. An-ski's "Mendl Terk" (1892), *Gezamlte shriftn, zibeter band* ("Collected Writings," vol. 7) (Warsaw: Farlag An-ski, 1922), 61–102. For an English translation see "Mendl Turk," in S. An-sky, *The Dybbuk and Other Writings*, ed. David G. Roskies (New York: Schocken Books, 1992), 93–117. An-ski's narrative takes place during the Russian-Turkish War of 1877—roughly the same distance separates An-ski's writing from the events depicted as the period intervening between the Crimean War and *Benyomin hashlishi*—and therefore depicts a more modern shtetl, complete with maskilim and Russian newspapers, in a style that mixes literary impressionism with realism, rather than parodic allegory and mock-epic. One can thus trace a quick history of nineteenth-century Yiddish literature through the treatment of historical conflicts, from *Dos Shterntikhl*'s depiction of the Napoleonic Wars, to *Benyomin hashlishi*'s use of the Crimean War, to *Mendl Terk*'s setting during the Russian-Turkish war. Each of these narratives responds to a previous generation's war, and each of them treats the war as a backdrop against which an internal drama within the (imaginary) shtetl plays out; the progression from farce to satire to literary impressionism analogously conveys the major aesthetic preoccupations of this fiction, as well as its slow and idiosyncratic convergence with the formal concerns of other European literatures in the same era.

15. Or as the great American musical parodist Mickey Katz (1909–1985) would put it, *mit aza pisk an episkopelyen?* ("With a beak like that, an Episcopalian?") See

the monologue included on his compact disc *Simcha Time: Mickey Katz Plays Music for Weddings, Bar Mitzvahs, & Brisses* (Hollywood, CA: Capitol Records, 1994), CDP 7243 8 30453 2 7.

16. Abramovitsh's depiction of this shtetl conversation about the Crimean War should be understood in the context of Steven Zipperstein's comment that "the Napoleonic wars . . . made little impression (on the values, at least) of the cloistered Lithuanian Jews, with whom the French came into direct contact. . . . By contrast, the war conducted in the remote Crimea four decades later apparently evoked considerable interest." See *The Jews of Odessa: A Cultural History, 1794–1881* (Stanford, CA: Stanford University Press, 1986), 17. Similarly, Aksenfeld's *Dos Shterntikhl* is set in the era of the Napoleonic Wars, but the protagonists of this novel scarcely mention this fact, and the narrator discusses it only in the context of the money-making opportunities it provides for the hero, Mikhl!

17. For a far more detailed structural analysis of *Benyomin hashlishi*—one that nonetheless underscores the importance of analogy, correspondence, and repetition suggested here—see Menahem Perry, *Ha'analogiah umakoma b'mivneh haroman shel Mendele Moykher-Sforim* ("Analogy and Its Role as a Structural Principle in the Novels of Mendele Moykher-Sforim"), *Hasifrut* 1, no. 1 (Spring 1968): 65–100. As Perry summarizes his argument in the English abstract to his article, "Numerous details of situation and language, and even some main happenings in the first chapters of the novel (*Benyomin hashlishi*), are found to correspond with similar elements in the final chapters of the book. . . . On similar principles are based the analogical links between elements of style and language in one part of the novel and events and situations in the other part. A simile in one plot becomes a real object or event in the parallel plot. Words appearing in a metaphor or an idiom . . . reappear as real events, based on their literal meanings, in the other plot" (IX–X). Perry's comments connect the novel's organization to the principle of *fantasy*, whereby metaphors are *embodied* literally—even though the actual story of *Benyomin hashlishi* is much less fantastic than *Di Klyatshe*. This in turn offers further evidence of Benyomin's fundamentally *textual* apprehension of reality, to the extent that he sees the world in terms set for him by the works of medieval Jewish fantasy that inspire his "travels."

18. See "The Mirror of Erised," chap. 12 of J. K. Rowling's *Harry Potter and the Sorcerer's Stone* (New York: Scholastic, 1997; 1998), 194–214.

19. To this example could be added countless others throughout the novel. For example, "I don't need a chaperone in order to unburden the secrets of my heart to you" (Y 182; E 198). Again, "'My soul, let me give you a kiss!' Benyomin exclaimed with great joy, and with love embraced Senderl the *yidene*" (Y 185; E 200); "'Now, dearest, I could kiss each and every one of your limbs,' Benyomin said loudly and animatedly he embraced Senderl the *yidene*" (Y 186; E 201–202).

20. For an analysis of this translation project and its place in Abramovitsh's creativity, see Chone Shmeruk, *Mendeles tilim-iberzetsung* ("Mendele's Translation

of the Psalms"), *Di Goldene Keyt* 62/63 (1968): 290–312; the primary exception to the rule of maskilic antipathy toward Yiddish poetry would be M. M. Lefin Satanover (1749–1826), who published a Yiddish translation of the Book of Proverbs in 1814, and also prepared manuscripts of translations of the Psalms, Job, and Ecclesiastes. For a brief discussion of these projects, see Miron, *A Traveler Disguised*, 40–41. Additionally significant Yiddish poets of the maskilic era include Shloyme Ettinger, who is better known as a pioneering Yiddish dramatist, and Elyokem Tsunzer (1836–1913).

21. As Michael Stanislawski explains, "Finally [in 1853], Nicholas hit on the most radical solution to the problem of Jewish conscription arrears. He decreed that any Jewish community could arrest any Jew found traveling without a passport and present him as a recruit under its own quota; in this way an individual Jew could catch a passportless Jew and substitute him for a family member eligible for the draft" (*Tsar Nicholas I and the Jews*, 184).

22. Mikhail Krutikov writes of this incident, " . . . [I]n Abramovitsh's novel *The Brief Travels of Benjamin the Third* . . . the positive state authority is represented by a Russian official who appears at the end of the story and puts things straight, in the deus ex machina manner. . . . The final episode of the novel leaves open the possibility of further development and can be read as an open end, suggesting another cycle in the potentially endless chain of adventures. . . . " See Krutikov, *Yiddish Fiction and the Crisis of Modernity, 1905–1914* (Stanford, CA: Stanford University Press, 2001), 70. Krutikov's analysis of the officer's role in the narrative is of course correct, but it overlooks the fact that Benyomin and Senderl's fantastic, analogical sense of the world remains intact because neither they nor the officer are able to *understand* one another; the Russian bureaucracy represents one layer of objective reality, but the Russian language represents another. As long as Benyomin and Senderl are ignorant of the imperial language, they are impervious to the social order it imposes—and this in turn becomes their unwitting survival strategy.

23. In fact, Olga Litvak offers a diametrically opposed interpretation of the novel's conclusion, arguing that Benyomin and Senderl will return directly to their homes in the shtetl and thus reclaim their patriarchal authority within a restored Jewish tradition. See her book *Conscription and the Search for Modern Russian Jewry* (Bloomington: Indiana University Press, 2006), 113–121. I see little in the novel itself to justify this interpretation and much to counter it; indeed, the very fact that the book was first published with the subtitle "Volume 1" (Y 155) indicates that Abramovitsh originally intended to extend Benyomin and Senderl's adventures over subsequent installments, carrying them further and further away from the shtetl. That Abramovitsh never completed a sequel merely situates this project among several other unrealized ambitions in his career.

24. The first sociological examination of adolescence in Jewish Eastern Europe is Max Weinreich's extraordinary study, *Der Veg tsu undzer yugnt: yesoydes, metodn,*

problemen fun yidisher yugnt-forshung ("The Way to Our Youth: Foundations, Methods, and Problems in Jewish Youth-Research") (Vilna: YIVO, 1935). Weinreich coins the Yiddish term for adolescence, *dervaksling*, in a footnote on page 10. The absence of the word "adolescent" doesn't preclude Abramovitsh from evoking the concept, particularly in the metaphorical sense used here. In this context one can consider that Dostoyevsky's 1875 novel *Podrostok* ("The Raw Youth") has more recently been translated as "The Adolescent." By the same token, the absence of a formal autobiographical genre during the eighteenth century doesn't preclude authors of the Enlightenment from writing pseudo-autobiographical novels.

25. Christopher Miller notes that *La Race Nègre* published a single article in *petit-Nègre*, a Francophone creole, in 1927. As he states, this is the first effort in Francophone Africa "to elevate a 'patois' to the level of a language of communication." See Christopher L. Miller, *Nationalists and Nomads: Essays on Francophone African Literature and Culture* (Chicago: University of Chicago Press, 1998), 43. Nonetheless, with the partial and complicated exception of Bakary Diallo's (and Lucie Cousturier's) *Force-Bonté*, it would be more than forty years before this journalistic experiment would be joined by Kourouma and his contemporaries to integrate African varieties of French into Francophone literature.

26. As Miller explains, the events in the third part refer to an actual coup attempt that occurred in the Cote d'Ivoire: "The incipient insurrection in *Les Soleils des indépendances* roughly corresponds to events that took place in the Ivory Coast beginning in 1962: an alleged plot against the regime, the arrest of conspirators, followed by a magnanimous pardon and political 're-education' of the seditionaries, who included many notables" (*Theories of Africans*, 240–241).

27. Ahmadou Kourouma, *Les Soleils des indépendances* (Paris: Éditions du Seuil, 1970; 1998), 9. Subsequent references incorporated in text as "F." Translated as *The Suns of Independence* by Adrian Adams (New York: Africana, 1981), 3. Subsequent references incorporated in text as "E," although my translations will depart slightly from the published version.

28. As Miller explains, "Francophonie is built on the myth of universalism: Charles de Gaulle identified the French language as the root of France's mission in the world, a mission 'to make available to the world a language perfectly adapted to the universal nature of thought'" (*Theories of Africans*, 184).

29. Quoted in Christiane Yandé Diop's Foreword to *The Surreptitious Speech: Présence Africaine and the Politics of Otherness 1947–1987*, ed. V. Y. Mudimbe (Chicago: University of Chicago Press, 1992), xv–xvi.

30. As Miller states: "French colonialism, built around a doctrine of assimilation, did little to encourage local language literacy. The British . . . worked to establish African language literacy and to encourage the development of literatures in local languages. . . . The style and freedom of the respective literatures seemed to follow suit: anglophone writing seemed more open and 'creole'; francophone literature remained wedded to the academism of Paris" (*Theories of Africans*, 193).

31. Quoted in Adrien Huannou, «La technique du récit et le style dans 'les soleils des indépendances'» ("The Narrative Technique and Style of *Les Soleils des indépendances*"), *L'afrique Litteraire et Artistique* 38 (1975), 38. The translation is my own.

32. Quoted in Lilyan Kesteloot, *Black Writers in French: A Literary History of Negritude*, trans. Ellen Conroy Kennedy (Washington, DC: Howard University Press, 1963; 1991), 337.

33. In this context consider the episode in Amos Tutuola's novel *The Witch-Herbalist of the Remote Town*, in which the eponymous witch-herbalist interrogates the protagonist in all the languages of the animal and human kingdoms, yet the protagonist is only able to understand her when she speaks "in plain language, in Yoruba, the language of Western Nigeria." Yoruba, for Tutuola, apparently remains the "plain language," even though he writes exclusively in English! See *The Witch-Herbalist of the Remote Town* (London: Faber and Faber, 1981), 146.

34. One should add to this list the Malian novelist Yambo Ouologuem (b. 1940), whose 1968 novel *Le Devoir de violence* ("Bound to Violence") offers in historical terms a mock-epic, spanning from the year 1202 to the era of decolonization, directly comparable to the parodic geographical "quest romance" of *Les Soleils des indépendances*.

35. Manthia Diawara, *In Search of Africa* (Cambridge, MA: Harvard University Press, 1998), 46.

36. As when Kourouma writes, "At Mayako [the prison], praying deeply and very often, he [Fama] had resigned himself, he had come to accept his fate, and was ready to meet the shades of the ancestors, ready for the judgment of Allah. Death had become his sole companion; they knew and loved each other" (F 185; E 129).

37. "Salimata went back to consult Abdoulaye, the marabout she had stabbed with a knife still red with the blood of the sacrificial cock. Abdoulaye no longer frightened her, no longer reeked of Tiécoura [the marabout in her village who had raped her following her excision ceremony]" (F 177; E 123). It is significant that both in this passage, and the one quoted previously, the measure of the character's existential condition is determined vis-à-vis his or her relationship to religion.

Part 3 Conclusion

1. Mendele's function in *Benyomin hashlishi* compares with Reb Nakhman's presence in the *sipurey mayses*, at once narrator and hero of the stories.

2. See on this score Dan Miron, "Sholem Aleichem: Person, Persona, Presence," in *The Image of the Shtetl* (Syracuse, NY: Syracuse University Press, 1972; 2000), 128–156.

3. Consider for example Frantz Fanon's dismissal of "the native artist who wishes at whatever cost to create a national work of art" and who "shuts himself up in a stereotyped reproduction of details. . . . The artist who has decided to

illustrate the truths of the nation turns paradoxically toward the past and away from actual events. What he ultimately intends to embrace are in fact the castoffs of thought, its shells and corpses. . . . " See *The Wretched of the Earth*, trans. Constance Farrington (New York: Grove Press, 1961; 1963), 224–225.

Conclusion

1. Consider in this regard Michel de Certeau's observation, "Marginality is today no longer limited to minority groups, but is rather massive and pervasive; this cultural activity of the non-producers of culture, an activity that is unsigned, unreadable, and unsymbolized, remains the only one possible for all those who nevertheless buy and pay for the showy products through which a productivist economy articulates itself. Marginality is becoming universal. A marginal group has now become a silent majority." See Michel de Certeau, *The Practice of Everyday Life*, trans. Steven Rendall (Berkeley: University of California Press, 1984; 1988), xvii.

2. Kenneth B. Moss, "Jewish Culture between Renaissance and Decadence: *Di Literarishe Monatsshriften* and Its Critical Reception," *Jewish Social Studies* 8, no. 1, n.s. (Fall 2001), 158–159.

3. For a comprehensive study of the Czernowitz conference and its significance to twentieth-century "Yiddishism," see Emanuel S. Goldsmith, *Modern Yiddish Culture: The Story of the Yiddish Language Movement* (New York: Fordham University Press, 1976; 1997). For a precursor to this conference within the context of peripheral linguistic cultures, see Holger Nath, "The First International Conference of the Catalan Language in Barcelona (1906): A Spiritual Precursor to Czernowitz (1908)?" in *The Politics of Yiddish: Studies in Language, Literature, & Society*, ed. Dov-Ber Kerler (Walnut Creek, CA: AltaMira Press, 1998), 51–61. The correspondences between Yiddish and Catalan are, of course, a topic meriting much more extensive and intensive comparative research.

4. It may be noted that Singer's monologue stories often appeared in small literary journals, whereas his novels were typically serialized in the mass-circulation *Forverts* newspaper, in New York. This points not only to the development of a differentiated Yiddish readership over the course of the twentieth century, but also to differentiated aspects of Singer's creativity—reflected often by differing pseudonyms for these respective literary markets. Inevitably, the translation of Singer's work into English and other languages has bulldozed over these subtleties.

5. In a different sense, although Sutzkever was *the* central figure in postwar Yiddish literature, he could only function as a peripheral writer in the context of Israeli literature because of his choice of language. In more theoretical terms, it may be noted that this study has largely excluded poetry from its purview precisely because the formal model it draws from, of "minor" literary theory, was conceived in response to the challenges of Modernist prose; if Deleuze and Guattari had

intended to consider poetry in their conceptualization of "minor" literature, they might well have devoted their monograph to Rainer Maria Rilke rather than Franz Kafka.

6. One can also point to an emergent trend in American, Canadian, and German literature over the past decade of young authors from the former Soviet Union writing belletristically in the national language of their adopted countries. Speaking provisionally, this emerging, ostensibly deterritorialized language seems to bear more similarity with other examples of immigrant writing, in choice of theme, genre, and voice, than with either the Jewish writing of native authors in these nations or the Yiddish literature that precedes and anticipates it.

7. This list includes Ruth R. Wisse's *The Modern Jewish Canon: A Journey through Language and Culture* (New York: Free Press, 2000); the collection *Ideology and Jewish Identity in Israeli and American Literature*, ed. Emily Miller Budick (Albany: State University of New York Press, 2001); Hannan Hever's *Producing the Modern Hebrew Canon* (New York: New York University Press, 2002); and in a more attenuated sense Robert Alter's *Canon and Creativity: Modern Writing and the Authority of Scripture* (New Haven: Yale University Press, 2000). For a critique of the homogenizing trend of canon-formation in contemporary Jewish criticism, particularly as exemplified by Wisse's book, see Dan Miron, *From Continuity to Contiguity: Toward a New Jewish Literary Thinking* (Stanford, CA: Stanford University Press, 2010). For additional meta-commentary, consider *Arguing the Modern Jewish Canon: Essays on Literature and Culture in Honor of Ruth R. Wisse*, ed. Justin Cammy, Dara Horn, Alyssa Quint, and Rachel Rubinstein (Cambridge, MA: Harvard University Press, 2008).

8. Immanuel Etkes, "Magic and Miracle-Workers in the Literature of the Haskalah," in *New Perspectives on the Haskalah*, ed. Shmuel Feiner and David Sorkin (London: Littman Library of Jewish Civilization, 2001), 121.

9. See Haym Soloveitchik, "Rupture and Reconstruction: The Transformation of Contemporary Orthodoxy," *Tradition* 28, no. 4 (1994): 64–130. See as well Lawrence Kaplan, "The Hazon Ish: Haredi ["Ultra-Orthodox"] Critic of Traditional Orthodoxy," and Menachem Friedman, "The Lost *Kiddush* Cup: Changes in Ashkenazic Haredi Culture—A Tradition in Crisis," in *The Uses of Tradition: Jewish Continuity in the Modern Era*, ed. Jack Wertheimer (New York: Jewish Theological Seminary, 1992), 145–173; 175–186.

10. As Ernst Renan reminds us, forgetfulness is also the necessary precondition for the liberal nation-state: "forgetting . . . is a crucial factor in the creation of a nation." See his "What Is a Nation?" trans. Martin Thom, in *Nation and Narration*, ed. Homi K. Bhabha (London: Routledge, 1990; 1995), 11. For a commentary from the perspective of Jewish literature, see Sidra DeKoven Ezrahi, *Booking Passage: Exile and Homecoming in the Modern Jewish Imagination* (Berkeley: University of California Press, 2000), 21; 251n43.

11. Ralph Ellison, "Richard Wright's Blues" (1945), *Shadow and Act* (New York:

Vintage Books, 1972), 78. In *Black Boy*, the autobiography that Ellison discusses in this essay, Richard Wright expresses the same idea more starkly by writing, "[W]hen I brooded upon the cultural barrenness of black life, I wondered if clean, positive tenderness, love, honor, loyalty, *and the capacity to remember* were native to man. I asked myself if these human qualities were not fostered, won, struggled and suffered for, *preserved in ritual* from one generation to another" (quoted in "Richard Wright's Blues," 93, emphasis added).

12. Benedict Anderson, *Imagined Communities: Reflections on the Origin and Spread of Nationalism* (London: Verso, 1983; 1994), 133–134.

13. For a discussion of this statistic, see Eyamba G. Bokamba, "The Africanization of English," in *The Other Tongue: English across Cultures*, ed. Braj B. Kachru (Urbana: University of Illinois Press, 1982; 1992), 125.

14. As Kwame Appiah has written, "in sub-Saharan Africa, most literate people are literate in the colonial languages; most writing with a substantial readership (with the important exception of Swahili) is in those languages, and the only writing with a genuinely subcontinental audience and address is in English or French." Kwame Anthony Appiah, *In My Father's House: Africa in the Philosophy of Culture* (New York: Oxford University Press, 1992; 1993), 54. By way of comparison, it is worth recalling that in traditional Jewish society, literacy meant literacy in *Loshn-koydesh* (although generally anyone in Ashkenazic society able to read the Hebrew alphabet should have been able to read Yiddish as well). Indeed, the word in Yiddish for "literate" is *ivredik*—from the Hebrew word for Hebrew, *ivrit*.

15. Albert Memmi, *The Colonizer and the Colonized*, trans. Howard Greenfeld (Boston: Beacon Press, 1957; 1965; 1991), 111.

16. Oyekan Owomoyela, "The Question of Language in African Literatures," in *A History of Twentieth Century African Literatures*, ed. Oyekan Owomoyela (Lincoln: University of Nebraska Press, 1993), 347.

17. Mikhail Krutikov, *Sh. An-ski un zayn* Dibek: *naye faktn un heshores* ("Sh. An-ski and his *Dybbuk*: new facts and theories"), *Der Forverts* newspaper (January 3, 2003), 19. The translation from the Yiddish is my own.

18. Achille Mbembe, *On the Postcolony* (Berkeley: University of California Press, 2001), 11–12.

Bibliography

Aberbach, David. *Realism, Caricature, and Bias: The Fiction of Mendele Mocher Se-farim.* London: Littman Library of Jewish Civilization, 1993.

Abramovitsh, Sh. Y. *Dos Vintshfingerl.* Warsaw: Yoysef Lebnzon, 1865.

Achebe, Chinua. *Hopes and Impediments: Selected Essays.* New York: Anchor, 1977; 1989.

Adler, Elkan Nathan, ed. *Jewish Travellers in the Middle Ages: 19 Firsthand Accounts.* New York: Dover, 1930; 1987.

Adorno, Theodor W. *Mahler: A Musical Physiognomy.* Trans. Edmund Jephcott. Chicago: University of Chicago Press, 1971; 1992.

———. *Beethoven: The Philosophy of Music.* Ed. Rolf Tiedemann and trans. Edmund Jephcott. Stanford, CA: Stanford University Press 1993; 1998.

Aire, Victor O. "Mort et devenir: Lecture thanato-sociologique de *L'Aventure am-biguë.*" *French Review* 55, no. 6 (May 1982): 752–760.

Aksenfeld, Yisroel. *Dos Shterntikhl.* Ed. Meir Wiener. Moscow: Emes, 1938.

———. *Dos Shtern-tikhl un Der Ershter yiddisher rekrut.* Vol. 47, Musterverk. Library of Yiddish Literature. Buenos Aires: Ateneo Literario en el IWO, 1971.

Alter, Robert. *The Invention of Hebrew Prose: Modern Fiction and the Language of Realism.* Seattle: University of Washington Press, 1988.

———. *Hebrew & Modernity.* Bloomington: Indiana University Press, 1994.

———. *Canon and Creativity: Modern Writing and the Authority of Scripture.* New Haven: Yale University Press, 2000.

Anderson, Benedict. *Imagined Communities: Reflections on the Origin and Spread of Nationalism.* London: Verso, 1983; 1994.

An-ski, Sh. *Gezamlte shriftn, zibeter band.* Warsaw: Farlag An-ski, 1922.

Ansky, S. *The Dybbuk and Other Writings.* Ed. David G. Roskies. New York: Schocken Books, 1992.

Appiah, Kwame Anthony. *In My Father's House: Africa in the Philosophy of Culture.* New York: Oxford University Press, 1992; 1993.

Aschheim, Steven E. *Brothers and Strangers: The East European Jew in German and*

German Jewish Consciousness, 1800–1923. Madison: University of Wisconsin Press 1982.

Assaf, David. *Breslav bibliografyah mu'eret: R. Nahman mi-breslov, toldatav u'morashto hasifrutit*. Jerusalem: Zalman Shazar Center, 2000.

Baker, Houston A., Jr. *Modernism and the Harlem Renaissance*. Chicago: University of Chicago Press, 1987; 1989.

Bakhtin, M. M. *The Dialogic Imagination: Four Essays*. Trans. Caryl Emerson and Michael Holquist. Austin: University of Texas Press, 1981; 1987.

Bakhtin, Mikhail. *Problems of Dostoevsky's Poetics*. Ed. and trans. Caryl Emerson. Minneapolis: University of Minnesota Press, 1984.

Band, Arnold J. *Nahman of Bratslav: The Tales*. New York: Paulist Press, 1978.

Bartal, Israel. *The Jews of Eastern Europe, 1772–1881*. Trans. Chaya Naor. Philadelphia: University of Pennsylvania Press, 2002; 2005.

Baumgarten, Jean. *Introduction to Old Yiddish Literature*. Ed. and trans. Jerold C. Frakes. New York: Oxford University Press, 2005.

Beckett, Samuel. "Dante . . . Bruno. Vico . . Joyce." In *James Joyce/Finnegans Wake: A Symposium*. New York: New Directions, 1929; 1972, 3–22.

Bemporad, Elissa. "From Literature of the People to History of the People: Simon Dubnow and the Origins of Russian Jewish Historiography." Published as "Da letteratura del popolo a storia del popolo: Simon Dubnow e l'origine della storiografia russo-ebraica." *Annali di Storia dell'Esegesi*. Universita' degli Studi di Bologna 18, no. 2 (2001): 533–557.

Ben-Amos, Dan, and Jerome R. Mintz, eds. *In Praise of the Baal Shem Tov*. Northvale, NJ: Jason Aronson, 1970; 1993.

Berkowitz, Joel, and Jeremy Dauber, eds. *Landmark Yiddish Plays: A Critical Anthology*. Albany: State University of New York Press, 2006.

Bhabha, Homi K., ed. *Nation and Narration*. London: Routledge, 1990; 1995.

Biakolo, Emevwo. "On the Theoretical Foundations of Orality and Literacy." *Research in African Literatures* 30, no. 2 (Summer 1999): 42–65.

Buber, Martin. *The Tales of Rabbi Nachman*. Trans. M. Friedman. Bloomington: University of Indiana Press, 1906; 1956.

Budick, Emily Miller, ed. *Ideology and Jewish Identity in Israeli and American Literature*. Albany: State University of New York Press, 2001.

Camara Laye. *The Dark Child*. Trans. James Kirkup and Ernest Jones. New York: Noonday Press, 1954; 1994.

———. *L'enfant noir*. Paris: Librairie Plon, 1954; 1998.

Cammy, Justin, Dara Horn, Alyssa Quint, and Rachel Rubinstein, eds. *Arguing the Modern Jewish Canon: Essays on Literature and Culture in Honor of Ruth R. Wisse*. Cambridge, MA: Harvard University Press, 2008.

Casanova, Pascale. *The World Republic of Letters*. Trans. M. B. DeBevoise. Cambridge, MA: Harvard University Press, 2004.

Certeau, Michel de. *The Practice of Everyday Life*. Trans. Steven Rendall. Berkeley: University of California Press, 1984; 1988.

Chadwick, Owen. *The Secularization of the European Mind in the 19th Century*. Cambridge, UK: Cambridge University Press, 1975; 1995.

Chinweizu, Onwuchekwa Jemie, and Ihechukwu Madubuike. *Toward the Decolonization of African Literature*, vol. 1. Washington, DC: Howard University Press, 1983.

Curtin, Philip D., ed. *Africa & the West: Intellectual Responses to European Culture*. Madison: University of Wisconsin Press, 1972.

Dan, Joseph. *Hasippur ha-hasidi*. Jerusalem: Keter Publishing House, 1975.

Deleuze, Gilles, and Félix Guattari. *Kafka: Toward a Minor Literature*. Trans. Dana Polan. Minneapolis: University of Minnesota Press, 1975; 1994.

Derrida, Jacques. *Monolingualism of the Other: or, The Prosthesis of Origin*. Trans. Patrick Mensah. Stanford, CA: Stanford University Press, 1996; 1998.

Diawara, Manthia. *In Search of Africa*. Cambridge, MA: Harvard University Press, 1998.

Dik, Isaac Meyer. *Geklibene verk*. Ed. Sh. Niger. New York: Congress for Jewish Culture, 1954.

Dostoyevsky, Fyodor. *Crime and Punishment*. Trans. Sidney Monas. New York: Signet Classic, 1968.

Drewal, Henry John. "Performing the Other: Mami Wata Worship in Africa." *Drama Review* 32, no. 2 (Summer 1988): 160–185.

Drewal, Margaret Thompson. *Yoruba Ritual: Performers, Play, Agency*. Bloomington: University of Indiana Press, 1992.

Dubnow, Shimen. *Geshikhte fun khasidizm*. Translated from Hebrew into Yiddish by Zelig Kalmanovitch under the supervision of the author. Vilna: Farlag fun B. Kletskin, 1930.

Duffy, Enda. *The Subaltern Ulysses*. Minneapolis: University of Minnesota Press, 1994.

Dunton, Chris. "Pupils, Witch Doctor, Vengeance: Amos Tutuola as Playwright." *Research in African Literatures* 37, no. 4 (Winter 2006): 1–14.

Dylan, Bob. *"Love & Theft."* New York: Columbia Records, 2001, CK 86076.

Ellison, Ralph. *Shadow and Act*. New York: Vintage Books, 1972.

Elstein, Yoav. *Pa-amei bat melekh*. Ramat-Gan: Bar-Ilan University, 1984.

Epstein, Edmund L., and Robert Kole, eds. *The Language of African Literature*. Trenton, NJ: Africa World Press, 1998.

Erik, Max. *Vegn altyidshn roman un novele, fertsenter-zektsenter yorhundert*. Kowel: Der Veg tsum visn, 1926.

Ezrahi, Sidra DeKoven. *Booking Passage: Exile and Homecoming in the Modern Jewish Imagination*. Berkeley: University of California Press, 2000.

Fanon, Frantz. *The Wretched of the Earth*. Trans. Constance Farrington. New York: Grove Press, 1961; 1963.

Feiner, Shmuel, and David Sorkin. *New Perspectives on the Haskalah*. London: Littman Library of Jewish Civilization, 2001.

Fernandez, James W. *Persuasions and Performances: The Play of Tropes in Culture.* Bloomington: Indiana University Press, 1986.

Foucault, Michel. *Discipline & Punish: The Birth of the Prison.* Trans. Alan Sheridan. New York: Vintage Books, 1975; 1995.

——. "What Is an Author?" In *Textual Strategies: Perspectives in Post-Structuralist Criticism.* Ed. Josue V. Harari. Ithaca, NY: Cornell University Press, 1979; 1986, 141–160.

Gaster, Moses. *Ma'aseh Book.* Philadelphia: Jewish Publication Society of America, 1934; 1981.

Gates, Henry Louis, Jr. *Black Literature and Literary Theory.* New York: Routledge, 1984; 1990.

——. *The Signifying Monkey: A Theory of African-American Literary Criticism.* New York: Oxford University Press, 1988; 1989.

George, Olakunle. *Relocating Agency: Modernity and African Letters.* Albany: State University of New York Press, 2003.

Gibbs, James, ed. *Critical Perspectives on Wole Soyinka.* Washington, DC: Three Continents Press, 1980.

Gibbs, James, and Bernth Lindfors, eds. *Research on Wole Soyinka.* Trenton, NJ: Africa World Press, 1993.

Gilman, Sander L. *Jewish Self-Hatred: Anti-Semitism and the Hidden Language of the Jews.* Baltimore: Johns Hopkins University Press, 1986.

Goldsmith, Emanuel S. *Modern Yiddish Culture: The Story of the Yiddish Language Movement.* New York: Fordham University Press, 1976; 1997.

Gramsci, Antonio. *Selections from the Prison Notebooks.* Ed. and trans. Quintin Hoare and Geoffrey Nowell Smith. New York: International Publishers, 1971; 1995.

Green, Arthur. *Tormented Master: The Life and Spiritual Quest of Rabbi Nahman of Bratslav.* Woodstock, VT: Jewish Lights Publishing, 1979; 1992.

Harris, Jay M. *Nachman Krochmal: Guiding the Perplexed of the Modern Age.* New York: New York University Press, 1991.

Harrow, Kenneth W., ed. *Faces of Islam in African Literature.* Portsmouth, NH: Heinemann, 1991.

Harshav, Benjamin. "Chagall: Postmodernism and Fictional Worlds in Painting." In *Marc Chagall and the Jewish Theater.* New York: Guggenheim Museum, 1992.

Hersh, Seymour M. "The Twentieth Man." *The New Yorker,* September 30, 2002, 56–76.

Herzog, Marvin I., Barbara Kirshenblatt-Gimblett, Dan Miron, and Ruth Wisse, eds. *The Field of Yiddish: Fourth Collection.* Philadelphia: Institute for the Study of Human Issues, 1980.

Hobsbawm, E. J. *Nations and Nationalism since 1780: Programme, Myth, Reality.* Cambridge, UK: Cambridge University Press, 1990; 1997.

Hobsbawm, Eric, and Terence Ranger, eds. *The Invention of Tradition.* Cambridge, UK: Cambridge University Press, 1983; 1997.

Horkheimer, Max, and Theodor W. Adorno. *Dialectic of Enlightenment: Philosophi-*

cal Fragments. Trans. Edmund Jephcott and ed. Gunzelin Schmid Noerr. Stanford, CA: Stanford University Press, 2002.

Huannou, Adrien. "La technique du récit et le style dans 'les soleils des indépendances.'" *L'Afrique littéraire et artistique* 38 (1975): 31–38.

Hundert, Gershon, ed. *Essential Papers on Hasidism: Origins to the Present*. New York: New York University Press, 1991.

Hundert, Gershon David. *Jews in Poland-Lithuania in the Eighteenth Century: A Genealogy of Modernity*. Berkeley: University of California Press, 2004.

Hutton, Christopher. "Normativism and the Notion of Authenticity in Yiddish Linguistics." In *The Field of Yiddish: Studies in Language, Folklore, and Literature, Fifth Collection*. Ed. David Goldberg. Evanston, IL: Northwestern University Press, 1993, 11–57.

Irele, Abiola. *The African Experience in Literature and Ideology*. Bloomington: Indiana University Press, 1975; 1990.

Irele, F. Abiola. "In Search of Camara Laye." *Research in African Literatures* 37, no. 1 (Spring 2006): 110–127.

JanMohamed, Abdul R., and David Lloyd, eds. *The Nature and Context of Minority Discourse*. New York: Oxford University Press, 1990.

Joseph, George. "Free Indirect Discourse in *Soleils des indépendances*." *American Journal of Semiotics* 6, no. 1 (1988–1989): 69–84.

Kachru, Braj. B. *The Other Tongue: English across Cultures*. Urbana: University of Illinois Press, 1982; 1992.

Kane, Cheikh Hamidou. *L'aventure ambiguë*. Paris: Éditions 10/18, 1961; 1998.

——. *Ambiguous Adventure*. Trans. Katherine Woods. Oxford: Heinemann, 1963; 1972.

——. *Les Gardiens du Temple*. Paris: Roman Editions Stock, 1995; 1997.

Kaplan, Rabbi Aryeh, trans. *Rabbi Nachman's Wisdom*. Brooklyn, NY: Breslov Research Institute, 1973.

——. *Rabbi Nachman's Stories*. New York: Breslov Research Institute, 1983.

Katz, Mickey. *Simcha Time: Mickey Katz Plays Music for Weddings, Bar Mitzvahs, & Brisses*. Hollywood, CA: Capitol Records, 1994, CDP 7243 8 30453 2 7.

Kerler, Dov-Ber. *The Origins of Modern Literary Yiddish*. Oxford: Clarendon Press, 1999.

Kerler, Dov-Ber, ed. *The Politics of Yiddish: Studies in Language, Literature, & Society*. Walnut Creek, CA: AltaMira Press, 1998.

Kesteloot, Lilyan. *Black Writers in French: A Literary History of Negritude*. Trans. Ellen Conroy Kennedy. Washington, DC: Howard University Press, 1963; 1974; 1991.

Kourouma, Ahmadou. *Les Soleils des indépendences*. Paris: Éditions du Seuil, 1970; 1998.

——. *The Suns of Independence*. Trans. Adrian Adams. New York: Africana Publishing, 1981.

Krutikov, Mikhail. *Yiddish Fiction and the Crisis of Modernity, 1905–1914*. Stanford, CA: Stanford University Press, 2001.

———. *Sh. An-ski un zayn* Dibek: *naye faktn un heshores. Der Forverts* newspaper (January 3, 2003): 19.

Larson, Charles R. *The Emergence of African Fiction*. Bloomington: Indiana University Press, 1971; 1972.

Leskov, Nikolai. *Lady Macbeth of Mtsensk and Other Stories*. New York: Penguin Books, 1987.

Liberman, Kh. "Rabbi Nakhman Bratslaver and the Maskilim of Uman." In *YIVO Annual of Jewish Social Science*, vol. 6. Ed. Koppel S. Pinson. New York: Yiddish Scientific Institute—YIVO, 1951, 287–301.

Lifschutz, E. "Merrymakers and Jesters among Jews (Materials for a Lexicon)." *YIVO Annual of Jewish Social Science* 7 (1952): 43–83.

Lindfors, Bernth. *African Textualities: Texts, Pre-Texts, and Contexts of African Literature*. Trenton, NJ: Africa World Press, 1997.

———. *The Blind Men and the Elephant and Other Essays in Biographical Criticism*. Trenton, NJ: Africa World Press, 1999.

Lindfors, Bernth, ed. *Critical Perspectives on Amos Tutuola*. Boulder, CO: Three Continents Press, 1975.

Linetski, Y. Y. *Dos Poylishe yingl*. Odessa: Hameylits, 1869.

Lionnet, Françoise, and Shu-mei Shih, eds. *Minor Transnationalism*. Durham, NC: Duke University Press, 2005.

Litvak, Olga. *Conscription and the Search for Modern Russian Jewry*. Bloomington: Indiana University Press, 2006.

Lott, Eric. *Love & Theft: Blackface Minstrelsy and the American Working Class*. New York: Oxford University Press, 1995.

Luria, Shalom, ed. *Dos Kleyne mentshele*. Literature Department of the University of Haifa, Israel, 1994.

Magid, Shaul, ed. *God's Voice from the Void: Old and New Studies in Bratslav Hasidism*. Albany: State University of New York Press, 2002.

Mahler, Raphael. "The Social and Political Aspects of the Haskalah in Galicia." *YIVO Annual of Jewish Social Science* 1 (1946): 64–85.

Maimon, Solomon. *Solomon Maimon: An Autobiography*. Trans. J. Clark Murray. Urbana: University of Illinois Press, 2001.

Maja-Pearce, Adewale, ed. *Wole Soyinka: An Appraisal*. Oxford: Heinemann, 1994.

Mandelker, Amy, ed. *Bakhtin in Contexts: Across the Disciplines*. Evanston, IL: Northwestern University Press, 1995.

Mark, Yudl. *Mendele loshn. Yidishe Shprakh* 27, no. 1 (June 1967): 1–17; no. 2 (September 1967): 33–47; no. 3 (December 1967): 65–79; 28, no. 2 (September 1968): 33–51.

Mark, Zvi. *The Scroll of Secrets: The Hidden Messianic Vision of R. Nachman of Breslav*. Trans. Naftali Moses. Brighton, MA: Academic Studies Press, 2010.

Mbembe, Achille. *On the Postcolony*. Berkeley: University of California Press, 2001.

Memmi, Albert. *The Colonizer and the Colonized*. Trans. Howard Greenfield. Boston, MA: Beacon Press, 1957; 1965; 1991.

Mendele Moykher-Sforim. *Kol Kitvey Mendele Mokher Sforim, Seyfer shlishi.* Berlin: "Moriah" Publishers, 1922.

——. *Geklibene verk, band 1–5.* New York: Ikuf, 1947.

——. *Selected Works of Mendele Moykher-Sforim.* Ed. Marvin Zuckerman, Gerald Stillman, and Marion Herbst. Malibu, CA: Pangloss Press, 1991.

Mendes-Flohr, Paul. "Fin-de-Siecle Orientalism, the *Ostjuden* and the Aesthetics of Jewish Self-Affirmation." In *Divided Passions: Jewish Intellectuals and the Experience of Modernity.* Detroit: Wayne State University, 1991, 77–132.

Miller, Christopher L. *Theories of Africans: Francophone Literature and Anthropology in Africa.* Chicago: University of Chicago Press, 1990.

——. *Nationalists and Nomads: Essays on Francophone African Literature and Culture.* Chicago: University of Chicago Press, 1998.

Miller, Tyrus. *Late Modernism: Politics, Fiction, and the Arts between the World Wars.* Berkeley: University of California Press, 1999.

Miron, Dan. *A Traveler Disguised: The Rise of Modern Yiddish Fiction in the Nineteenth Century.* Syracuse, NY: Syracuse University Press, 1973; 1996.

——. "The Discovery of Mendele Moykher-Sforim and the Beginnings of Modern Yiddish Literature." *YIVO Annual* 15 (1974): 66–81.

——. *Der Imazh fun shtetl: Dray literarishe shtudyes.* Tel Aviv: I. L. Peretz Publishing House, 1981.

——. "Rediscovering Haskalah Poetry." *Prooftexts: A Journal of Jewish Literary History* 1, no. 3 (September 1981): 292–305.

——. *The Image of the Shtetl and Other Studies of Modern Jewish Literary Imagination.* Syracuse, NY: Syracuse University Press, 2000.

——. *From Continuity to Contiguity: Toward a New Jewish Literary Thinking.* Stanford, CA: Stanford University Press, 2010.

Mongo Beti, *Mission terminée.* Paris: Buchet/Chastel, 1957; 1999.

——. *Mission to Kala.* Trans. Peter Green. Portsmouth, NH: Heinemann, 1964.

Mortimer, Mildred. *Journeys through the French African Novel.* Portsmouth, NH: Heinemann, 1990.

Mosley, Marcus. *Being for Myself Alone: Origins of Jewish Autobiography.* Stanford, CA: Stanford University Press, 2006.

Moss, Kenneth. "Jewish Culture between Renaissance and Decadence: *Di Literarishe Monatsshriften* and Its Critical Reception." *Jewish Social Studies* 8, no. 1, n.s. (Fall 2001): 153–198.

Mudimbe, V. Y. *L'autre face du royaume: une introduction à la critique des langages en folie.* Paris: L'age d'homme, 1973.

——. *The Invention of Africa: Gnosis, Philosophy, and the Order of Knowledge.* Bloomington: Indiana University Press, 1988.

Mudimbe, V. Y., ed. *The Surreptitious Speech: Présence Africaine and the Politics of Otherness, 1947–1987.* Chicago: University of Chicago Press, 1992.

Murphy, David. "Birth of a Nation? The Origins of Senegalese Literature in French." *Research in African Literatures* 39, no. 1 (2008): 48–69.

Nadal, Sara. "Introduction: Around . . . Peripheries/Propositions." *Around: Planning the Periphery*. Barcelona: Editorial Gustavo Gili, 2002.

Nakhman of Breslov. *Seyfer sipurey mayses*. Jerusalem: Makhon "Toyres haNetsakh" Breslov, 1991.

Nathans, Benjamin. *Beyond the Pale: The Jewish Encounter with Late Imperial Russia*. Berkeley: University of California Press, 2004.

Neugroschel, Joachim, trans. and ed. *The Great Works of Jewish Fantasy and Occult*. Woodstock, NY: Overlook Press, 1976; 1986.

———. *The Shtetl: A Creative Anthology of Jewish Life in Eastern Europe*. Woodstock, NY: Overlook Press, 1979; 1989.

———. *No Star Too Beautiful: An Anthology of Yiddish Stories from 1382 to the Present*. New York: W. W. Norton, 2002.

Neumarkt, Paul. "Amos Tutuola: Emerging African Literature." *American Imago* 28 (1971): 129–145.

Ngugi wa Thiong'o. *Decolonising the Mind: The Politics of Language in African Literature*. London: James Currey, 1986; 1988.

Niane, D. T. *Soundjata, ou l'Epopée Mandingue*. Paris: *Présence Africaine*, 1960.

———. *Sundiata: An Epic of Old Mali*. Trans. G. D. Pickett. Harlow, UK: Longman, 1965; 1994.

Niger, Sh. *A Maskils utopye*, *YIVO-Bleter* 36 (1952): 136–190.

Niger, Shmuel. *Dertseylers un romanistn*. New York: Tsiko farlag, 1946.

Nwapa, Flora. *Efuru*. London: Heinemann, 1966; 1986.

Obiechina, Emmanuel. *An African Popular Literature: A Study of Onitsha Market Pamphlets*. New York: Cambridge University Press, 1973.

Obiechina, Emmanuel N. *Language and Theme: Essays on African Literature*. Washington, DC: Howard University Press, 1990.

Okpewho, Isidore. *African Oral Literature: Backgrounds, Character, and Continuity*. Bloomington: Indiana University Press, 1992.

Ong, Walter. *Orality and Literacy: The Technologizing of the Word*. London: Routledge, 1982; 1995.

Osaghae, Eghosa E. *Crippled Giant: Nigeria since Independence*. Bloomington: Indiana University Press, 1998.

Owomoyela, Oyekan, ed. *A History of Twentieth Century African Literatures*. Lincoln: University of Nebraska Press, 1993.

Oyono, Ferdinand. *Une Vie de boy*. Paris: Pocket, 1956; 1998.

———. *Houseboy*. Trans. John Reed. Oxford: Heinemann, 1966; 1990.

Parush, Iris. *Reading Jewish Women: Marginality and Modernization in Nineteenth-Century Eastern European Jewish Society*. Trans. Saadya Sternberg. Waltham, MA: Brandeis University Press, 2004.

Peterson, Dale E. *Up from Bondage: The Literatures of Russian and African American Soul*. Durham, NC: Duke University Press, 2000.

Peretz, Y. L. *Ale verk fun Y. L. Peretz*. Vol. 4. New York: "CYCO" *Bicher-Farlag*, 1947.

Perl, Joseph. *Revealer of Secrets: The First Hebrew Novel*. Ed. Dov Taylor. Boulder, CO: Westview Press, 1997.

Perry, Menahem. *Ha'analogiah umakoma b'mivneh haroman shel Mendele Moykher-Sforim*. *Hasifrut* 1, no. 1 (Spring 1968): 65–100.

Philipson, Robert. *The Identity Question: Blacks and Jews in Europe and America*. Jackson: University of Mississippi Press, 2000.

Poe, Edgar Allan. *Complete Tales & Poems*. New York: Vintage Books, 1938; 1975.

Polansky, Antony, ed. *Studies from Polin: From* Shtetl *to Socialism*. London: Littman Library of Jewish Civilization, 1993.

———. *Polin: Studies in Polish Jewry*. Vol. 17, *The Shtetl: Myth and Reality*. Oxford: Littman Library of Jewish Civilization, 2004.

Portnoy, Eddy. "Do You Know What Time It Isn't?" *Pakn-Treger* (Fall 2007): 14–21.

Propp, Vladimir. *Morphology of the Folktale*. Trans. Laurence Scott. 2nd ed. rev. and ed. Louis A. Wagner. Austin: University of Texas Press, 1968; 1994.

Quayson, Ato. "Wole Soyinka and Autobiography as Political Unconscious." *Journal of Commonwealth Literature* 31, no. 2 (1996): 19–32.

———. *Strategic Transformations in Nigerian Writing: Orality & History in the Work of Rev. Samuel Johnson, Amos Tutuola, Wole Soyinka & Ben Okri*. Bloomington: Indiana University Press, 1997.

Rapoport-Albert, Ada, ed. *Hasidism Reappraised*. London: Littman Library of Jewish Civilization, 1997.

Reyzn, Zalman. *Fun Mendelssohn biz Mendele*. Warsaw: Farlag Kultur-Lige, 1923.

Rosen, Jody, curator. *Jewface*. Reboot Stereophonic 2006, RSR 006.

Rosenfeld, Isaac. *Passage from Home*. New York: Markus Wiener, 1946; 1988.

Roskies, David G. *Against the Apocalypse: Responses to Catastrophe in Modern Jewish Culture*. Cambridge, MA: Harvard University Press, 1984.

———. *A Bridge of Longing: The Lost Art of Yiddish Storytelling*. Cambridge, MA: Harvard University Press, 1995.

Rowling, J. K. *Harry Potter and the Sorcerer's Stone*. New York: Scholastic, 1997; 1998.

Sartre, Jean-Paul. "Black Orpheus." Trans. S. W. Allen. Paris: *Présence Africaine*, n.d.

Schaechter, Mordkhe. *Laytish mame-loshn*. New York: League for Yiddish. 1986.

Scholem, Gershom G. *Major Trends in Jewish Mysticism*. New York: Schocken Books, 1941; 1974.

Seidman, Naomi. *A Marriage Made in Heaven: The Sexual Politics of Hebrew and Yiddish*. Berkeley: University of California Press, 1997.

Senghor, Léopold Sédar, ed. *Anthologie de la nouvelle poésie nègre et malagache de langue française*. Paris: Presses Universitaires de France, 1948; 1997.

———. *Liberté 1: Négritude et Humanisme*. Paris: Éditions du Seuil, 1964.

———. *Léopold Sédar Senghor: The Collected Poetry*. Trans. Melvin Dixon. Charlottesville: University Press of Virginia, 1991.

Shapiro, Rabbi Dovid, ed. *Until the Mashiach: The Life of Rabbi Nachman*. Trans. Rabbi Aryeh Kaplan. Far Rockaway, NY: Breslov Research Institute, 1985.

Shiver, William S. "A Summary of Interior Monologue in Cheikh Hamidou Kane's 'Ambiguous Adventure.'" *Présence Africaine* 101/102 (1977): 207–215.

Shmeruk, Chone. *Mendeles tilim-iberzetsung*. *Di Goldene keyt* 62/63 (1968): 290–312.

———. *Prokim fun der yidisher literatur-geshikhte*. Tel Aviv: I. L. Peretz Publishing House, 1988.

Sholem Aleichem. *Monologen, Ale verk fun Sholem-Aleichem*. Vol. 25. New York: Morgen-Frayhayt Edition, 1937.

———. *Collected Stories of Sholom Aleichem*. Trans. Frances Butwin. New York: Crown, 1949.

Shtif, Nokhem, ed. *Mendele Moykher-Sforims briv*. *Shriftn*, vol. 1. Kiev: Farlag Kultur-Lige, 1928.

Sklamberg, Lorin, and Paula Teitelbaum, producers. *Di Grine Katshke / The Green Duck: A Menagerie of Yiddish Animal-Songs for Children*. Living Traditions CD LTD 1801, 1997.

Slobin, Mark. *Tenement Songs: The Popular Music of Jewish Immigrants*. Urbana: University of Illinois Press, 1982; 1996.

Soloveitchik, Haym. "Rupture and Reconstruction: The Transformation of Contemporary Orthodoxy." *Tradition* 28, no. 4 (1994): 64–130.

Soyinka, Wole. *The Interpreters*. Portsmouth, NH: Heinemann, 1965; 1986.

———. *The Man Died: Prison Notes of Wole Soyinka*. New York: Farrar, Straus, and Giroux, 1972; 1988.

———. *Collected Plays 1*. Oxford: Oxford University Press, 1973; 1986.

———. *Death and the King's Horseman*. New York: Noonday Press, 1975; 1991.

———. *Myth, Literature, and the African World*. Cambridge, UK: Cambridge University Press, 1976; 1992.

———. *The Burden of Memory, The Muse of Forgiveness*. New York: Oxford University Press, 1999; 2000.

Stanislawski, Michael. *Tsar Nicholas I and the Jews: The Transformation of Jewish Society in Russia, 1825–1855*. Philadelphia: Jewish Publication Society of America, 1983.

———. *For Whom Do I Toil? Judah Leib Gordon and the Crisis of Russian Jewry*. New York: Oxford University Press, 1988.

Starck, Astrid, trans. and ed. *Un beau livre d'histoires; Eyn shön Mayse bukh*. 2 vols. Basel: Schwabe Verlag, 2004.

Stern, David, and Mark Jay Mirsky, eds. *Rabbinic Fantasies: Imaginative Narratives from Classical Hebrew Literature*. New Haven: Yale University Press, 1990.

Stock, Brian. *Listening for the Text: On the Uses of the Past*. Philadelphia: University of Pennsylvania Press, 1990; 1996.

Sullivan, Joanna. "The Question of a National Literature for Nigeria." *Research in African Literatures* 32, no. 3 (Fall 2001): 71–85.

Teller, Adam. "Hasidism and the Challenge of Geography: The Polish Background to the Spread of the Hasidic Movement." *AJS Review* 30, no. 1 (2006): 1–29.

Tidjani-Serpos, Nouréini. "De l'école coranique à l'école étrangère ou le passage tragique de l'Ancien au Nouveau dans 'L'Aventure ambiguë' de Cheikh Hamidou Kane." *Préscence Africaine* 101/102 (1977): 188–206.

Trouillot, Michel-Rolph. *Silencing the Past: Power and the Production of History.* Boston: Beacon Press, 1995.

Tsinberg, Dr. Yisroyl. *Di Geshikhte fun der literatur ba yidn.* Vol. 8, book 2. Vilna: "Tomor" Publishing, 1937.

Turniansky, Chava, ed. *Di Yidishe literatur in nayntsntn yorhundert: zamlung fun yidisher literatur-forshung un kritik in ratn-farband.* Jerusalem: Magnes Press, 1993.

Tutuola, Amos. *The Palm-Wine Drinkard and My Life in the Bush of Ghosts.* New York: Grove Press, 1954; 1984.

——. *The Brave African Huntress.* New York: Grove Press, 1958; 1970.

——. *The Witch-Herbalist of the Remote Town.* London: Faber and Faber, 1981.

——. *The Wild Hunter in the Bush of Ghosts.* Ed. Bernth Lindfors. Washington, DC: Three Continents Press, 1982; 1989.

Vaillant, Janet G. *Black, French, and African: A Life of Léopld Sédar Senghor.* Cambridge, MA: Harvard University Press, 1990.

Vaynlez, Yisroyl, ed. *Yoysef Perl's yidishe ksovim.* Vilna: YIVO Institute, 1937.

Weinreich, Max. *Bilder fun der yidisher literaturgeshikhte: fun di onheybn biz Mendele Moykher-Sforim.* Vilna: Farlag "Tomor," 1928.

——. *Der Veg tsu undzer yugnt: yesoydes, metodn, problemen fun yidisher yugnt-forshung.* Vilna: YIVO, 1935.

——. *Geshikhte fun der yidisher shprakh: Bagrifn, faktn, metodn.* New York: YIVO Institute for Jewish Research, 1973.

Weinreich, Uriel. *Languages in Contact.* The Hague: Mouton, 1963.

Weiss, Joseph. *Mekhkarim bekhasidut breslov.* Jerusalem: Bialik Institute, 1974.

——. *Studies in East European Jewish Mysticism & Hasidism.* Ed. David Goldstein. London: Littman Library of Jewish Civilization, 1997.

Werses, Shmuel. *Tsvishn dray shprakhn: vegn yoysef perls yidishe ksovim in likht fun naye materialn. Di goldene keyt* 89 (1976): 150–177.

Wertheimer, Jack, ed. *The Uses of Tradition: Jewish Continuity in the Modern Era.* New York: Jewish Theological Seminary, 1992.

Wiener, Leo. *The History of Yiddish Literature in the Nineteenth Century.* New York: Charles Scribner's, 1899.

Wiener, Meyer. *Tsu der Geshikhte fun der yidisher literatur in 19tn yorhundert: Ershter un Tsveyter band.* New York: YKUF, 1945.

Wiskind-Elper, Ora. *Tradition and Fantasy in the Tales of Reb Nahman of Bratslav.* Albany: State University of New York Press, 1998.

Wisse, Ruth R. *The Schlemiel as Modern Hero.* Chicago: University of Chicago Press, 1971.

———. *I. L. Peretz and the Making of Modern Jewish Culture.* Seattle: University of Washington Press, 1991.

———. "The Jewish Intellectual and the Jews: The Case of *Di Kliatshe* (The Mare) by Mendele Mocher Sforim." Daniel E. Koshland Memorial Lecture of the Congregation Emanu-El, San Francisco (uncollected), March 24, 1992.

———. *The Modern Jewish Canon: A Journey through Language and Culture.* New York: Free Press, 2000.

Zeitlin, Hillel. *Reb Nakhman Braslaver: Der zeyr fun padolye.* New York: Matones, 1952.

Zipperstein, Steven J. *The Jews of Odessa: A Cultural History, 1794–1881.* Stanford, CA: Stanford University Press, 1986.

Zumthor, Paul. *Oral Poetry: An Introduction.* Trans. Kathryn Murphy-Judy. Minneapolis: University of Minnesota Press, 1990.

Index